EARLY GREEK PHILOSOPHY

UNIFORM WITH THIS BOOK

STUDIES OF THE GREEK POETS

by

John Addington Symonds

Third Edition

ADAM & CHARLES BLACK : LONDON

EARLY
GREEK PHILOSOPHY

BY

JOHN BURNET
M.A., LL.D., F.B.A.
EMERITUS PROFESSOR OF GREEK, UNIVERSITY OF ST. ANDREWS

Περὶ μὲν τῶν ὄντων τὴν ἀλήθειαν ἐσκόπουν, τὰ δ᾽ ὄντα ὑπέλαβον
εἶναι τὰ αἰσθητὰ μόνον.—ARISTOTLE.

FOURTH EDITION

LONDON
ADAM & CHARLES BLACK

Printed in Great Britain by
Hollen Street Press Ltd at Slough
First Edition published April 1892
Second Edition June 1908. *Third Edition September* 1920
Fourth Edition 1930.
Reprinted 1945, 1948, 1952, 1958, 1963, 1971 *and* 1975.

A. AND C. BLACK LTD
4, 5 AND 6 SOHO SQUARE LONDON W1V 6AD

ISBN 0 7136 0337 2

NOTE ON THE FOURTH EDITION

The present is a reprint of the third edition, but the opportunity has been taken to incorporate a couple of additional references and one correction which the author had noted in his own copy and to correct some misprints and trivial slips.
St. Andrews, *March*, 1930   W. L. LORIMER

PREFACE TO THIRD EDITION

As a third edition of this work has been called for, and as it has been translated into German [1] and into French,[2] it must have served some useful purpose, in spite of its imperfections, of which I am naturally more conscious than any one. The present edition was prepared under the stress of war conditions, which much abridged the leisure of university teachers, and its publication has been delayed longer than I could have wished for the same reason.

My aim has been to show that a new thing came into the world with the early Ionian teachers—the thing we call science—and that they first pointed the way which Europe has followed ever since, so that, as I have said elsewhere, it is an adequate description of science to say that it is " thinking about the world in the Greek way." That is why science has never existed except among peoples who have come under the influence of Greece.

When the first edition of *Early Greek Philosophy* was published, twenty-eight years ago, the subject was still generally treated in this country from a Hegelian point of view, and many of my conclusions were regarded as paradoxes. Some of these are now accepted by most people, but there are two which still provoke opposition. In the first place, I ventured to call Parmenides " the father of Materialism," and it is still maintained in some quarters that he was an Idealist (a modern term, which is most

[1] *Die Anfänge der griechischen Philosophie, aus dem Englischen übersetzt von Else Schenkl* (Berlin, Teubner, 1913).

[2] *L'Aurore de la Philosophie grecque, édition française, par Aug. Reymond* (Paris, Payot, 1919).

misleading when applied to Greek philosophy) on the ground
that " the very essence of materialism is that this material
world, this world of sense, is the real world," [1] and that
Parmenides certainly denied all reality to the world of sense.
Undoubtedly he did, and, if I had used the term Materialism
in the sense alleged, I should have been talking nonsense.
As I understand it, however, the " matter " of the Materialist
is not a possible object of sense at all ; it is as much, or
more, an *ens rationis* as Spirit, and the " being " of Parmenides is the first clear attempt to apprehend this non-
sensuous reality.   That is, in fact, the main thesis of my
book, and the vital point of the argument is my insistence
on the derivation of Atomism (which is admittedly material-
istic) from Eleaticism, in accordance with the express statements of Aristotle and Theophrastos (pp. 333 *sqq.*).   If that
is wrong, my whole treatment of the subject is wrong.

The other paradox which has still to win acceptance is
my contention that the opposite view which finds reality
not in matter, but in form, the Platonist view in short, goes
back to the Pythagoreans, and was already familiar to
Sokrates, though it was not formulated in a perfectly clear
way till the days of the Platonic Academy.   I am convinced
that this can only be made good by a fresh interpretation
in detail of the Platonic dialogues, and I am now engaged
on that task.   It is necessary to make it quite clear that
the interpretation current in the nineteenth century was
based on certain assumptions, for which no evidence has
ever been offered, and which are most improbable in themselves.   I cannot discuss this further here, but I hope to
have an early opportunity of doing so.

J. B.

St. Andrews, *July* 1920.

[1] W. T. Stace, *A Critical History of Greek Philosophy* (London, 1920),
pp. 46 *sqq.*

CONTENTS

vii

ABBREVIATIONS

Arch.   *Archiv für Geschichte der Philosophie.*   Berlin, 1888–1920.

BEARE.   *Greek Theories of Elementary Cognition*, by John I. Beare.   Oxford, 1906.

DIELS *Dox.*   *Doxographi graeci.*   Hermannus Diels.   Berlin, 1879.

DIELS *Vors.*   *Die Fragmente der Vorsokratiker*, von Hermann Diels, Dritte Auflage.   Berlin, 1912.

GOMPERZ.   *Greek Thinkers*, by Theodor Gomperz, Authorised (English) Edition, vol. i.   London, 1901.

JACOBY.   *Apollodors Chronik*, von Felix Jacoby (*Philol. Unters.* Heft xvi.).   Berlin, 1902.

R. P.   *Historia Philosophiae Graecae*, H. Ritter et L. Preller. Editio octava, quam curavit Eduardus Wellmann. Gotha, 1898.

ZELLER.   *Die Philosophie der Griechen, dargestellt von Dr. Eduard Zeller.*   Erster Theil, Fünfte Auflage.   Leipzig, 1892.

EARLY GREEK PHILOSOPHY

INTRODUCTION

I. IT was not till the traditional view of the world and the customary rules of life had broken down, that the Greeks began to feel the needs which philosophies of nature and of conduct seek to satisfy. Nor were those needs felt all at once. The ancestral maxims of conduct were not seriously questioned till the old view of nature had passed away ; and, for this reason, the earliest philosophers busied themselves mainly with speculations about the world around them. In due season, Logic was called into being to meet a fresh want. The pursuit of cosmological inquiry had brought to light a wide divergence between science and common sense, which was itself a problem that demanded solution, and moreover constrained philosophers to study the means of defending their paradoxes against the pre-judices of the unscientific. Later still, the prevailing interest in logical matters raised the question of the origin and validity of knowledge ; while, about the same time, the break-down of traditional morality gave rise to Ethics. The period which precedes the rise of Logic and Ethics has thus a distinctive character of its own, and may fitly be treated apart.[1]

[1] It will be observed that Demokritos falls outside the period thus defined. The common practice of treating this younger contemporary of Sokrates along with the " Pre-Socratics " obscures the historical develop-ment altogether. Demokritos comes after Protagoras, and he has to face the problems of knowledge and conduct far more seriously than his pre-decessors had done (see Brochard, " Protagoras et Démocrite," *Arch.* ii. p. 368).

The
traditional
view of
the world.

II. It must, however, be remembered that the world was already very old when science and philosophy began. In particular, the Aegean Sea had been the seat of a high civilisation from the Neolithic age onwards, a civilisation as ancient as that of Egypt or of Babylon, and superior to either in most things that matter. It is becoming clearer every day that the Greek civilisation of later days was mainly the revival and continuation of this, though it no doubt received certain new and important elements from the less civilised northern peoples who for a time arrested its development. The original Mediterranean population must have far outnumbered the intruders, and must have assimilated and absorbed them in a few generations, except in a state like Sparta, which deliberately set itself to resist the process. At any rate, it is to the older race we owe Greek Art and Greek Science.[1] It is a remarkable fact

[1] See Sir Arthur Evans, " The Minoan and Mycenean Element in Hellenic Life " (*J.H.S.* xxxii. 277 *sqq.*), where it is contended (p. 278) that " The people whom we discern in the new dawn are not the pale-skinned northerners—the ' yellow-haired Achaeans ' and the rest—but essentially the dark-haired, brown-complexioned race . . . of whom we find the earlier portraiture in the Minoan and Mycenean wall-paintings." But, if the Greeks of historical times were the same people as the " Minoans," why should Sir Arthur Evans hesitate to call the " Minoans " Greeks ? The Achaians and Dorians have no special claim to the name ; for the Graes of Boiotia, who brought it to Cumae, were of the older race. I can attach no intelligible meaning either to the term " pre-Hellenic." If it means that the Aegean race was there before the somewhat un-important Achaian tribe which accidentally gave its name later to the whole nation, that is true, but irrelevant. If, on the other hand, it implies that there was a real change in the population of the Aegean at any time since the end of the Neolithic age, that is untrue, as Sir Arthur Evans himself maintains. If it means (as it probably does) that the Greek language was introduced into the Aegean by the northerners, there is no evidence of that, and it is contrary to analogy. The Greek language, as we know it, is in its vocabulary a mixed speech, like our own, but its essential structure is far liker that of the Indo-Iranian languages than that of any northern branch of Indo-European speech. For instance, the augment is common and peculiar to Sanskrit, Old Persian, and Greek. The Greek language cannot have differed very much from the Persian in the second millennium B.C. The popular distinction between *centum* and *satem* languages is wholly misleading and based on a secondary phenomenon, as is shown by the fact that the Romance languages have become *satem* languages in historical times. It would be more to the point to note that Greek, like Old Indian and Old Persian, represents the

that every one of the men whose work we are about to study was an Ionian, except Empedokles of Akragas, and this exception is perhaps more apparent than real. Akragas was founded from the Rhodian colony of Gela, its οἰκιστής was himself a Rhodian, and Rhodes, though officially Dorian, had been a centre of the early Aegean civilisation. We may fairly assume that the emigrants belonged mainly to the older population rather than to the new Dorian aristocracy. Pythagoras founded his society in the Achaian city of Kroton, but he himself was an Ionian from Samos.

This being so, we must be prepared to find that the Greeks of historical times who first tried to understand the world were not at all in the position of men setting out on a hitherto untrodden path. The remains of Aegean art prove that there must have been a tolerably consistent view of the world in existence already, though we cannot hope to recover it in detail till the records are deciphered. The ceremony represented on the sarcophagus of Hagia Triada implies some quite definite view as to the state of the dead, and we may be sure that the Aegean people were as capable of developing theological speculation as were the Egyptians and Babylonians. We shall expect to find traces of this in later days, and it may be said at once that things like the fragments of Pherekydes of Syros are inexplicable except as survivals of some such speculation. There is no ground for supposing that this was borrowed from Egypt, though no doubt these early civilisations all influenced one another. The Egyptians may have borrowed from Crete as readily as the Cretans from Egypt, and there was a seed of life in the sea civilisation which was somehow lacking in that of the great rivers.

On the other hand, it is clear that the northern invaders must have assisted the free development of the Greek

---

sonant *n* in the word for "hundred" (ἑκατόν = śatam, satem) by *a*, and to classify it with them as a *satem* language on that ground.

genius by breaking up the powerful monarchies of earlier days and, above all, by checking the growth of a superstition like that which ultimately stifled Egypt and Babylon. That there was once a real danger of this is suggested by certain features in the Aegean remains.　On the other hand, the worship of Apollo seems to have been brought from the North by the Achaians,[1] and indeed what has been called the Olympian religion was, so far as we can see, derived mainly from that source.　Still, the artistic form it assumed bears the stamp of the Mediterranean peoples, and it was chiefly in that form it appealed to them.　It could not become oppressive to them as the old Aegean religion might very possibly have done.　It was probably due to the Achaians that the Greeks never had a priestly class, and that may well have had something to do with the rise of free science among them.

1. Homer.　III. We see the working of these influences clearly in Homer.　Though he doubtless belonged to the older race himself and used its language,[2] it is for the courts of Achaian princes he sings, and the gods and heroes he celebrates are mostly Achaian.[3]　That is why we find so few traces of the traditional view of the world in the epic.　The gods have become frankly human, and everything primitive is kept out of sight.　There are, of course, vestiges of the early

[1] See Farnell, *Cults of the Greek States*, vol. iv. pp. 98 *sqq.*

[2] This is surely a simpler hypothesis than that of Sir Arthur Evans, who postulates (*loc. cit.* p. 288) " an earlier Minoan epic taken over into Greek." The epic dialect has most points of contact with Arcadian and Cypriote, and it is wholly improbable that the Arcadians came from the North. There are sufficient parallels for the prowess of the conqueror being celebrated by a bard of the conquered race (Ridgeway, *Early Age of Greece*, vol. i. p. 664).　Does this explain the name Ὅμηρος, " hostage " ?

[3] Professor Ridgeway (*Early Age of Greece*, i. p. 674) points out that the specifically Achaian names, such as Achilles, Odysseus, Aiakos, Aias, Laertes and Peleus, cannot be explained from the Greek language, while the names of the older race, such as Herakles, Erichthonios, Erysichthon, etc., can.　No doubt Agamemnon and Menelaos have Greek names, but that is because Atreus owed his kingship to the marriage of Pelops with a princess of the older race.　It is an instance of the process of assimilation which was going on everywhere.

beliefs and practices, but they are exceptional.[1] It has often been noted that Homer never speaks of the primitive custom of purification for homicide. The dead heroes are burned, not buried, as the kings of the older race were. Ghosts play hardly any part. In the *Iliad* we have, to be sure, the ghost of Patroklos, in close connexion with the solitary instance of human sacrifice in Homer. There is also the *Nekyia* in the Eleventh Book of the *Odyssey*.[2] Such things, however, are rare, and we may fairly infer that, at least in a certain society, that of the Achaian princes for whom Homer sang, the traditional view of the world was already discredited at a comparatively early date,[3] though it naturally emerges here and there.

IV. When we come to Hesiod, we seem to be in another world. We hear stories of the gods which are not only irrational but repulsive, and these are told quite seriously. Hesiod makes the Muses say : " We know how to tell many false things that are like the truth ; but we know too, when we will, to utter what is true."[4] This means that he was conscious of the difference between the Homeric spirit and his own. The old light-heartedness is gone, and it is important to tell the truth about the gods. Hesiod knows, too, that he belongs to a later and a sadder time than Homer. In describing the Ages of the World, he inserts a fifth age between those of Bronze and Iron. That is the Age of the Heroes, the age Homer sang of. It was better than the Bronze Age which came before it, and far better than that which followed it, the Age of Iron, in which Hesiod

2. Hesiod.

---

[1] There are traces of cosmogonical ideas in the Διὸς ἀπάτη (*Il.* xiv.).

[2] *Od.* xi. has been referred to a late date because it is supposed to contain Orphic ideas. In the light of our present knowledge, such a hypothesis is quite unnecessary. The ideas in question are primitive, and were probably generally accepted in the Aegean. Orphicism was essentially a revival of primitive beliefs.

[3] On all this, see especially Rohde, *Psyche*[3], i. pp. 37 *sqq.* (=*Ps.*[1] pp. 34 *sqq.*).

[4] Hes. *Theog.* 27 (the words of the first verse are borrowed from *Od.* xix. 203). The Muses are the same as those who inspired Homer, which means that Hesiod wrote in hexameters and used the Epic dialect.

lives.[1] He also feels that he is singing for another class. It is to shepherds and husbandmen of the older race he addresses himself, and the Achaian princes for whom Homer sang have become remote persons who give " crooked dooms." The romance and splendour of the Achaian Middle Ages meant nothing to the common people. The primitive view of the world had never really died out among them ; so it was natural for their first spokesman to assume it in his poems. That is why we find in Hesiod these old savage tales, which Homer disdained.

Yet it would be wrong to see in the *Theogony* a mere revival of the old superstition. Hesiod could not help being affected by the new spirit, and he became a pioneer in spite of himself. The rudiments of what grew into Ionic science and history are to be found in his poems, and he really did more than any one to hasten that decay of the old ideas which he was seeking to arrest. The *Theogony* is an attempt to reduce all the stories about the gods into a single system, and system is fatal to so wayward a thing as mythology. Moreover, though the spirit in which Hesiod treats his theme is that of the older race, the gods of whom he sings are for the most part those of the Achaians. This introduces an element of contradiction into the system from first to last. Herodotos tells us that it was Homer and Hesiod who made a theogony for the Hellenes, who gave the gods their names, and distributed among them their offices and arts,[2] and it is perfectly true. The Olympian pantheon took the place of the older gods in men's minds, and this was quite as much the doing of Hesiod as of Homer. The ordinary man would hardly recognise his gods in the humanised figures, detached from all local associations, which poetry had substituted for the older objects of worship. Such gods were incapable of satisfying the needs of the people, and

---

[1] There is great historical insight here. It was Hesiod, not our modern historians, who first pointed out that the " Greek Middle Ages " were a break in the normal development.

[2] Herod. ii. 53.

that is the secret of the religious revival we shall have to consider later.

V. Nor is it only in this way that Hesiod shows himself a child of his time. His *Theogony* is at the same time a Cosmogony, though it would seem that here he was following the older tradition rather than working out a thought of his own. At any rate, he only mentions the two great cosmo-. gonical figures, Chaos and Eros, and does not really bring them into connexion with his system. They seem to belong, in fact, to an older stratum of speculation. The conception of Chaos represents a distinct effort to picture the beginning of things. It is not a formless mixture, but rather, as its etymology indicates, the yawning gulf or gap where nothing is as yet.[1] We may be sure that this is not primitive. Primitive man does not feel called on to form an idea of the very beginning of all things ; he takes for granted that there was something to begin with. The other figure, that of Eros, was doubtless intended to explain the impulse to production which gave rise to the whole process. These are clearly speculative ideas, but in Hesiod they are blurred and confused.

We have records of great activity in the production of cosmogonies during the whole of the sixth century B.C., and we know something of the systems of Epimenides, Pherekydes,[2] and Akousilaos. If there were speculations of this kind even before Hesiod, we need have no hesitation in believing that the earliest Orphic cosmogony goes back to that century too.[3] The feature common to all these systems is the attempt to get behind the Gap, and to put Kronos or Zeus in the first place. That is what Aristotle has in view when he distinguishes the " theologians " from

[1] The word χάος certainly means the " gape " or " yawn," the χάσμα πελώριον of the Rhapsodic Theogony (fr. 52). Grimm compared it with the Scandinavian *Ginnunga-Gap*.

[2] For the remains of Pherekydes, see Diels, *Vorsokratiker*, 71 B, and the interesting account in Gomperz, *Greek Thinkers*, vol. i. pp. 85 *sqq.*

[3] This was the view of Lobeck with regard to the so-called " Rhapsodic Theogony " described by Damaskios.

those who were half theologians and half philosophers, and who put what was best in the beginning.[1] It is obvious, however, that this process is the very reverse of scientific, and might be carried on indefinitely ; so we have nothing to do with the cosmogonists in our present inquiry, except so far as they can be shown to have influenced the course of more sober investigations.

General character-istics of Greek cos-mology.

VI. The Ionians, as we can see from their literature, were deeply impressed by the transitoriness of things. There is, in fact, a fundamental pessimism in their outlook on life, such as is natural to an over-civilised age with no very definite religious convictions. We find Mimnermos of Kolophon preoccupied with the sadness of the coming of old age, while at a later date the lament of Simonides, that the generations of men fall like the leaves of the forest, touches a chord that Homer had already struck.[2] Now this sentiment always finds its best illustrations in the changes of the seasons, and the cycle of growth and decay is a far more striking phenomenon in Aegean lands than in the North, and takes still more clearly the form of a war of opposites, hot and cold, wet and dry. It is, accordingly, from that point of view the early cosmologists regard the world. The opposition of day and night, summer and winter, with their suggestive parallelism in sleep and waking, birth and death, are the outstanding features of the world as they saw it.[3]

The changes of the seasons are plainly brought about by the encroachments of one pair of opposites, the cold and the wet, on the other pair, the hot and the dry, which in

[1] Arist. *Met.* N, 4. 1091 b 8.

[2] See Butcher, " The Melancholy of the Greeks," in *Some Aspects of the Greek Genius*, pp. 130 *sqq.*

[3] This is well brought out by Prof. J. L. Myres in a paper entitled " The Background of Greek Science " (*University of Chicago Chronicle*, vol. xvi. No. 4). There is no need to derive the doctrine of the " opposites " from a " religious representation " as Mr. Cornford does in the first chapter of *From Religion to Philosophy*. In Greece these force themselves upon our attention quite apart from anything of the sort. Of course they are also important in agrarian magic for practical reasons.

their turn encroach on the other pair. This process was
naturally described in terms borrowed from human society ;
for in early days the regularity and constancy of human
life was far more clearly realised than the uniformity of
nature. Man lived in a charmed circle of social law and
custom, but the world around him at first seemed lawless.
That is why the encroachment of one opposite on another
was spoken of as injustice (ἀδικία) and the due observance of a balance between them as justice (δίκη). The
later word κόσμος is based on this notion too. It meant
originally the discipline of an army, and next the ordered
constitution of a state.

That, however, was not enough. The earliest cosmologists could find no satisfaction in the view of the world
as a perpetual contest between opposites. They felt that
these must somehow have a common ground, from which
they had issued and to which they must return once more.
They were in search of something more primary than the
opposites, something which persisted through all change,
and ceased to exist in one form only to reappear in another.
That this was really the spirit in which they entered on their
quest is shown by the fact that they spoke of this something
as " ageless " and " deathless." [1] If, as is sometimes held,
their real interest had been in the process of growth and
becoming, they would hardly have applied epithets so
charged with poetical emotion and association to what is
alone permanent in a world of change and decay. That
is the true meaning of Ionian " Monism." [2]

[1] Ar. *Phys.* Γ, 4. 203 b 14 ἀθάνατον γὰρ καὶ ἀνώλεθρον (sc. τὸ ἄπειρον), ὥς
φησιν Ἀναξίμανδρος καὶ οἱ πλεῖστοι τῶν φυσιολόγων, Hipp. *Ref.* i. 6, 1 φύσιν
τινὰ τοῦ ἀπείρου . . . ταύτην δ' ἀίδιον εἶναι καὶ ἀγήρω. The epithets come from
the Epic, where ἀθάνατος καὶ ἀγήρως is a standing phrase to mark the
difference between gods and men.

[2] As it has been suggested that the Monism ascribed by later writers
to the early cosmologists is only based on Aristotle's distinction between
those who postulated one ἀρχή and those who postulated more than one
(*Phys.* A, 2. 184 b 15 sqq.), and is not therefore strictly historical, it will
be well to quote a pre-Aristotelian testimony for it. In the Hippokratean
Περὶ φύσιος ἀνθρώπου (Littré, vi. 32) we read φασί τε γὰρ ἕν τι εἶναι ὅτι ἐστι,

φύσις.   VII. Now, Ionian science was introduced into Athens by Anaxagoras about the time Euripides was born, and there are sufficient traces of its influence on him.[1] It is, therefore, significant that, in a fragment which portrays the blessedness of a life devoted to scientific research (ἱστορία),[2] he uses the very epithets " ageless and deathless " which Anaximander had applied to the one primary substance, and that he associates them with the term φύσις. The passage is so important for our present purpose that I quote it in full :

ὄλβιος ὅστις τῆς ἱστορίας
ἔσχε μάθησιν, μήτε πολιτῶν
ἐπὶ πημοσύνας μήτ' εἰς ἀδίκους
πράξεις ὁρμῶν,
ἀλλ' ἀθανάτου καθορῶν φύσεως
κόσμον ἀγήρω, τίς τε συνέστη
καὶ ὅπῃ καὶ ὅπως·
τοῖς τοιούτοις οὐδέποτ' αἰσχρῶν
ἔργων μελέτημα προσίζει.[3]

This fragment is clear evidence that, in the fifth century B.C., the name φύσις was given to the everlasting something of which the world was made. That is quite in accordance with the history of the word, so far as we can make it out. Its original meaning appears to be the " stuff " of which

---

καὶ τοῦτ' εἶναι τὸ ἓν καὶ τὸ πᾶν, κατὰ δὲ τὰ ὀνόματα οὐκ ὁμολογέουσι· λέγει δ' αὐτῶν ὁ μέν τις φάσκων ἀέρα εἶναι τοῦτο τὸ ἓν καὶ τὸ πᾶν, ὁ δὲ πῦρ, ὁ δὲ ὕδωρ, ὁ δὲ γῆν, καὶ ἐπιλέγει ἕκαστος τῷ ἑωυτοῦ λόγῳ μαρτύριά τε καὶ τεκμήρια, ἅ γε ἔστιν οὐδέν.

[1] See below, § 123.

[2] Cf. Plato, _Phaedo_, 96 a 7 ταύτης τῆς σοφίας ἣν δὴ καλοῦσι περὶ φύσεως ἱστορίαν. This is the oldest and most trustworthy statement as to the name originally given to science. I lay no stress on the fact that the books of the early cosmologists are generally quoted under the title Περὶ φύσεως, as such titles are probably of later date.

[3] Eur. fr. inc. 910. The word κόσμος here means, of course, " ordering," " arrangement," and ἀγήρω is genitive. The object of research is _firstly_ what is " the ordering of immortal ageless φύσις," and _secondly_, how it arose. Anaxagoras, who introduced Ionian science to Athens, had belonged to the school of Anaximenes (§ 122). We know from Aristotle (_loc. cit._ p. 9 _n._ 1) that not only Anaximander, but most of the φυσιολόγοι, applied epithets like this to the Boundless.

anything is made, a meaning which easily passes into that of its " make-up," its general character or constitution. Those early cosmologists who were seeking for an " undying and ageless " something, would naturally express the idea by saying there was " one φύσις "[1] of all things. When that was given up, under the influence of Eleatic criticism, the old word was still used. Empedokles held there were four such primitive stuffs, each with a φύσις of its own, while the Atomists believed in an infinite number, to which they also applied the term.[2]

The term ἀρχή, which is often used in our authorities, is in this sense [3] purely Aristotelian. It is very natural that it should have been adopted by Theophrastos and later writers ; for they all start from the well-known passage of the *Physics* in which Aristotle classifies his predecessors according as they postulated one or more ἀρχαί.[4] But Plato never uses the term in this connexion, and it does not occur once in the genuine fragments of the early philosophers, which would be very strange on the assumption that they employed it.

Now, if this is so, we can understand at once why the Ionians called science Περὶ φύσεως ἱστορίη. We shall see

---

[1] Arist. *Phys.* A, 6. 189 b 2 οἱ μίαν τινὰ φύσιν εἶναι λέγοντες τὸ πᾶν, οἷον ὕδωρ ἢ πῦρ ἢ τὸ μεταξὺ τούτων, Β, I. 193 a 21 οἱ μὲν πῦρ, οἱ δὲ γῆν, οἱ δ' ἀέρα φασίν, οἱ δὲ ὕδωρ, οἱ δ' ἔνια τούτων (Parmenides), οἱ δὲ πάντα ταῦτα (Empedokles) τὴν φύσιν εἶναι τὴν τῶν ὄντων.

[2] For the history of the term φύσις, see Appendix I.

[3] Professor W. A. Heidel has shown that the cosmologists might have used ἀρχή in a sense different from Aristotle's, that, namely, of " source," " store," or " collective mass," from which particular things are derived (*Class. Phil.* vii. pp. 217 *sqq.*). I should be quite willing to accept this account of the matter if I could find any evidence that they used the term at all. It is only in the case of Anaximander that there is even a semblance of such evidence, and I believe that to be illusory (p. 54, *n.* 2). Moreover, Diels has shown that the first book of Theophrastos's great work dealt with the ἀρχή *in the Aristotelian sense*, and it is very unlikely that the word should have been used in one sense of Anaximander and in another of the rest.

[4] *Phys.* A, 2. 184 b 15 *sqq.* It is of great importance to remember that Theophrastos and his followers simply adopted the classification of this chapter, which has no claim to be regarded as historical.

that the growing thought which may be traced through the successive representatives of any school is always that which concerns the primary substance,[1] whereas the astronomical and other theories are, in the main, peculiar to the individual thinkers. The chief interest of all is the quest for what is abiding in the flux of things.[2]

Motion and Rest.

VIII. According to Aristotle and his followers, the early cosmologists believed also in an " eternal motion " ($\dot{a}t\delta\iota os$ $\kappa\dot{\iota}\nu\eta\sigma\iota s$), but that is probably their own way of putting the thing. It is not at all likely that the Ionians said anything about the eternity of motion in their writings. In early times, it is not movement but rest that has to be accounted for, and it is unlikely that the origin of motion was discussed till its possibility had been denied. As we shall see, that was done by Parmenides ; and accordingly his successors, accepting the fact of motion, were bound to show how it originated. I understand Aristotle's statement, then, as meaning no more than that the early thinkers did not feel the need of assigning an origin for motion. The eternity of motion is an inference, which is substantially correct, but is misleading in so far as it suggests deliberate rejection of a doctrine not yet formulated.[3]

[1] I am conscious of the unsatisfactory character of the phrase " primary substance " ($\pi\rho\hat{\omega}\tau ov$ $\dot{v}\pi o\kappa\epsilon\dot{\iota}\mu\epsilon vov$), but it is hard to find a better. The German *Urstoff* is less misleading in its associations, but the English " stuff " is not very satisfactory.

[2] The view of O. Gilbert (*Die meteorologischen Theorien des griechischen Altertums*, Leipzig, 1907) that the early cosmologists started from the traditional and popular theory of " the four elements " derives all its plausibility from the ambiguity of the term " element." If we only mean the great aggregates of Fire, Air, Water and Earth, there is no doubt that these were distinguished from an early date. But that is not what is meant by an " element " ($\sigma\tau o\iota\chi\epsilon\hat{\iota}ov$) in cosmology, where it is always an irreducible something with a $\phi\dot{v}\sigma\iota s$ of its own. The remarkable thing really is that the early cosmologists went behind the theory of " elements " in the popular sense, and it was only the accident that Empedokles, the first to maintain a plurality of elements, selected the four that have become traditional that has led to the loose use of the word " element " for the great aggregates referred to.

[3] This way of thinking is often called Hylozoism, but that is still more misleading. No doubt the early cosmologists said things about the world and the primary substance which, from our point of view, imply

A more important question is the nature of this motion. It is clear that it must have existed before the beginning of the world, since it is what brought the world into being. It cannot, therefore, be identified with the diurnal revolution of the heavens, as it has been by many writers, or with any other purely mundane motion.[1] The Pythagorean doctrine, as expounded in Plato's *Timaeus*,[2] is that the original motion was irregular and disorderly, and we shall see reason for believing that the Atomists ascribed a motion of that kind to the atoms. It is safer, then, not to attribute any regular or well-defined motion to the primary substance of the early cosmologists at this stage.[3]

IX. In all this, there is no trace of theological speculation. We have seen that there had been a complete break with the early Aegean religion, and that the Olympian polytheism never had a firm hold on the Ionian mind. It is therefore quite wrong to look for the origins of Ionian science in mythological ideas of any kind. No doubt there were many vestiges of the older beliefs and practices in

The secular character of Ionian science.

---

that they are alive ; but that is a very different thing from ascribing a " plastic power " to " matter." The concept of " matter " did not yet exist, and the underlying assumption is simply that everything, life included, can be explained mechanically, as we say, that is, by body in motion. Even that is not stated explicitly, but taken for granted.

[1] It was Aristotle who first took the fateful step of identifying the " eternal motion " with the diurnal revolution of the heavens.

[2] Plato, *Tim.* 30 a.

[3] As I understand him, Prof. W. A. Heidel regards the " eternal motion " as a rotary or vortex motion ($\delta\iota\nu\eta$), on the ground that it is hazardous to assume that an early thinker, such as Anaximenes, " distinguished between the primordial motion of the infinite Air and the original motion in the cosmos " (see his article, " The $\delta\iota\nu\eta$ in Anaximenes and Anaximander," *Classical Philology*, i. p. 279). It seems to me, on the other hand, that any one who held the world had come into being must have made such a distinction, especially if he also held the doctrine of innumerable worlds. As will be seen later, I adopt Prof. Heidel's view that the " original motion of the cosmos " was a rotary one in the earliest cosmological systems, but it was certainly not " eternal," and I do not think we can infer anything from it as to the pre-mundane motion, except that it must have been of such a nature that it could give rise to the $\delta\iota\nu\eta$.

those parts of Greece which had not come under the rule
of the Northerners, and we shall see presently how they
reasserted themselves in the Orphic and other mysteries,
but the case of Ionia was different.   It was only after the
coming of the Achaians that the Greeks were able to establish
their settlements on the coast of Asia Minor, which had
been closed to them by the Hittites,[1] and there was no
traditional background there at all.   In the islands of the
Aegean it was otherwise, but Ionia proper was a country
without a past.   That explains the secular character of the
earliest Ionian philosophy.

We must not be misled by the use of the word θεός in
the remains that have come down to us.   It is quite true
that the Ionians applied it to the " primary substance "
and to the world or worlds, but that means no more and no
less than the use of the divine epithets " ageless " and
" deathless " to which we have referred already.   In its
religious sense the word " god " always means first and
foremost an object of worship, but already in Homer that
has ceased to be its only signification.   Hesiod's *Theogony*
is the best evidence of the change.   It is clear that many
of the gods mentioned there were never worshipped by
any one, and some of them are mere personifications of
natural phenomena, or even of human passions.[2]   This
non-religious use of the word " god " is characteristic of
the whole period we are dealing with, and it is of the first
importance to realise it.   No one who does so will fall into
the error of deriving science from mythology.[3]

We see this, above all, from the fact that, while primitive

---

[1] See Hogarth, *Ionia and the East,* pp. 68 *sqq.*

[2] No one worshipped Okeanos and Tethys, or even Ouranos, and still
less can Phobos and Deimos be regarded as gods in the religious sense.

[3] This is, I venture to think, the fundamental error of Mr. Cornford's
interesting book, *From Religion to Philosophy* (1912).   He fails to realise
how completely the old " collective representations " had lost their hold
in Ionia.   We shall see that his method is more applicable when he comes
to deal with the western regions, but even there he does not recognise
sufficiently the contrast between Ionian science and the old tradition.

religion regards the heavenly bodies and the heavens
themselves as divine, and therefore of a wholly different
nature from anything on this earth, the Ionians from the
very first set their faces against any such distinction, though
it must have been perfectly familiar to them from popular
beliefs. Aristotle revived the distinction at a later date,
but Greek science began by rejecting it.[1]

X. We have also to face the question of the nature and
extent of the influence exercised by what we call Eastern
wisdom on the Greek mind. It is a common idea even
now that the Greeks in some way derived their philosophy
from Egypt and Babylon, and we must therefore try to
understand as clearly as possible what such a statement
really means. To begin with, we must observe that the
question wears a very different aspect now that we know
the great antiquity of the Aegean civilisation. Much that
has been regarded as Oriental may just as well be native.
As for later influences, we must insist that no writer of the
period during which Greek philosophy flourished knows
anything of its having come from the East. Herodotos
would not have omitted to say so, had he heard of it ; for it
would have confirmed his own belief in the Egyptian origin
of Greek religion and civilisation.[2] Plato, who had a great
respect for the Egyptians on other grounds, classes them as
a business-like rather than a philosophical people.[3] Aristotle
speaks only of the origin of mathematics in Egypt[4] (a point

Alleged
Oriental
origin of
philo-
sophy.

[1] The importance of this point can hardly be exaggerated. See
Prof. A. E. Taylor, *Aristotle*, p. 58.

[2] All he can say is that the worship of Dionysos and the doctrine of
transmigration came from Egypt (ii. 49, 123). We shall see that both these
statements are incorrect, and in any case they do not imply anything
directly as to philosophy.

[3] In *Rep.* 435 e, after saying that τὸ θυμοειδές is characteristic of the
Thracians and Scythians, and τὸ φιλομαθές of the Hellenes, he refers us to
Phoenicia and Egypt for τὸ φιλοχρήματον. In the *Laws* he says (747 b 6)
that arithmetical studies are valuable only if we remove all ἀνελευθερία
and φιλοχρηματία from the souls of the learners. Otherwise, we produce
πανουργία instead of σοφία, as we can see that the Phoenicians, the Egyptians,
and many other peoples do.

[4] Arist. *Met.* A, 1. 981 b 23.

to which we shall return), though, if he had known of an
Egyptian philosophy, it would have suited his argument
better to mention that. It is not till later, when Egyptian
priests and Alexandrian Jews began to vie with one another
in discovering the sources of Greek philosophy in their
own past, that we have definite statements to the effect
that it came from Phoenicia or Egypt. But the so-called
Egyptian philosophy was only arrived at by a process of
turning primitive myths into allegories. We are still able
to judge Philo's Old Testament interpretation for ourselves,
and we may be sure that the Egyptian allegorists were even
more arbitrary; for they had far less promising material
to work on. The myth of Isis and Osiris, for instance, is first
interpreted according to the ideas of later Greek philosophy,
and then declared to be the source of that philosophy.

This method of interpretation culminated with the
Neopythagorean Noumenios, from whom it passed to the
Christian Apologists. It is Noumenios who asks, " What is
Plato but Moses speaking Attic ? " [1] Clement and Eusebios
give the remark a still wider application.[2] At the Renaissance, this farrago was revived along with everything else,
and certain ideas derived from the *Praeparatio Evangelica*
continued for long to colour accepted views.[3] Cudworth
speaks of the ancient " Moschical or Mosaical philosophy "
taught by Thales and Pythagoras.[4] It is important to
realise the true origin of this prejudice against the originality
of the Greeks. It does not come from modern researches

---

[1] Noumenios, fr. 13 (R. P. 624), Τί γάρ ἐστι Πλάτων ἢ Μωυσῆς ἀττικίζων ;

[2] Clement (*Strom.* i. p. 8, 5, Stählin) calls Plato ὁ ἐξ Ἑβραίων φιλόσοφος.

[3] Exaggerated notions of Oriental wisdom were popularised by the
Encyclopédie, which accounts for their diffusion and persistence. Bailly
(*Lettres sur l'origine des sciences*) assumed that the Orientals had received
fragments of highly advanced science from a people which had disappeared,
but which he identified with the inhabitants of Plato's Atlantis !

[4] We learn from Strabo (xvi. p. 757) that it was Poseidonios who
introduced Mochos of Sidon into the history of philosophy. He attributes
the atomic theory to him. His identification with Moses, however, is a
later *tour de force* due to Philon of Byblos, who published a translation
of an ancient Phoenician history by Sanchuniathon, which was used by
Porphyry and afterwards by Eusebios.

into the beliefs of ancient peoples ; for these have disclosed nothing in the way of evidence for a Phoenician or Egyptian philosophy. It is a mere residuum of the Alexandrian passion for allegory.

Of course no one nowadays would rest the case for the Oriental origin of Greek philosophy on the evidence of Clement or Eusebios ; the favourite argument in recent times has been the analogy of the arts. We are seeing more and more, it is said, that the Greeks derived their art from the East ; and it is urged that the same will in all probability prove true of their philosophy. That is a specious argument, but not at all conclusive. It ignores the difference in the way these things are transmitted from people to people. Material civilisation and the arts may pass easily from one people to another, though they have not a common language, but philosophy can only be expressed in abstract language, and can only be transmitted by educated men, whether by means of books or oral teaching. Now we know of no Greek, in the times we are dealing with, who could read an Egyptian book or even listen to the discourse of an Egyptian priest, and we never hear till a late date of Oriental teachers who wrote or spoke in Greek. The Greek traveller in Egypt would no doubt pick up a few words of Egyptian, and it is taken for granted that the priests could make themselves understood by the Greeks.[1] But they must have made use of interpreters, and it is impossible to conceive of philosophical ideas being communicated through an uneducated dragoman.[2]

But really it is not worth while to ask whether the communication of philosophical ideas was possible or not, till some evidence has been produced that any of these

[1] Herod. ii. 143 (where they boast to Hekataios of their superior antiquity) ; Plato, *Tim.* 22 b 3 (where they do the same to Solon).

[2] Gomperz's " native bride," who discusses the wisdom of her people with her Greek lord (*Greek Thinkers*, vol. i. p. 95), does not convince me either. She would probably teach her maids the rites of strange goddesses ; but she would not be likely to talk theology with her husband, and still less philosophy or science.

peoples had a philosophy to communicate. No such evidence has yet been discovered, and, so far as we know, the Indians were the only ancient people besides the Greeks who ever had anything that deserves the name. No one now will suggest that Greek philosophy came from India, and indeed everything points to the conclusion that Indian philosophy arose under Greek influence. The chronology of Sanskrit literature is an extremely difficult subject ; but, so far as we can see, the great Indian systems are later in date than the Greek philosophies they most nearly resemble. Of course the mysticism of the Upanishads and of Buddhism was of native growth ; but, though these influenced philosophy in the strict sense profoundly, they were related to it only as Hesiod and the Orphics were related to Greek scientific thought.

Egyptian mathematics.

XI. It would, however, be another thing to say that Greek philosophy originated quite independently of Oriental influences. The Greeks themselves believed their mathematical science to be of Egyptian origin, and they must have known something of Babylonian astronomy. It cannot be an accident that philosophy originated just at the time when communication with these two countries was easiest, and that the very man who was said to have introduced geometry from Egypt is also regarded as the first philosopher. It thus becomes important for us to discover what Egyptian mathematics meant. We shall see that, even here, the Greeks were really original.

The Rhind papyrus in the British Museum [1] gives us a glimpse of arithmetic and geometry as they were understood on the banks of the Nile. It is the work of one Aahmes,

[1] I am indebted for most of the information which follows to Cantor's *Vorlesungen über Geschichte der Mathematik*, vol. i. pp. 46-63. See also Gow's *Short History of Greek Mathematics*, §§ 73-80 ; and Milhaud, *La Science grecque*, pp. 91 *sqq.* The discussion in the last-named work is of special value because it is based on M. Rodet's paper in the *Bulletin de la Société Mathématique*, vol. vi., which in some important respects supplements the interpretation of Eisenlohr, on which the earlier accounts depend.

and contains rules for calculations both of an arithmetical and a geometrical character. The arithmetical problems mostly concern measures of corn and fruit, and deal particularly with such questions as the division of a number of measures among a given number of persons, the number of loaves or jars of beer that certain measures will yield, and the wages due to the workmen for a certain piece of work. It corresponds exactly, in fact, to the description of Egyptian arithmetic Plato gives us in the *Laws*, where he tells us that children learnt along with their letters to solve problems in the distribution of apples and wreaths to greater or smaller numbers of people, the pairing of boxers and wrestlers, and so forth.[1] This is clearly the origin of the art which the Greeks called λογιστική, and they probably borrowed that from Egypt, where it was highly developed ; but there is no trace of what the Greeks called ἀριθμητική, the scientific study of numbers.

The geometry of the Rhind papyrus is of a similar character, and Herodotos, who tells us that Egyptian geometry arose from the necessity of measuring the land afresh after the inundations, is clearly far nearer the mark than Aristotle, who says it grew out of the leisure enjoyed by the priestly caste.[2] The rules given for calculating areas are only exact when these are rectangular. As fields are usually more or less rectangular, this would be sufficient for practical purposes. It is even assumed that a right-angled triangle can be equilateral. The rule for finding what is called the *seqt* of a pyramid is, however, on a rather higher level, as we should expect. It comes to this. Given the " length across the sole of the foot," that is, the diagonal of the base, and that of the *piremus* or " ridge," to find a number which represents the ratio between them. This is

[1] Plato, *Laws*, 819 b 4 μήλων τέ τινων διανομαὶ καὶ στεφάνων πλείοσιν ἅμα καὶ ἐλάττοσιν ἁρμοττόντων ἀριθμῶν τῶν αὐτῶν, καὶ πυκτῶν καὶ παλαιστῶν ἐφεδρείας τε καὶ συλλήξεως ἐν μέρει καὶ ἐφεξῆς καὶ ὡς πεφύκασι γίγνεσθαι. καὶ δὴ καὶ παίζοντες, φιάλας ἅμα χρυσοῦ καὶ χαλκοῦ καὶ ἀργύρου καὶ τοιούτων τινῶν ἄλλων κεραννύντες, οἱ δὲ καὶ ὅλας πως διαδιδόντες.

[2] Herod. ii. 109 ; Arist. *Met.* A, 1. 981 b 23.

done by dividing half the diagonal of the base by the " ridge," and it is obvious that such a method might quite well be discovered empirically. It seems an anachronism to speak of elementary trigonometry in connexion with a rule like this, and there is nothing to suggest that the Egyptians went any further.[1] That the Greeks learnt as much from them is highly probable, though we shall see also that, from the very first, they generalised it so as to make it of use in measuring the distances of inaccessible objects, such as ships at sea. It was probably this generalisation that suggested the idea of a science of geometry, which was really the creation of the Pythagoreans, and we can see how far the Greeks soon surpassed their teachers from a remark attributed to Demokritos. It runs (fr. 299) : " I have listened to many learned men, but no one has yet surpassed me in the construction of figures out of lines accompanied by demonstration, not even the Egyptian *arpedonapts*, as they call them." [2]   Now the word ἀρπεδονάπτης is not Egyptian but Greek. It means " cord-fastener," [3] and it is a striking coincidence that the oldest Indian geometrical treatise is called the *Śulvasūtras* or " rules of the cord." These things point to the use of the triangle of which the sides are as 3, 4, 5, and which has always a right angle. We know that this was used from an early date among the Chinese and the Hindus, who doubtless got it from Babylon, and we shall see that Thales probably learnt the use of it in Egypt.[4] There is no reason for

---

[1] For a fuller account of this method see Gow, *Short History of Greek Mathematics*, pp. 127 *sqq.* ; and Milhaud, *Science grecque*, p. 99.

[2] R. P. 188. It should be stated that Diels now considers this fragment spurious (*Vors.*³ ii. p. 124). He regards it, in fact, as from an Alexandrian forgery intended to show the derivative character of Greek science, while insisting on its superiority. However that may be, the word ἀρπεδονάπται is no doubt a real one, and the inference drawn from it in the text is justified.

[3] The real meaning of ἀρπεδονάπτης was first pointed out by Cantor. The gardener laying out a flower-bed is the true modern representative of he " arpedonapts."

[4] See Milhaud, *Science grecque*, p. 103.

supposing that any of these peoples had troubled themselves
to give a theoretical demonstration of its properties, though
Demokritos would certainly have been able to do so. As
we shall see, however, there is no real evidence that Thales
had any mathematical knowledge which went beyond the
Rhind papyrus, and we must conclude that mathematics
in the strict sense arose in Greece after his time. It is
significant in this connexion that all mathematical terms
are purely Greek in their origin.[1]

XII. The other source from which the Ionians were
supposed to have derived their science is Babylonian
astronomy. It is certain, of course, that the Babylonians
had observed the heavens from an early date. They had
planned out the fixed stars, and especially those of the
zodiac, in constellations.[2] That is useful for purposes of
observational astronomy, but in itself it belongs rather to
mythology or folklore. They had distinguished and named
the planets and noted their apparent motions. They were
well aware of their stations and retrograde movements,
and they were familiar with the solstices and equinoxes.

Babylonian astronomy.

---

[1] Cf. *e.g.* κύκλος, κύλινδρος. Very often these terms are derived from
the names of tools; *e.g.* γνώμων, which is the carpenter's square, and τομεύς,
"sector," which is a cobbler's knife. The word πυραμίς is sometimes
supposed to be an exception and has been derived from the term *piremus*
used in the Rhind papyrus, which, however, does not mean "pyramid"
(p. 19) ; but it too is Greek. Πυραμίς (or πυραμοῦς) means a "wheat-
cake," and is formed from πυροί on the analogy of σησαμίς (or σησαμοῦς).
The Greeks had a tendency to give jocular names to things Egyptian.
Cf. κροκόδειλος, ὀβελίσκος, στρουθός, καταράκτης (lit. "sluice"). We seem to
hear an echo of the slang of the mercenaries who cut their names on the
colossus at Abu-Simbel.

[2] That is not quite the same thing as dividing the zodiac into twelve
signs of 30° each. There is no evidence of this before the sixth century
B.C. It is also to be noted that, while a certain number of names for
constellations appear to have reached the Greeks from Babylon, most of
them are derived from Greek mythology, and from its oldest stratum,
which became localised in Crete, Arkadia, and Boiotia. That points to
the conclusion that the constellations were already named in "Minoan"
times. The disproportionate space occupied by Andromeda and her
relatives points to the time when Crete and Philistia were in close contact.
There is a clue here which has been obscured by the theory of "astral
mythology."

They had also noted the occurrence of eclipses with a view
to predicting their return for purposes of divination.   But
we must not exaggerate the antiquity or accuracy of these
observations.   It was long before the Babylonians had a
satisfactory calendar, and they kept the year right only by
intercalating a thirteenth month when it seemed desirable.
That made a trustworthy chronology impossible, and
therefore there were not and could not be any data available for astronomical purposes before the so-called era of
Nabonassar (747 B.C.).   The oldest astronomical document
of a really scientific character which had come to light up
to 1907 is dated 523 B.C., in the reign of Kambyses, when
Pythagoras had already founded his school at Kroton.
Moreover, the golden age of Babylonian observational
astronomy is now assigned to the period after Alexander the
Great, when Babylon was a Hellenistic city.   Even then,
though great accuracy of observation was attained, and
data were accumulated which were of service to the Alexandrian astronomers, there is no evidence that Babylonian
astronomy had passed beyond the empirical stage.[1]

   We shall see that Thales probably knew the cycle by
means of which the Babylonians tried to predict eclipses
(§ 3) ; but it would be a mistake to suppose that the pioneers
of Greek science had any detailed knowledge of Babylonian

---

[1] All this has been placed beyond doubt by the researches of Father
Kugler (*Sternkunde und Sterndienst in Babel*, 1907).   There is a most interesting account and discussion of his results by Schiaparelli in *Scientia*,
vol. iii. pp. 213 *sqq.*, and vol. iv. pp. 24 *sqq.*, the last work of the great
astronomer.   These discussions were not available when I published my
second edition, and I made some quite unnecessary concessions as to
Babylonian astronomy there.   In particular, I was led by some remarks
of Ginzel (*Klio*, i. p. 205) to admit that the Babylonians might have
observed the precession of the equinoxes, but this is practically impossible
in the light of our present knowledge.   There is a good note on the
subject in Schiaparelli's second article (*Scientia*, iv. p. 34).   The chief
reason why the Babylonians could have no records of astronomical records
from an early date is that they had no method of keeping the lunar and
the solar year together, nor was there any control such as is furnished by
the Egyptian Sothis period.   Neither the ὀκταετηρίς or the ἐννεακαιδεκαετηρίς
was known to them till the close of the sixth century B.C.   They are
purely Greek inventions.

observations. The Babylonian names of the planets do not occur earlier than the writings of Plato's old age.[1] We shall find, indeed, that the earliest cosmologists paid no attention to the planets, and it is hard to say what they thought about the fixed stars. That, in itself, shows that they started for themselves, and were quite independent of Babylonian observations, and the recorded observations were only made fully available in Alexandrian times.[2] But, even if the Ionians had known them, their originality would remain. The Babylonians recorded celestial phenomena for astrological purposes, not from any scientific interest. There is no evidence that they attempted to account for what they saw in any but the crudest way. The Greeks, on the other hand, made at least three discoveries of capital importance in the course of two or three generations. In the first place, they discovered that the earth is a sphere and does not rest on anything.[3] In the second place, they discovered the true theory of lunar and solar eclipses ; and, in close connexion with that, they came to see, in the third place, that the earth is not the centre of our system, but revolves round the centre like the planets. Not much later, certain Greeks took, at least tentatively, the final step of identifying the centre round which the earth and planets revolve with the sun. These discoveries will be discussed in their proper place ; they are only mentioned here to show the gulf between Greek astronomy and everything that had preceded it. On the

[1] In classical Greek literature, no planets but Ἕσπερος and Ἑωσφόρος are mentioned by name at all. Parmenides (or Pythagoras) first identified these as a single planet (§ 94). Mercury appears for the first time by name in *Tim.* 38 e, and the other divine names are given in *Epin.* 987 b *sq.*, where they are said to be " Syrian." The Greek names Φαίνων, Φαέθων, Πυρόεις, Φωσφόρος, Στίλβων, are no doubt older, though they do not happen to occur earlier.

[2] The earliest reference to them is in Plato's *Epinomis*, 987 a. They are also referred to by Aristotle, *De caelo*, B, 12. 292 a 8.

[3] The view of Berger (*Erdkunde*, pp. 171 *sqq.*) that the sphericity of the earth was known in Egypt and Babylon is flatly contradicted by all the evidence known to me.

other hand, the Greeks rejected astrology, and it was not till the third century B.C. that it was introduced among them.[1]

We may sum up all this by saying that the Greeks did not borrow either their philosophy or their science from the East. They did, however, get from Egypt certain rules of mensuration which, when generalised, gave birth to geometry ; while from Babylon they learnt that the phenomena of the heavens recur in cycles. This piece of knowledge doubtless had a great deal to do with the rise of science ; for to the Greek it suggested further questions such as no Babylonian ever dreamt of.[2]

The scientific character of the early Greek cosmology.

XIII. It is necessary to insist on the scientific character of the philosophy we are about to study. We have seen that the Eastern peoples were considerably richer than the Greeks in accumulated facts, though these facts had not been observed for any scientific purpose, and never suggested a revision of the primitive view of the world. The Greeks, however, saw in them something that could be turned to account, and they were never as a people slow to act on the maxim, *Chacun prend son bien partout où il le trouve.* The visit of Solon to Croesus which Herodotos describes, however unhistorical it may be, gives us a good idea of this

---

[1] The earliest reference to astrology among the Greeks appears to be Plato, *Tim.* 40 c 9 (of conjunctions, oppositions, occultations, etc.), φόβους καὶ σημεῖα τῶν μετὰ ταῦτα γενησομένων τοῖς οὐ δυναμένοις λογίζεσθαι πέμπουσιν. That is quite general, but Theophrastos was more definite. Cf. the commentary of Proclus on the passage : θαυμασιωτάτην εἶναί φησιν ἐν τοῖς κατ' αὐτὸν χρόνοις τὴν τῶν Χαλδαίων θεωρίαν τά τε ἄλλα προλέγουσαν καὶ τοὺς βίους ἑκάστων καὶ τοὺς θανάτους καὶ οὐ τὰ κοινὰ μόνον. The Stoics, and especially Poseidonios, were responsible for the introduction of astrology into Greece, and it has recently been shown that the fully developed system known in later days was based on the Stoic doctrine of εἱμαρμένη. See the very important article by Boll in *Neue Jahrb.* xxi. (1908), p. 108.

[2] The Platonic account of this matter is to be found in the *Epinomis*, 986 e 9 *sqq.*, and is summed up by the words λάβωμεν δὲ ὡς ὅτιπερ ἂν Ἕλληνες βαρβάρων παραλάβωσι, κάλλιον τοῦτο εἰς τέλος ἀπεργάζονται (987 d 9). The point is well put by Theon (Adrastos), *Exp.* p. 177, 20 Hiller, who speaks of the Chaldaeans and Egyptians as ἄνευ φυσιολογίας ἀτελεῖς ποιούμενοι τὰς μεθόδους, δέον ἅμα καὶ φυσικῶς περὶ τούτων ἐπισκοπεῖν · ὅπερ οἱ παρὰ τοῖς Ἕλλησιν ἀστρολογήσαντες ἐπειρῶντο ποιεῖν, τὰς παρὰ τούτων λαβόντες ἀρχὰς καὶ τῶν φαινομένων τηρήσεις. This gives the view taken at Alexandria, where the facts were accurately known.

spirit. Croesus tells Solon that he has heard much of " his wisdom and his wanderings," and how, from love of knowledge (φιλοσοφέων), he has travelled over much land for the purpose of seeing what was to be seen (θεωρίης εἵνεκεν). The words θεωρίη, φιλοσοφίη, and ἱστορίη are, in fact, the catchwords of the time, though they had, no doubt, a somewhat different meaning from that they were afterwards made to bear at Athens.[1] The idea that underlies them all may, perhaps, be rendered in English by the word *Curiosity* ; and it was just this great gift of curiosity, and the desire to see all the wonderful things—pyramids, inundations, and so forth—that were to be seen, which enabled the Ionians to pick up and turn to their own use such scraps of knowledge as they could come by among the barbarians. No sooner did an Ionian philosopher learn half-a-dozen geometrical propositions, and hear that the phenomena of the heavens recur in cycles, than he set to work to look for law everywhere in nature, and, with an audacity almost amounting to ὕβρις, to construct a system of the universe. We may smile at the medley of childish fancy and scientific insight which these efforts display, and sometimes we feel disposed to sympathise with the sages of the day who warned their more daring contemporaries " to think the thoughts befitting man's estate " (ἀνθρώπινα φρονεῖν). But we shall do well to remember that even now it is just such hardy anticipations of experience that make scientific progress possible, and that nearly every one of these early inquirers made some permanent addition to positive knowledge, besides opening up new views of the world in every direction.

There is no justification either for the idea that Greek science was built up by more or less lucky guesswork, instead of by observation and experiment. The nature

---

[1] Still, the word θεωρία never lost its early associations, and the Greeks always felt that the θεωρητικὸς βίος meant literally '' the life of the spectator." Its special use and the whole theory of the " three lives" seem to be Pythagorean. (See § 45.)

of our tradition, which mostly consists of *Placita*—that is, of what we call " results "—tends, no doubt, to create this impression. We are seldom told why any early philosopher held the views he did, and the appearance of a string of " opinions " suggests dogmatism. There are, however, certain exceptions to the general character of the tradition ; and we may reasonably suppose that, if the later Greeks had been interested in the matter, there would have been many more. We shall see that Anaximander made some remarkable discoveries in marine biology, which the researches of the nineteenth century have confirmed (§ 22), and even Xenophanes supported one of his theories by referring to the fossils and petrifactions of such widely separated places as Malta, Paros, and Syracuse (§ 59). This is enough to show that the theory, so commonly held by the earlier philosophers, that the earth had been originally in a moist state, was not purely mythological in origin, but based on biological and palaeontological observations. It would surely be absurd to imagine that the men who could make these observations had not the curiosity or the ability to make many others of which the memory is lost. Indeed, the idea that the Greeks were not observers is ludicrously wrong, as is proved by the anatomical accuracy of their sculpture, which bears witness to trained habits of observation, while the Hippokratean corpus contains models of scientific observation at its best. We know, then, that the Greeks could observe well, and we know that they were curious about the world. Is it conceivable that they did not use their powers of observation to gratify that curiosity ? It is true that they had not our instruments of precision ; but a great deal can be discovered by the help of very simple apparatus. It is not to be supposed that Anaximander erected his *gnomon* merely that the Spartans might know the seasons.[1]

---

[1] As we saw, the word γνώμων properly means a carpenter's square (p. 21, *n.* 1), and we learn from Proclus (*in Eucl..I.* p. 283, 7) that Oinopides of Chios used it in the sense of a perpendicular (κάθετος). The instrument

Nor is it true that the Greeks made no use of experiment. The rise of the experimental method dates from the time when the medical schools began to influence the development of philosophy, and accordingly we find that the first recorded experiment of a modern type is that of Empedokles with the *klepsydra*. We have his own account of this (fr. 100), and we can see how it brought him to the verge of anticipating Harvey and Torricelli. It is inconceivable that an inquisitive people should have applied the experimental method in a single case without extending it to other problems.

Of course the great difficulty for us is the geocentric hypothesis from which science inevitably started, though only to outgrow it in a surprisingly short time. So long as the earth is supposed to be in the centre of the world, meteorology, in the later sense of the word, is necessarily identified with astronomy. It is difficult for us to feel at home in this point of view, and indeed we have no suitable word to express what the Greeks at first called an οὐρανός. It will be convenient to use the term " world " for it ; but then we must remember that it does not refer solely, or even chiefly, to the earth, though it includes that along with the heavenly bodies.

The science of the sixth century was mainly concerned, therefore, with those parts of the world that are " aloft " (τὰ μετέωρα), and these include such things as clouds, rainbows, and lightning, as well as the heavenly bodies.[1] That is how the latter came sometimes to be explained as ignited

---

so called was simply an upright erected on a flat surface, and its chief use was to indicate the solstices and the equinoxes by means of its shadow. It was not a sundial ; for it afforded no means of dividing the day into equal hours, though the time of day would be approximately inferred from the length of the shadow cast by it. For the geometrical use of the term, see below, p. 103, *n.* 1.

[1] The restricted sense of μετεωρολογία only arose when Aristotle introduced for the first time the fateful distinction between the οὐρανός and the " sublunary " region, to which it was now confined. In so far as they make no such distinction, the early cosmologists were more scientific than Aristotle. Their views admitted of correction and development ; Aristotle's theory arrested the growth of science.

clouds, an idea which seems astonishing to us.[1] But even that is better than to regard the sun, moon, and stars as having a different nature from the earth, and science inevitably and rightly began with the most obvious hypothesis, and it was only the thorough working out of this that could show its inadequacy. It is just because the Greeks were the first people to take the geocentric hypothesis seriously that they were able to go beyond it. Of course the pioneers of Greek thought had no clear idea of the nature of scientific hypothesis, and supposed themselves to be dealing with ultimate reality, but a sure instinct guided them to the right method, and we can see how it was the effort to " save appearances " [2] that really operated from the first. It is to those men we owe the conception of an exact science which should ultimately take in the whole world as its object. They fancied they could work out this science at once. We sometimes make the same mistake nowadays, and forget that all scientific progress consists in the advance from a less to a more adequate hypothesis. The Greeks were the first to follow this method, and that is their title to be regarded as the originators of science.

Schools of philosophy.

XIV. Theophrastos, the first writer to treat the history of Greek philosophy in a systematic way,[3] represented the early cosmologists as standing to one another in the relation of master and scholar, and as members of regular societies. This has been regarded as an anachronism, and some have even denied the existence of " schools " of philosophy altogether. But the statements of Theophrastos on such a subject are not to be lightly set aside. As this point is of

---

[1] It is well, however, to remember that Galileo himself regarded comets as meteorological phenomena.

[2] This phrase originated in the school of Plato.   The method of research in use there was for the leader to " propound " (προτείνειν, προβάλλεσθαι) it as a " problem " (πρόβλημα) to find the simplest " hypothesis " (τίνων ὑποτεθέντων) on which it is possible to account for and do justice to all the observed facts (σώζειν τὰ φαινόμενα). Cf. Milton, *Paradise Lost*, viii. 81, " how build, unbuild, contrive | To save appearances."

[3] See Note on Sources, § 7.

great importance, it will be necessary to elucidate it before we enter on our story.

In almost every department of life, the corporation at first is everything and the individual nothing. The peoples of the East hardly got beyond this stage ; their science, such as it is, is anonymous, the inherited property of a caste or guild, and we still see clearly in some cases that it was once the same among the Greeks. Medicine, for instance, was originally the " mystery " of the Asklepiads. What distinguished the Greeks from other peoples was that at an early date these crafts came under the influence of out-standing individuals, who gave them a fresh direction and a new impulse. But this does not destroy the corporate character of the craft ; it rather intensifies it. The guild becomes what we call a " school," and the disciple takes the place of the apprentice. That is a vital change. A close guild with none but official heads is essentially conservative, while a band of disciples attached to a master they revere is the greatest progressive force the world knows.

It is certain that the later Athenian schools were legally recognised corporations, the oldest of which, the Academy, maintained its existence as such for some nine hundred years, and the only question we have to decide is whether this was an innovation made in the fourth century B.C., or rather the continuance of an old tradition. Now we have the authority of Plato for speaking of the chief early systems as handed down in schools. He makes Sokrates speak of " the men of Ephesos," the Herakleiteans, as forming a strong body in his own day,[1] and the stranger of the *Sophist* and the *Statesman* speaks of his school as still in existence at Elea.[2] We also hear of " Anaxagoreans," [3] and no one, of

---

[1] *Theaet.* 179 e 4, αὐτοῖς . . . τοῖς περὶ τὴν Ἔφεσον. The humorous denial that the Herakleiteans had any disciples (180 b 8, Ποίοις μαθηταῖς, ὦ δαιμόνιε ;) implies that this was the normal and recognised relation.

[2] *Soph.* 242 d 4, τὸ . . . παρ᾽ ἡμῖν Ἐλεατικὸν ἔθνος. Cf. *ib.* 216 a 3, ἑταῖρον δὲ τῶν ἀμφὶ Παρμενίδην καὶ Ζήνωνα [ἑταίρων] (where ἑταίρων is probably interpolated, but gives the right sense) ; 217 a 1, οἱ περὶ τὸν ἐκεῖ τόπον.

[3] *Crat.* 409 b 6, εἴπερ ἀληθῆ οἱ Ἀναξαγόρειοι λέγουσιν. Cf. also the Δισσοὶ

course, can doubt that the Pythagoreans were a society.
In fact, there is hardly any school but that of Miletos for
which we have not external evidence of the strongest kind ;
and even as regards it, we have the significant fact that
Theophrastos speaks of philosophers of a later date as
having been " associates of the philosophy of Anaximenes." [1]
We shall see too in the first chapter that the internal evidence
in favour of the existence of a Milesian school is very strong
indeed.   It is from this point of view, then, that we shall
now proceed to consider the men who created Greek science.

λόγοι (Diels, Vors.³ ii. p. 343) τί δὲ ᾿Αναξαγόρειοι καὶ Πυθαγόρειοι ἦεν ;   This is
independent of Plato.
   [1] Cf. Chap. VI. § 122.

NOTE ON THE SOURCES

A.—PHILOSOPHERS

1. IT is not very often that Plato allows himself to dwell on Plato. the history of philosophy as it was before the rise of ethical and epistemological inquiry ; but when he does, he is always illuminating. His artistic gift and his power of entering into the thoughts of other men enabled him to describe the views of early philosophers in a sympathetic manner, and he never, except in a playful and ironical way, sought to read unthought-of meanings into the words of his predecessors. He has, in fact, a historical sense, which was a rare thing in antiquity.

The passage of the *Phaedo* (96 a *sqq.*) where he describes the state of scientific opinion at Athens in the middle of the fifth century is invaluable for our purposes.

2. As a rule, Aristotle's statements about early philoso- Aristotle. phers are far less historical than Plato's. He nearly always discusses the facts from the point of view of his own system, and that system, resting as it does on the deification of the apparent diurnal revolution of the heavens, made it very hard for him to appreciate more scientific views. He is convinced that his own philosophy accomplishes what all previous philosophers had aimed at, and their systems are therefore regarded as " lisping " attempts to formulate it (*Met.* A, 10, 993 a 15). It is also to be noted that Aristotle regards some systems in a much more sympathetic way than others. He is distinctly unfair to the Eleatics, for

31

instance, and in general, wherever mathematical considerations come into play, he is an untrustworthy guide.

It is often forgotten that Aristotle derived much of his information from Plato, and we must specially observe that he more than once takes Plato's humorous remarks too literally.

Stoics.

3. The Stoics, and especially Chrysippos, paid great attention to early philosophy, but their way of regarding it was simply an exaggeration of Aristotle's. They did not content themselves with criticising their predecessors from their own point of view ; they seem really to have believed that the early poets and thinkers taught doctrines hardly distinguishable from their own. The word συνοικειοῦν, which Cicero renders by *accommodare*, was used by Philodemos to denote this method of interpretation,[1] which has had serious results upon our tradition, especially in the case of Herakleitos.

Skeptics.

4. The same remarks apply *mutatis mutandis* to the Skeptics. The interest of such a writer as Sextus Empiricus in early philosophy is mainly to exhibit its contradictions. But what he tells us is often of value ; for he frequently quotes early views as to knowledge and sensation in support of his thesis.

Neo-platonists.

5. Under this head we have chiefly to consider the commentators on Aristotle in so far as they are independent of the Theophrastean tradition. Their chief characteristic is what Simplicius calls εὐγνωμοσύνη, that is, a liberal spirit of interpretation, which makes all early philosophers agree with one another in upholding the doctrine of a Sensible and an Intelligible World. It is, however, to Simplicius

---

[1] Cf. Cic. *De nat. d.* i. 15, 41 : " Et haec quidem (Chrysippus) in primo libro de natura deorum, in secundo autem vult Orphei, Musaei, Hesiodi Homerique fabellas accommodare ad ea quae ipse primo libro de deis immortalibus dixerat, ut etiam veterrimi poetae, qui haec ne suspicati quidem sunt, Stoici fuisse videantur." Cf. Philod. *De piet. fr.* c. 13, ἐν δὲ τῷ δευτέρῳ τά τε εἰς Ὀρφέα καὶ Μουσαῖον ἀναφερόμενα καὶ τὰ παρ' Ὁμήρῳ καὶ Ἡσιόδῳ καὶ Εὐριπίδῃ καὶ ποιηταῖς ἄλλοις, ὡς καὶ Κλεάνθης, πειρᾶται συνοικειοῦν ταῖς δόξαις αὐτῶν.

more than any one else that we owe the preservation of the fragments. He had, of course, the library of the Academy at his disposal, at any rate up to A.D. 529.

B.—DOXOGRAPHERS

6. The *Doxographi Graeci* of Professor Hermann Diels (1879) threw an entirely new light upon the filiation of the later sources ; and we can only estimate justly the value of statements derived from these if we bear constantly in mind the results of his investigation. Here it will only be possible to give an outline which may help the reader to find his way in the *Doxographi Graeci* itself.

The Doxographi Graeci.

7. By the term *doxographers* we understand all those writers who relate the opinions of the Greek philosophers, and who derive their material, directly or indirectly, from the great work of Theophrastos, Φυσικῶν δοξῶν ιη' (Diog. v. 46). Of this work, one considerable chapter, that entitled Περὶ αἰσθήσεων, has been preserved (*Dox.* pp. 499-527). And Usener, following Brandis, further showed that there were important fragments of it contained in the commentary of Simplicius ·(sixth cent. A.D.) on the First Book of Aristotle's Φυσικὴ ἀκρόασις (Usener, *Analecta Theophrastea*, pp. 25 *sqq*.). These extracts Simplicius seems to have borrowed in turn from Alexander of Aphrodisias (*c*. A.D. 200); cf. *Dox.* p. 112 *sqq*. We thus possess a very considerable portion of the First Book, which dealt with the ἀρχαί, as well as practically the whole of the last Book.

The "Opinions" of Theophrastos.

From these remains it clearly appears that the method of Theophrastos was to discuss in separate books the leading topics which had engaged the attention of philosophers from Thales to Plato. The chronological order was not observed ; the philosophers were grouped according to the affinity of their doctrine, the differences between those who appeared to agree most closely being carefully noted. The First Book, however, was in some degree exceptional ; for in it the order was that of the successive schools, and short historical and chronological notices were inserted.

8. A work of this kind was, of course, a godsend to the epitomators and compilers of handbooks, who flourished more and more as the Greek genius declined. These either followed Theophrastos in arranging the subject-matter under heads, or else they broke up his work, and rearranged his statements under the names of the various philosophers to whom they applied. This latter class form the natural transition between the doxographers proper and the biographers, so I have ventured to distinguish them by the name of *biographical doxographers*.

I. DOXOGRAPHERS PROPER

9. These are now mainly represented by two works, viz. the *Placita Philosophorum*, included among the writings ascribed to Plutarch, and the *Eclogae Physicae* of John Stobaios (*c.* A.D. 470). The latter originally formed one work with the *Florilegium* of the same author, and includes a transcript of some epitome substantially identical with the pseudo-Plutarchean *Placita*. It is, however, demonstrable that neither the *Placita* nor the doxography of the *Eclogae* is the original of the other. The latter is usually the fuller of the two, and yet the former must be earlier ; for it was used by Athenagoras for his defence of the Christians in A.D. 177 (*Dox.* p. 4). It was also the source of the notices in Eusebios and Cyril, and of the *History of Philosophy* ascribed to Galen. From these writers many important corrections of the text have been derived (*Dox.* pp. 5 *sqq.*).

Another writer who made use of the *Placita* is Achilles (*not* Achilles Tatius). For his Εἰσαγωγή to the *Phaenomena* of Aratos see Maass, *Commentariorum in Aratum reliquiae*, pp. 25-75. His date is uncertain, but probably he belongs to the third century A.D. (*Dox.* p. 18).

10. What, then, was the common source of the *Placita*

and the *Eclogae* ? Diels has shown that Theodoret (*c.*
A.D. 445) had access to it ; for in some cases he gives a fuller
form of statements made in these two works. Not only
so, but he also names that source ; for he refers us (*Gr. aff.
cur.* iv. 31) to Ἀετίου τὴν περὶ ἀρεσκόντων συναγωγήν. Diels
has accordingly printed the *Placita* in parallel columns with
the relevant parts of the *Eclogae*, under the title of *Aetii
Placita*. The quotations from " Plutarch " by later writers,
and the extracts of Theodoret from Aetios, are also given
at the foot of each page.

11. Diels has shown further, however, that Aetios did The Vetusta Placita.
not draw directly from Theophrastos, but from an intermediate epitome which he calls the *Vetusta Placita*, traces
of which may be found in Cicero (*infra*, § 12), and in
Censorinus (*De die natali*), who follows Varro. The *Vetusta
Placita* were composed in the school of Poseidonios, and
Diels now calls them the Poseidonian Ἀρέσκοντα (*Über das
phys. System des Straton*, p. 2). There are also traces of
them in the " Homeric Allegorists."

It is quite possible, by discounting the somewhat unin-
telligent additions which Aetios made from Epicurean and
other sources, to form a pretty accurate table of the contents
of the *Vetusta Placita* (*Dox*. pp. 181 *sqq.*), and this gives us
a fair idea of the arrangement of the original work by
Theophrastos.

12. So far as what he tells us of the earliest Greek Cicero.
philosophy goes, Cicero must be classed with the doxographers, and not with the philosophers ; for he gives us
nothing but extracts at second or third hand from the work
of Theophrastos. Two passages in his writings fall to be
considered under this head, namely, " Lucullus " (*Acad.* ii.),
118, and *De natura deorum*, i. 25-41.

(*a*) *Doxography of the " Lucullus."*—This contains a
meagre and inaccurately-rendered summary of the various
opinions held by philosophers with regard to the ἀρχή (*Dox*.
pp. 119 *sqq.*), and would be quite useless if it did not in one

case enable us to verify the exact words of Theophrastos (Chap. I. p. 50, *n.* 4). The doxography has come through the hands of Kleitomachos, who succeeded Karneades in the headship of the Academy (129 B.C.).

(b) *Doxography of the " De natura deorum."*—A fresh light was thrown upon this important passage by the discovery at Herculaneum of a roll containing fragments of an Epicurean treatise, so like it as to be at once regarded as its original. This treatise was at first ascribed to Phaidros, on the ground of the reference in *Epp. ad Att.* xiii. 39. 2 ; but the real title, Φιλοδήμου περὶ εὐσεβείας, was afterwards restored (*Dox.* p. 530). Diels, however, has shown (*Dox.* pp. 122 *sqq.*) that there is much to be said for the view that Cicero did not copy Philodemos, but that both drew from a common source (no doubt Phaidros, Περὶ θεῶν) which itself went back to a Stoïc epitome of Theophrastos. The passage of Cicero and the relevant fragments of Philodemos are edited in parallel columns by Diels (*Dox.* pp. 531 *sqq.*).

II. BIOGRAPHICAL DOXOGRAPHERS

Hippolytos. 13. Of the "biographical doxographies," the most important is Book I. of the *Refutation of all Heresies* by Hippolytos. This had long been known as the *Philosophoumena* of Origen ; but the discovery of the remaining books, which were first published at Oxford in 1854, showed finally that it could nòt belong to him. It is drawn mainly from some good epitome of Theophrastos, in which the matter was already rearranged under the names of the various philosophers. We must note, however, that the sections dealing with Thales, Pythagoras, Herakleitos, and Empedokles come from an inferior source, some merely biographical compendium full of apocryphal anecdotes and doubtful statements.

The 14. The fragments of the pseudo-Plutarchean *Stromateis*, Stromateis. quoted by Eusebios in his *Praeparatio Evangelica*, come from a source similar to that of the best portions of the *Philosophoumena*. So far as we can judge, they differ chiefly in two points. In the first place, they are mostly taken from the earliest sections of the work, and therefore most of them deal with the primary substance, the heavenly bodies and the earth. In the second place, the language is a much less faithful transcript of the original.

15. The scrap-book which goes by the name of Diogenes Laertios, or Laertios Diogenes (cf. Usener, *Epicurea*, pp. 1 *sqq.*), contains large fragments of two distinct doxographies. One is of the merely biographical, anecdotic, and apophthegmatic kind used by Hippolytos in his first four chapters ; the other is of a better class, more like the source of Hippolytos' remaining chapters. An attempt is made to disguise this " contamination " by referring to the first doxography as a " summary " (κεφαλαιώδης) account, while the second is called " particular " (ἐπὶ μέρους). **" Diogenes Laertios."**

16. Short doxographical summaries are to be found in Eusebios (*P. E.* x., xiv., xv.), Theodoret (*Gr. aff. cur.* ii. 9-11), Irenaeus (*C. haer.* ii. 14), Arnobius (*Adv. nat.* ii. 9), Augustine (*Civ. Dei*, viii. 2). These depend mainly upon the writers of " Successions," whom we shall have to consider in the next section. **Patristic doxographies.**

C.—BIOGRAPHERS

17. The first to write a work entitled *Successions of the Philosophers* was Sotion (Diog. ii. 12 ; R. P. 4 a), about 200 B.C. The arrangement of his work is explained in *Dox.* p. 147. It was epitomised by Herakleides Lembos. Other writers of Διαδοχαί were Antisthenes, Sosikrates, and Alexander. All these compositions were accompanied by a very meagre doxography, and made interesting by the addition of unauthentic apophthegms and apocryphal anecdotes. **Successions.**

18. The peripatetic Hermippos of Smyrna, known as Καλλιμάχειος (*c.* 200 B.C.), wrote several biographical works **Hermippos.**

which are frequently quoted. The biographical details are very untrustworthy ; but sometimes bibliogι. phical information is added, which doubtless rests upon the Πίνακες of Kallimachos.

Satyros.   19. Another peripatetic, Satyros, the pupil of Aristarchos, wrote (*c.* 160 B.C.) *Lives of Famous Men.* The same remarks apply to him as to Hermippos. His work was epitomised by Herakleides Lembos.

" Diogenes Laertios."   20. The work which goes by the name of Laertios Diogenes is, in its biographical parts, a mere patchwork of all earlier learning. It has not been digested or composed by any single mind at all, but is little more than a collection of extracts made at haphazard. But, of course, it contains much that is of the greatest value.

D.—CHRONOLOGISTS

Eratosthenes and Apollodoros.   21. The founder of ancient chronology was Eratosthenes of Kyrene (275-194 B.C.) ; but his work was soon supplanted by the metrical version of Apollodoros (*c.* 140 B.C.), from which most of our information as to the dates of early philosophers is derived. See Diels' paper on the Χρονικά of Apollodoros in *Rhein. Mus.* xxxi. ; and Jacoby, *Apollodors Chronik* (1902).

The method adopted is as follows :—If the date of some striking event in a philosopher's life is known, that is taken as his *floruit* (ἀκμή), and he is assumed to have been forty years old at that date. In default of this, some historical era is taken as the *floruit.* Of these the chief are the eclipse of Thales 586/5 B.C., the taking of Sardeis in 546/5 B.C., the accession of Polykrates in 532/1 B.C., and the foundation of Thourioi in 444/3 B.C. It is usual to attach far too much weight to these combinations, and we can often show that Apollodoros is wrong from our other evidence. His dates can only be accepted as a makeshift, when nothing better is available.

CHAPTER I

THE MILESIAN SCHOOL

1. It was at Miletos that the earliest school of scientific Miletos and Lydia. cosmology had its home, and it is not, perhaps, without significance that Miletos is just the place where the continuity of Aegean and Ionian civilisation is most clearly marked.[1] The Milesians had come into conflict more than once with the Lydians, whose rulers were bent on extending their dominion to the coast ; but, towards the end of the seventh century B.C., the tyrant Thrasyboulos succeeded in making terms with King Alyattes, and an alliance was concluded which secured Miletos against molestation for the future. Even half a century later, when Croesus, resuming his father's forward policy, made war upon and conquered Ephesos, Miletos was able to maintain the old treaty-relation, and never, strictly speaking, became subject to the Lydians at all. The Lydian connexion, moreover, favoured the growth of science at Miletos. What was called at a later date Hellenism seems to have been traditional in the dynasty of the Mermnadai, and Herodotos says that all the " sophists " of the time flocked to the court of Sardeis.[2] The tradition which represents Croesus as

[1] See Introd. § II. Ephoros said that Old Miletos was colonised from Milatos in Crete at an earlier date than the fortification of the new city by Neleus (Strabo, xiv. p. 634), and recent excavation has shown that the Aegean civilisation passed here by gradual transition into the early Ionic. The dwellings of the old Ionians stand on and among the *débris* of the " Mycenean " period. There is no " geometrical " interlude.

[2] Herod. i. 29. See Radet, *La Lydie et le monde grec au temḟ des Mermnades* (Paris, 1893).

the " patron " of Greek wisdom was fully developed in the fifth century ; and, however unhistorical its details may be, it must clearly have some foundation in fact. Particularly noteworthy is " the common tale among the Greeks," that Thales accompanied Croesus on his luckless campaign against Pteria, apparently in the capacity of military engineer. Herodotos disbelieves the story that he diverted the course of the Halys, but only because he knew there were bridges there already. It is clear that the Ionians were great engineers, and that they were employed as such by the eastern kings.[1]

It should be added that the Lydian alliance would facilitate intercourse with Babylon and Egypt. Lydia was an advanced post of Babylonian culture, and Croesus was on friendly terms with the kings of Egypt and Babylon. Amasis of Egypt had the same Hellenic sympathies as Croesus, and the Milesians possessed a temple of their own at Naukratis.

I. THALES

Origin.　　2. The founder of the Milesian school, and therefore the first man of science, was Thales ;[2] but all we can really be said to know of him comes from Herodotos, and the Tale

[1] Herod. i. 75. It is important for a right estimate of Ionian science to remember the high development of engineering in these days. Mandrokles of Samos built the bridge over the Bosporos for King Dareios (Herod. iv. 88), and Harpalos of Tenedos bridged the Hellespont for Xerxes when the Egyptians and Phoenicians had failed in the attempt (Diels, *Abh. der Berl. Akad.*, 1904, p. 8). The tunnel through the hill above Samos described by Herodotos (iii. 60) has been discovered by German excavators. It is about a kilometre long, but the levels are almost accurate. On the whole subject see Diels, " Wissenschaft und Technik bei den Hellenen " (*Neue Jahrb.* xxxiii. pp. 3, 4). Here, as in other things, the Ionians carried on " Minoan " traditions.

[2] Simplicius quotes Theophrastos as saying that Thales had many predecessors (*Dox.* p. 475, 11). This need not trouble us ; for the scholiast on Apollonios Rhodios (ii. 1248) tells us that he made Prometheus the first philosopher, which is merely an application of Peripatetic literalism to a phrase of Plato's (*Phileb.* 16 c 6). Cf. Note on Sources, § 2.

of the Seven Wise Men was already in existence when he wrote. He says that Thales was of Phoenician descent, a statement which other writers explained by saying he belonged to a noble house descended from Kadmos and Agenor.[1] Herodotos probably mentions the supposed descent of Thales simply because he was believed to have introduced certain improvements in navigation from Phoenicia.[2] At any rate, his father's name, Examyes, lends no support to the view that he was a Semite. It is Karian, and the Karians had been almost completely assimilated by the Ionians. On the monuments we find Greek and Karian names alternating in the same families, while the name Thales is otherwise known as Cretan. There is therefore no reason to doubt that Thales was of pure Milesian descent, though he probably had Karian blood in his veins.[3]

3. The most remarkable statement Herodotos makes about Thales is that he foretold the eclipse of the sun which put an end to the war between the Lydians and the Medes.[4] Now, he was quite ignorant of the cause of eclipses. Anaximander and his successors certainly were so,[5] and it is incredible that the explanation should have been given and forgotten so soon. Even supposing Thales had known the cause of eclipses, such scraps of elementary geometry

The eclipse foretold by Thales.

---

[1] Herod. i. 170 (R. P. 9 d) ; Diog. i. 22 (R. P. 9). This is no doubt connected with the fact mentioned by Herodotos (i. 146) that there were Kadmeians from Boiotia among the original Ionian colonists. Cf. also. Strabo, xiv. pp. 633, 636 ; Pausan. vii. 2, 7. These, however, were not Semites.

[2] Diog. i. 23, Καλλίμαχος δ' αὐτὸν οἶδεν εὑρετὴν τῆς ἄρκτου τῆς μικρᾶς λέγων ἐν τοῖς Ἰάμβοις οὕτως—

καὶ τῆς ἁμάξης ἐλέγετο σταθμήσασθαι
τοὺς ἀστερίσκους, ᾗ πλέουσι Φοίνικες.

[3] See Diels, " Thales ein Semite ? " (*Arch.* ii. 165 sqq.), and Immisch, " Zu Thales Abkunft " (*ib.* p. 515). The name Examyes occurs also in Kolophon (Hermesianax, *Leontion,* fr. 2, 38 Bgk.), and may be compared with other Karian names such as Cheramyes and Panamyes.

[4] Herod. i. 74.

[5] For the theories held by Anaximander and Herakleitos, see *infra,* §§ 19, 71.

as he picked up in Egypt would never have enabled him to calculate one. Yet the evidence for the prediction is too strong to be rejected off-hand. The testimony of Herodotos is said to have been confirmed by Xenophanes,[1] and according to Theophrastos Xenophanes was a disciple of Anaximander. In any case, he must have known scores of people who were able to remember what happened. The prediction of the eclipse is therefore better attested than any other fact about Thales whatsoever.

Now it is possible to predict eclipses of the moon approximately without knowing their true cause, and there is no doubt that the Babylonians actually did so. It is generally stated, further, that they had made out a cycle of 223 lunar months, within which eclipses of the sun and moon recurred at equal intervals of time.[2] This, however, would not have enabled them to predict eclipses of the sun for a given spot on the earth's surface ; for these phenomena are not visible at all places where the sun is above the horizon at the time. We do not occupy a position at the centre of the earth, and the geocentric parallax has to be taken into account. It would only, therefore, be possible to tell by means of the cycle that an eclipse of the sun would be visible somewhere, and that it might be worth while to look out for it, though an observer at a given place

---

[1] Diog. i. 23, δοκεῖ δὲ κατά τινας πρῶτος ἀστρολογῆσαι καὶ ἡλιακὰς ἐκλείψεις καὶ τροπὰς προειπεῖν, ὥς φησιν Εὔδημος ἐν τῇ περὶ τῶν ἀστρολογουμένων ἱστορίᾳ, ὅθεν αὐτὸν καὶ Ξενοφάνης καὶ Ἡρόδοτος θαυμάζει. The statement that Thales " predicted " solstices as well as eclipses is not so absurd as has been thought. Eudemos may very well have meant that he fixed the dates of the solstices and equinoxes more accurately than had been done before. That he would do by observing the length of the shadow cast by an upright (γνώμων), and we shall see (p. 47) that popular tradition ascribed observations of the kind to him. This interpretation is favoured by another remark of Eudemos, preserved by Derkyllides (ap. Theon. p. 198, 17 Hiller), that Thales discovered τὴν κατὰ τὰς τροπὰς αὐτοῦ (τοῦ ἡλίου) περίοδον, ὡς οὐκ ἴση ἀεὶ συμβαίνει. In other words, he discovered the inequality of the four seasons which is due to the solar anomaly.

[2] It is wrong to call this the *Saros* with Souidas ; for *sar* on the monuments always means $60^2 = 3600$, the number of the Great Year. The period of 223 lunations is, of course, that of the retrograde movement of the nodes.

might be disappointed five times out of six. Now, if we may judge from reports by Chaldaean astronomers which have been preserved, this was just the position of the Babylonians in the eighth century B.C. They watched for eclipses at the proper dates; and, if they did not occur, they announced the fact as a good omen.[1] To explain what we are told about Thales no more is required. He said there would be an eclipse by a certain date; and luckily it was visible in Asia Minor, and on a striking occasion.[2]

4. The prediction of the eclipse does not, then, throw any light on the scientific attainments of Thales; but, if we can fix its date, it will give us an indication of the time at which he lived. Astronomers have calculated that there was an eclipse of the sun, probably visible in Asia Minor, on May 28 (O.S.), 585 B.C., while Pliny gives the date of the eclipse foretold by Thales as Ol. XLVIII. 4 (585/4 B.C.).[3] This does not exactly tally; for May 585 belongs to the year 586/5 B.C. It is near enough, however, to justify us in

Date of Thales.

[1] See George Smith, *Assyrian Discoveries* (1875), p. 409. The inscription which follows was found at Kouyunjik :—
" To the king my lord, thy servant Abil-Istar.

.   .   .   .

" Concerning the eclipse of the moon of which the king my lord sent to me; in the cities of Akkad, Borsippa, and Nipur, observations they made, and then in the city of Akkad, we saw part. . . . The observation was made, and the eclipse took place.

.   .   .   .

" And when for the eclipse of the sun we made an observation, the observation was made and it did not take place. That which I saw with my eyes to the king my lord I send." See further R. C. Thomson, *Reports of the Magicians and Astrologers of Nineveh and Babylon* (1900).

[2] Cf. Schiaparelli, " I primordi dell' Astronomia presso i Babilonesi " (*Scientia*, 1908, p. 247). His conclusion is that " the law which regulates the circumstances of the visibility of solar eclipses is too complex to be discovered by simple observation," and that the Babylonians were not in a position to formulate it. " Such a triumph was reserved to the geometrical genius of the Greeks."

[3] Pliny, *N.H.* ii. 53. It should be noted that this date is inconsistent with the chronology of Herodotos, but that is vitiated by the assumption that the fall of the Median kingdom synchronised with the accession of Cyrus to the throne of Persia. If we make the necessary correction, Cyaxares was still reigning in 585 B.C.

identifying the eclipse as that of Thales,[1] and this is confirmed by Apollodoros, who fixed his *floruit* in the same year.[2] The further statement in Diogenes that, according to Demetrios Phalereus, Thales " received the name of wise " in the archonship of Damasias at Athens, really refers to the Tale of the Seven Wise Men, as is shown by the words which follow, and is doubtless based on the story of the Delphic tripod ; for the archonship of Damasias is the era of the restoration of the Pythian Games.[3]

Thales in Egypt.

5. The introduction of Egyptian geometry into Hellas is ascribed to Thales,[4] and it is probable that he did visit Egypt ; for he had a theory of the inundations of the Nile. Herodotos [5] gives three explanations of the fact that this alone of all rivers rises in summer and falls in winter ; but, as his custom is, he does not name their authors. The first, however, which attributes the rise of the Nile to the Etesian winds, is ascribed to Thales in the *Placita*,[6] and by

---

[1] The words of Herodotos (i. 74), οὖρον προθέμενος ἐνιαυτὸν τοῦτον ἐν τῷ δὴ καὶ ἐγένετο, mean at first sight that he only said the eclipse would occur before the end of a certain year, but Diels suggests (*Neue Jahrb.* xxxiii. p. 2) that ἐνιαυτός has here its original sense of " summer solstice " (cf. Brugmann, *Idg. Forsch.* xv. p. 87). In that case Thales would have fixed the date within a month. He may have observed the eclipse of May 18, 603 B.C. in Egypt, and predicted another in eighteen years and some days, not later than the solstice.

[2] For Apollodoros, see Note on Sources, § 21. The dates in our text of Diogenes (i. 37 ; R. P. 8) cannot be reconciled with one another. That given for the death of Thales is probably right ; for it is the year before the fall of Sardeis in 546/5 B.C., which is one of the regular eras of Apollodoros. It no doubt seemed natural to make Thales die the year before the " ruin of Ionia " which he foresaw. Seventy-eight years before this brings us to 624/3 B.C. for the birth of Thales, and this gives us 585/4 B.C. for his fortieth year. That is Pliny's date for the eclipse, and Pliny's dates come from Apollodoros through Nepos.

[3] Diog. i. 22 (R. P. 9), especially the words καθ' ὃν καὶ οἱ ἑπτὰ σοφοὶ ἐκλήθησαν. The story of the tripod was told in many versions (cf. Diog. i. 28-33 ; *Vors.* i. p. 2, 26 *sqq.*). It clearly belongs to the Delphian Tale of the Seven Wise Men, which is already alluded to by Plato (*Prot.* 343 a, b). Now Demetrios of Phaleron dated this in the archonship of Damasias at Athens (582/1 B.C.), and the Marmor Parium dates the restoration of the ἀγὼν στεφανίτης at Delphoi in the same year, and also identifies it with that of Damasias (cf. Jacoby, p. 170, *n.* 12).

[4] Proclus, *in Eucl. I.* p. 65, Friedlein (from Eudemos).

[5] Herod. ii. 20.   [6] Aet. iv. 1. 1 (*Dox.* p. 384).

many later writers. Now, this comes from a treatise on
the Rise of the Nile attributed to Aristotle and known to
the Greek commentators, but extant only in a Latin epitome
of the thirteenth century.[1] In this the first of the theories
mentioned by Herodotos is ascribed to Thales, the second
to Euthymenes of Massalia, and the third to Anaxagoras.
Where did Aristotle, or whoever wrote the book, get these
names ? We think naturally of Hekataios ; and this
conjecture is strengthened when we find that Hekataios
mentioned Euthymenes.[2] We may conclude that Thales
really was in Egypt ; and, perhaps, that Hekataios, in
describing the Nile, took account, as was natural, of his
fellow-citizen's views.

6. As to the nature and extent of the mathematical Thales
knowledge brought back by Thales from Egypt, it must be and
geometry.
pointed out that most writers have seriously misunderstood
the character of the tradition.[3] In his commentary on the
First Book of Euclid, Proclus enumerates, on the authority
of Eudemos, certain propositions which he says were known
to Thales,[4] one of which is that two triangles are equal
when they have one side and the two adjacent angles equal.
This he must have known, as otherwise he could not have
measured the distances of ships at sea in the way he was
said to have done.[5] Here we see how all these statements
arose. Certain feats in the way of measurement were
traditionally ascribed to Thales, and Eudemos assumed
that he must have known all the propositions these imply.

[1] *Dox.* pp. 226-229. The Latin epitome will be found in Rose's edition
of the Aristotelian fragments.
[2] Hekataios, fr. 278 (*F.H.G.* i. p. 19).
[3] See Cantor, *Vorlesungen über Geschichte der Mathematik*, vol. i. pp.
12 *sqq.* ; Allman, " Greek Geometry from Thales to Euclid " (*Hermathena*,
iii. pp. 164-174).
[4] Proclus, *in Eucl.* pp. 65, 7 ; 157, 10 ; 250, 20 ; 299, 1 ; 352, 14
(Friedlein). Eudemos wrote the first histories of astronomy and mathematics, just as Theophrastos wrote the first history of philosophy.
[5] Proclus, p. 352, 14, Εὔδημος δὲ ἐν ταῖς γεωμετρικαῖς ἱστορίαις εἰς Θαλῆν τοῦτο
ἀνάγει τὸ θεώρημα (*Eucl.* i. 26)· τὴν γὰρ τῶν ἐν θαλάττῃ πλοίων ἀπόστασιν δι' οὗ
τρόπου φασὶν αὐτὸν δεικνύναι τούτῳ προσχρῆσθαί φησιν ἀναγκαῖον.

But this is quite illusory. Both the measurement of the distance of ships at sea, and that of the height of the pyramids, which is also ascribed to him,[1] are easy applications of the rule given by Aahmes for finding the *seqt*.[2] What the tradition really points to is that Thales applied this empirical rule to practical problems which the Egyptians had never faced, and that he was thus the originator of general methods. That is a sufficient title to fame.

Thales as a politician.
7. Thales appears once more in Herodotos some time before the fall of the Lydian monarchy. He is said to have urged the Ionian Greeks to unite in a federal state with its capital at Teos.[3] We shall have occasion to notice more than once that the early schools of philosophy by no means held aloof from politics ; and there are many things, for instance the part played by Hekataios in the Ionian revolt, which suggest that the scientific men of Miletos took up a very decided position in the stirring times that followed the death of Thales. It is this political action which has gained the founder of the Milesian school his undisputed place among the Seven Wise Men ; and it is owing to his inclusion among those worthies that the numerous anecdotes told of him in later days attached themselves to his name.[4]

Uncertain character of the tradition.
8. So far as we know, Thales wrote nothing, and no writer earlier than Aristotle knows anything of him as a scientific man and a philosopher ; in the older tradition he

[1] The oldest version of this story is given in Diog. i. 27, ὁ δὲ Ἱερώνυμος καὶ ἐκμετρῆσαί φησιν αὐτὸν τὰς πυραμίδας, ἐκ τῆς σκιᾶς παρατηρήσαντα ὅτε ἡμῖν ἰσομεγέθης ἐστίν. Cf. Pliny, *H. Nat.* xxxvi. 82, *mensuram altitudinis earum deprehendere invenit Thales Milesius umbram metiendo qua hora par esse corpori solet*. (Hieronymos of Rhodes was contemporary with Eudemos.) This need imply no more than the reflexion that the shadows of all objects will be equal to the objects at the same hour. Plutarch (*Conv. sept. sap.* 147 a) gives a more elaborate method, τὴν βακτηρίαν στήσας ἐπὶ τῷ πέρατι τῆς σκιᾶς ἣν ἡ πυραμὶς ἐποίει, γενομένων τῇ ἐπαφῇ τῆς ἀκτῖνος δυοῖν τριγώνων, ἔδειξας ὃν ἡ σκιὰ πρὸς τὴν σκιὰν λόγον εἶχε, τὴν πυραμίδα πρὸς τὴν βακτηρίαν ἔχουσαν.

[2] See Gow, *Short History of Greek Mathematics*, § 84.

[3] Herod. i. 170 (R. P. 9 d).

[4] The story of Thales falling into a well (Plato, *Theaet.* 174 a) is nothing but a fable teaching the uselessness of σοφία ; the anecdote about the " corner " in oil (Ar. *Pol.* A, 11. 1259 a 6) is intended to inculcate the opposite lesson.

is simply an engineer and an inventor.[1] It is obvious,
however, that the requirements of Milesian enterprise and
commerce would necessarily turn his attention to problems
which we should call astronomical. He was said, we saw,
to have introduced the practice of steering a ship's course
by *Ursa minor* ;[2] and there is a remarkable persistence in
the tradition that he tried to do something for the calendar,
though the details are not sufficiently well attested to find
a place here.[3] No doubt he constructed a παράπηγμα like
those of much later date which have been discovered at
Miletos.[4] The παράπηγμα was the oldest form of almanac,
and gave, for a series of years, the equinoxes and solstices,
the phases of the moon, the heliacal risings and settings of
certain stars, and also weather predictions. Even Aristotle
does not pretend to know how Thales arrived at the views he
ascribes to him or by what arguments they were supported.
This very reserve, however, makes it hard to doubt that
he was correctly informed with regard to the few points
about them he mentions, so we may venture on a conjectural restoration of his cosmology. This, of course, must
be taken for just what it is worth.

9. The statements of Aristotle may be reduced to three : The cos-
  (1) The earth floats on the water.[5]   mology of Thales.
  (2) Water is the material cause [6] of all things.

---

[1] Cf. Aristophanes, *Clouds* 180 (after a burlesque description of how
Sokrates provided himself with a cloak) τί δῆτ' ἐκεῖνον τὸν Θαλῆν θαυμάζομεν ;
Birds 1009 (of Meton's town-planning, ἄνθρωπος Θαλῆς). Plato's way of
speaking is remarkable. Cf. *Rep.* 600 a ἀλλ' οἷα δὴ εἰς τὰ ἔργα σοφοῦ ἀνδρὸς
πολλαὶ ἐπίνοιαι καὶ εὐμήχανοι εἰς τέχνας ἤ τινας ἄλλας πράξεις λέγονται, ὥσπερ αὖ
Θάλεώ τε πέρι τοῦ Μιλησίου καὶ 'Αναχάρσιος τοῦ Σκύθου.
[2] See p. 41, *n.* 2.
[3] If he tried to introduce the year of 360 days and the month of
30 days, he may have learnt that in Egypt.
[4] For the Milesian παραπήγματα see Rehm, *Berl. Sitzungsber.*, 1893,
p. 101 *sqq.*, 752 *sqq.*
[5] Ar. *Met.* A, 3. 983 b 21 (R. P. 10) ; *De caelo*, B, 13. 294 a 28
(R. P. 11).
[6] *Met.* A, 3. 983 b 21 (R. P. 10). We must translate ἀρχή here by
" material cause," for τῆς τοιαύτης ἀρχῆς (b 19) means τῆς ἐν ὕλης εἴδει ἀρχῆς
(b 7). The word, then, is used here in a strictly Aristotelian sense. Cf.
Introd. p. 11, *n.* 3.

(3) All things are full of gods. The magnet is alive ;
for it has the power of moving iron.[1]

The first of these statements must be understood in
the light of the second, which is expressed in Aristotelian
terminology, but would undoubtedly mean that Thales
had said water was the stuff of which all other things were
transient forms. We have seen that this was the great
question of the day.

Water.   10. Aristotle and Theophrastos, followed by Simplicius
and the doxographers, suggest several explanations of this
doctrine. Aristotle gives them as conjectures ; it is only
later writers that repeat them as if they were quite certain.[2]
The most probable view seems to be that Aristotle ascribed
to Thales the arguments used at a later date by Hippon of
Samos in support of a similar thesis.[3] That would account
for their physiological character. The rise of scientific
medicine had made biological arguments popular in the
fifth century ; but, in the days of Thales, the prevailing
interest was not physiological, but meteorological, and it is
from this point of view we must try to understand the
theory.

Now it is not hard to see how meteorological considera-

---

[1] Arist. *De an.* A, 5. 411 a 7 (R. P. 13) ; *ib.* 2. 405 a 19 (R. P. 13 a).
Diog. i. 24 (R. P. *ib.*) adds amber.

[2] *Met.* A, 3. 983 b 22 ; Aet. i. 3, 1 ; Simpl. *Phys.* p. 36, 10 (R. P. 10,
12, 12 a). The last of Aristotle's explanations, that Thales was influenced
by cosmogonical theories about Okeanos and Tethys, has strangely been
supposed to be more historical than the rest, whereas it is merely a fancy
of Plato's taken literally. Plato says (*Theaet.* 180 d 2 ; *Crat.* 402 b 4)
that Herakleitos and his predecessors (οἱ ῥέοντες) derived their philosophy
from Homer (*Il.* xiv. 201), and even earlier sources (Orph. frag. 2, Diels,
Vors. 66 B 2). In quoting this suggestion, Aristotle refers it to " some "
—a word which often means Plato—and he calls the originators of the
theory παμπαλαίους, as Plato had done (*Met.* A, 3. 983 b 28 ; cf. *Theaet.*
181 b 3). This is how Aristotle gets history out of Plato. See Note on
Sources, § 2.

[3] Compare Arist. *De an.* A, 2. 405 b 2 (R. P. 220) with the passages
referred to in the last note. We now know that, though Aristotle declines
to consider Hippon as a philosopher (*Met.* A, 3. 984 a 3 ; R. P. 219 a),
he was discussed in the Peripatetic history of medicine known as Menon's
Iatrika. See § 185.

tions may have led Thales to adopt the view he did. Of all the things we know, water seems to take the most various shapes. It is familiar to us in a solid, a liquid, and a vaporous form, and so Thales may well have thought he saw the world-process from water and back to water again going on before his eyes. The phenomenon of evaporation naturally suggests that the fire of the heavenly bodies is kept up by the moisture they draw from the sea. Even at the present day people speak of " the sun drawing water." Water comes down again in rain ; and lastly, so the early cosmologists thought, it turns to earth. This may have seemed natural enough to men familiar with the river of Egypt which had formed the Delta, and the torrents of Asia Minor which bring down large alluvial deposits. At the present day the Gulf of Latmos, on which Miletos used to stand, is filled up. Lastly, they thought, earth turns once more to water—an idea derived from the observation of dew, night-mists, and subterranean springs. For these last were not in early times supposed to have anything to do with the rain. The " waters under the earth " were regarded as an independent source of moisture.[1]

11. The third of the statements mentioned above is Theology. supposed by Aristotle to imply that Thales believed in a " soul of the world," though he is careful to mark this as no more than an inference.[2] The doctrine of the world-soul is then attributed quite positively to Thales by Aetios, who gives it in the Stoic phraseology which he found in his immediate source, and identifies the world-intellect with God.[3] Cicero found a similar statement in the Epicurean manual which he followed, but he goes a step further. Eliminating the Stoic pantheism, he turns the world-intellect into a Platonic *demiourgos*, and says that Thales

[1] The view here taken most resembles that of the " Homeric allegorist " Herakleitos (R. P. 12 a). That, however, is also a conjecture, probably of Stoic, as the others are of Peripatetic, origin.

[2] Arist. *De an.* A, 5. 411 a 7 (R. P. 13).

[3] Aet. i. 7, 11=Stob. i. 56 (R. P. 14). On the sources here referred to, see Note on Sources, §§ 11, 12.

held there was a divine mind which formed all things out of water.[1] All this is derived from Aristotle's cautious statement, and can have no greater authority than its source. We need not enter, then, on the old controversy whether Thales was an atheist or not. If we may judge from his successors, he may very possibly have called water a " god " ; but that would not imply any definite religious belief.[2]

Nor must we make too much of the saying that " all things are full of gods." It is not safe to regard an apophthegm as evidence, and the chances are that it belongs to Thales as one of the Seven Wise Men, rather than as founder of the Milesian school. Further, such sayings are, as a rule, anonymous to begin with, and are attributed now to one sage and now to another.[3] On the other hand, it is probable that Thales did say the magnet and amber had souls. That is no apophthegm, but more on the level of the statement that the earth floats on the water. It is just the sort of thing we should expect Hekataios to record about Thales. It would be wrong, however, to draw any inference from it as to his view of the world ; for to say the magnet and amber are alive is to imply, if anything, that other things are not.

II. ANAXIMANDER

Life.　　12. Anaximander, son of Praxiades, was also a citizen of Miletos, and Theophrastos described him as an " associate " of Thales.[4] We have seen how that expression is to be understood (§ XIV.).

---

[1] Cicero, De nat. d. 1. 25 (R. P. 13 b). On Cicero's source, see Dox. pp. 125, 128. The Herculanean papyrus of Philodemos is defective at this point, but it is not likely that he anticipated Cicero's mistake.

[2] See Introd. § IX.

[3] Plato refers to the saying πάντα πλήρη θεῶν in Laws, 899 b 9 (R. P. 14 b), without mentioning Thales. That ascribed to Herakleitos in the De part. an. A, 5. 645 a 7 seems to be a mere variation on it. In any case it means only that nothing is more divine than anything else.

[4] R. P. 15 d. That the words πολίτης καὶ ἑταῖρος, given by Simplicius, De caelo, p. 615, 13, are from Theophrastos is shown by the agreement of Cic. Acad. ii. 118, popularis et sodalis. The two passages represent independent branches of the tradition. See Note on Sources, §§ 7, 12.

According to Apollodoros, Anaximander was sixty-four years old in Ol. LVIII. 2 (547/6 B.C.) ; and this is confirmed by Hippolytos, who says he was born in Ol. XLII. 3 (610/9 B.C.), and by Pliny, who assigns his great discovery of the obliquity of the zodiac to Ol. LVIII.[1] We seem to have something more here than a combination of the ordinary type ; for, according to all the rules, Anaximander should have " flourished " in 565 B.C., half-way between Thales and Anaximenes, and this would make him sixty, not sixty-four, in 546. Now Apollodoros appears to have said that he had met with the work of Anaximander ; and the only reason he can have had for mentioning this must be that he found in it some indication which enabled him to fix its date. Now 547/6 is just the year before the fall of Sardeis, and we may perhaps conjecture that Anaximander mentioned what his age had been at the time of that event. We know from Xenophanes that the question, " How old were you when the Mede appeared ? " was considered an interesting one in those days.[2] At all events, Anaximander was apparently a generation younger than Thales.[3]

Like his predecessor, he distinguished himself by certain practical inventions. Some writers credited him with that of the *gnomon* ; but that can hardly be correct. Herodotos tells us this instrument came from Babylon, and Thales must have used it to determine the solstices and equinoxes.[4] Anaximander was also the first to construct a map, and Eratosthenes said this was the map elaborated by Hekataios. No doubt it was intended to be of service to Milesian enterprise in the Black Sea. Anaximander himself conducted

[1] Diog. ii. 2 (R. P. 15); Hipp. *Ref.* i. 6 (*Dox.* p. 560); Plin. *N.H.* ii. 31.
[2] Xenophanes, fr. 22 (= fr. 17 Karsten; R. P. 95 a).
[3] The statement that he " died soon after " (Diog. ii. 2 ; R. P. 15) seems to mean that Apollodoros made him die in the year of Sardeis (546/5), one of his regular epochs.
[4] For the gnomon, see Introd. p. 26, *n.* 1 ; and cf. Diog. ii. 1 (R. P. 15) ; Herod. ii. 109 (R. P. 15 a). Pliny, on the other hand, ascribes the invention of the gnomon to Anaximenes (*N.H.* ii. 187).

a colony to Apollonia,[1] and his fellow-citizens erected a
statue to him.[2]

Theo-
phrastos
on Anaxi-
mander's
theory of
the
primary
substance.

13. Nearly all we know of Anaximander's system is
derived in the last resort from Theophrastos, who certainly
knew his book.[3] He seems once at least to have quoted
Anaximander's own words, and he criticised his style.
Here are the remains of what he said of him in the First
Book :

Anaximander of Miletos, son of Praxiades, a fellow-citizen
and associate of Thales,[4] said that the material cause and first
element of things was the Infinite, he being the first to introduce
this name of the material cause. He says it is neither water nor
any other of the so-called [5] elements, but a substance different
from them which is infinite, from which arise all the heavens and
the worlds within them.—*Phys. Op.* fr. 2 (*Dox.* p. 476 ; R. P. 16).

He says that this is " eternal and ageless," and that it " encompasses all the worlds."—Hipp. *Ref.* i. 6 (R. P. 17 a).

And into that from which things take their rise they pass
away once more, " as is meet ; for they make reparation and
satisfaction to one another for their injustice according to the
ordering of time," as he says [6] in these somewhat poetical terms.
—*Phys. Op.* fr. 2 (R. P. 16).

And besides this, there was an eternal motion, in which
was brought about the origin of the worlds.—Hipp. *Ref.* i. 6
(R. P. 17 a).

---

[1] Aelian, *V.H.* iii. 17. Presumably Apollonia on the Pontos is meant.
[2] The lower part of a contemporary statue has been discovered at
Miletos (Wiegand, *Milet*, ii. 88), with the inscription ANJAΞIMANΔPO.
It was not, we may be sure, for his thec᷄ ᷄ of the Boundless that
Anaximander received this honour ; he w᷄ ᷄ a statesman and an inventor
like Thales and Hekataios.
[3] In this and other cases, where t᷄e words of the original have been
preserved by Simplicius, I have given them alone. On the various writers
quoted, see Note on Sources, §§ 9 *sqq.*
[4] Simplicius says " successor and disciple " (διάδοχος καὶ μαθητής) in his
Commentary on the *Physics* ; but see above, p. 50, *n.* 4.
[5] For the expression τὰ καλούμενα στοιχεῖα, see Diels, *Elementum*,
p. 25, *n.* 4.
[6] Diels (*Vors.* 2, 9) begins the actual quotation with the words ἐξ ὧν δὲ
ἡ γένεσις . . . The Greek practice of blending quotations with the text
tells against this. Further, it is safer not to ascribe the terms γένεσις and
φθορά in their technical Platonic sense to Anaximander, and it is not
likely that Anaximander said anything about τὰ ὄντα.

He did not ascribe the origin of things to any alteration in matter, but said that the oppositions in the substratum, which was a boundless body, were separated out.—Simpl. *Phys.* p. 150, 20 (R. P. 18).

14. Anaximander taught, then, that there was an eternal, indestructible something out of which everything arises, and into which everything returns ; a boundless stock from which the waste of existence is continually made good. That is only the natural development of the thought we have ascribed to Thales, and there can be no doubt that Anaximander at least formulated it distinctly. Indeed, we can still follow to some extent the reasoning which led him to do so. Thales had regarded water as the most likely thing to be that of which all others are forms ; Anaximander appears to have asked how the primary substance could be one of these particular things. His argument seems to be preserved by Aristotle, who has the following passage in his discussion of the Infinite :

The primary substance is not one of the "elements."

Further, there cannot be a single, simple body which is infinite, either, as some hold, one distinct from the elements, which they then derive from it, or without this qualification. For there are some who make this (*i.e.* a body distinct from the elements) the infinite, and not air or water,· in order that the other things may not be destroyed by their infinity. *They are in opposition one to another*—air is cold, water moist, and fire hot—and therefore, *if any one of them were infinite, the rest would have ceased to be by this time.* Accordingly they say that what is infinite is something other than the elements, and from it the elements arise.—Arist. *Phys.* Γ, 5. 204 b 22 (R. P. 16 b).

It is clear that Anaximander is here contrasted with Thales and with Anaximenes. Nor is there any reason to doubt that the account given of his reasoning is substantially correct, though the form is Aristotle's own, and in particular the "elements" are an anachronism.[1] Anaximander started, it would seem, from the strife between the opposites which

---

[1] See p. 12, *n.* 2.

go to make up the world; the warm was opposed to the cold, the dry to the wet. These were at war, and any predominance of one over the other was an "injustice" for which they must make reparation to one another at the appointed time.[1] If Thales had been right in saying that water was the fundamental reality, it would not be easy to see how anything else could ever have existed. One side of the opposition, the cold and moist, would have had its way unchecked, and the warm and dry would have been driven from the field long ago. We must, then, have something not itself one of the warring opposites, something more primitive, out of which they arise, and into which they once more pass away. That Anaximander called this something by the name of φύσις is the natural interpretation of what Theophrastos says; the current statement that the term ἀρχή was introduced by him appears to be due to a misunderstanding.[2] We have seen that, when Aristotle used

[1] The important word ἀλλήλοις is in all the MSS. of Simplicius, though omitted in the Aldine. This omission made the sentence appear to mean that the existence of individual things (ὄντα) was somehow a wrong (ἀδικία) for which they must be punished. With ἀλλήλοις restored, this fanciful interpretation disappears. It is *to one another* that whatever the subject of the verb may be make reparation and give satisfaction, and therefore the injustice must be a wrong which they commit *against one another*. Now, as δίκη is regularly used of the observance of an equal balance between the opposites hot and cold, dry and wet, the ἀδικία here referred to must be the undue encroachment of one opposite on another, such as we see, for example, in the alternation of day and night, winter and summer, which have to be made good by an equal encroachment of the other. I stated this view in my first edition (1892), pp. 60-62, and am glad to find it confirmed by Professor Heidel (*Class. Phil.* vii., 1912, p. 233 *sq.*).

[2] The words of Theophrastos, as given by Simplicius (*Phys.* p. 24, 15: R. P. 16), are ἀρχήν τε καὶ στοιχεῖον εἴρηκε τῶν ὄντων τὸ ἄπειρον, πρῶτος τοῦτο τοὔνομα κομίσας τῆς ἀρχῆς, the natural meaning of which is "he being the first to introduce this name (τὸ ἄπειρον) of the material cause." Hippolytos, however, says (*Ref.* i. 6, 2) πρῶτος τοὔνομα καλέσας τῆς ἀρχῆς, and this has led most writers to take the words in the sense that Anaximander introduced the term ἀρχή. Hippolytos, however, is not an independent authority (see Note on Sources, § 13), and the only question is what Theophrastos wrote. Now Simplicius quotes Theophrastos from Alexander, who used the original, while Hippolytos represents a much more indirect tradition. Obviously, καλέσας is a corruption of the characteristically Peripatetic κομίσας, and the omission of τοῦτο is much more likely than its inter-

the term in discussing Thales, he meant what is called the " material cause," [1] and it is hard to believe that it means anything else here.

15. It was natural for Aristotle to regard this theory as an anticipation or presentiment of his own doctrine of " indeterminate matter," [2] and that he should sometimes express the views of Anaximander in terms of the later theory of " elements." He knew that the Boundless was a body,[3] though in his own system there was no room for anything corporeal prior to the elements ; so he had to speak of it as a boundless body " alongside of " or " distinct from " the elements (παρὰ τὰ στοιχεῖα). So far as I know no one has doubted that, when he uses this phrase, he is referring to Anaximander.

In a number of other places Aristotle speaks of some one who held the primary substance to be something " intermediate between " the elements or between two of them.[4]

Aristotle's account of the theory.

---

polation by Alexander or Simplicius. But, if τοῦτο is genuine, the ὄνομα referred to must be τὸ ἄπειρον, and this interpretation is confirmed by Simpl. *De caelo* 615, 15, ἄπειρον δὲ πρῶτος ὑπέθετο. In another place (p. 150, 23) Simplicius says πρῶτος αὐτὸς ἀρχὴν ὀνομάσας τὸ ὑποκείμενον, which must mean, as the context shows, " being the first to name the substratum of the opposites as the material cause," which is another point altogether. Theophrastos is always interested in noting who it was that " first " introduced a concept, and both ἄπειρον and ὑποκείμενον were important enough to be noted. Of course he does not mean that Anaximander used the *word* ὑποκείμενον. He only infers that he had the idea from the doctrine that the opposites which are " in " the ἄπειρον are " separated out." Lastly, the whole book from which these extracts were taken was Περὶ τῶν ἀρχῶν, and the thing to note was who first applied various predicates to the ἀρχή or ἀρχαί.

[1] See p. 47 *n.* 6 and Introd. p. 11 *n.* 3.
[2] Arist. *Met.* Λ, 2. 1069 b 18 (R. P. 16 c).
[3] This is taken for granted in *Phys.* Γ, 4. 203 a 16 ; 204 b 22 (R. P. 16 b), and stated in Γ, 8. 208 a 8 (R. P. 16 a). Cf. Simpl. *Phys.* p. 150, 20 (R. P. 18).
[4] Aristotle speaks four times of something intermediate between Fire and Air (*Gen. Corr.* B, 1. 328 b 35 ; *ib.* 5. 332 a 21 ; *Phys.* A, 4. 187 a 14 ; *Met.* A, 7. 988 a 30). In five places we have something intermediate between Water and Air (*Met.* A, 7. 988 a 13 ; *Gen. Corr.* B, 5. 332 a 21 ; *Phys.* Γ, 4. 203 a 18 ; *ib.* 5. 205 a 27 ; *De caelo*, Γ, 5. 303 b 12). Once (*Phys.* A, 6. 189 b 1) we hear of something between Water and Fire. This variation shows at once that he is not speaking historically. If any one

Nearly all the Greek commentators referred this to Anaximander also, but most modern writers refuse to follow them. It is, no doubt, easy to show that Anaximander himself cannot have said anything of the sort, but that is no real objection. Aristotle puts things in his own way regardless of historical considerations, and it is difficult to see that it is more of an anachronism to call the Boundless " intermediate between the elements " than to say that it is " distinct from the elements." Indeed, if once we introduce the elements at all, the former description is the more adequate of the two. At any rate, if we refuse to understand these passages as referring to Anaximander, we shall have to say that Aristotle paid a great deal of attention to some one whose very name has been lost, and who not only agreed with some of Anaximander's views, but also used some of his most characteristic expressions.[1] We may add that in one or two places Aristotle certainly seems to identify the " intermediate " with the something " distinct from " the elements.[2]

There is even one passage in which he speaks of Anaximander's Boundless as a " mixture," though his words may perhaps admit of another interpretation.[3] But this is of no consequence for our interpretation of Anaximander. It is certain that he cannot have said anything about " elements," which no one thought of before Empedokles,

---

ever held the doctrine of τὸ μεταξύ, he must have known which " elements " he meant.

[1] Arist. De caelo, Γ, 5. 303 b 12, ὕδατος μὲν λεπτότερον, ἀέρος δὲ πυκνότερον, ὃ περιέχειν φασὶ πάντας τοὺς οὐρανοὺς ἄπειρον ὄν.

[2] Cf. Phys. Γ, 5. 204 b 22 (R. P. 16 b), where Zeller rightly refers τὸ παρὰ τὰ στοιχεῖα to Anaximander. Now, at the end (205 a 25) the whole passage is summarised thus : καὶ διὰ τοῦτ' οὐθεὶς τὸ ἓν καὶ ἄπειρον πῦρ ἐποίησεν οὐδὲ γῆν τῶν φυσιολόγων, ἀλλ' ἢ ὕδωρ ἢ ἀέρα ἢ τὸ μέσον αὐτῶν. In Gen. Corr. B, 1. 328 b 35 we have first τι μεταξὺ τούτων σῶμά τε ὂν καὶ χωριστόν, and a little further on (329 a 9) μίαν ὕλην παρὰ τὰ εἰρημένα. In B, 5. 332 a 20 we have οὐ μὴν οὐδ' ἄλλο τί γε παρὰ ταῦτα, οἷον μέσον τι ἀέρος καὶ ὕδατος ἢ ἀέρος καὶ πυρός.

[3] Met. Λ, 2. 1069 b 18 (R. P. 16 c). Zeller (p. 205, n. 1) assumes an " easy zeugma."

and no one could think of before Parmenides. The question has only been mentioned because it has given rise to a lengthy controversy, and because it throws light on the historical value of Aristotle's statements. From the point of view of his own system, these may be justified; but we shall have to remember in other cases that, when he seems to attribute an idea to some earlier thinker, we are not bound to take what he says in an historical sense.[1]

16. Anaximander's reason for conceiving the primary substance as boundless was, no doubt, as indicated by Aristotle, "that becoming might not fail."[2] It is not clear, however, that these words are his own, though the doxographers speak as if they were. It is enough for us that Theophrastos, who had seen his book, attributed the thought to him. And certainly his view of the world would bring home to him the need of a boundless stock of matter. The "opposites" are, we have seen, at war with one another, and their strife is marked by "unjust" encroachments on either side. The warm commits "injustice" in summer,

The primary substance is infinite.

---

[1] For the literature of this controversy, see R. P. 15. Professor Heidel has shown in his "Qualitative Change in Pre-Socratic Philosophy" (*Arch.* xix. p. 333) that Aristotle misunderstood the Milesians because he could only think of their doctrine in terms of his own theory of ἀλλοίωσις. That is quite true, but it is equally true that they had no definite theory of their own with regard to the transformations of substance. The theory of an original "mixture" is quite as unhistorical as that of ἀλλοίωσις. Qualities were not yet distinguished from "things," and Thales doubtless said that water turned into vapour or ice without dreaming of any further questions. They all believed that in the long run there was only one "thing," and at last they came to the conclusion that all apparent differences were due to rarefaction and condensation. Theophrastos (*ap.* Simpl. *Phys.* 150, 22) says ἐνούσας γὰρ τὰς ἐναντιότητας ἐν τῷ ὑποκειμένῳ . . . ἐκκρίνεσθαι. I do not believe these words are even a paraphrase of anything Anaximander said. They are merely an attempt to "accommodate" his views to Peripatetic ideas, and ἐνούσας is as unhistorical as the ὑποκείμενον.

[2] *Phys.* Γ, 8. 208 a 8 (R. P. 16 a). Cf. Aet. i. 3, 3 (R. P. 16 a). The same argument is given in *Phys.* Γ, 4. 203 b 18, a passage where Anaximander has just been named, τῷ οὕτως ἂν μόνον μὴ ὑπολείπειν γένεσιν καὶ φθοράν, εἰ ἄπειρον εἴη ὅθεν ἀφαιρεῖται τὸ γιγνόμενον. I cannot, however, believe that the arguments at the beginning of this chapter (203 b 7; R. P. 17) are Anaximander's. They bear the stamp of the Eleatic dialectic, and are, in fact, those of Melissos.

C

the cold in winter, and this would lead in the long run to the destruction of everything but the Boundless itself, if there were not an inexhaustible supply of it from which opposites might continually be separated out afresh. We must picture, then, an endless mass, which is not any one of the opposites we know, stretching out without limit on every side of the world we live in.[1] This mass is a body, out of which our world once emerged, and into which it will one day be absorbed again.

The innumerable worlds.

17. We are told that Anaximander believed there were " innumerable worlds in the Boundless," [2] and we have to decide between the interpretation that, though all the worlds are perishable, there are an unlimited number of them in existence at the same time, and Zeller's view that a new world never comes into existence till the old one has passed away, so that there is never more than one world at a time. As this point is of fundamental importance, it will be necessary to examine the evidence carefully.

In the first place, the doxographical tradition proves that Theophrastos discussed the views of all the early philosophers as to whether there was one world or an infinite number, and there can be no doubt that, when he ascribed " innumerable worlds " to the Atomists, he meant coexistent and not successive worlds. Now, if he had classed two such different views under one head, he would

---

[1] I have assumed that the word ἄπειρον means *spatially infinite*, not *qualitatively indeterminate*, as maintained by Teichmüller and Tannery. The decisive reasons for holding that the sense of the word is ' boundless in extent " are as follows : (1) Theophrastos said the primary substance of Anaximander was ἄπειρον and contained all the worlds, and the word περιέχειν everywhere means " to encompass," not, as has been suggested, " to contain potentially." (2) Aristotle says (*Phys.* Γ, 4. 203 b 23) διὰ γὰρ τὸ ἐν τῇ νοήσει μὴ ὑπολείπειν καὶ ὁ ἀριθμὸς δοκεῖ ἄπειρος εἶναι καὶ τὰ μαθηματικὰ μεγέθη καὶ τὰ ἔξω τοῦ οὐρανοῦ· ἀπείρου δ' ὄντος τοῦ ἔξω, καὶ σῶμα ἄπειρον εἶναι δοκεῖ καὶ κόσμοι. The mention of σῶμα shows that this does not refer to the Atomists. (3) Anaximander's theory of the ἄπειρον was adopted by Anaximenes, and he identified it with Air, which is not qualitatively indeterminate.

[2] Cf. [Plut.] *Strom.* fr. 2 (R. P. 21 b).

have been careful to point out in what respect they differed, and there is no trace of any such distinction. On the contrary, Anaximander, Anaximenes, Archelaos, Xenophanes, Diogenes, Leukippos, Demokritos, and Epicurus are all mentioned together as holding the doctrine of " innumerable worlds " on every side of this one,[1] and the only distinction is that, while Epicurus made the distances between these worlds unequal, Anaximander said all the worlds were equidistant.[2] Zeller rejected this evidence [3] on the ground that we can have no confidence in a writer who attributes " innumerable worlds " to Anaximenes, Archelaos, and Xenophanes. With regard to the first two, I hope to show that the statement is correct, and that it is at least intelligible in the case of the last.[4] In any case, the passage comes from Aetios,[5] and there is no reason for doubting that it is derived from Theophrastos, though the name of Epicurus has been added later. This is confirmed by what Simplicius says :

Those who assumed innumerable worlds, *e.g.* Anaximander, Leukippos, Demokritos, and, at a later date, Epicurus, held that they came into being and passed away *ad infinitum*, some always coming into being and others passing away.[6]

It is practically certain that this too comes from Theophrastos through Alexander.

---

[1] Aet. ii. 1, 3 (*Dox.* p. 327). Zeller seems to be wrong in understanding κατὰ πᾶσαν περιαγωγήν here of revolution. It must mean " in every direction we turn," as is shown by the alternative phrase κατὰ πᾶσαν περίστασιν. The six περιστάσεις are πρόσω, ὀπίσω, ἄνω, κάτω, δεξιά, ἀριστερά (Nicom. *Introd.* p. 85, 11, Hoche).

[2] Aet. ii. 1, 8 (*Dox.* p. 329), τῶν ἀπείρους ἀποφηναμένων τοὺς κόσμους Ἀναξίμανδρος τὸ ἴσον αὐτοὺς ἀπέχειν ἀλλήλων, Ἐπίκουρος ἄνισον εἶναι τὸ μεταξὺ τῶν κόσμων διάστημα.

[3] He supposed it to be only that of Stobaios. The filiation of the sources had not been traced when he wrote.

[4] For Anaximenes see § 30 ; Xenophanes, § 59 ; Archelaos, § 192.

[5] This is proved by the fact that the list of names is given also by Theodoret. See Note on Sources, § 10.

[6] Simpl. *Phys.* p. 1121, 5 (R. P. 21 b). Cf. Simpl. *De caelo*, p. 202, 14, οἱ δὲ καὶ τῷ πλήθει ἀπείρους κόσμους, ὡς Ἀναξίμανδρος . . . ἄπειρον τῷ μεγέθει τὴν ἀρχὴν θέμενος ἀπείρους ἐξ αὐτοῦ τῷ πλήθει κόσμους ποιεῖν δοκεῖ.

We come next to a very important statement which
Cicero has copied from Philodemos, the author of the
Epicurean treatise on Religion found at Herculaneum, or
perhaps from the immediate source of that work. " Anaximander's opinion was," he makes Velleius say, " that there
were gods who came into being, rising and passing away
at long intervals, and that these were the innumerable
worlds " ; [1] and this must clearly be taken along with the
statement of Aetios that, according to Anaximander, the
" innumerable heavens " were gods.[2] Now it is much
more natural to understand the " long intervals " as
intervals of space than as intervals of time ; [3] and, if
that is right, we have a perfect agreement among our
authorities.

It may be added that it is very unnatural to understand
the statement that the Boundless " encompasses all the
worlds " of worlds succeeding one another in time ; for on
this view there is at a given time only one world to " encompass." Moreover, the argument mentioned by Aristotle
that, if what is outside the heavens is infinite, body must
be infinite, and there must be innumerable worlds, can only
be understood in one sense, and is certainly intended to
represent the reasoning of the Milesians ; for they were
the only cosmologists who held there was a boundless
body outside the heavens.[4] Lastly, we happen to know
that Petron, one of the earliest Pythagoreans, held
there were just one hundred and eighty - three worlds

---

[1] Cicero, De nat. d. i. 25 (R. P. 21).

[2] Aet. i. 7, 12 (R. P. 21 a). The reading of Stob., ἀπείρους οὐρανούς,
is guaranteed by the ἀπείρους κόσμους of Cyril, and the ἀπείρους νοῦς
(i.e. οὐνούς) of the pseudo-Galen. See Dox. p. 11.

[3] It is natural to suppose that Cicero found διαστήμασιν in his Epicurean
source, and that is a technical term for the intermundia.

[4] Arist. Phys. Γ. 4. 203 b 25, ἀπείρου δ' ὄντος τοῦ ἔξω (sc. τοῦ οὐρανοῦ),
καὶ σῶμα ἄπειρον εἶναι δοκεῖ καὶ κόσμοι (sc. ἄπειροι). The next words—τί γὰρ
μᾶλλον τοῦ κενοῦ ἐνταῦθα ἢ ἐνταῦθα ;—show that this refers to the Atomists
as well ; but the ἄπειρον σῶμα will not apply to them. The meaning is
that both those who made the Boundless a body and those who made
it a κενόν held the doctrine of ἄπειροι κόσμοι in the same sense.

arranged in a triangle,[1] which shows at least that the doctrine of a plurality of worlds was much older than the Atomists.

18. The doxographers say it was the " eternal motion " that brought into being " all the heavens and all the worlds within them." We have seen (§ VIII.) that this is probably only the Aristotelian way of putting the thing, and that we must not identify the primordial motion of the Boundless with any purely mundane movement such as the diurnal revolution. That would be quite inconsistent, moreover, with the doctrine of innumerable worlds, each of which has, presumably, its own centre and its own diurnal revolution. As to the true nature of this motion, we have no definite statement, but the term " separating off " (ἀπόκρισις) rather suggests some process of shaking and sifting as in a riddle or sieve. That is given in Plato's *Timaeus* as the Pythagorean doctrine,[2] and the Pythagoreans followed Anaximander pretty closely in their cosmology (§ 54). The school of Abdera, as will be shown (§ 179), attributed a motion of the same kind to their atoms, and they too were mainly dependent on the Milesians for the details of their system. This, however, must remain a conjecture in the absence of express testimony.

When, however, we come to the motion of the world once it has been " separated off," we are on safer ground. It is certain that one of the chief features of early cosmology is the part played in it by the analogy of an eddy in water or in wind, a δίνη (or δῖνος),[3] and there seems to be little

Marginal note: " Eternal motion " and the δίνη.

---

[1] See below, § 53. Cf. Diels, *Elementum*, pp. 63 *sqq.*

[2] Plato, *Tim.* 52 e. There the elemental figures (which have taken the place of the " opposites ") " being thus stirred (by the irregular motion of the τιθήνη), are carried in different directions and separated, just as by sieves and instruments for winnowing corn the grain is shaken and sifted ; and the dense and heavy parts go one way, while the rare and light are carried to a different place and settle there."

[3] Aristophanes, referring to the Ionian cosmology, says (*Clouds*, 828) Δῖνος βασιλεύει τὸν Δί' ἐξεληλακώς, which is nearer the truth than the modern theory of its religious origin.

doubt that we are entitled to regard this as the doctrine of Anaximander and Anaximenes.[1] It would arise very naturally in the minds of thinkers who started with water as the primary substance and ended with " air," and it would account admirably for the position of earth and water in the centre and fire at the circumference, with " air " between them. Heavy things tend to the centre of a vortex and light things are forced out to the periphery. It is to be observed that there is no question of a sphere in revolution at this date ; what we have to picture is rotary motion in a plane or planes more or less inclined to the earth's surface.[2] It is in favour of the conjecture given above as to the nature of the primordial motion that it provides a satisfactory dynamical explanation of the formation of the δίνη, and we shall find once more (§ 180) that the Atomists held precisely this view of its origin.

Origin of the heavenly bodies.

19. The doxographers also give us some indications of the process by which the different parts of the world arose from the Boundless. The following statement comes ultimately from Theophrastos :

He says that something capable of begetting hot and cold out of the eternal was separated off at the origin of this world. From this arose a sphere of flame which fitted close round the air surrounding the earth as the bark round a tree. When this had been torn off and shut up in certain rings, the sun,

---

[1] I gratefully accept the view propounded by Prof. W. A. Heidel (" The δίνη in Anaximenes and Anaximander," *Class. Phil.* i. 279), so far as the cosmical motion goes, though I cannot identify that with the " eternal motion." I had already done what I could to show that the " spheres " of Eudoxos and Aristotle must not be imported into Pythagoreanism, and it strengthens the position considerably if we ascribe a rotary motion in a plane to Anaximander's world.

[2] This is the plain meaning of Aet. ii. 2, 4, οἱ δὲ τροχοῦ δίκην περι-δινεῖσθαι τὸν κόσμον, which is referred to Anaximander by Diels (*Dox.* p. 46). Zeller's objections to the ascription of the δίνη to Anaximander are mainly based on an inadmissible rendering of the word τροπαί (p. 63 *n.* 2). Of course, the rotations are not all in the same plane ; the ecliptic, for instance, is inclined to the equator, and the Milky Way to both.

moon and stars came into existence.—Ps.-Plut. *Strom.* fr. 2 (R. P. 19).[1]

We see from this that, when a portion of the Boundless was separated off from the rest to form a world, it first differentiated itself into the two opposites, hot and cold. The hot appears as flame surrounding the cold ; the cold, as earth with air surrounding it. We are not told here how the cold was differentiated into earth, water and air, but there is a passage in Aristotle's *Meteorology* which throws some light on the question. After discussing the views of the " theologians " regarding the sea, he says :

But those who are wiser in the wisdom of men give an origin for the sea. At first, they say, all the terrestrial region was moist ; and, as it was dried up by the sun, the portion of it that evaporated produced the winds and the turnings back of the sun and moon,[2] while the portion left behind was the sea. So

---

[1] This passage has been discussed by Heidel (*Proceedings of the American Academy*, xlviii. 686). I agree that ἀπὸ τοῦ ἀπείρου must be supplied with ἀποκριθῆναι, and I formerly thought that ἐκ τοῦ ἀιδίου might be equivalent to that, and might have been displaced if the order of words was too harsh. I cannot believe that it means " from eternity," as Heidel thinks. On the other hand, he is clearly right in his interpretation of περιφυῆναι and ἀπορραγείσης. He also points out correctly that " the *sphere* of flame " is an inaccuracy. The comparison to the bark of a tree distinctly suggests something annular.

[2] Zeller (p. 223, *n.* 5) asks what can be meant by τροπαὶ τῆς σελήνης, but his difficulty is an imaginary one. The moon has certainly a movement in declination and therefore τροπαί. In other words, the moon does not always rise at the same point of the horizon any more than the sun. This is admitted by Sir T. L. Heath (*Aristarchus*, p. 33, *n.* 3), though he has unfortunately followed Zeller in supposing that τροπαί here means " revolutions." This seems to me impossible ; for τρέπεσθαι means " to turn back " or " to turn aside," never " to turn round," which is στρέφεσθαι. It is conceivable, indeed, that τροπαὶ ἠελίοιο in *Od.* xv. 404 means the place where the sun sets and turns *back* from west to east, though it is not very likely, as Hesiod already uses τροπαὶ ἠελίοιο of the winter and summer solstices (*O.D.* 479, 564, 663). Zeller's statement (repeated by Heath) that Aristotle speaks of τροπαί of the fixed stars in *De caelo*, B, 14. 296 b 4, is erroneous. What Aristotle does say is that, if the earth is in motion, there ought to be πάροδοι (movements in latitude) and τροπαί of the fixed stars, *which there are not.* The passage is correctly rendered by Sir T. L. Heath himself in a subsequent chapter (p. 241). For the other passages referred to, see p. 64, *n.* 1, and p. 76, *n.* 3.

they think the sea is becoming smaller by being dried up, and that at last it will all be dry.—*Meteor*, B, 1. 353 b 5.

And the same absurdity arises for those who say the earth too was at first moist, and that, when the region of the world about the earth was heated by the sun, air was produced and the whole heavens were increased, and that it (the air) produced winds and caused its (the sun's) turnings back.[1]—*Ib*. 2. 355 a 21 (R. P. 20 a).

In his commentary on the passage, Alexander says this was the view of Anaximander and Diogenes, and cites Theophrastos as his authority for the statement. This is confirmed by Anaximander's theory of the sea as given by the doxographers (§ 20). We conclude, then, that after the first separation of the hot and the cold by the δίνη, the heat of the flame turned part of the moist, cold interior of the world into air or vapour—it is all one at this date—and that the expansion of this mist broke up the flame itself into rings. We shall come back to these rings presently, but we must look first at what we are told of the earth.

Earth
and sea.
20. The origin of earth and sea from the moist, cold matter which was " separated off " in the beginning is thus described :

The sea is what is left of the original moisture. The fire has dried up most of it and turned the rest salt by scorching it.— Aet. iii. 16, 1 (R. P. 20 a).

He says that the earth is cylindrical in form, and that its depth is as a third part of its breadth.—Ps.-Plut. *Strom*. fr. 2 (R. P. *ib*.).

The earth swings free, held in its place by nothing. It stays where it is because of its equal distance from everything. Its

---

[1] From the whole context it is plain that τὰς τροπὰς αὐτοῦ means τὰς τοῦ ἡλίου τροπάς, and not τὰς τοῦ οὐρανοῦ, as Zeller and Heath say. The " air " in this passage answers to " the portion that evaporated " (τὸ διατμίσαν) in that previously quoted, and τοῦτον must therefore refer to it. Cf. the paraphrase of Alexander (p. 67, 3 from Theophrastos, *Dox*. p. 494), τὸ μέν τι τῆς ὑγρότητος ὑπὸ τοῦ ἡλίου ἐξατμίζεσθαι καὶ γίνεσθαι πνεύματά τε ἐξ αὐτοῦ καὶ τροπὰς ἡλίου τε καὶ σελήνης (see last note). In this chapter of the *Meteorology*, Aristctle is discussing the doctrine that the sun is " fed " by moisture and the relation of that doctrine to its τροπαί at the solstices, and we must interpret accordingly.

shape is hollow and round, and like a stone pillar. We are on one of the surfaces, and the other is on the opposite side.[1]—Hipp. *Ref.* i. 6 (R. P. 20).

Adopting for a moment the popular theory of "elements," we see that Anaximander put fire on one side as the hot and dry, and all the rest on the other as the cold, which is also moist. This may explain how Aristotle came to speak of the Boundless as intermediate between fire and water. And we have seen also that the moist element was partly turned into "air" or vapour by the fire, which explains how Aristotle could say the Boundless was something between fire and air, or between air and water.[2]

The moist, cold interior of the world is not, in fact, water. It is always called "the moist" or "the moist state." That is because it has to be still further differentiated under the influence of heat into earth, water, and vapour. The gradual drying up of the water by the fire is a good example of what Anaximander meant by "injustice."

Thales had said that the earth floated on the water, but Anaximander realised that it was freely suspended in space (μετέωρος) and did not require any support. Aristotle has preserved the argument he used. The earth is equally distant from the circumference of the vortex in every direction, and there is no reason for it to move up or down

---

[1] The MSS. of Hippolytos have ὑγρὸν στρογγύλον, and so has Cedrenus, a writer of the eleventh century who made extracts from him. Roeper read γυρὸν [στρογγύλον], supposing the second word to be a gloss on the first. Diels (*Dox.* p. 218) holds that the first applies to the *surface* of the earth ; while the second refers to its circuit. Professor A. E. Taylor has pointed out to me, however, the great improbability of the view that γυρόν means convex. The Ionians down to Archelaos (§ 192) and Demokritos (Aet. iii. 10, 5, κοίλην τῷ μέσῳ) regularly regarded the surface of the earth as concave, and γυρός can just as well mean that. The next words are also of doubtful meaning. The MSS. of Hippolytos have χίονι λίθῳ, while Aetios (iii. 10, 2) has λίθῳ κίονι. Diels doubtfully conjectures λιθῷ κίονι, which he suggests might represent an original λιθέη κίονι (*Dox.* p. 219). In any case the pillar seems genuine, and the general sense is guaranteed by the Plutarchean *Stromateis* (*loc. cit.*), ὑπάρχειν . . . τῷ μὲν σχήματι τὴν γῆν κυλινδροειδῆ.

[2] See above, p. 55, n. 4.

or sideways.[1] The doctrine of innumerable worlds was inconsistent with the existence of an absolute up and down in the universe, so the argument is quite sound. The central position of the earth is due to the δίνη ; for the greater masses tend to the centre of an eddy.[2] There is good evidence that Anaximander made the earth share in the rotary movement.[3] It is not, however, a sphere, so we must not speak of an axial revolution. The shape given to the earth by Anaximander is easily explained if we adopt the view that the world is a system of rotating rings. It is just a solid ring in the middle of the vortex.

The heavenly bodies.

21. We have seen that the flame which had been forced to the circumference of the vortex was broken up into rings by the pressure of expanding vapour produced by its own heat. I give the statements of Hippolytos and Aetios as to the formation of the heavenly bodies from these rings.

The heavenly bodies are a wheel of fire, separated off from the fire of the world, and surrounded by air. And there are breathing-holes, certain pipe-like passages, at which the heavenly bodies show themselves. That is why, when the breathing-holes are stopped, eclipses take place. And the moon appears now to wax and now to wane because of the stopping and opening of

---

[1] Arist. *De caelo*, B, 13. 295 b 10 εἰσὶ δέ τινες οἳ διὰ τὴν ὁμοιότητά φασιν αὐτὴν (τὴν γῆν) μένειν, ὥσπερ τῶν ἀρχαίων 'Αναξίμανδρος· μᾶλλον μὲν γὰρ οὐθὲν ἄνω ἢ κάτω ἢ εἰς τὰ πλάγια φέρεσθαι προσήκειν τὸ ἐπὶ τοῦ μέσου ἱδρυμένον καὶ ὁμοίως πρὸς τὰ ἔσχατα ἔχον. One point of the δίνη is no more "down" than another. Apparently, the Pythagoreans adopted this reasoning ; for Plato makes Sokrates in the *Phaedo* say (108 e) ἰσόρροπον γὰρ πρᾶγμα ὁμοίου τινὸς ἐν μέσῳ τεθὲν οὐχ ἕξει μᾶλλον οὐδὲ ἧττον οὐδαμόσε κλιθῆναι. From this it appears that ὁμοιότης means something like " indifference." There is nothing to differentiate one radius of a circle from another.

[2] Arist. *De caelo*, B, 13. 295 a 9 (ἡ γῆ) συνῆλθεν ἐπὶ τὸ μέσον φερομένη διὰ τὴν δίνησιν· ταύτην γὰρ τὴν αἰτίαν πάντες λέγουσιν ἐκ τῶν ἐν τοῖς ὑγροῖς καὶ περὶ τὸν ἀέρα συμβαινόντων· ἐν τούτοις γὰρ ἀεὶ φέρεται τὰ μείζω καὶ τὰ βαρύτερα πρὸς τὸ μέσον τῆς δίνης. διὸ δὴ καὶ τὴν γῆν πάντες ὅσοι τὸν οὐρανὸν γεννῶσιν ἐπὶ τὸ μέσον συνελθεῖν φασιν.

[3] This was expressly stated by Eudemos (*ap.* Theon. Smyrn. p. 198, 18), 'Αναξίμανδρος δὲ ὅτι ἐστὶν ἡ γῆ μετέωρος καὶ κινεῖται περὶ τὸ μέσον. Anaxagoras held the same view (§ 133).

the passages. The wheel of the sun is 27 times the size of (the earth, while that of) the moon is 18 times as large.[1] The sun is the highest of all, and lowest are the wheels of the stars. —Hipp. *Ref.* i. 6 (R. P. 20).

The heavenly bodies were hoop-like compressions of air, full of fire, breathing out flames at a certain point through orifices.— Aet. ii. 13, 7 (R. P. 19 a).

The sun was a wheel 28 times the size of the earth, like a chariot - wheel with the felloe hollow, full of fire, showing the fire at a certain point through an orifice, as through the nozzle of a pair of bellows.—Aet. ii. 20, 1 (R. P. 19 a).

The sun was equal to the earth, but the wheel from which it breathes out and by which it is carried round was 27 times the size of the earth.—Aet. ii. 21, 1.

The sun was eclipsed when the orifice of the fire's breathing-hole was stopped.—Aet. ii. 24, 2.

The moon was a wheel 19 times the size of the earth, like a chariot-wheel with its felloe hollow and full of fire like that of the sun, lying oblique also like it, with one breathing-hole like the nozzle of a pair of bellows. [It is eclipsed because of the turnings of the wheel.] [2]—Aet. ii. 25, 1.

The moon was eclipsed when the orifice of the wheel was stopped.—Aet. ii. 29, 1.

(Thunder and lightning, etc.) were all caused by the blast of the wind. When it is shut up in a thick cloud and bursts forth with violence, then the tearing of the cloud makes the noise, and the rift gives the appearance of a flash in contrast with the blackness of the cloud.—Aet. iii. 3, 1.

Wind was a current of air (*i.e.* vapour), which arose when its finest and moistest particles were stirred or melted by the sun.—Aet. iii. 7, 1.

---

[1] I assume with Diels (*Dox.* p. 560) that something has fallen out of the text, but I have made the moon's circle 18 and not 19 times as large, as agreeing better with the other figure, 27. See p. 68, *n.* 1.

[2] There is clearly some confusion here, as Anaximander's real account of lunar eclipses is given in the next extract. There is also some doubt about the reading. Both Plutarch and Eusebios (*P.E.* xv. 26, 1) have ἐπιστροφάς, so the τροπάς of Stob. may be neglected, especially as the *codex Sambuci* had στροφάς. It looks as if this were a stray reference to the theory of Herakleitos that eclipses were due to a στροφή or ἐπιστροφή of the σκάφη (§ 71). In any case, the passage cannot be relied on in support of the meaning given to τροπαί by Zeller and Heath (p. 63, *n.* 2).

There is a curious variation in the figures given for the size of the wheels of the heavenly bodies, and it seems most likely that 18 and 27 refer to their inner, while 19 and 28 refer to their outer circumference. We may, perhaps, infer that the wheels of the " stars " were nine times the size of the earth ; for the numbers 9, 18, 27 play a considerable part in primitive cosmogonies.[1] We do not see the wheels of fire as complete circles ; for the vapour or mist which formed them encloses the fire, and forms an outer ring except at one point of their circumference, through which the fire escapes, and that is the heavenly body we actually see.[2] It is possible that the theory of " wheels " was suggested by the Milky Way. If we ask how it is that the wheels of air can make the fire invisible to us without becoming visible themselves, the answer is that such is the property of what the Greeks at this date called " air." For instance, when a Homeric hero is made invisible by being clothed in " air," we can see right through both the " air " and the hero.[3] It should be added that lightning is explained in much the same way as the heavenly bodies. It, too, was fire breaking through condensed air, in this case storm-clouds. It seems probable that this was really the origin of the theory, and that Anaximander explained the heavenly bodies on the analogy of lightning, not *vice versa*. It must be remembered that meteorology and astronomy were still undifferentiated,[4] and that the theory of " wheels "

[1] See Tannery, *Science hellène*, p. 91 ; Diels, " Ueber Anaximanders Kosmos " (*Arch.* x. pp. 231 *sqq.*).

[2] The true meaning of this doctrine was first explained by Diels (*Dox.* pp. 25 *sqq.*). The flames issue *per magni circum spiracula mundi*, as Lucretius has it (vi. 493). The πρηστῆρος αὐλός, to which these are compared, is simply the mouthpiece of the smith's bellows, a sense the word πρηστήρ has in Apollonios of Rhodes (iv. 776), and has nothing to do with the meteorological phenomenon of the same name (see Chap. III. § 71), except that the Greek sailors very likely named the fiery waterspout after the familiar instrument. It is not necessary now to discuss the earlier interpretations of the phrase.

[3] This is not so strange a view as might appear. An island or a rock in the offing may disappear completely when shrouded in mist (ἀήρ), and we seem to ɛ the sky beyond it.   [4] See above, p. 27.

or rings is a natural inference from the idea of the vortex.

So far we seem to be justified, by the authority of Theophrastos, in going; and, if that is so, certain further inferences seem to be inevitable. In the first place, Anaximander had shaken himself free of the old idea that the heavens are a solid vault. There is nothing to prevent us from seeing right out into the Boundless, and it is hard to think that Anaximander did not believe he did. The traditional cosmos has given place to a much grander scheme, that of innumerable vortices in a boundless mass, which is neither water nor air. In that case, it is difficult to resist the belief that what we call the fixed stars were identified with the " innumerable worlds " which were also " gods." It would follow that the diurnal revolution is only apparent ; for the stars are at unequal distances from us, and can have no rotation in common. It must, then, be due to the rotation of the cylindrical earth in twenty-four hours. We have seen that the earth certainly shared in the rotation of the δίνη. That gets rid of one difficulty, the wheel of the " stars," which is between the earth and the moon ; for the fixed stars could not be explained by a " wheel " at all ; a sphere would be required. What, then, are the " stars " which are accounted for by this inner wheel ? I venture to suggest that they are the morning and the evening stars, which, we have seen (p. 23, n. 1), were not recognised yet as a single luminary. In other words, I believe that Anaximander regarded the fixed stars as stationary, each rotating in its own vortex. No doubt this involves us in a difficulty regarding the rotation of the sun and the moon. It follows from the nature of the vortex that they must rotate in the same direction as the earth, and, on the assumption just made, that must be from west to east, and it must be a slower rotation than that of the earth, which is inconsistent with the fact that the circumference of a vortex rotates more rapidly than the centre. That, however, is a difficulty which all the Ionian cosmologists down to Demokritos had to face. Holding, as they did, that the whole rotation was in the same direction, they had to say that what we call the greatest velocities were the least. The moon, for instance, did not rotate so rapidly as the sun, since the sun more nearly keeps up with the fixed stars.[1] That Anaximander failed to observe this difficulty is not surprising, if we remember that he was the first to attack the problem. It is not immediately obvious that the centre of the vortex must have a slower motion than the circumference. This serves to explain the origin of the theory that the heavenly bodies have a rotation of their own in the opposite direction to the diurnal revolution which we shall see reason for attributing to Pythagoras (§ 54).

Animals.   22. We have, in any case, seen enough to show us that the speculations of Anaximander about the world were of an extremely daring character. We come now to the crowning audacity of all, his theory of the origin of living creatures. The Theophrastean account of this has been well preserved by the doxographers :

Living creatures arose from the moist element as it was evaporated by the sun. Man was like another animal, namely, a fish, in the beginning.—Hipp. *Ref.* i. 6 (R. P. 22 a).

The first animals were produced in the moisture, each enclosed in a prickly bark. As they advanced in age, they came out upon the drier part. When the bark broke off,[2] they survived for a short time.[3]—Aet. v. 19, 4 (R. P. 22).

Further, he says that originally man was born from animals of another species. His reason is that while other animals

---

[1] Lucretius, v. 619 *sqq.*

[2] This is to be understood in the light of what we are told about γαλεοί below. Cf. Arist. *Hist. An.* Z, 10. 565 a 25, τοῖς μὲν οὖν σκυλίοις, οὓς καλοῦσί τινες νεβρίας γαλεούς, ὅταν περιρραγῇ καὶ ἐκπέσῃ τὸ ὄστρακον, γίνονται οἱ νεοττοί.

[3] The true reading is ἐπ' ὀλίγον χρόνον μεταβιῶναι, the omission of χρόνον by Diels in *Vors.*[1] and *Vors.*[2] being apparently a slip. In the Index to *Dox.*, Diels *s.v.* μεταβιοῦν says " mutare vitam [cf. μεταδιαιτᾶν]," and I followed him in my first edition. Heidel well compares Archelaos, *ap.* Hipp. *Ref.* i. 9, 5 (of the first animals) ἦν δὲ ὀλιγοχρόνια.

quickly find food by themselves, man alone requires a lengthy period of suckling. Hence, had he been originally as he is now, he would never have survived.—Ps.-Plut. *Strom.* fr. 2 (R. P. *ib.*).

He declares that at first human beings arose in the inside of fishes, and after having been reared like sharks,[1] and become capable of protecting themselves, they were finally cast ashore and took to land.—Plut. *Symp. Quaest.* 730 f (R. P. *ib.*).

The importance of these statements has sometimes been overrated and still more often underestimated. Anaximander has been called a precursor of Darwin by some, while others have treated the whole thing as a mythological survival. It is therefore important to notice that this is one of the rare cases where we have not merely a *placitum*, but an indication of the observations on which it was based. It is clear from this that Anaximander had an idea of what is meant by adaptation to environment and survival of the fittest, and that he saw the higher mammals could not represent the original type of animal. For this he looked to the sea, and he naturally fixed upon those fishes which present the closest analogy to the *mammalia*. The statements of Aristotle about the *galeus levis* were shown by Johannes Müller to be more accurate than those of later naturalists, and we now see that these observations were already made by Anaximander. The way in which the shark nourishes its young furnished him with the very thing he required to explain the survival of the earliest animals.[2]

[1] Reading ὥσπερ οἱ γαλεοί for ὥσπερ οἱ παλαιοί with Doehner, who compares Plut. *De soll. anim.* 982 a, where the φιλόστοργον of the shark is described.

[2] On Aristotle and the *galeus levis*, see Johannes Müller, " Ueber den glatten Hai des Aristoteles " (*K. Preuss. Akad.*, 1842), to which my attention was directed by my colleague, Professor D'Arcy Thompson. The precise point of the words τρεφόμενοι ὥσπερ οἱ γαλεοί appears from Arist. *Hist. An.* Z, 10. 565 b 1, οἱ δὲ καλούμενοι λεῖοι τῶν γαλεῶν τὰ μὲν ᾠὰ ἴσχουσι μεταξὺ τῶν ὑστερῶν ὁμοίως τοῖς σκυλίοις, περιστάντα δὲ ταῦτα εἰς ἑκατέραν τὴν δικρόαν τῆς ὑστέρας καταβαίνει, καὶ τὰ ζῷα γίνεται τὸν ὀμφαλὸν ἔχοντα πρὸς τῇ ὑστέρᾳ, ὥστε ἀναλισκομένων τῶν ᾠῶν ὁμοίως δοκεῖν ἔχειν τὸ ἔμβρυον τοῖς τετράποσιν. It is not necessary to suppose that Anaximander referred to the further phenomenon described by Aristotle, who more than once says that all the γαλεοί except the ἄκανθίας " send out their young and take them back again " (ἐξαφιᾶσι

III. ANAXIMENES

Life.
23. Anaximenes of Miletos, son of Eurystratos, was, according to Theophrastos, an " associate " of Anaximander.[1] Apollodoros said, it appears, that he " flourished " about the time of the fall of Sardeis (546/5 B.C.), and died in Ol. LXIII. (528/525 B.C.).[2] In other words, he was born when Thales " flourished," and " flourished " when Thales died, and this means that Apollodoros had no definite information about his date. He perhaps made him die in the sixty-third Olympiad because that gives just three generations for the Milesian school.[3] We cannot therefore say anything positive as to his date, except that he must have been younger than Anaximander.

His book.
24. Anaximenes wrote a book which survived until the age of literary criticism ; for we are told that he used a simple and unpretentious Ionic,[4] very different, we may suppose, from the poetical prose of Anaximander.[5] The speculations of Anaximander were distinguished for their hardihood and breadth ; those of Anaximenes are marked by the opposite quality. He appears to have thought out his system carefully, but he rejects the more audacious theories of his predecessor. The result is that, while his view of the world is less like the truth than Anaximander's,

---

καὶ δέχονται εἰς ἑαυτοὺς τοὺς νεοττούς, ib. 565 b 23), for which compare also Ael. i. 17 ; Plut. De amore prolis 494 c ; De soll. anim. 982 a. The placenta and umbilical cord described by Johannes Müller will account sufficiently for all he says.

[1] Theophr. Phys. Op. fr. 2 (R. P. 26).

[2] This follows from a comparison of Diog. ii. 3 with Hipp. Ref. i. 7 (R. P. 23) and Souidas (s.v.). In Hippolytos we must, however, read τρίτον for πρῶτον with Diels. The suggestion in R. P. 23 e that Apollodoros mentioned the Olympiad without giving the number of the year is inadequate ; for Apollodoros did not reckon by Olympiads, but Athenian archons.

[3] Jacoby (p. 194) brings the date into connexion with the floruit of Pythagoras, which seems to me less probable.

[4] Diog. ii. 3 (R. P. 23).

[5] Cf. the statement of Theophrastos above, § 13.

it is perhaps more fruitful in ideas that were destined to hold their ground.

25. Anaximenes is one of the philosophers on whom Theophrastos wrote a special monograph ;[1] and this gives us an additional guarantee for the trustworthiness of the tradition. The following [2] are the passages which contain the fullest account of the central feature of his system :

> Anaximenes of Miletos, son of Eurystratos, who had been an associate of Anaximander, said, like him, that the underlying substance was one and infinite. He did not, however, say it was indeterminate, like Anaximander, but determinate ; for he said it was Air.—*Phys. Op.* fr. 2 (R. P. 26).
>
> From it, he said, the things that are, and have been, and shall be, the gods and things divine, took their rise, while other things come from its offspring.—Hipp. *Ref.* i. 7 (R. P. 28).
>
> " Just as," he said, " our soul, being air, holds us together, so do breath and air encompass the whole world."—Aet. i. 3, 4 (R. P. 24).
>
> And the form of the air is as follows. Where it is most even, it is invisible to our sight ; but cold and heat, moisture and motion, make it visible. It is always in motion ; for, if it were not, it would not change so much as it does.—Hipp. *Ref.* i. 7 (R. P. 28).
>
> It differs in different substances in virtue of its rarefaction and condensation.—*Phys. Op.* fr. 2 (R. P. 26).
>
> When it is dilated so as to be rarer, it becomes fire ; while winds, on the other hand, are condensed Air. Cloud is formed from Air by felting ;[3] and this, still further condensed, becomes water. Water, condensed still more, turns to earth ; and when condensed as much as it can be, to stones.—Hipp. *Ref.* i. 7 (R. P. 28).

26. At first, this looks like a falling off from the more refined doctrine of Anaximander to a cruder view ; but this is not really the case. On the contrary, the introduction of rarefaction and condensation into the theory is a notable

---

[1] On these monographs, see *Dox.* p. 103.

[2] See the conspectus of extracts from Theophrastos given in *Dox.* p. 135.

[3] " Felting " (πίλησις) is the regular term for this process with all the early cosmologists, from whom Plato has taken it (*Tim.* 58 b 4 ; 76 c 3).

advance.[1] In fact, it makes the Milesian cosmology consistent for the first time ; since a theory which explains everything as a form of a single substance is clearly bound to regard all differences as quantitative. The only way to save the unity of the primary substance is to say that all diversities are due to the presence of more or less of it in a given space. And when once this step has been taken, it is no longer necessary to make the primary substance something " distinct from the elements," to use Aristotle's inaccurate but convenient phrase ; it may just as well be one of them.

Air.

27. The air Anaximenes speaks of includes a good deal that we should not call by the name. In its normal condition, when most evenly distributed, it is invisible, and it then corresponds to our " air " ; it is the breath we inhale and the wind that blows. That is why he called it πνεῦμα. On the other hand, the old idea that mist or vapour is condensed air, is still accepted without question. It was Empedokles, we shall see, who first discovered that what we call air was a distinct corporeal substance, and not identical either with vapour or with empty space. In the earlier cosmologists " air " is always a form of vapour, and even darkness is a form of " air." It was Empedokles who cleared up this point too by showing that darkness is a shadow.[2]

---

[1] Simplicius, *Phys.* p. 149, 32 (R. P. 26 b), says that Theophrastos spoke of rarefaction and condensation in the case of Anaximenes *alone*. It should be noted, however, that Aristotle, *Phys.* A, 4. 187 a 12, seems to imply that Anaximander too had spoken of rarefaction and condensation, especially if ὅ ἐστι πυρὸς μὲν πυκνότερον ἀέρος δὲ λεπτότερον is referred to him. On the other hand, at 20, οἱ δ' ἐκ τοῦ ἑνὸς ἐνούσας τὰς ἐναντιότητας ἐκκρίνεσθαι, ὥσπερ Ἀναξίμανδρός φησι seems to be opposed to a 12, οἱ μὲν κτλ. As I have indicated already, it looks as if we were dealing here with Aristotle's own inferences and interpretations, which are far from clear. They are outweighed by the definite statement quoted by Simplicius from Theophrastos, though Simplicius himself adds δῆλον δὲ ὡς καὶ οἱ ἄλλοι τῇ μανότητι καὶ πυκνότητι ἐχρῶντο. That, however, is only his own inference from Aristotle's somewhat confused statement.

[2] For the meaning of ἀήρ in Homer, cf. *e.g. Od.* viii. 1, ἠέρι καὶ νεφέλῃ κεκαλυμμέναι ; and for its survival in Ionic prose, Hippokrates, Περὶ

It was natural for Anaximenes to fix upon " air " as the primary substance ; for, in the system of Anaximander, it occupied an intermediate place between the two fundamental opposites, the ring of flame and the cold, moist mass within it (§ 19). We know from Plutarch that he fancied air became warmer when rarefied, and colder when condensed. Of this he satisfied himself by a curious experimental proof. When we breathe with our mouths open, the air is warm ; when our lips are closed, it is cold.[1]

28. This argument brings us to an important point in the theory, which is attested by the single fragment that has come down to us.[2] " Just as our soul, being air, holds us together, so do breath and air encompass the whole world." The primary substance bears the same relation to the life of the world as to that of man. Now this was the Pythagorean view ; [3] and it is also an early instance of the argument from the microcosm to the macrocosm, and so marks the beginning of an interest in physiological matters.

The world breathes.

29. We turn now to the doxographical tradition concerning the formation of the world and its parts :

The parts of the world.

He says that, as the air was felted, the earth first came into being. It is very broad and is accordingly supported by the air.—Ps.-Plut. *Strom.* fr. 3 (R. P. 25).

In the same way the sun and the moon and the other heavenly bodies, which are of a fiery nature, are supported by the air

---

ἀέρων, ὑδάτων, τόπων, 15, ἀήρ τε πολὺς κατέχει τὴν χώρην ἀπὸ τῶν ὑδάτων. Plato is still conscious of the old meaning ; for he makes Timaios say ἀέρος (γένη) τὸ μὲν εὐαγέστατον ἐπίκλην αἰθὴρ καλούμενος, ὁ δὲ θολερώτατος ὁμίχλη καὶ σκότος (*Tim.* 58 d). For the identification of ἀήρ with darkness, cf. Plut. *De prim. frig.* 948 e, ὅτι δ' ἀὴρ τὸ πρώτως σκοτεινόν ἐστιν οὐδὲ τοὺς ποιητὰς λέληθεν· ἀέρα γὰρ τὸ σκότος καλοῦσιν. My view has been criticised by Tannery, " Une nouvelle hypothèse sur Anaximandre " (*Arch.* viii. pp. 443 *sqq.*), and I have slightly altered my expression of it to meet these criticisms. The point is of fundamental importance for the interpretation of Pythagoreanism.

[1] Plut. *De prim. frig.* 947 f (R. P. 27), where we are told that he used the term τὸ χαλαρόν for the rarefied air.

[2] Aet. i. 3, 4 (R. P. 24).   [3] See Chap. II. § 53.

because of their breadth. The heavenly bodies were produced from the earth by moisture rising from it. When this is rarefied, fire comes into being, and the stars are composed of the fire thus raised aloft. There were also bodies of earthy substance in the region of the stars, revolving along with them. And he says that the heavenly bodies do not move under the earth, as others suppose, but round it, as a cap turns round our head. The sun is hidden from sight, not because it goes under the earth, but because it is concealed by the higher parts of the earth, and because its distance from us becomes greater. The stars give no heat because of the greatness of their distance.—Hipp. *Ref.* i. 7, 4-6 (R. P. 28).

Winds are produced when air is condensed and rushes along under propulsion ; but when it is concentrated and thickened still more, clouds are generated ; and, lastly, it turns to water.[1] —Hipp. *Ref.* i. 7, 7 (*Dox.* p. 561).

The stars [are fixed like nails in the crystalline vault of the heavens, but some say they] are fiery leaves, like paintings.[2]— Aet. ii. 14, 3 (*Dox.* p. 344).

They do not go under the earth, but turn round it.—*Ib.* 16, 6 (*Dox.* p. 348).

The sun is fiery.—*Ib.* 20, 2 (*Dox.* p. 348).

It is broad like a leaf.—*Ib.* 22, 1 (*Dox.* p. 352).

The heavenly bodies turn back in their courses [3] owing to the resistance of compressed air.—*Ib.* 23, 1 (*Dox.* p. 352).

The moon is of fire.—*Ib.* 25, 2 (*Dox.* p. 356).

Anaximenes explained lightning like Anaximander, adding as an illustration what happens in the case of the sea, which flashes when divided by the oars.—*Ib.* iii. 3, 2 (*Dox.* p. 368).

Hail is produced when water freezes in falling ; snow, when there is some air imprisoned in the water.—Aet. iii. 4, 1 (*Dox.* p. 370).

The rainbow is produced when the beams of the sun fall on thick condensed air. Hence the anterior part of it seems red, being burnt by the sun's rays, while the other part is dark,

---

[1] The text is very corrupt here. I retain ἐκπεπυκνωμένος, because we are told above that winds are condensed air.

[2] See below, p. 77, *n.* 4.

[3] This can only refer to the τροπαί of the sun, though it is loosely stated of τὰ ἄστρα generally. It occurs in the chapter Περὶ τροπῶν ἡλίου, and we cannot interpret it as if it were a detached statement.

owing to the predominance of moisture. And he says that a
rainbow is produced at night by the moon, but not often, because
there is not constantly a full moon, and because the moon's light
is weaker than that of the sun.—*Schol. Arat.*[1] (*Dox.* p. 231).

The earth was like a table in shape.—Aet. iii. 10, 3 (*Dox.*
p. 377).

The cause of earthquakes was the dryness and moisture of
the earth, occasioned by droughts and heavy rains respectively.
—*Ib.* 15, 3 (*Dox.* p. 379).

We have seen that Anaximenes was justified in going
back to Thales in regard to the nature of primary substance ;
but the effect upon the details of his cosmology was unfortunate. The earth is once more imagined as a table-like
disc floating on the air. The sun, moon, and stars are also
fiery discs which float on the air " like leaves " ; an idea
naturally suggested by the " eddy " (δίνη). It follows that
the heavenly bodies cannot go under the earth at night, as
Anaximander must have held, but only round it laterally
like a cap or a millstone.[2] This view is also mentioned in
Aristotle's *Meteorology*,[3] where the elevation of the northern
parts of the earth, which makes it possible for the heavenly
bodies to be hidden from sight, is referred to. This is only
meant to explain why the stars outside the Arctic circle
appear to rise and set, and the explanation is fairly adequate
if we remember that the world is regarded as rotating in a
plane. It is quite inconsistent with the theory of a celestial
sphere.[4]

[1] The source of this is Poseidonios, who used Theophrastos. *Dox.*
p. 231.

[2] Theodoret (iv. 16) speaks of those who believe in a revolution like that
of a millstone, as contrasted with one like that of a wheel. Diels (*Dox.*
p. 46) refers these similes to Anaximenes and Anaximander respectively.
They come, of course, from Aetios (Note on Sources, § 10), though they
are given neither by Stobaios nor in the *Placita*.

[3] B. 1. 354 a 28 (R. P. 28 c).

[4] For this reason, I now reject the statement of Aetios, ii. 14, 3 (p. 76),
'Αναξιμένης ἥλων δίκην καταπεπηγέναι τῷ κρυσταλλοειδεῖ. That there is some
confusion of names here is strongly suggested by the words which
immediately follow, ἔνιοι δὲ πέταλα εἶναι πύρινα ὥσπερ τὰ ζωγραφήματα,
which is surely the genuine doctrine of Anaximenes. I understand

The earthy bodies, which circulate among the planets, are doubtless intended to account for eclipses and the phases of the moon.[1]

Innumerable worlds. 30. As might be expected, there is much the same difficulty about the "innumerable worlds" ascribed to Anaximenes as there is about those of Anaximander. The evidence, however, is far less satisfactory. Cicero says that Anaximenes regarded air as a god, and adds that it came into being.[2] That cannot be right. Air, as the primary substance, is certainly eternal, and it is quite likely that Anaximenes called it "divine," as Anaximander did the Boundless ; but it is certain that he also spoke of gods who came into being and passed away. These arose, he said, from the air. This is expressly stated by Hippolytos,[3] and also by St. Augustine.[4] These gods are probably to be explained like Anaximander's. Simplicius, indeed, takes another view ; but he may have been misled by a Stoic authority.[5]

Influence of Anaximenes. 31. It is not easy for us to realise that, in the eyes of his contemporaries, and for long after, Anaximenes was a much more important figure than Anaximander. And yet the fact is certain. We shall see that Pythagoras, though he followed Anaximander in his account of the heavenly bodies,

---

ζωγραφήματα of the constellations (cf. Plato, *Tim.* 55 c). To regard the stars as fixed to a crystalline sphere is quite inconsistent with the far better attested doctrine that they do not go under the earth.

[1] See Tannery, *Science hellène*, p. 153. For the precisely similar bodies assumed by Anaxagoras, see below, Chap. VI. § 135. See further Chap. VII. § 151.

[2] Cic. *De nat. d.* i. 26 (R. P. 28 b).

[3] Hipp. *Ref.* i. 7, 1 (R. P. 28).

[4] Aug. *De civ. D.* viii. 2 : " Anaximenes omnes rerum causas infinito aëri dedit : nec deos negavit aut tacuit ; non tamen ab ipsis aërem factum, sed ipsos ex aëre ortos credidit " (R. P. 28 b).

[5] Simpl. *Phys.* p. 1121, 12 (R. P. 28 a). The passage from the *Placita* is of higher authority than this from Simplicius. It is only to Anaximenes, Herakleitos, and Diogenes that successive worlds are ascribed even here. For the Stoic view of Herakleitos, see Chap. III. § 78 ; and for Diogenes, Chap. X. § 188. That Simplicius is following a Stoic authority is suggested by the words καὶ ὕστερον οἱ ἀπὸ τῆς Στοᾶς.

was far more indebted to Anaximenes for his general theory of the world (§ 53). We shall see further that when, at a later date, science revived once more in Ionia, it was " the philosophy of Anaximenes " to which it attached itself (§ 122). Anaxagoras adopted many of his most characteristic views (§ 135), and so did the Atomists.[1] Diogenes of Apollonia went back to the central doctrine of Anaximenes, and made Air the primary substance, though he also tried to combine it with the theories of Anaxagoras (§ 188). We shall come to all this later ; but it seemed desirable to point out at once that Anaximenes marks the culminating point of the line of thought which started with Thales, and to show how the " philosophy of Anaximenes " came to mean the Milesian doctrine as a whole. This it can only have done because it was really the work of a school, of which Anaximenes was the last distinguished representative, and because his contribution to it was one that completed the system he had inherited from his predecessors. That the theory of rarefaction and condensation was really such a completion of the Milesian system, we have seen (§ 26), and it need only be added that a clear realisation of this fact will be the best clue at once to the understanding of the Milesian cosmology itself and to that of the systems which followed it. In the main, it is from Anaximenes they all start.

[1] In particular, both Leukippos and Demokritos adhered to his theory of a flat earth. Cf. Aet. iii. 10, 3-5 (Περὶ σχήματος γῆς), 'Αναξιμένης τραπεζοειδῆ (τὴν γῆν). Λεύκιππος τυμπανοειδῆ. Δημόκριτος δισκοειδῆ μὲν τῷ πλάτει, κοίλην δὲ τῷ μέσῳ. And yet the spherical form of the earth was already a commonplace in circles affected by Pythagoreanism.

CHAPTER II

SCIENCE AND RELIGION

Ionia and
the West. 32. THE spirit of the Ionians in Asia was, as we have seen, thoroughly secular ; and, so far as we can judge, the Milesians wholly ignored traditional beliefs. Their use of the term " god " for the primary substance and the innumerable worlds had no religious significance.[1] It was different in the Aegean islands, which had been the home of the Ionians long before the Anatolian coasts were open to colonisation, and where there were many memories of a remote past. These seem to have centred round the sanctuary of Delos, and the fragments of Pherekydes, who belonged to the neighbouring island of Syros, read like belated utterances of an earlier age.[2] No doubt it was also different in the Chalkidian and Ionian colonies of the West, which were founded at a time when Hesiod and his followers still held unchallenged authority.

Now Pythagoras and Xenophanes, the most striking figures of the generation that saw the Greek cities in Asia become subject to Persia, were both Ionians, but both spent the greater part of their lives in the West. There it was no longer possible to ignore religion, especially when reinforced by the revival that now swept over the Greek world. Henceforth the leaders of enlightenment must either seek to reform and deepen traditional religion, like Pythagoras, or oppose it openly, like Xenophanes.

[1] See p. 14.   [2] See p. 3.

33 The revival was not, however, a mere recrudescence The Delian religion.
of the old Aegean religion, but was profoundly influenced
by the diffusion of certain ideas originating in what was then
the far North. The temple legend of Delos is certainly
ancient, and it connects the worship of Apollo with the
Hyperboreans, who were thought of as living on the banks
of the Danube.[1] The "holy things wrapped in straw,"
which were passed on from people to people till they reached
Delos by way of the head of the Adriatic, Dodona, and the
Malian Gulf,[2] bear witness to a real connexion between the
Danubian and Aegean civilisations at an early date, and it
is natural to associate this with the coming of the Achaians.
The stories of Abaris the Hyperborean [3] and Aristeas of
Prokonnesos [4] belong to the same religious movement and
prove that it was based on a view of the soul which was
new, so far as we can see, in the Aegean. Now the connexion
of Pythagoras with Delos is well attested, and it is certain
that he founded his society in cities which gloried in the
Achaian name. If the Delian religion was really Achaian,
we have a clue to certain things in the life of Pythagoras
which are otherwise puzzling. We shall come back to these
later.[5]

34. It was not, however, in its Delian form that the Orphicism.
northern religion had most influence. In Thrace it had
attached itself to the wild worship of Dionysos, and was
associated with the name of Orpheus. In this religion the
new beliefs were mainly based on the phenomenon of
"ecstasy" (ἔκστασις, "stepping out"). It was supposed
that it was only when "out of the body" that the soul
revealed its true nature. It was not merely a feeble double
of the self, as in Homer, but a fallen god, which might be

[1] Pindar, Ol. iii. 14-16.
[2] Herod. iv. 33. Cf. Farnell, Cults of the Greek States, iv. pp. 99 sqq.
[3] Herod. iv. 36.
[4] Ibid. iv. 13-15.
[5] I have discussed the origin of the Pythagorist religion in the Encyclopaedia of Religion and Ethics (s.v. Pythagoras) rather more fully than would be appropriate here.

restored to its high estate by a system of " purifications "
(καθαρμοί) and sacraments (ὄργια). In this form, the new
religion made an immediate appeal to all sorts and conditions of men who could not find satisfaction in the worship
of the secularised anthropomorphic gods of the poets and
the state religions.

The Orphic religion had two features which were new
in Greece. It looked to a written revelation as the source
of religious authority, and its adherents were organised in
communities, based, not on any real or supposed tie of
blood, but on voluntary adhesion and initiation. Most of
the Orphic literature that has come down to us is of late
date and uncertain origin, but the thin gold plates, with
Orphic verses inscribed on them, discovered at Thourioi
and Petelia take us back to a time when Orphicism was still
a living creed.[1] From them we learn that it had some
striking resemblances to the beliefs prevalent in India
about the same time, though it is really impossible to
assume any Indian influence in Greece at this date.[2] In
any case, the main purpose of the Orphic observances and
rites was to release the soul from the " wheel of birth," that
is, from reincarnation in animal or vegetable forms. The
soul so released became once more a god and enjoyed
everlasting bliss.

**Philo-
sophy as
a way of
life.**   35. The chief reason for taking account of the Orphic
communities here is that their organisation seems to have

---

[1] For these gold plates, see the Appendix to Miss Harrison's *Prolego-
mena to the Study of Greek Religion*, where the texts are discussed and
translated by Professor Gilbert Murray.

[2] The earliest attested case of a Greek coming under Indian influence
is that of Pyrrho of Elis (see my article " Sceptics " in the *Encyclopaedia of Religion and Ethics*). I venture to suggest that the religious
ideas referred to may have reached India from the same northern source
as they reached Greece, a source which we may vaguely call "Scythian."
If, as Caesar tells us (*B.G.* vi. 14, 5), the Gallic Druids taught the doctrine
of transmigration, this suggestion is strongly confirmed. The theories of
L. von Schroeder (*Pythagoras und die Inder*, 1884) are based on a mistaken view of Pythagoreanism, and appear also to involve chronological
impossibilities. See A. Berriedale Keith, " Pythagoras and the Doctrine
of Transmigration " (*Journal of the Royal Asiatic Society*, 1909, pp. 569 *sqq.*).

suggested the idea that philosophy is above all a " way of life." In Ionia, as we have seen, φιλοσοφία meant something like " curiosity," and from that use of it the common Athenian sense of " culture," as we find it in Isokrates, seems to have been derived. On the other hand, wherever we can trace the influence of Pythagoras, the word has a far deeper meaning. Philosophy is itself a " purification " and a way of escape from the " wheel." That is the idea so nobly expressed in the *Phaedo*, which is manifestly inspired by Pythagorean doctrine.[1] This way of regarding philosophy is henceforth characteristic of the best Greek thought. Aristotle is as much influenced by it as any one, as we may see from the Tenth Book of the *Ethics*, and as we should see still more clearly if we possessed his Προτρεπτικός in its entirety.[2] There was a danger that this attitude should degenerate into mere quietism and " otherworldliness," a danger Plato saw and sought to avert. It was he that insisted on philosophers taking their turn to descend once more into the Cave to help their former fellow-prisoners.[3] If the other view ultimately prevailed, that was hardly the fault of the philosophers.

36. Science, then, became a religion, and to that extent it is true that philosophy was influenced by religion. It would be wrong, however, to suppose that even now philosophy took over any particular doctrines from religion. The religious revival implied, we have seen, a new view of the soul, and we might expect to find that it profoundly influenced the teaching of philosophers on that subject. The remarkable thing is that this did not happen. Even the Pythagoreans and Empedokles, who took part in the

Relation of religion and philosophy.

---

[1] The *Phaedo* is dedicated, as it were, to the Pythagorean community at Phleious. Plato speaks in *Rep*. x. 600 b of Pythagoras as the originator of a private ὁδός τις βίου. Cf. the ἄτραπος of *Phaed.* 66 b.

[2] For the Προτρεπτικός, see Bywater in *J. Phil.* ii. p. 35. It was the original of Cicero's *Hortensius*, which had such an effect on Augustine.

[3] Plato, *Rep*. 520 c 1, καταβατέον οὖν ἐν μέρει. The Allegory of the Cave seems clearly to be of Orphic origin (Stewart, *Myths of Plato*, p. 252, n. 2).

religious movement themselves, held views about the soul which flatly contradicted the beliefs implied in their religious practices.[1] There is no room for an immortal soul in any philosophy of this period, as we shall see. Sokrates was the first philosopher to assert the doctrine on rational grounds,[2] and it is significant that Plato represents him as only half serious in appealing to the Orphics for confirmation of his own teaching.[3]

The reason is that ancient religion was not a body of doctrine. Nothing was required but that the ritual should be performed correctly and in a proper frame of mind ; the worshipper was free to give any explanation of it he pleased. It might be as exalted as that of Pindar and Sophokles or as debased as that of the itinerant mystery-mongers described in Plato's *Republic*. " The initiated," said Aristotle, " are not supposed to learn anything, but to be affected in a certain way and put into a certain frame of mind." [4] That is why the religious revival could inspire philosophy with a new spirit, but could not at first graft new doctrines on it.

I. PYTHAGORAS OF SAMOS

Character of the tradition.

37. It is not easy to give any account of Pythagoras that can claim to be regarded as historical. The earliest reference to him, indeed, is practically a contemporary one. Some verses are quoted from Xenophanes, in which we are told that Pythagoras once heard a dog howling and appealed to its master not to beat it, as he recognised the voice of a departed friend.[5] From this we know that he taught the

---

[1] For Empedokles, see § 117 ; for the Pythagoreans, see § 149.

[2] I have discussed this point fully in " The Socratic Doctrine of the Soul " (*Proceedings of the British Academy*, 1915–16, p. 235).

[3] Plato, *Phaed.* 69 c 3, καὶ κινδυνεύουσι καὶ οἱ τὰς τελετὰς ἡμῖν οὗτοι καταστήσαντες οὐ φαῦλοί τινες εἶναι, ἀλλὰ τῷ ὄντι πάλαι αἰνίττεσθαι κτλ. The irony of this and similar passages should be unmistakable.

[4] Arist. fr. 45 (1483 a 19), τοὺς τελουμένους οὐ μαθεῖν τι δεῖν, ἀλλὰ παθεῖν καὶ διατεθῆναι.

[5] Xenophanes, fr. 7.

doctrine of transmigration. Herakleitos, in the next generation, speaks of his having carried scientific investigation (ἱστορίη) further than any one, though he made use of it for purposes of imposture.[1] Later, though still within the century, Herodotos [2] speaks of him as " not the weakest scientific man (σοφιστής) among the Hellenes," and he says he had been told by the Greeks of the Hellespont that the legendary Scythian Salmoxis had been a slave of Pythagoras at Samos. He does not believe that ; for he knew Salmoxis lived many years before Pythagoras. The story, however, is evidence that Pythagoras was well known in the fifth century, both as a scientific man and as a preacher of immortality. That takes us some way.

Plato was deeply interested in Pythagoreanism, but he is curiously reserved about Pythagoras. He only mentions him once by name in all his writings, and all we are told then is that he won the affections of his followers in an unusual degree (διαφερόντως ἠγαπήθη) by teaching them a " way of life," which was still called Pythagorean.[3] Even the Pythagoreans are only once mentioned by name, in the passage where Sokrates is made to say that they regard music and astronomy as sister sciences.[4] On the other hand, Plato tells us a good deal about men whom we know from other sources to have been Pythagoreans, but he avoids the name. For all he says, we should only have been able to guess that Echekrates and Philolaos belonged to the school. Usually Pythagorean views are given anonymously, as those of " ingenious persons " (κομψοί τινες) or the like, and we are not even told expressly that Timaios the Lokrian, into whose mouth Plato has placed an unmistakably Pythagorean cosmology, belonged to the society. We are left to infer it from the fact that he comes from Italy. Aristotle imitates his master's reserve in this matter. The

[1] Herakleitos, fr. 17. For the meaning given to κακοτεχνίη, see note in loc.
[2] Herod. iv. 95.
[3] Plato, Rep. x. 600 b.   [4] Ibid. vii. 530 d.

name of Pythagoras occurs only twice in the genuine works that have come down to us. In one place we are told that Alkmaion was a young man in the old age of Pythagoras,[1] and the other is a quotation from Alkidamas to the effect that "the men of Italy honoured Pythagoras." [2] Aristotle is not so shy of the word " Pythagorean " as Plato, but he uses it in a curious way. He says such things as " the men of Italy who are called Pythagoreans," [3] and he usually refers to particular doctrines as those of " some of the Pythagoreans." It looks as if there was some doubt in the fourth century as to who the genuine Pythagoreans were. We shall see why as we go on.

Aristotle also wrote a special treatise on the Pythagoreans which has not come down to us, but from which quotations are found in later writers. These are of great value, as they have to do with the religious side of Pythagoreanism.

The only other ancient authorities on Pythagoras were Aristoxenos of Taras, Dikaiarchos of Messene, and Timaios of Tauromenion, who all had special opportunities of knowing something about him. The account of the Pythagorean Order in the Life of Pythagoras by Iamblichos is based mainly on Timaios,[4] who was no doubt an uncritical historian, but who had access to information about Italy and Sicily which makes his testimony very valuable when it can be recovered. Aristoxenos had been personally acquainted with the last generation of the Pythagorean society at Phleious. It is evident, however, that he wished to represent Pythagoras simply as a man of science, and was anxious to refute the idea that he was a religious teacher. In the same way, Dikaiarchos tried to make out that Pythagoras was simply a statesman and reformer.[5]

---

[1] Arist. *Met.* A, 5. 986 a 29.   [2] Arist. *Rhet.* B, 23. 1398 b 14.

[3] Cf. *e.g. Met.* A, 5. 985 b 23 ; *De caelo*, B, 13. 293 a 20.

[4] See Rostagni, " Pitagora e i Pitagorici in Timeo " (*Atti della R. Accademia delle Scienze di Torino*, vol. 49 (1913-14), pp. 373 *sqq.*

[5] See E. Rohde's papers, " Die Quellen des Iamblichos in seiner Biographie des Pythagoras," in *Rh. Mus.* xxvi. and xxvii.

When we come to the Lives of Pythagoras, by Porphyry, Iamblichos, and Diogenes Laertios,[1] we find ourselves once more in the region of the miraculous. They are based on authorities of a very suspicious character,[2] and the result is a mass of incredible fiction. It would be quite wrong, however, to ignore the miraculous elements in the legend of Pythagoras ; for some of the most striking miracles are quoted from Aristotle's work on the Pythagoreans[3] and from the *Tripod* of Andron of Ephesos,[4] both of which belong to the fourth century B.C., and cannot have been influenced by Neopythagorean fancies. The fact is that the oldest and the latest accounts agree in representing Pythagoras as a wonder-worker ; but, for some reason, an attempt was made in the fourth century to save his memory from that imputation. This helps to account for the cautious references of Plato and Aristotle, but its full significance will only appear later.

38. We may be said to know for certain that Pythagoras passed his early manhood at Samos, and was the son of Mnesarchos ;[5] and he " flourished," we are told, in the reign

Life of Pythagoras.

---

[1] Porphyry's *Life of Pythagoras* is the only considerable extract from his *History of Philosophy* that has survived. The *Life* by Iamblichos has been edited by Nauck (1884).

[2] Iamblichos made a compilation from the arithmetician Nikomachos of Gerasa and the romance of Apollonios of Tyana. Porphyry used Nikomachos and Antonius Diogenes, who wrote a work called *Marvels from beyond Thule*, which is parodied in Lucian's *Vera Historia*.

[3] It is Aristotle who told how Pythagoras killed a deadly snake by biting it, how he was seen at Kroton and Metapontion at the same time, how he exhibited his golden thigh at Olympia, and how he was addressed by a voice from heaven when crossing the river Kasas. It was also Aristotle who preserved the valuable piece of information that the Krotoniates identified Pythagoras with Apollo Hyperboreios, and that the Pythagoreans had a division of the λογικὸν ζῷον into τὸ μὲν . . . θεός, τὸ δὲ ἄνθρωπος, τὸ δὲ οἷον Πυθαγόρας. For these and other statements of the same kind, see Diels, *Vors.* 4, 7. It looks as if Aristotle took special pains to emphasise this aspect of Pythagoras out of opposition to the later Pythagoreans who tried to ignore it.

[4] Andron wrote a work on the Seven Wise Men, and the title refers to the well-known story (p. 44, *n.* 3).

[5] Cf. Herod. iv. 95, and Herakleitos, fr. 17 (R. P. 31 a). Timaios, however, gave his father's name as Demaratos. Herodotos represents him as living at Samos. Aristoxenos said his family came from one of

of Polykrates (532 B.C.).[1]   This date cannot be far wrong ;
for Herakleitos already speaks of him in the past tense.[2]

The extensive travels attributed to Pythagoras by late
writers are, of course, apocryphal.   Even the statement
that he visited Egypt, though far from improbable if we
consider the close relations between Polykrates of Samos
and Amasis, rests on no sufficient authority.[3]   Herodotos,
it is true, observes that the Egyptians agreed in certain
practices with the rules called Orphic and Bacchic, which
are really Egyptian, and with the Pythagoreans ; [4] but this
does not imply that the Pythagoreans derived these directly
from Egypt.   He says also that the belief in transmigration
came from Egypt, though certain Greeks, both at an earlier
and a later date, had passed it off as their own.   He refuses,
however, to give their names, so he can hardly be referring
to Pythagoras.[5]   Nor does it matter ; for the Egyptians

---

the islands which the Athenians occupied after expelling the Tyrrhenians
(Diog. viii. 1).   This suggests Lemnos or Imbros, from which the Tyr-
rhenian "Pelasgians" were expelled by Miltiades (Herod. vi. 140).   That
explains the story that he was an Etrurian or a Tyrian.   Other accounts
bring him into connexion with Phleious, but that may be a pious invention of the society which flourished there at the beginning of the
fourth century B.C.   Pausanias (ii. 13, 1) gives it as a Phleiasian tradition
that Hippasos, the great-grandfather of Pythagoras, had emigrated from
Phleious to Samos.

[1] Eratosthenes wrongly identified Pythagoras with the Olympic victor
of Ol. XLVIII. 1 (588/7 B.C.), but Apollodoros gave his *floruit* as 532/1,
the era of Polykrates.   He doubtless based this on the statement of
Aristoxenos quoted by Porphyry (*V. Pyth.* 9), that Pythagoras left Samos
from dislike to the tyranny of Polykrates (R. P. 53 a).

[2] Herakl. fr. 16, 17 (R. P. 31, 31 a).

[3] It occurs first in the *Bousiris* of Isokrates, § 28 (R. P. 52).

[4] Herod. ii. 81 (R. P. 52 a).   The comma at Αἰγυπτίοισι is clearly right.
Herodotos believed that the cult of Dionysos was introduced by Melampous
(ii. 49), and he means that the Orphics got these practices from the wor-
shippers of Bakchos, while the Pythagoreans got them from the Orphics.

[5] Herod. ii. 123 (R. P. *ib.*).   The words " whose names I know, but
do not write " cannot refer to Pythagoras ; for it is only of contemporaries
Herodotos speaks in this way (cf. i. 51, iv. 48).   Stein's suggestion that
he meant Empedokles seems convincing.   Herodotos must have met him
at Thourioi.   If Herodotos had ever heard of Pythagoras visiting Egypt,
he would surely have said so in one or other of these passages.   There
was no occasion for reserve, as Pythagoras must have died before Herodotos
was born.

did not believe in transmigration at all, and Herodotos was deceived by the priests or the symbolism of the monuments.

Aristoxenos said that Pythagoras left Samos in order to escape from the tyranny of Polykrates.[1] It was at Kroton, a city which had long been in friendly relations with Samos and was famed for its athletes and its doctors,[2] that he founded his society. Timaios appears to have said that he came to Italy in 529 B.C. and remained at Kroton for twenty years. He died at Metapontion, whither he had retired when the Krotoniates rose in revolt against his authority.[3]

39. The Pythagorean Order was simply, in its origin, The Order. a religious fraternity, and not, as has been maintained, a political league.[4] Nor had it anything whatever to do with the "Dorian aristocratic ideal." Pythagoras was an Ionian, and the Order was originally confined to Achaian states.[5] Moreover the "Dorian aristocratic ideal" is a

---

[1] Porph. *V. Pyth.* 9 (R. P. 53 a).

[2] From what Herodotos tells us of Demokedes (iii. 131) we may infer that the medical school of Kroton was founded before the time of Pythagoras. The series of Olympian victories won by Krotoniates in the sixth century B.C. is remarkable.

[3] For a full discussion of the chronological problem, see Rostagni, *op. cit.* pp. 376 *sqq.* It seems clear that Timaios made the rising of Kylon take place just after the destruction of Sybaris (510 B.C.), with which he connected it. The statement that Pythagoras then retired to Metapontion is confirmed by Cicero, who speaks (*De fin.* v. 4) of the honours still paid to his memory in that city (R. P. 57 c). Aristoxenos (*ap.* Iambl. *V. Pyth.* 249) referred to the same thing (R. P. 57 c). Cf. also Andron, fr. 6 (*F.H.G.* ii. 347).

[4] Plato, *Rep.* x. 600 a 9, clearly implies that Pythagoras held no public office. The view that the Pythagorean sect was a political league, maintained in modern times by Krische (*De societatis a Pythagora conditae scopo politico*, 1830), goes back, as Rohde has shown (*loc. cit.*), to Dikaiarchos, the champion of the "Practical Life," just as the view that it was primarily a scientific society goes back to the mathematician and musician Aristoxenos.

[5] The idea that the Pythagoreans represented the "Dorian ideal" dies very hard. In his *Kulturhistorische Beiträge* (Heft i. p. 59), Max C. P. Schmidt imagines that later writers call the founder of the sect Pythagoras instead of Pythagores, as he is called by Herakleitos and Demokritos, because he had become "a Dorian of the Dorians." The fact is simply that Πυθαγόρας is the Attic form of Πυθαγόρης, and is no more "Doric" than Ἀναξαγόρας. Even in the reign of Trajan, the Samians still knew that Πυθαγόρης was the correct spelling. Cf. the title vignette in Diels, *Vors.*

D

fiction based on the Sokratic idealisation of Sparta and Crete. Corinth, Argos, and Syracuse are quite forgotten. Nor is there any evidence that the Pythagoreans favoured the aristocratic party.[1] The main purpose of the Order was the cultivation of holiness. In this respect it resembled an Orphic society, though Apollo, and not Dionysos, was the chief Pythagorean god. That is doubtless due to the connexion of Pythagoras with Delos, and explains why the Krotoniates identified him with Apollo Hyperboreios.[2]

Downfall of the Order. 40. For a time the new Order succeeded in securing supreme power in the Achaian cities, but reaction soon came. Our accounts of these events are much confused by failure to distinguish between the revolt of Kylon in the lifetime of Pythagoras himself, and the later risings which led to the expulsion of the Pythagoreans from Italy. It is only if we keep these apart that we begin to see our way. Timaios appears to have connected the rising of Kylon closely with

[1] The only statement which might suggest that Pythagoras took the aristocratic side is the remark in Diogenes (viii. 3) ὥστε σχεδὸν εἶναι ἀριστοκρατίαν τὴν πολιτείαν. That may come from Timaios, but (as the adverb σχεδόν shows) it is not to be taken literally. The Pythagorean rule was no doubt an ἀριστοκρατία in the sense given to the word by Sokrates in Plato's *Republic*, but it was not based either on birth or on wealth, so that it was not an aristocracy in the common Greek sense of the word, and still less an oligarchy. It was more like the " Rule of the Saints." Kylon, the chief opponent of the Pythagoreans, is described by Aristoxenos (Iambl. *V. Pyth.* 248) as γένει καὶ δόξῃ καὶ πλούτῳ πρωτεύων τῶν πολιτῶν. Taras, later the chief seat of the Pythagoreans, was a democracy. (Cf. Strabo, vi. p. 280, ἴσχυσαν δέ ποτε οἱ Ταραντῖνοι καθ' ὑπερβολὴν πολιτευόμενοι δημοκρατικῶς . . . ἀπεδέξαντο δὲ καὶ τὴν Πυθαγόρειον φιλοσοφίαν κτλ.) The truth is that, at this time, the new religion appealed to the people rather than the aristocracies, which were apt to be " free-thinking." Xenophanes, not Pythagoras, is their man.

[2] We have the authority of Aristotle, fr. 186. 1510 b 20, for this identification. The names of Abaris and Aristeas stand for a mystical movement parallel to the Orphic, but based on the worship of Apollo. The later tradition makes them predecessors of Pythagoras ; and that this has some historical basis appears from Herod. iv. 13 *sqq.*, and above all from the statement that Aristeas had a statue at Metapontion, where Pythagoras died. The connexion of Pythagoras with Salmoxis belongs to the same order of ideas. As the legend of the Hyperboreans is Delian, we see that the religion taught by Pythagoras was genuinely Ionian in its origin, and had nothing to do with Dionysos.

the events which led to the destruction of Sybaris (510 B.C.). We gather that in some way Pythagoras had shown sympathy with the Sybarites, and had urged the people of Kroton to receive certain refugees who had been expelled by the tyrant Telys. There is no ground for the assertion that he sympathised with these refugees because they were " aristocrats " ; they were victims of a tyrant and suppliants, and it is not hard to understand that the Ionian Pythagoras should have felt a certain kindness for the men of the great but unfortunate Ionian city. Kylon, who is expressly stated by Aristoxenos to have been one of the first men of Kroton in wealth and birth,[1] was able to bring about the retirement of Pythagoras to Metapontion, another Achaian city, and it was there that he passed his remaining years.

Disturbances still went on, however, at Kroton after the departure of Pythagoras for Metapontion and after his death. At last, we are told, the Kyloneans set fire to the house of the athlete Milo, where the Pythagoreans were assembled. Of those in the house only two, who were young and strong, Archippos and Lysis, escaped. Archippos retired to Taras, a democratic Dorian state ; Lysis, first to Achaia and afterwards to Thebes, where he was later the teacher of Epameinondas.[2] It is impossible to date these events accurately, but the mention of Lysis proves that they were spread over more than one generation. The *coup d'État* of Kroton can hardly have occurred before 450 B.C., if the teacher of Epameinondas escaped from it, nor can it have been much later or we should have heard of it in connexion with the foundation of Thourioi in 444 B.C. In a valuable passage, doubtless derived from Timaios, Polybios tells us of the burning of the Pythagorean

---

[1] See p. 90, *n*. 1. I do not know why modern historians call him a democratic leader.

[2] Rohde, *Rhein. Mus.* xxxvi. p. 565, *n*. 1. The later accounts telescope these events into a single catastrophe. Some have it that Pythagoras himself was burned to death in the house of Milo.

" lodges " (συνέδρια) in all the Achaian cities, and the way in which he speaks suggests that this went on for a considerable time, till at last peace and order were restored by the Achaians of Peloponnesos.[1] We shall see that at a later date some of the Pythagoreans were able to return to Italy, and once more acquired great influence there.

Want of evidence as to the teaching of Pythagoras. 41. Of the opinions of Pythagoras we know even less than of his life. Plato and Aristotle clearly knew nothing for certain of ethical or physical doctrines going back to the founder himself.[2] Aristoxenos gave a string of moral precepts.[3] Dikaiarchos said hardly anything of what Pythagoras taught his disciples was known except the doctrine of transmigration, the periodic cycle, and the kinship of all living creatures.[4] Pythagoras apparently preferred oral instruction to the dissemination of his opinions by writing, and it was not till Alexandrian times that any one ventured to forge books in his name. The writings ascribed to the first Pythagoreans were also forgeries of the same period.[5] The early history of Pythagoreanism is, therefore, wholly conjectural ; but we may still make an attempt to understand, in a very general way, what the position of Pythagoras in the history of Greek thought must have been.

[1] Polyb. ii. 39, καθ' οὓς γὰρ καιροὺς ἐν τοῖς κατὰ τὴν Ἰταλίαν τόποις κατὰ τὴν μεγάλην Ἑλλάδα τότε προσαγορευομένην ἐνέπρησαν τὰ συνέδρια τῶν Πυθαγορείων, μετὰ ταῦτα γινομένου κινήματος ὁλοσχεροῦς περὶ τὰς πολιτείας (ὅπερ εἰκός, ὡς ἂν τῶν πρώτων ἀνδρῶν ἐξ ἑκάστης πόλεως οὕτω παραλόγως διαφθαρέντων) συνέβη τὰς κατ' ἐκείνους τοὺς τόπους Ἑλληνικὰς πόλεις ἀναπλησθῆναι φόνου καὶ στάσεως καὶ παντοδαπῆς ταραχῆς. ἐν οἷς καιροῖς, ἀπὸ τῶν πλείστων μερῶν τῆς Ἑλλάδος πρεσβευόντων ἐπὶ τὰς διαλύσεις, Ἀχαιοῖς καὶ τῇ τούτων πίστει συνεχρήσαντο πρὸς τὴν τῶν παρόντων κακῶν ἐξαγωγήν.

[2] When discussing the Pythagorean system, Aristotle always refers it to " the Pythagoreans," not to Pythagoras himself. He is quite clear that what he knew as the Pythagorean system belonged in the main to the days of Empedokles, Anaxagoras, and Leukippos ; for, after mentioning these, he goes on to describe the Pythagoreans as " contemporary with and earlier than them " (ἐν δὲ τούτοις καὶ πρὸ τούτων, *Met.* A, 5. 985 b 23).

[3] The fragments of the Πυθαγορικαὶ ἀποφάσεις of Aristoxenos are given by Diels, *Vors.* 45 D.

[4] Porphyry, *V. Pyth.* 19 (R. P. 55).

[5] See Diels, *Dox.* p. 150, and " Ein gefälschtes Pythagorasbuch " (*Arch.* iii. pp. 451 sqq.) ; Bernays, *Die heraklitischen Briefe*, n. 1.

42. In the first place, as we have seen,[1] he taught the doctrine of transmigration.[2] Now this is most easily to be explained as a development of the primitive belief in the kinship of men and beasts, a view which Dikaiarchos said Pythagoras held. Further, this belief is commonly associated with a system of taboos on certain kinds of food, and the Pythagorean rule is best known for its prescription of similar forms of abstinence. It seems certain that Pythagoras brought this with him from Ionia. Timaios told how at Delos he refused to sacrifice on any but the oldest altar, that of Apollo the Father, where only bloodless sacrifices were allowed.[3] *Trans-migration.*

43. It has indeed been doubted whether we can accept what we are told by such late writers as Porphyry on the subject of Pythagorean abstinence. Aristoxenos undoubtedly said Pythagoras did not abstain from animal flesh in general, but only from that of the ploughing ox and the ram.[4] He also said that Pythagoras preferred beans to every other vegetable, as being the most laxative, and that he was partial to sucking-pigs and tender kids.[5] The palpable exaggeration of these statements shows, however, that he is endeavouring to combat a belief which existed in *Abstinence.*

---

[1] See above, p. 84.

[2] The proper Greek for this is παλιγγενεσία, and the inaccurate term μετεμψύχωσις only occurs in late writers. Some of the Neoplatonists and Christian apologists say μετενσωμάτωσις, which is accurate but cumbrous. Cf. Olympiodoros *in Phaed.* p. 54, 25 (Norvin), τὴν μετεμψύχωσιν, ἤτοι τὴν μετενσωμάτωσιν, διότι οὐ πολλαὶ ψυχαὶ ἓν σῶμα εἰδοποιοῦσιν, ἐπεὶ αὕτη μετεμψύχωσις ἦν, ἀλλὰ μία ψυχὴ διάφορα σώματα μεταμπίσχεται. See Rohde, *Psyche,* p. 428, *n.* 2.

[3] See Diog. viii. 13.

[4] Aristoxenos *ap.* Diog. viii. 20, πάντα μὲν τὰ ἄλλα συγχωρεῖν αὐτὸν ἐσθίειν ἔμψυχα, μόνον δ' ἀπέχεσθαι βοὸς ἀροτῆρος καὶ κριοῦ.

[5] Aristoxenos *ap.* Gell. iv. 11, 5, Πυθαγόρας δὲ τῶν ὀσπρίων μάλιστα τὸν κύαμον ἐδοκίμασεν· λειαντικόν τε γὰρ εἶναι καὶ διαχωρητικόν· διὸ καὶ μάλιστα κέχρηται αὐτῷ; *ib.* 6, " porculis quoque minusculis et haedis tenerioribus victitasse, idem Aristoxenus refert." It is just possible that Aristoxenos may be right about the taboo on beans. We know that it was Orphic, and it may have been transferred to the Pythagoreans by mistake. That, however, would not affect the general conclusion that at least some Pythagoreans practised abstinence from various kinds of animal food, which is all that is required.

his own day, so we can show, out of his own mouth, that the tradition which made the Pythagoreans abstain from animal flesh and beans goes back to a time long before the Neopythagoreans. The explanation is that Aristoxenos had been the friend of the last of the Pythagoreans ; and, in their time, the strict observance had been relaxed, except by some zealots whom the heads of the Society refused to acknowledge.[1] The " Pythagorists " who clung to the old practices were now regarded as heretics, and it was said that the Akousmatics, as they were called, were really followers of Hippasos, who had been excommunicated for revealing secret doctrines. The genuine followers of Pythagoras were the Mathematicians.[2] The satire of the poets of the Middle Comedy proves, however, that, even though the friends of Aristoxenos did not practise abstinence, there were plenty of people in the fourth century, calling themselves followers of Pythagoras, who did.[3] We know also from Isokrates that they still observed the rule of

[1] Yet even Aristoxenos recorded that, when Pherekydes died, he was buried by Pythagoras at Delos (Diog. i. 118). It was, perhaps, too notorious to be denied.

[2] Hippasos of Kroton or Metapontion (in the catalogue of Iamblichos he is a Sybarite) is, we shall see, the regular scapegoat of the Pythagoreans. Iamblichos, who here follows Nikomachos, says (V. Pyth. 81 ; R. P. 56) that the μαθηματικοί were admitted to be Pythagoreans by the ἀκουσματικοί, but did not recognise them in return. We are told (Diog. viii. 7) that the μυστικὸς λόγος ascribed to Pythagoras was really by Hippasos, who wrote it ἐπὶ διαβολῇ Πυθαγόρου, i.e. to throw discredit on him by representing him as a purely religious teacher. The term Πυθαγοριστής seems to have been used specially of the Akousmatics, while the scientific Pythagoreans were called Πυθαγόρειοι in the same way as the followers of other schools were called Ἀναξαγόρειοι, Ἡρακλείτειοι, and like.

[3] For the fragments, see Diels, Vors. 45 E. The most striking are Antiphanes, fr. 135, Kock, ὥσπερ Πυθαγορίζων ἐσθίει | ἔμψυχον οὐδέν; Alexis, fr. 220, οἱ Πυθαγορίζοντες γάρ, ὡς ἀκούομεν, | οὔτ' ὄψον ἐσθίουσιν οὔτ' ἄλλ' οὐδὲ ἓν | ἔμψυχον; fr. 196 (from the Πυθαγορίζουσα), ἡ δ' ἑστίασις ἰσχάδες καὶ στέμφυλα | καὶ τυρὸς ἔσται· ταῦτα γὰρ θύειν νόμος | τοῖς Πυθαγορείοις; Aristophon, fr. 9 (from the Πυθαγοριστής), πρὸς τῶν θεῶν οἰόμεθα τοὺς πάλαι ποτέ, | τοὺς Πυθαγοριστὰς γενομένους ὄντως ῥυπᾶν | ἑκόντας ἢ φορεῖν τρίβωνας ἡδέως; Mnesimachos, fr. 1, ὡς Πυθαγοριστὶ θύομεν τῷ Λοξίᾳ | ἔμψυχον οὐδὲν ἐσθίοντες παντελῶς. See also Theokritos xiv. 5, τοιοῦτος καὶ πρᾶν τις ἀφίκετο Πυθαγορικτάς, | ὠχρὸς κἀνυπόδητός· Ἀθηναῖος δ' ἔφατ' ἦμεν.

silence.[1] History has not been kind to the Akousmatics, but they never wholly died out. The names of Diodoros of Aspendos and Nigidius Figulus help to bridge the gulf between them and Apollonios of Tyana.

We have seen that Pythagoras taught the kinship of beasts and men, and we infer that his rule of abstinence from flesh was based, not on humanitarian or ascetic grounds, but on taboo. This is strikingly confirmed by a statement in Porphyry's *Defence of Abstinence*, to the effect that, though the Pythagoreans did as a rule abstain from flesh, they nevertheless ate it when they sacrificed to the gods.[2] Now, among primitive peoples, we often find that the sacred animal is slain and eaten on certain solemn occasions, though in ordinary circumstances this would be the greatest of all impieties. Here, again, we have a primitive belief ; and we need not attach any weight to the denials of Aristoxenos.[3]

44. We shall now know what to think of the Pythagorean *Akousmata.* rules and precepts that have come down to us. These are

---

[1] *Bousiris*, § 28, ἔτι γὰρ καὶ νῦν τοὺς προσποιουμένους ἐκείνου μαθητὰς εἶναι μᾶλλον σιγῶντας θαυμάζουσιν ἢ τοὺς ἐπὶ τῷ λέγειν μεγίστην δόξαν ἔχοντας. The Pythagorean silence was called ἐχεμυθία or ἐχερρημοσύνη, both of which seem to be good Ionic words. It is ' probable that the silence was disciplinary rather than a means of keeping the doctrine secret.

[2] See Bernays, *Theophrastos' Schrift über Frömmigkeit.* Porphyry's tract, Περὶ ἀποχῆς ἐμψύχων, is addressed to Castricius Firmus, who had fallen away from the strict vegetarianism of the Pythagoreans. The passage referred to is *De abst.* p. 58, 25 Nauck, ἱστοροῦσι δέ τινες καὶ αὐτοὺς ἅπτεσθαι τῶν ἐμψύχων τοὺς Πυθαγορείους, ὅτε θύοιεν θεοῖς. This does not come, like most of Porphyry's tract, from Theophrastos, but it is in all probability from Herakleides of Pontos. See Bernays, *op. cit.* p. 11. Cf. also Plutarch, *Q. conv.* 729 c (οἱ Πυθαγορικοὶ) ἐγεύοντο τῶν ἱεροθύτων ἀπαρξάμενοι τοῖς θεοῖς.

[3] Porphyry (*V. Pyth.* c 15) has preserved a tradition to the effect that Pythagoras recommended a flesh diet for athletes (Milo ?). This story must have originated at the same time as those related by Aristoxenos, and in a similar way. In fact, Bernays has shown that it comes from Herakleides of Pontos (*Theophr. Schr.* n. 8). Iamblichos (*V. Pyth.* 5. 25) and others (Diog. viii. 13, 47) got out of this by supposing it referred to a gymnast of the same name. We see here how the Neoplatonists endeavoured to go back to the original form of the Pythagorean legend, and to explain away the fourth-century reconstruction.

of two kinds, and have different sources. Some of them, derived from Aristoxenos, and for the most part preserved by Iamblichos, are mere precepts of morality. They do not pretend to go back to Pythagoras himself ; they are only the sayings which the last generation of " Mathematicians " heard from their predecessors.[1] The second class is of a different nature, and consists of rules called *Akousmata*,[2] which points to their being the property of the sect which had faithfully preserved the old customs. Later writers interpret them as " symbols " of moral truth ; but it does not require a practised eye to see that they are genuine taboos. I give a few examples to show what the Pythagorean rule was really like.

1. To abstain from beans.
2. Not to pick up what has fallen.
3. Not to touch a white cock.
4. Not to break bread.
5. Not to step over a crossbar.
6. Not to stir the fire with iron.
7. Not to eat from a whole loaf.
8. Not to pluck a garland.
9. Not to sit on a quart measure.
10. Not to eat the heart.
11. Not to walk on highways.
12. Not to let swallows share one's roof.
13. When the pot is taken off the fire, not to leave the mark of it in the ashes, but to stir them together.
14. Do not look in a mirror beside a light.
15. When you rise from the bedclothes, roll them together and smooth out the impress of the body.

It would be easy to multiply proofs of the close connexion between Pythagoreanism and primitive modes of thought, but what has been said is sufficient for our purpose.

---

[1] For the Πυθαγορικαὶ ἀποφάσεις of Aristoxenos, see Diels, *Vors.* 45 D.
[2] There is a collection of ᾿Ακούσματα καὶ σύμβολα in Diels, *Vors.* 45 C.

45. Now, were this all, we should be tempted to delete the name of Pythagoras from the history of philosophy, and relegate him to the class of " medicine-men " (γόητες) along with Epimenides and Onomakritos. That, however, would be quite wrong. The Pythagorean Society became the chief scientific school of Greece, and it is certain that Pythagorean science goes back to the early years of the fifth century, and therefore to the founder. Herakleitos, who is not partial to him, says that Pythagoras had pursued scientific investigation further than other men.[1] Herodotos called Pythagoras " by no means the weakest sophist of the Hellenes," a title which at this date does not imply the slightest disparagement, but does imply scientific studies.[2] Aristotle said that Pythagoras at first busied himself with mathematics and numbers, though he adds that later he did not renounce the miracle-mongering of Pherekydes.[3] Can we trace any connexion between these two sides of his activity ?

Pythagoras as a man of science.

We have seen that the aim of the Orphic and other *Orgia* was to obtain release from the " wheel of birth " by means of " purifications " of a primitive type. The new thing in the society founded by Pythagoras seems to have been that, while it admitted all these old practices, it at the same time suggested a deeper idea of what " purification " really is. Aristoxenos said that the Pythagoreans employed music to purge the soul as they used medicine to purge the body.[4] Such methods of purifying the soul were familiar in the *Orgia* of the Kory-

[1] Herakl. fr. 17 (R. P. 31 a). The word ἱστορίη is in itself quite general. What it chiefly means here we see from a valuable notice preserved by Iamblichos, *V. Pyth.* 89, ἐκαλεῖτο δὲ ἡ γεωμετρία πρὸς Πυθαγόρου ἱστορία.

[2] Herod. iv. 95.

[3] Arist. Περὶ τῶν Πυθαγορείων, fr. 186, 1510 a 39, Πυθαγόρας Μνησάρχου υἱὸς τὸ μὲν πρῶτον διεπονεῖτο περὶ τὰ μαθήματα καὶ τοὺς ἀριθμούς, ὕστερον δέ ποτε καὶ τῆς Φερεκύδου τερατοποιίας οὐκ ἀπέστη.

[4] See Cramer, *An. Par.* i. 172, ὅτι οἱ Πυθαγορικοί, ὡς ἔφη Ἀριστόξενος, καθάρσει ἐχρῶντο τοῦ μὲν σώματος διὰ τῆς ἰατρικῆς, τῆς δὲ ψυχῆς διὰ τῆς μουσικῆς.

bantes,[1] and will serve to explain the Pythagorean interest
in Harmonics. But there is more than this. If we can
trust Herakleides, it was Pythagoras who first distinguished
the " three lives," the Theoretic, the Practical, and the
Apolaustic, which Aristotle made use of in the *Ethics*. The
doctrine is to this effect. We are strangers in this world,
and the body is the tomb of the soul, and yet we must not
seek to escape by self-murder ; for we are the chattels of
God who is our herdsman, and without his command we
have no right to make our escape.[2] In this life there are
three kinds of men, just as there are three sorts of people
who come to the Olympic Games. The lowest class is made
up of those who come to buy and sell, and next above them
are those who come to compete. Best of all, however, are
those who come to look on (θεωρεῖν). The greatest purification of all is, therefore, science, and it is the man who
devotes himself to that, the true philosopher, who has most
effectually released himself from the " wheel of birth." It
would be rash to say that Pythagoras expressed himself
exactly in this manner ; but all these ideas are genuinely
Pythagorean, and it is only in some such way that we can
bridge the gulf which separates Pythagoras the man of
science from Pythagoras the religious teacher.[3] It is easy
to understand that most of his followers would rest content
with the humbler kinds of purification, and this will account
for the sect of the Akousmatics. A few would rise to the
higher doctrine, and we have now to ask how much of the

[1] These are mentioned in Plato, *Laws*, 790 d, a passage which is the
origin of Aristotle's doctrine of κάθαρσις. For a full account see Rohde,
Psyche, ii. 48, *n.* 1.

[2] Plato gives this as the Pythagorean view in *Phaed.* 62 b. The
passage distinctly implies that it was not merely the theory of Philolaos,
but something older.

[3] See Döring in *Arch.* v. pp. 505 *sqq.* There seems to be a reference
to the theory of the " three lives " in Herakleitos, fr. 111. It was
apparently taught in the Pythagorean Society of Phleious ; for Herakleides
made Pythagoras expound it in a conversation with the tyrant of Phleious
(Cic. *Tusc.* v. 3 ; Diog. pr. 12, viii. 8), and Plato makes Sokrates argue
from it in the *Phaedo* (see my note on 68 c 2).

later Pythagorean science may be ascribed to Pythagoras himself.

46. In his treatise on Arithmetic, Aristoxenos said that Arithmetic. Pythagoras was the first to carry that study beyond the needs of commerce,[1] and his statement is confirmed by everything we otherwise know. By the end of the fifth century B.C. we find that there is a widespread interest in such subjects and that these are studied for their own sake. Now this new interest cannot have been wholly the work of a school ; it must have originated with some great man, and there is no one but Pythagoras to whom we can refer it. As, however, he wrote nothing, we have no sure means of distinguishing his own teaching from that of his followers in the next generation or two. All we can safely say is that, the more primitive any Pythagorean doctrine appears, the more likely it is to be that of Pythagoras himself, and all the more so if it can be shown to have points of contact with views which we know to have been held in his own time or shortly before it. In particular, when we find the later Pythagoreans teaching things that were already something of an anachronism in their own day, we may be pretty sure we are dealing with survivals which only the authority of the master's name could have preserved. Some of these must be mentioned at once, though the developed system belongs to a later part of our story. It is only by separating its earliest form from its later that the place of Pythagoreanism in Greek thought can be made clear, though we must remember that no one can now pretend to draw the line between its successive stages with any certainty.

47. One of the most remarkable statements we have The figures. about Pythagoreanism is what we are told of Eurytos on the unimpeachable authority of Archytas. Eurytos was

---

[1] Stob. i. p. 20, 1, ἐκ τῶν ᾿Αριστοξένου περὶ ἀριθμητικῆς, Τὴν δὲ περὶ τοὺς ἀριθμοὺς πραγματείαν μάλιστα πάντων τιμῆσαι δοκεῖ Πυθαγόρας καὶ προαγαγεῖν ἐπὶ τὸ πρόσθεν ἀπαγαγὼν ἀπὸ τῆς τῶν ἐμπόρων χρείας.

the disciple of Philolaos, and Aristoxenos mentioned him along with Philolaos as having taught the last of the Pythagoreans, the men with whom he himself was acquainted. He therefore belongs to the beginning of the fourth century B.C., by which time the Pythagorean system was fully developed, and he was no eccentric enthusiast, but one of the foremost men in the school.[1] We are told of him, then, that he used to give the number of all sorts of things, such as horses and men, and that he demonstrated these by arranging pebbles in a certain way. Moreover, Aristotle compares his procedure to that of those who bring numbers into figures (σχήματα) like the triangle and the square.[2]

Now these statements, and especially the remark of Aristotle last quoted, seem to imply the existence at this date, and earlier, of a numerical symbolism quite distinct from the alphabetical notation on the one hand and from the Euclidean representation of numbers by lines on the other. The former was inconvenient for arithmetical purposes, because the zero was not yet invented.[3] The representation of numbers by lines was adopted to avoid

[1] Apart from the story in Iamblichos (*V. Pyth.* 148) that Eurytos heard the voice of Philolaos from the grave after he had been many years dead, it is to be noticed that he is mentioned after him in the statement of Aristoxenos referred to (Diog. viii. 46 ; R. P. 62).

[2] Arist. *Met.* N, 5. 1092 b 8 (R. P. 76 a). Aristotle does not quote the authority of Archytas here, but the source of his statement is made quite clear by Theophr. *Met.* p. vi. a 19 (Usener), τοῦτο γὰρ (sc. τὸ μὴ μέχρι του προελθόντα παύεσθαι) τελέου καὶ φρονοῦντος, ὅπερ Ἀρχύτας ποτ' ἔφη ποιεῖν Εὔρυτον διατιθέντα τινὰς ψήφους· λέγειν γὰρ ὡς ὅδε μὲν ἀνθρώπου ὁ ἀριθμός, ὅδε δὲ ἵππου, ὅδε δ' ἄλλου τινὸς τυγχάνει.

[3] The notation used in Greek arithmetical treatises must have originated at a date and in a region where the *Vau* and the *Koppa* were still recognised as letters of the alphabet and retained their original position in it. That points to a Dorian state (Taras or Syracuse ?), and to a date not later than the early fourth century B.C. The so-called Arabic figures are usually credited to the Indians, but M. Carra de Vaux has shown (*Scientia*, xxi. pp. 273 *sqq.*) that this idea (which only makes its appearance in the tenth century A.D.) is due to a confusion between the Arabic *hindi*, " Indian," and *hindasi*, " arithmetical." He comes to the conclusion that the " Arabic " numerals were invented by the Neopythagoreans, and brought by the Neoplatonists to Persia, whence they reached the Indians and later the Arabs. The zero, on which the value of the whole system depends, appears to be the initial letter of οὐδέν.

the difficulties raised by the discovery of irrational quantities, and is of much later date. It seems rather that numbers were originally represented by dots arranged in symmetrical and easily recognised patterns, of which the marking of dice or dominoes gives us the best idea. And these markings are, in fact, the best proof that this is a genuinely primitive method of indicating numbers ; for they are of unknown antiquity, and go back to the time when men could only count by arranging numbers in such patterns, each of which became, as it were, a fresh unit.

It is, therefore, significant that we do not find any clue to what Aristotle meant by " those who bring numbers into figures like the triangle and the square " till we come to certain late writers who called themselves Pythagoreans, and revived the study of arithmetic as a science independent of geometry. These men not only abandoned the linear symbolism of Euclid, but also regarded the alphabetical notation, which they did use, as inadequate to represent the true nature of number. Nikomachos of Gerasa says expressly that the letters used to represent numbers are purely conventional.[1] The natural thing would be to represent linear or prime numbers by a row of units, polygonal numbers by units arranged so as to mark out the various plane figures, and solid numbers by units disposed in pyramids and so forth.[2] We therefore find figures like this :

```
                          a           a a a
        a     a a     a      aaa     a a a
 a  aa  a a   a a   a a      aaa     a a a
                     a a             a a a
```

[1] Nikomachos of Gerasa, *Introd. Arithm.* p. 83, 12, Hoche, Πρότερον δὲ ἐπιγνωστέον ὅτι ἕκαστον γράμμα ᾧ σημειούμεθα ἀριθμόν, οἷον τὸ ι, ᾧ τὸ δέκα, τὸ κ, ᾧ τὰ εἴκοσι, τὸ ω, ᾧ τὰ ὀκτακόσια, νόμῳ καὶ συνθήματι ἀνθρωπίνῳ, ἀλλ' οὐ φύσει σημαντικόν ἐστι τοῦ ἀριθμοῦ κτλ.   Cf. also Iambl. *in Nicom.* p. 56, 27, Pistelli, ἰστέον γὰρ ὡς τὸ παλαιὸν φυσικώτερον οἱ πρόσθεν ἐσημαίνοντο τὰς τοῦ ἀριθμοῦ ποσότητας, ἀλλ' οὐχ ὥσπερ οἱ νῦν συμβολικῶς.
[2] For the prime or rectilinear numbers, cf. Iambl. *in Nicom.* p. 26, 25, Pistelli, πρῶτος μὲν οὖν καὶ ἀσύνθετος ἀριθμός ἐστι περισσὸς ὃς ὑπὸ μόνης μονάδος πληρούντως μετρεῖται, οὐκέτι δὲ καὶ ὑπ' ἄλλου τινὸς μέρους, καὶ ἐπὶ μίαν

Now it ought to be obvious that this is no innovation. Of course the employment of the letter *alpha* to represent the units is derived from the conventional notation ; but otherwise we are clearly in presence of something which belongs to the very earliest stage of the science. We also gather that the dots were supposed to represent pebbles (ψῆφοι), and this throws light on early methods of what we still call *calculation.*

Triangular, square, and oblong numbers.

48. That Aristotle refers to this seems clear, and is confirmed by the tradition that the great revelation made by Pythagoras to mankind was precisely a figure of this kind, the *tetraktys,* by which the Pythagoreans used to swear,[1] and we have the authority of Speusippos for holding that the whole theory was Pythagorean.[2] In later days there were many kinds of *tetraktys,*[3] but the original one, that by which the Pythagoreans swore, was the " tetraktys of the dekad." It was a figure like this :

and represented the number ten as the triangle of four.

δὲ διάστασιν προβήσεται ὁ τοιοῦτος, διὰ τοῦτο δὲ αὐτὸν καὶ εὐθυμετρικόν τινες καλοῦσι, Θυμαρίδας δὲ καὶ εὐθυγραμμικόν· ἁπλατὴς γὰρ ἐν τῇ ἐκθέσει ἐφ' ἓν μόνον διιστάμενος. It is generally recognised now that Thymaridas was an early Pythagorean (Tannery, *Mém. scient.* vol. i. *n.* 9 ; G. Loria, *Scienze esatte,* p. 807) ; and, if that is so, we have a complete proof that this theory goes back to the early days of the school. For the triangular, oblong, and square numbers, etc., see Theon of Smyrna, pp. 27-37, Hiller, and Nicom. *loc. cit.*

[1] Cf. the formula Οὐ μὰ τὸν ἀμετέρᾳ γενεᾷ παραδόντα τετρακτύν, which is all the more likely to be old that it is put into the mouth of Pythagoras by the forger of the Χρυσᾶ ἔπη, thus making him swear by himself ! See Diels, *Arch.* iii. p. 457.

[2] Speusippos wrote a work on the Pythagorean numbers, based chiefly on Philolaos, and a considerable fragment of it is preserved in the *Theologumena Arithmetica.* It will be found in Diels, *Vorsokratiker,* 32 A 13, and is discussed by Tannery, *Science hellène,* pp. 374 *sqq.*

[3] See Theon, *Expositio,* pp. 93 *sqq.,* Hiller. The τετρακτύς used in the *Timaeus* is the second described by Theon (*Exp.* p. 94, 10 *sqq.*).

It showed at a glance that $1+2+3+4=10$. Speusippos tells us of several properties which the Pythagoreans discovered in the dekad. It is, for instance, the first number that has in it an equal number of prime and composite numbers. How much of this goes back to Pythagoras himself, we cannot tell ; but we are probably justified in referring to him the conclusion that it is " according to nature " that all Hellenes and barbarians count up to ten and then begin over again.

It is obvious that the *tetraktys* may be indefinitely extended so as to exhibit the sums of the series of successive integers in a graphic form, and these sums are accordingly called " triangular numbers."

For similar reasons, the sums of the series of successive odd numbers are called " square numbers," and those of successive even numbers " oblong." If odd numbers are added in the form of *gnomons*,[1] the result is always a similar figure, namely a square, while, if even numbers are added, we get a series of rectangles,[2] as shown by the figure :

Square Numbers.   Oblong Numbers.

---

[1] In accordance with analogy (p. 21, *n.* 1), the original meaning of the word γνώμων must have been that of the carpenter's square. From that are derived its use (1) for the instrument ; (2) for the figure added to a square or rectangle to form another square or rectangle. In Euclid (ii. def. 2) this is extended to all parallelograms, and finally the γνώμων is defined by Heron (ed. Heiberg, vol. iv. def. 58) thus : καθόλου δὲ γνώμων ἐστὶν πᾶν, ὃ προσλαβὸν ὁτιοῦν, ἀριθμὸς ἢ σχῆμα, ποιεῖ τὸ ὅλον ὅμοιον ᾧ προσείληφεν. These, however, are later developments ; for the use of γνώμων in the sense of "perpendicular" by Oinopides of Chios shows that, in the fifth century B.C., it only applied to rectangular figures.

[2] Cf. Milhaud, *Philosophes géomètres*, pp. 115 *sqq.* Aristotle puts the matter thus (*Phys.* Γ, 4. 203 a 13) : περιτιθεμένων γὰρ τῶν γνωμόνων περὶ τὸ ἓν καὶ χωρὶς ὁτὲ μὲν ἄλλο ἀεὶ γίγνεσθαι τὸ εἶδος, ὁτὲ δὲ ἕν. This is more clearly stated by Ps.-Plut. (Stob. i. p. 22, 16), ἔτι δὲ τῇ μονάδι τῶν ἐφεξῆς περισσῶν περιτιθεμένων ὁ γινόμενος ἀεὶ τετράγωνός ἐστι · τῶν δὲ ἀρτίων ὁμοίως

It is clear, then, that we are entitled to refer the study of sums of series to Pythagoras himself ; but whether he went beyond the oblong, and studied pyramidal or cubic numbers, we cannot say.[1]

Geometry and harmonics.

49. It is easy to see how this way of representing numbers would suggest problems of a geometrical nature. The dots which stand for the pebbles are regularly called " boundary-stones " (ὅροι, *termini*, " terms "), and the area they mark out is the " field " (χώρα).[2] This is evidently an early way of speaking, and may be referred to Pythagoras himself. Now it must have struck him that " fields " could be compared as well as numbers,[3] and it is likely that he knew the rough methods of doing this traditional in Egypt, though certainly these would fail to satisfy him. Once more the tradition is helpful in suggesting the direction his thoughts must have taken. He knew, of course, the use of the triangle 3, 4, 5 in constructing right angles. We have seen (p. 20) that it was familiar in the East from a very early date, and that Thales introduced it to the Hellenes, if they did not know it already. In later writers it is actually called the " Pythagorean triangle." Now the Pythagorean proposition *par excellence* is just that, in a right-angled

---

περιτιθεμένων ἑτερομήκεις καὶ ἄνισοι πάντες ἀποβαίνουσιν, ἴσως δὲ ἰσάκις οὐδείς. It will be observed that Aristotle here uses εἶδος in the sense of "figure." The words καὶ χωρὶς apparently mean χωρὶς τοῦ ἑνός, *i.e.* starting from 2, not from 1.

[1] Speusippos (cf. p. 102, *n.* 2) speaks of four as the first pyramidal number ; but this is taken from Philolaos, so we cannot safely ascribe it to Pythagoras.

[2] Proclus, *in Eucl. I.* p. 136, 8, ἔστι δὲ τὸ ὄνομα (sc. ὅρος) οἰκεῖον τῇ ἐξ ἀρχῆς γεωμετρίᾳ, καθ' ἥν τὰ χωρία ἐμέτρουν καὶ τοὺς ὅρους αὐτῶν ἐφύλαττον ἀσυγχύτους. We have ὅροι of a series (ἔκθεσις), then of a proportion, and in later times of a syllogism. The signs :, ::, and ∴ seem to be derived from this. The term χώρα is often used by the later Pythagoreans, though Attic usage required χωρίον for a rectangle. The spaces between the γραμμαί of the *abacus* and the chess-board were also called χῶραι.

[3] In his commentary on Euclid i. 44, Proclus tells us on the authority of Eudemos that the παραβολή, ἔλλειψις, and ὑπερβολή of χωρία were Pythagorean inventions. For these and the later application of the terms in Conic Sections, see Milhaud, *Philosophes géomètres*, pp. 81 *sqq.*

triangle, the square on the hypotenuse is equal to the squares on the other two sides, and the so-called Pythagorean triangle is the application of its converse to a particular case. The very name " hypotenuse " (ὑποτείνουσα) affords strong confirmation of the intimate connexion between the two things. It means literally " the cord stretching over against," and this is surely just the rope of the " arpedonapt." It is, therefore, quite possible that this proposition was really discovered by Pythagoras, though we cannot be sure of that, and though the demonstration of it which Euclid gives is certainly not his.[1]

50. One great disappointment, however, awaited him. It follows at once from the Pythagorean proposition that the square on the diagonal of a square is double the square on its side, and this ought surely to be capable of arithmetical expression. As a matter of fact, however, there is no square number which can be divided into two equal square numbers, and so the problem cannot be solved. In this sense, it may be true that Pythagoras discovered the incommensurability of the diagonal and the side of a square, and the proof mentioned by Aristotle, namely, that, if they were commensurable, we should have to say that an even number was equal to an odd number, is distinctly Pythagorean in character.[2] However that may be, it is certain that Pythagoras did not care to pursue the subject any further. He may have stumbled on the fact that the square root of two is a surd, but we know that it was left for Plato's friends, Theodoros of Kyrene and Theaitetos, to give a complete theory of irrationals.[3] For the present, the incommensurability of the diagonal and the square remained, as has been said, a " scandalous exception." Our tradition says that

Incommensurability.

---

[1] See Proclus's commentary on Euclid i. 47.

[2] Arist. *An. Pr.* A, 23. 41 a 26, ὅτι ἀσύμμετρος ἡ διάμετρος διὰ τὸ γίγνεσθαι τὰ περιττὰ ἴσα τοῖς ἀρτίοις συμμέτρου τεθείσης. The proofs given at the end of Euclid's Tenth Book (vol. iii. pp. 408 *sqq.*, Heiberg) turn on this very point. They are not Euclidean, and may be substantially Pythagorean. Cf. Milhaud, *Philosophes géomètres,* p. 94.

[3] Plato, *Theaet.* 147 d 3 *sqq.*

Hippasos of Metapontion was drowned at sea for revealing this skeleton in the cupboard.[1]

Proportion and harmony.

51. These last considerations show that, while it is quite safe to attribute the substance of the early books of Euclid to the early Pythagoreans, his arithmetical method is certainly not theirs. It operates with lines instead of with units, and it can therefore be applied to relations which are not capable of being expressed as equations between rational numbers. That is doubtless why arithmetic is not treated in Euclid till after plane geometry, a complete inversion of the original order. For the same reason, the doctrine of proportion which we find in Euclid cannot be Pythagorean, and is indeed the work of Eudoxos. Yet it is clear that the early Pythagoreans, and probably Pythagoras himself, studied proportion in their own way, and that the three " medieties " (μεσότητες) in particular go back to the founder, especially as the most complicated of them, the " harmonic," stands in close relation to his discovery of the octave. If we take the harmonic proportion 12 : 8 : 6,[2] we find that 12 : 6 is the octave, 12 : 8 the fifth, and 8 : 6 the fourth, and it can hardly be doubted that Pythagoras himself discovered these intervals. The stories about his observing the harmonic intervals in a smithy, and then weighing the hammers that produced them, or suspending weights corresponding to those of the hammers to equal strings, are, indeed, impossible and absurd ; but it is sheer waste of time to rationalise them.[3]

---

[1] This version of the tradition is mentioned in Iamblichos, *V. Pyth.* 247, and looks older than the other, which we shall come to later (§ 148). The excommunicated Hippasos is the *enfant terrible* of Pythagoreanism, and the traditions about him are full of instruction. See p. 94, *n.* 2.

[2] The harmonic mean is thus defined by Archytas (fr. 2, Diels) ἁ δὲ ὑπεναντία (μεσότας), ἃν καλοῦμεν ἁρμονικάν, ὅκκα ἔωντι ⟨τοῖοι (sc. οἱ ὅροι) · ᾧ⟩ ὁ πρῶτος ὅρος ὑπερέχει τοῦ δευτέρου αὐταύτου μέρει, τωὐτῷ ὁ μέσος τοῦ τρίτου ὑπερέχει τοῦ τρίτου μέρει. Cf. Plato, *Tim.* 36 a 3, τὴν . . . ταὐτῷ μέρει τῶν ἄκρων αὐτῶν ὑπερέχουσαν καὶ ὑπερεχομένην. The harmonic mean of 12 and 6 is, therefore, 8 ; for 8 = 12 − ¼² = 6 + ⅔.

[3] The smith's hammers belong to the region of *Märchen*, and it is not true that the notes would correspond to the weight of the hammers, or

For our purpose their absurdity is their chief merit. They
are not stories which any Greek mathematician could possibly have invented, but popular tales bearing witness to
the existence of a real tradition that Pythagoras was the
author of this momentous discovery. On the other hand,
the statement that he discovered the " consonances " by
measuring the lengths corresponding to them on the mono-
chord is quite credible and involves no error in acoustics.

52. It was this, no doubt, that led Pythagoras to say all
things were numbers. We shall see that, at a later date, the
Pythagoreans identified these numbers with geometrical
figures ; but the mere fact that they called them " numbers,"
taken in connexion with what we are told about the method
of Eurytos, is sufficient to show this was not the original
sense of the doctrine. It is enough to suppose that Pythagoras reasoned somewhat as follows. If musical sounds can
be reduced to numbers, why not everything else ? There
are many likenesses to number in things, and it may well
be that a lucky experiment, like that by which the octave
was discovered, will reveal their true numerical nature.
The Neopythagorean writers, going back in this as in other
matters to the earliest tradition of the school, indulge their
fancy in tracing out analogies between things and numbers
in endless variety ; but we are fortunately dispensed from
following them in these vagaries. Aristotle tells us distinctly that the Pythagoreans explained only a few things
by means of numbers,[1] which means that Pythagoras himself left no developed doctrine on the subject, while the
Pythagoreans of the fifth century did not care to add anything of the sort to the tradition. Aristotle does imply,
however, that according to them the " right time " (καιρός)

Things are numbers.

that, if they did, the weights hung to equal strings would produce the
notes. The number of vibrations really varies with the square root of
the weights. These inaccuracies were pointed out by Montucla (Martin,
Études sur le Timée, i. p. 391).

[1] Arist. *Met.* M, 4. 1078 b 21 (R. P. 78). The *Theologumena Arithmetica*
is full of such fancies (R. P. 78 a). Alexander, *in Met.* p. 38, 8, gives a
few definitions which may be old (R. P. 78 c).

was seven, justice was four, and marriage three. These identifications, with a few others like them, we may safely refer to Pythagoras or his immediate successors ; but we must not attach too much importance to them. We must start, not from them, but from any statements we can find that present points of contact with the teaching of the Milesian school. These, we may fairly infer, belong to the system in its most primitive form.

Cosmology.   53. Now the most striking statement of this kind is one of Aristotle's. The Pythagoreans held, he tells us, that there was " boundless breath " outside the heavens, and that it was inhaled by the world.[1] In substance, that is the doctrine of Anaximenes, and it becomes practically certain that it was taught by Pythagoras, when we find that Xenophanes denied it.[2] We may infer that the further development of the idea is also due to Pythagoras. We are told that, after the first unit had been formed—however that may have taken place—the nearest part of the Boundless was first drawn in and limited ; [3] and that it is the Boundless thus inhaled that keeps the units separate from each other.[4] It represents the interval between them. This is a primitive way of describing discrete quantity.

---

[1] Arist. *Phys.* Δ, 6. 213 b 22 (R. P. 75).

[2] Diog. ix. 19 (R. P. 103 c), ὅλον δ' ὁρᾶν καὶ ὅλον ἀκούειν, μὴ μέντοι ἀναπνεῖν (φησι Ξενοφάνης). So in [Plut.] *Strom.* fr. 4 we read that Xenophanes held μὴ κατὰ πᾶν μέρος περιέχεσθαι ὑπὸ ἀέρος (τὴν γῆν). We may therefore ascribe the statement to Theophrastos without hesitation, in spite of the fact that Diogenes is here drawing on an inferior (biographical) source, as shown by Diels (*Dox.* p. 168). Cf. also Hipp. *Ref.* i. 14, 2, τὴν δὲ γῆν ἄπειρον εἶναι καὶ μήτε ὑπ' ἀέρος μήτε ὑπὸ τοῦ οὐρανοῦ περιέχεσθαι (Ξενοφάνης λέγει).

[3] Arist. *Met.* N, 3. 1091 a 13 (R. P. 74).

[4] Arist. *Phys.* Δ, 6. 213 b 23 (R. P. 75 a). The words διορίζει τὰς φύσεις have caused unnecessary difficulty, because they have been supposed to attribute the function of limiting to the ἄπειρον. Aristotle makes it quite clear that his meaning is that stated in the text. Cf. especially the words χωρισμοῦ τινος τῶν ἐφεξῆς καὶ διορίσεως. The term διωρισμένον, " discrete," is the proper antithesis to συνεχές, " continuous." In his work on the Pythagorean philosophy, Aristotle used instead the phrase διορίζει τὰς χώρας (Stob. i. p. 156, 8 ; R. P. 75), which is also quite intelligible if we remember what the Pythagoreans meant by χώρα (cf. p. 104, *n.* 2).

In these passages of Aristotle, the " breath " is also spoken of as the void or empty. This is a confusion we have already met with in Anaximenes, and it need not surprise us to find it here.[1] We find also clear traces of the other confusion, that of air and vapour. It seems certain, in fact, that Pythagoras identified the Limit with fire, and the Boundless with darkness. We are told by Aristotle that Hippasos made Fire the first principle,[2] and we shall see that Parmenides, in discussing the opinions of his contemporaries, attributes to them the view that there were two primary " forms," Fire and Night.[3] We also find that Light and Darkness appear in the Pythagorean table of opposites under the heads of the Limit and the Unlimited respectively.[4] The identification of breath with darkness here implied is a strong proof of the primitive character of the doctrine ; for in the sixth century darkness was supposed to be a sort of vapour, while in the fifth its true nature was known. Plato, with his usual historical tact, makes the Pythagorean Timaios describe mist and darkness as condensed air.[5] We must think, then, of a " field " of darkness or breath marked out by luminous units, an imagination the starry heavens would naturally suggest. It is even probable that we should ascribe to Pythagoras the Milesian view of a plurality of worlds, though it would not have been natural for him to speak of an infinite number. We know, at least, that Petron, one of the early Pythagoreans, said there were just a hundred and eighty-three worlds arranged in a triangle.[6]

[1] Cf. Arist. *Phys.* Δ, 6. 213 a 27, οἱ δ' ἄνθρωποι . . . φασὶν ἐν ᾧ ὅλως μηδέν ἐστι, τοῦτ' εἶναι κενόν, διὸ τὸ πλῆρες ἀέρος κενὸν εἶναι; *De part. an.* B, 10. 656 b 15, τὸ γὰρ κενὸν καλούμενον ἀέρος πλῆρές ἐστι ; *De an.* B, 10. 419 b 34, δοκεῖ γὰρ εἶναι κενὸν ὁ ἀήρ.

[2] Arist. *Met.* A, 3. 984 a 7 (R. P. 56 c).   [3] See Chap. IV. § 91.

[4] Arist. *Met.* A, 5. 986 a 25 (R. P. 66).   [5] Plato, *Tim.* 58 d 2.

[6] This is quoted by Plutarch, *De def. orac.* 422 b, d, from Phanias of Eresos, who gave it on the authority of Hippys of Rhegion. If we may follow Wilamowitz (*Hermes*, xix. p. 444) in supposing that this really means Hippasos of Metapontion (and it was in Rhegion that the Pythagoreans took refuge), this is a very valuable piece of evidence.

54. Anaximander had regarded the heavenly bodies as wheels of " air " filled with fire which escapes through certain orifices (§ 21), and there is evidence that Pythagoras adopted the same view.[1] We have seen that Anaximander only assumed the existence of three such wheels, and it is extremely probable that Pythagoras identified the intervals between these with the three musical intervals he had discovered, the fourth, the fifth, and the octave. That would be the most natural beginning for the doctrine of the " harmony of the spheres," though the expression would be doubly misleading if applied to any theory we can properly ascribe to Pythagoras himself. The word ἁρμονία does not mean harmony, but octave, and the " spheres " are an anachronism. We are still at the stage when wheels or rings were considered sufficient to account for the heavenly bodies.

The distinction between the diurnal revolution of the heavens from east to west, and the slower revolutions of the sun, moon, and planets from west to east, may also be referred to the early days of the school, and probably to Pythagoras himself.[2] It obviously involves a complete break with the theory of a vortex, and suggests that the heavens are spherical. That, however, was the only way to get out of the difficulties of Anaximander's system. If it is to be taken seriously, we must suppose that the motions of the sun, moon, and planets are composite. On the one

[1] This will be found in Chap. IV. § 93.

[2] I formerly doubted this on the ground that Plato appeared to represent the theory as a novelty in *Laws*, 822 a, but Professor Taylor has convinced me that I was wrong. What Plato is denying in that passage is this very doctrine, and the theory he is commending must be that of a simple motion in a new form. This was a discovery of Plato's old age ; in the Myth of Er in the *Republic* and in the *Timaeus* we still have the Pythagorean theory of a composite motion. It is true that no writer earlier than Theon of Smyrna (p. 150, 12) expressly ascribes this theory to Pythagoras, but Aetios (ii. 16, 2) says that Alkmaion, a younger contemporary of Pythagoras, agreed with the mathematicians in holding that the planets had an opposite motion to the fixed stars. His other astronomical views were so crude (§ 96) that he can hardly have invented this.

hand, they have their own revolutions with varying angular velocities from west to east, but they are also carried along by the diurnal revolution from east to west. Apparently this was expressed by saying that the motions of the planetary orbits, which are oblique to the celestial equator, are mastered ($\kappa\rho\alpha\tau\epsilon\hat{\iota}\tau\alpha\iota$) by the diurnal revolution. The Ionians, down to the time of Demokritos, never accepted this view. They clung to the theory of the vortex, which made it necessary to hold that all the heavenly bodies revolved in the same direction, so that those which, on the Pythagorean system, have the greatest angular velocity have the least on theirs. On the Pythagorean view, Saturn, for instance, takes about thirty years to complete its revolution; on the Ionian view it is "left behind" far less than any other planet, that is, it more nearly keeps pace with the signs of the Zodiac.[1]

For reasons which will appear later, we may confidently attribute to Pythagoras himself the discovery of the sphericity of the earth, which the Ionians, even Anaxagoras and Demokritos, refused to accept. It is probable, however, that he still adhered to the geocentric system, and that the discovery that the earth was a planet belongs to a later generation (§ 150).

The account just given of the views of Pythagoras is, no doubt, conjectural and incomplete. We have simply assigned to him those portions of the Pythagorean system which appear to be the oldest, and it has not even been possible at this stage to cite fully the evidence on which our discussion is based. It will only appear in its true light when we have examined the second part of the poem of Parmenides and the system of the later Pythagoreans.[2]

---

[1] See the account of the theory of Demokritos in Lucretius, v. 621 *sqq.*, and cf. above, p. 70. The technical term is $\dot{\upsilon}\pi\dot{o}\lambda\epsilon\iota\psi\iota\varsigma$. Strictly speaking, the Ionian view is only another way of describing the same phenomena, but it does not lend itself so easily to a consistent theory of the real planetary motions.

[2] See Chap. IV. §§ 92-93, and Chap. VII. §§ 150-152.

It is clear at any rate that the great contribution of Pythagoras to science was his discovery that the concordant intervals could be expressed by simple numerical ratios. In principle, at least, that suggests an entirely new view of the relation between the traditional " opposites." If a perfect attunement (ἁρμονία) of the high and the low can be attained by observing these ratios, it is clear that other opposites may be similarly harmonised. The hot and the cold, the wet and the dry, may be united in a just blend (κρᾶσις), an idea to which our word " temperature " still bears witness.[1] The medical doctrine of the " temperaments " is derived from the same source. Moreover, the famous doctrine of the Mean is only an application of the same idea to the problem of conduct.[2] It is not too much to say that Greek philosophy was henceforward to be dominated by the notion of the perfectly tuned string.

II. XENOPHANES OF KOLOPHON

Life.

55. We have seen how Pythagoras gave a deeper meaning to the religious movement of his time ; we have now to consider a very different manifestation of the reaction against the view of the gods which the poets had made familiar. Xenophanes denied the anthropomorphic gods altogether, but was quite unaffected by the revival of religion going on all round him. We still have a fragment of an elegy in which he ridiculed Pythagoras and the doctrine of transmigration.[3] We are also told that he opposed the views of Thales and Pythagoras, and attacked Epimenides,

---

[1] It is impossible not to be struck by the resemblance between this doctrine and Dalton's theory of chemical combination. A formula like H_2O is a beautiful example of a μεσότης. The diagrams of modern stereochemistry have also a curiously Pythagorean appearance. We sometimes feel tempted to say that Pythagoras had really hit upon the secret of the world when he said, " Things are numbers."

[2] Aristotle derived his doctrine of the Mean from Plato's *Philebus*, where it is clearly expounded as a Pythagorean doctrine.

[3] See fr. 7, below.

which is likely enough, though no fragments of the kind have come down to us.[1]

It is not easy to determine the date of Xenophanes. Timaios, whose testimony in such matters carries weight, said he was a contemporary of Hieron and Epicharmos, and he certainly seems to have played a part in the anecdotical romance of Hieron's court which amused the Greeks of the fourth century as that of Croesus and the Seven Wise Men amused those of the fifth.[2] As Hieron reigned from 478 to 467 B.C., that would make it impossible to date the birth of Xenophanes earlier than 570 B.C., even if we suppose him to have lived till the age of a hundred. On the other hand, Clement says that Apollodoros gave Ol. XL. (620–616 B.C) as the date of his birth, and adds that his days were prolonged till the time of Dareios and Cyrus.[3] Again, Diogenes, whose information on such matters mostly comes from Apollodoros, says he flourished in Ol. LX. (540–537 B.C.), and Diels holds that Apollodoros really said so.[4] However that may be, it is evident that the date 540 B.C. is based on the assumption that he went to Elea in the year of its foundation, and is, therefore, a mere combination, which need not be taken into account.[5]

[1] Diog. ix. 18 (R. P. 97). We know that Xenophanes referred to the prediction of an eclipse by Thales (Chap. I. p. 42, *n.* 1).

[2] Timaios *ap.* Clem. *Strom.* i. p. 353 (R. P. 95). There is only one anecdote which actually represents Xenophanes in conversation with Hieron (Plut. *Reg. apophth.* 175 e), but it is natural to understand Arist. *Met.* Γ, 5. 1010 a 4 as an allusion to a remark made by Epicharmos to him. Aristotle's anecdotes about Xenophanes probably come from the romance of which Xenophon's *Hieron* is also an echo.

[3] Clem. *loc cit.* The mention of Cyrus is confirmed by Hipp. *Ref.* i. 94. Diels thinks Dareios was mentioned first for metrical reasons ; but no one has satisfactorily explained why Cyrus should be mentioned at all, unless the early date was intended. On the whole subject, see Jacoby, pp. 204 *sqq.*, who is certainly wrong in supposing that ἄχρι τῶν Δαρείου καὶ Κύρου χρόνων can mean " during the times of Dareios and Cyrus."

[4] *Rh. Mus.* xxxi. p. 22. He adopts the suggestion of Ritter to read πεντηκόστην for τεσσαρακόστην in Clem. *loc. cit.* (N for M). But Apollodoros gave Athenian archons, not Olympiads.

[5] As Elea was founded by the Phokaians six years after they left Phokaia (Herod. i. 164 *sqq.*) its date is just 540–39 B.C. Cf. the way in which Apollodoros dated Empedokles by the era of Thourioi (§ 98).

What we do know for certain is that Xenophanes had
led a wandering life from the age of twenty-five, and that
he was still alive and making poetry at the age of ninety-two.
He says himself (fr. 8 = 24 Karst. ; R. P. 97) :

There are by this time threescore years and seven that have
tossed my careworn soul [1] up and down the land of Hellas ; and
there were then five-and-twenty years from my birth, if I can
say aught truly about these matters.

It is tempting to suppose that in this passage Xenophanes
was referring to the conquest of Ionia by Harpagos, and
that he is, in fact, answering the question asked in another
poem [2] (fr. 22 = 17 Karst. ; R. P. 95 a) :

This is the sort of thing we should say by the fireside in the
winter-time, as we lie on soft couches after a good meal, drinking
sweet wine and crunching chickpeas : " Of what country are you,
and how old are you, good sir ?   And how old were you when
the Mede appeared ? "

In that case, his birth would fall in 565 B.C., and his
connexion with Hieron would be quite credible. We note
also that he referred to Pythagoras in the past tense, and
is in turn so referred to by Herakleitos.[3]

Theophrastos said that Xenophanes had " heard "
Anaximander,[4] and we shall see that he was acquainted
with the Ionian cosmology. When driven from his native
city, he lived in Sicily, chiefly, we are told, at Zankle and
Katana.[5] Like Archilochos before him, he unburdened his
soul in elegies and satires, which he recited at the banquets
where, we may suppose, the refugees tried to keep up the

---

[1] Bergk (*Litteraturgesch.* ii. p. 418, *n.* 23) took φροντίς here to mean
the literary work of Xenophanes, but it is surely an anachronism to
suppose that at this date it could be used like the Latin *cura.*

[2] It was certainly another poem ; for it is in hexameters, while the
preceding fragment is in elegiacs.

[3] Xenophanes, fr. 7 ; Herakleitos, frs. 16, 17.

[4] Diog. ix. 21 (R. P. 96 a).

[5] Diog. ix. 18 (R. P. 96). The use of the old name Zankle, instead of
the later Messene, points to an early source for this statement—probably
the elegies of Xenophanes himself.

usages of good Ionian society. The statement that he was
a rhapsode has no foundation at all.[1] The singer of elegies
was no professional like the rhapsode, but the social equal
of his listeners. In his ninety-second year he was still, we
have seen, leading a wandering life, which is hardly consistent with the statement that he settled at Elea and founded
a school there, especially if we are to think of him as
spending his last days at Hieron's court.[2] It is very
remarkable that no ancient writer expressly says he ever
was at Elea,[3] and all the evidence we have seems inconsistent
with his having settled there at all.

56. According to Diogenes, Xenophanes wrote in hexa- Poems.
meters and also composed elegies and iambics against
Homer and Hesiod.[4] No good authority says anything
of his having written a philosophical poem.[5] Simplicius
tells us he had never met with the verses about the earth

---

[1] Diog. ix. 18 (R. P. 97) says αὐτὸς ἐρραψῴδει τὰ ἑαυτοῦ, which is a very
different thing. Nothing is said anywhere of his reciting Homer. Gomperz's imaginative picture (Greek Thinkers, vol. i. p. 155) has no further
support than this single word.

[2] Diog. ix. 20 (R. P. 97) says he wrote a poem in 2000 hexameters
on the colonisation of Elea. Even if true, this would not prove he
lived there ; for the foundation of Elea would be a subject of interest
to all the Ionian émigrés. Moreover, the statement is very suspicious.
The stichometric notices of the Seven Wise Men, Epimenides, etc., in
Diogenes come from the forger Lobon, and this seems to be from the
same source.

[3] The only passage which brings him into connexion with Elea is
Aristotle's anecdote about the answer he gave the Eleates when they
asked him whether they should sacrifice to Leukothea. " If you think
her a goddess," he said, "do not lament her ; if you do not, do not
sacrifice to her " (Rhet. B, 26. 1400 b 5 ; R. P. 98 a). Even this does
not necessarily imply that he settled at Elea, and in any case such
anecdotes are really anonymous. Plutarch tells the story more than
once, but he makes it a remark of Xenophanes to the Egyptians (Diels,
Vors. 11 A 13), while others tell it of Herakleitos.

[4] Diog. ix. 18 (R. P. 97). The word ἐπικόπτων is a reminiscence of
Timon, fr. 60 (Diels), Ξεινοφάνης ὑπάτυφος Ὁμηραπάτης ἐπικόπτης.

[5] The oldest reference to a poem Περὶ φύσεως is in the Geneva scholium
on Il. xxi. 196 (quoting fr. 30), and this goes back to Krates of Mallos.
We must remember that such titles are of later date, and Xenophanes
had been given a place among philosophers long before the time of Krates.
All we can say, therefore, is that the Pergamene librarians gave the title
Περὶ φύσεως to some poem of Xenophanes.

stretching infinitely downwards (fr. 28),[1] and this means that
the Academy possessed no copy of such a poem, which would
be very strange if it had ever existed. Simplicius was able
to find the complete works of much smaller men. Nor does
internal evidence lend any support to the view that Xenophanes wrote a philosophical poem.   Diels refers about
twenty-eight lines to it, but they would all come in quite
as naturally in his attacks on Homer and Hesiod, as I have
endeavoured to show. It is also significant that a number
of them are derived from commentators on Homer.[2] It
is more probable, then, that Xenophanes expressed such
scientific opinions as he had incidentally in his satires. That
would be in the manner of the time, as we can see from the
remains of Epicharmos.

The satires are called *Silloi* by late writers, and this
name may go back to Xenophanes himself. It may, however, originate in the fact that Timon of Phleious, the
' sillographer '' (c. 259 B.C.), put much of his satire upon
philosophers into the mouth of Xenophanes. Only one
iambic line has been preserved, and that is immediately
followed by a hexameter (fr. 14). This suggests that Xenophanes inserted iambic lines among his hexameters in the
manner of the *Margites*.

The fragments.　57. I give the fragments according to the text and
arrangement of Diels.

ELEGIES

(1)

Now is the floor clean, and the hands and cups of all ; one
sets twisted garlands on our heads, another hands us fragrant
ointment on a salver. The mixing bowl stands ready, full of

---

[1] Simpl. *De caelo*, p. 522, 7 (R. P. 97 b). It is true that two of our
fragments (25 and 26) are preserved by Simplicius, but he got them from
Alexander. Probably they were quoted by Theophrastos ; for it is plain
that Alexander had no first-hand knowledge of Xenophanes, or he would
not have been taken in by *M.X.G.* (See p. 126.)

[2] Three fragments (27, 31, 33) come from the *Homeric Allegories*, two
(30, 32) are from Homeric scholia.

gladness, and there is more wine at hand that promises never to leave us in the lurch, soft and smelling of flowers in the jars. In the midst the frankincense sends up its holy scent, and there is cold water, sweet and clean. Brown loaves are set before us and a lordly table laden with cheese and rich honey. The altar in the midst is clustered round with flowers ; song and revel fill the halls.

But first it is meet that men should hymn the god with joy, with holy tales and pure words ; then after libation and prayer made that we may have strength to do right—for that is in truth the first thing to do—no sin is it to drink as much as a man can take and get home without an attendant, so he be not stricken in years. And of all men is he to be praised who after drinking gives goodly proof of himself in the trial of skill,[1] as memory and strength will serve him. Let him not sing of Titans and Giants —those fictions of the men of old—nor of turbulent civil broils in which is no good thing at all ; but to give heedful reverence to the gods is ever good.

(2)

What if a man win victory in swiftness of foot, or in the *pentathlon*, at Olympia, where is the precinct of Zeus by Pisa's springs, or in wrestling,—what if by cruel boxing or that fearful sport men call *pankration* he become more glorious in the citizens' eyes, and win a place of honour in the sight of all at the games, his food at the public cost from the State, and a gift to be an heir-loom for him,—what if he conquer in the chariot-race,—he will not deserve all this for his portion so much as I do. Far better is our art than the strength of men and of horses ! These are but thoughtless judgements, nor is it fitting to set strength before goodly art.[2] Even if there arise a mighty boxer among a people, or one great in the *pentathlon* or at wrestling, or one excelling in swiftness of foot—and that stands in honour before all tasks of men at the games—the city would be none the better governed for that. It is but little joy a city gets of it if a man conquer at the games by Pisa's banks ; it is not this that makes fat the store-houses of a city.

---

[1] So I understand ἀμφ' ἀρετῆς. The τόνος is "strength of lungs." The next verses are directed against Hesiod and Alkaios (Diels).

[2] At this date " art " is the natural translation of σοφίη in such a writer as Xenophanes.

(3)

They learnt dainty and unprofitable ways from the Lydians, so long as they were free from hateful tyranny ; they went to the market-place with cloaks of purple dye, not less than a thousand of them all told, vainglorious and proud of their comely tresses, reeking with fragrance from cunning salves.

(4)

Nor would a man mix wine in a cup by pouring out the wine first, but water first and wine on the top of it.

(5)

Thou didst send the thigh-bone of a kid and get for it the fat leg of a fatted bull, a worthy guerdon for a man to get, whose glory is to reach every part of Hellas and never to pass away, so long as Greek songs last.[1]

(7)

And now I will turn to another tale and point the way. . . . Once they say that he (Pythagoras) was passing by when a dog was being beaten and spoke this word : " Stop ! don't beat it ! For it is the soul of a friend that I recognised when I heard its voice." [2]

(8)

See p. 114.

(9)

Much weaker than an aged man.

SATIRES

(10)

Since all at first have learnt according to Homer. . . .

---

[1] Diels suggests that this is an attack on a poet like Simonides, whose greed was proverbial.

[2] The name of Pythagoras does not occur in the lines that have been preserved ; but the source of Diogenes viii. 36 must have had the complete elegy before him ; for he said the verses occurred ἐν ἐλεγείᾳ, ἧς ἀρχὴ Νῦν αὖτ' ἄλλον ἔπειμι λόγον κτλ.

(11)

Homer and Hesiod have ascribed to the gods all things that are a shame and a disgrace among mortals, stealings and adulteries and deceivings of one another. R. P. 99.

(12)

Since they have uttered many lawless deeds of the gods, stealings and adulteries and deceivings of one another. R. P. *ib.*

(14)

But mortals deem that the gods are begotten as they are, and have clothes like theirs, and voice and form. R. P. 100.

(15)

Yes, and if oxen and horses or lions had hands, and could paint with their hands, and produce works of art as men do, horses would paint the forms of the gods like horses, and oxen like oxen, and make their bodies in the image of their several kinds. R. P. *ib.*

(16)

The Ethiopians make their gods black and snub-nosed ; the Thracians say theirs have blue eyes and red hair. R. P. 100 b.

(18)

The gods have not revealed all things to men from the beginning, but by seeking they find in time what is better. R. P. 104 b.

(23)

One god, the greatest among gods and men, neither in form like unto mortals nor in thought. . . . R. P. 100.

(24)

He sees all over, thinks all over, and hears all over. R. P. 102.

(25)

But without toil he swayeth all things by the thought of his mind. R. P. 108 b.

(26)

And he abideth ever in the selfsame place, moving not at all ; nor doth it befit him to go about now hither now thither. R. P. 110 a.

(27)

All things come from the earth, and in earth all things end. R. P. 103 a.

(28)

This limit of the earth above is seen at our feet in contact with the air ; [1] below it reaches down without a limit.   R. P. 103.

(29)

All things are earth and water that come into being and grow. R. P. 103.

(30)

The sea is the source of water and the source of wind ; for neither in the clouds (would there be any blasts of wind blowing forth) from within without the mighty sea, nor rivers' streams nor rain-water from the sky.   The mighty sea is father of clouds and of winds and of rivers.[2]   R. P. 103.

(31)

The sun swinging over [3] the earth and warming it. . . .

(32)

She that they call Iris is a cloud likewise, purple, scarlet and green to behold.   R. P. 103.

(33)

For we all are born of earth and water.   R. P. *ib.*

---

[1] Reading ἠέρι for καὶ ῥεῖ with Diels.

[2] This fragment has been recovered from the Geneva scholia on Homer (see *Arch.* iv. p. 652).   The words in brackets are added by Diels.

[3] The word is ὑπεριέμενος.   This is quoted from the *Allegories* as an explanation of the name Hyperion, and doubtless Xenophanes so meant it.

(34)

There never was nor will be a man who has certain knowledge about the gods and about all the things I speak of. Even if he should chance to say the complete truth, yet he himself knows not that it is so. But all may have their fancy.[1]   R. P. 104.

(35)

Let these be taken as fancies [2] something like the truth. R. P. 104 a.

(36)

All of them [3] that are visible for mortals to behold.

(37)

And in some caves water drips. . . .

(38)

If god had not made brown honey, men would think figs far sweeter than they do.

58. Most of these fragments are not in any way philo- *The heavenly* sophical, and those that appear to be so are easily accounted *bodies.* for otherwise.   The intention of one of them (fr. 32) is clear. " Iris too " is a cloud, and we may infer that the same thing had been said of the sun, moon, and stars ; for the doxographers tell us that these were all explained as " clouds ignited by motion." [4]   To the same context clearly belongs the explanation of the St. Elmo's fire which Aetios has preserved.   "The things like stars that appear on ships," we

---

[1] It is more natural to take πᾶσι as masculine than as neuter, and ἐπὶ πᾶσι can mean " in the power of all."

[2] Reading δεδοξάσθω with Wilamowitz.

[3] As Diels suggests, this probably refers to the stars, which Xenophanes held to be clouds.

[4] Cf. Diels ad loc. (P. Ph. Fr. p. 44), " ut Sol et cetera astra, quae cum in nebulas evanescerent, deorum simul opinio casura erat."

E

are told, "which some call the Dioskouroi, are little clouds made luminous by motion." [1] In the doxographers the same explanation is repeated with trifling variations under the head of moon, stars, comets, lightning, shooting stars, and so forth, which gives the appearance of a systematic cosmology.[2] But the system is due to the arrangement of the work of Theophrastos, and not to Xenophanes; for it is obvious that a very few additional hexameters would amply account for the whole doxography.

What we hear of the sun presents some difficulties. We are told that it is an ignited cloud; but this is not very consistent with the statement that the evaporation of the sea from which clouds arise is due to the sun's heat. Theophrastos stated that the sun, according to Xenophanes, was a collection of sparks from the moist exhalation; but even this leaves the exhalation itself unexplained.[3] That, however, matters little, if the chief aim of Xenophanes was to discredit the anthropomorphic gods, rather than to give a scientific theory of the heavenly bodies. The important thing is that Helios too is a temporary phenomenon. The sun does not go round the earth, as Anaximander taught, but straight on, and the appearance of a circular path is solely due to its increasing distance. So it is not the same sun that rises next morning, but a new one altogether; while eclipses occur because the sun " tumbles into a hole " when it comes to certain uninhabited regions of the earth. An eclipse may last a month. Besides that, there are

---

[1] Aet. ii. 18, 1 (Dox. p. 347), Ξενοφάνης τοὺς ἐπὶ τῶν πλοίων φαινομένους οἷον ἀστέρας, οὓς καὶ Διοσκούρους καλοῦσί τινες, νεφέλια εἶναι κατὰ τὴν ποιὰν κίνησιν παραλάμποντα.

[2] The passages from Aetios are collected in Diels, Vors. 11 A 38 sqq.

[3] Aet. ii. 20, 3 (Dox. p. 348), Ξενοφάνης ἐκ νεφῶν πεπυρωμένων εἶναι τὸν ἥλιον. Θεόφραστος ἐν τοῖς Φυσικοῖς γέγραφεν ἐκ πυριδίων μὲν τῶν συναθροιζομένων ἐκ τῆς ὑγρᾶς ἀναθυμιάσεως, συναθροιζόντων δὲ τὸν ἥλιον. It seems likely from these words that Theophrastos pointed out the contradiction, as his manner was.

many suns and moons, one of each for every region of the
earth.¹

The vigorous expression " tumbling into a hole " ² seems
clearly to come from the verses of Xenophanes himself,
and there are others of a similar kind, which 've must
suppose were quoted by Theophrastos. The stars go out
in the daytime, but glow again at night " like charcoal
embers." ³ The sun is of some use in producing the world
and the living creatures in it, but the moon "does no work
in the boat." ⁴ Such expressions can only be meant to
make the heavenly bodies appear ridiculous, and it will
therefore be well to ask whether the other supposed cosmological fragments can be interpreted on the same principle.

59. In fr. 29 Xenophanes says that " all things are earth
and water," and Hippolytos has preserved the account
given by Theophrastos of the context in which this occurred.
It was as follows :

Earth and water.

Xenophanes said that a mixture of the earth with the sea is
taking place, and that it is being gradually dissolved by the
moisture. He says that he has the following proofs of this.
Shells are found in midland districts and on hills, and he says
that in the quarries at Syracuse has been found the imprint of
a fish and of seaweed, at Paros the form of a bayleaf in the depth
of the stone, and at Malta flat impressions of all marine animals.
These, he says, were produced when all things were formerly
mud, and the outlines were dried in the mud.   All human beings

----

¹ Aet. ii. 24, 9 (*Dox.* p. 355), πολλοὺς εἶναι ἡλίους καὶ σελήνας κατὰ
κλίματα τῆς γῆς καὶ ἀποτομὰς καὶ ζώνας, κατὰ δέ τινα καιρὸν ἐμπίπτειν τὸν
δίσκον εἴς τινα ἀποτομὴν τῆς γῆς οὐκ οἰκουμένην ὑφ' ἡμῶν καὶ οὕτως ὥσπερ κενεμ-
βατοῦντα ἔκλειψιν ὑποφαίνειν· ὁ δ' αὐτὸς τὸν ἥλιον εἰς ἄπειρον μὲν προιέναι, δοκεῖν
δὲ κυκλεῖσθαι διὰ τὴν ἀπόστασιν.
² That this is the meaning of κενεμβατέω appears sufficiently from
the passages referred to in Liddell and Scott, and it describes a total
eclipse very well.
³ Aet. ii. 13, 14 (*Dox.* p. 343), ἀναζωπυρεῖν νύκτωρ καθάπερ τοὺς ἄνθρακας.
⁴ Aet. ii. 30, 8 (*Dox.* p. 362), τὸν μὲν ἥλιον χρήσιμον εἶναι πρὸς τὴν
τοῦ κόσμου καὶ τὴν τῶν ἐν αὐτῷ ζώων γένεσίν τε καὶ διοίκησιν, τὴν δὲ σελήνην
παρέλκειν. The verb παρέλκειν means " to cork." (Cf. Aristophanes,
Pax, 1306.) In Hellenistic Greek the metaphor is no longer felt, and
παρέλκει means " is redundant," " is superfluous."

are destroyed when the earth has been carried down into the sea and turned to mud. This change takes place for all the worlds.—Hipp. *Ref.* i. 14 (R. P. 103 a).

This is, of course, the theory of Anaximander, and we may perhaps credit him rather than Xenophanes with the observations of fossils.[1] Most remarkable of all, however, is the statement that this change applies to " all the worlds." It seems impossible to doubt that Theophrastos attributed a belief in " innumerable worlds " to Xenophanes. As we have seen, Aetios includes him in his list of those who held this doctrine, and Diogenes ascribes it to him also,[2] while Hippolytos seems to take it for granted. We shall find, however, that in another connexion he said the World or God was one. If our interpretation of him is correct, there is no great difficulty here. The point is that, so far from being " a sure seat for all things ever," Gaia too is a passing appearance. That belongs to the attack on Hesiod, and if in this connexion Xenophanes spoke, with Anaximander, of "innumerable worlds," while elsewhere he said that God or the World was one, that may be connected with a still better attested contradiction which we have now to examine.

Finite or infinite ?

60. Aristotle tried without success to discover from the poems of Xenophanes whether he regarded the world as finite or infinite. " He made no clear pronouncement on the subject," he tells us.[3] Theophrastos, on the other hand,

---

[1] There is an interesting note on these in Gomperz's *Greek Thinkers* (Eng. trans. i. p. 551). I have translated his conjecture φυκῶν instead of the MS. φωκῶν, as this is said to involve a palaeontological impossibility, and impressions of fucoids are found, not indeed in the quarries of Syracuse, but near them. It is said also that there are no marine fossils in Paros, so the MS. reading δάφνης need not be changed to ἀφύης with Gronovius. The fact that the fossil was in the depth of the stone seemed to show that Parian marble was once mud. It was no doubt imaginary.

[2] Aet. ii. 1, 2 (*Dox.* p. 327) ; Diog. ix. 19 (R. P. 103 c). It is true that this passage of Diogenes comes from the biographical compendium (*Dox.* p. 168) ; but it is difficult to doubt the Theophrastean origin of a statement found in Aetios, Hippolytos, and Diogenes.

[3] Arist. *Met.* A, 5. 986 b 23 (R. P. 101), οὐδὲν διεσαφήνισεν.

decided that he regarded it as spherical and finite, because he said it was " equal every way." [1] It really appears that Xenophanes did not feel the contradiction involved in calling the world " equal every way " and infinite. We have seen that he said the sun went right on to infinity, and that agrees with his view of the earth as an infinitely extended plain. He also held (fr. 28) that, while the earth has an upper limit which we see, it has no limit below. This is attested by Aristotle, who speaks of the earth being " infinitely rooted," and adds that Empedokles criticised Xenophanes for holding this view.[2] It further appears from the fragment of Empedokles quoted by Aristotle that Xenophanes said the vast Air extended infinitely upwards.[3] We are therefore bound to try to find room for an infinite earth and an infinite air in a spherical finite world ! That comes of trying to find science in satire. If, on the other hand, we regard these statements from the same point of view as those about the heavenly bodies, we shall see what they probably mean. The story of Ouranos and Gaia was always the chief scandal of the *Theogony*, and the infinite air gets rid of Ouranos altogether. As to the earth stretching infinitely downwards, that gets rid of Tartaros, which Homer described as situated at the bottommost limit of earth and sea, as far beneath Hades as heaven is above the earth.[4] This is pure conjecture, of course ; but, if it is even possible, we are entitled to disbelieve that it was in a cosmological poem such startling contradictions occurred.

---

[1] This is given as an inference by Simpl. *Phys.* p. 23, 18 (R. P. 108 b), διὰ τὸ πανταχόθεν ὅμοιον. It does not merely come from *M.X.G.* (R. P. 108), πάντῃ δ' ὅμοιον ὄντα σφαιροειδῆ εἶναι. Hippolytos has it too (*Ref.* i. 14 ; R. P. 102 a), so it goes back to Theophrastos. Timon of Phleious understood Xenophanes in the same way ; for he makes him call the One ἶσον ἀπάντῃ (fr. 60, Diels ; R. P. 102 a).

[2] Arist. *De caelo*, B, 13. 294 a 21 (R. P. 103 b).

[3] I take δαψιλός as an attribute and ἀπείρονα as predicate to both subjects.

[4] *Il.* viii. 13-16, 478-481, especially the words οὐδ' εἴ κε τὰ νείατα πείραθ' ἵκηαι | γαίης καὶ πόντοιο κτλ. *Iliad* viii. must have seemed a particularly bad book to Xenophanes.

A more subtle explanation of the difficulty commended itself to the late Peripatetic who wrote an account of the Eleatic school, part of which is still extant in the Aristotelian corpus, and is generally known now as the treatise on *Melissos, Xenophanes, and Gorgias*.[1] He said that Xenophanes declared the world to be neither finite nor infinite, and composed a series of arguments in support of this thesis, to which he added another like it, namely, that the world is neither in motion nor at rest. This has introduced endless confusion into our sources. Alexander used this treatise as well as the work of Theophrastos, and Simplicius supposed the quotations from it to be from Theophrastos too. Having no copy of the poems he was completely baffled, and until recently all accounts of Xenophanes were vitiated by the same confusion. It may be suggested that, but for this, we should never have heard of the " philosophy of Xenophanes," a way of speaking which is really a survival from the days before this scholastic exercise was recognised as having no authority.

God and the world.

61. In the passage of the *Metaphysics* just referred to, Aristotle speaks of Xenophanes as " the first partisan of the One," [2] and the context shows he means to suggest he was the first of the Eleatics. We have seen already that

[1] In Bekker's edition this treatise bears the title Περὶ Ξενοφάνους, περὶ Ζήνωνος, περὶ Γοργίου, but the best MS. gives as the titles of its three sections : (1) Περὶ Ζήνωνος, (2) Περὶ Ξενοφάνους, (3) Περὶ Γοργίου. The first section, however, plainly refers to Melissos, so the whole treatise is now entitled *De Melisso, Xenophane, Gorgia* (*M.X.G.*). It has been edited by Apelt in the Teubner Series, and more recently by Diels (*Abh. der k. Preuss. Akad.* 1900), who has also given the section dealing with Xenophanes in *Vors.* 11 A 28. He has now withdrawn the view maintained in *Dox.* p. 108 that the work belongs to the third century B.C., and holds that it was *a Peripatetico eclectico* (i.e. *sceptica, platonica, stoica admiscente*) *circa Christi natalem conscriptum*. The writer would have no first-hand knowledge of his poems, and the order in which the philosophers are discussed is that of the passage in the *Metaphysics* which suggested the whole thing. It is possible that a section on Parmenides preceded what we now have.

[2] *Met.* A, 5. 986 b 21 (R. P. 101), πρῶτος τούτων ἐνίσας. The verb ἐνίζειν occurs nowhere else, but is plainly formed on the analogy of μηδίζειν, φιλιππίζειν, and the like.

the certain facts of his life make it very unlikely that he
settled at Elea and founded a school there, and it is probable
that, as usual in such cases, Aristotle is simply reproducing
certain statements of Plato. At any rate, Plato had spoken
of the Eleatics as the " partisans of the Whole," [1] and he
had also spoken of the school as " starting with Xenophanes
and even earlier." [2] The last words, however, show clearly
what he meant. Just as he called the Herakleiteans
" followers of Homer and still more ancient teachers," [3]
so he attached the Eleatics to Xenophanes and still earlier
authorities. We have seen before how these playful and
ironical remarks of Plato were taken seriously by his successors, and we must not make too much of this fresh
instance of Aristotelian literalness.

Aristotle goes on to tell us that Xenophanes, " referring
to the whole world,[4] said the One was god." This
clearly alludes to frs. 23-26, where all human attributes
are denied of a god who is said to be one and " the
greatest among gods and men." It may be added that
these verses gain much in point if we think of them
as closely connected with frs. 11-16, instead of referring
the one set of verses to the Satires and the other to a

---

[1] *Theaet.* 181 a 6, τοῦ ὅλου στασιῶται. The noun στασιώτης has no other
meaning than " partisan," and the context shows that this is what it
means here. The derivation στασιώτας . . . ἀπὸ τῆς στάσεως appears first
in Sext. *Math.* x. 46, where the term στασιῶται is incorrectly ascribed to
Aristotle and supposed to mean those who made the universe *stationary*,
an impossible interpretation.

[2] *Soph.* 242 d 5 (R. P. 101 b). If the passage implies that Xenophanes
settled at Elea, it equally implies this of his imaginary predecessors. But
Elea was not founded till Xenophanes was in the prime of life.

[3] *Theaet.* 179 e 3, τῶν Ἡρακλειτείων ἤ, ὥσπερ σὺ λέγεις, Ὁμηρείων καὶ ἔτι
παλαιοτέρων. Here Homer stands to the Herakleiteans in just the same
relation as Xenophanes does to the Eleatics in the *Sophist*. In just the
same spirit, Epicharmos, the contemporary of Xenophanes, is mentioned,
along with Homer, as a predecessor of the ῥέοντες (*Theaet.* 152 e).

[4] *Met.* 986 b 24. The words cannot mean " gazing up at the whole
heavens," or anything of that sort. They are taken as I take them by
Bonitz (*im Hinblicke auf den ganzen Himmel*) and Zeller (*im Hinblick auf
das Weltganze*). The word ἀποβλέπειν had become too colourless to mean
more, and οὐρανός means what was later called κόσμος.

cosmological poem. It was probably in the same context
that Xenophanes called the world or god " equal every
way "[1] and denied that it breathed.[2] The statement
that there is no mastership among the gods [3] also goes
very well with fr. 26. A god has no wants, nor is it
fitting for one god to be the servant of others, like Iris
and Hermes in Homer.

Mono-
theism or
poly-
theism.

62. That this " god " is just the world, Aristotle tells
us, and the use of the word θεός is quite in accordance
with Ionian usage. Xenophanes regarded it as sentient,
though without any special organs of sense, and it
sways all things by the thought of its mind. He
also calls it " one god," and, if that is monotheism,
then Xenophanes was a monotheist, though this is
surely not how the word is generally understood. The
fact is that the expression " one god " wakens all sorts
of associations in our mind which did not exist for the
Greeks of this time. What Xenophanes is really concerned to deny is the existence of any gods in the proper
sense, and the words " One god " mean " No god but the
world." [4]

It is certainly wrong, then, to say with Freudenthal
that Xenophanes was in any sense a polytheist.[5] That he
should use the language of polytheism in his elegies is only
what we should expect, and the other references to " gods "
can be best explained as incidental to his attack on the
anthropomorphic gods of Homer and Hesiod. In one case,
Freudenthal has pressed a proverbial way of speaking too

[1] See above, p. 125, n. 1.
[2] Diog. ix. 19 (R. P. 103 c), ὅλον δ' ὁρᾶν καὶ ὅλον ἀκούειν, μὴ μέντοι ἀναπνεῖν.
See above, p. 108, n. 2.
[3] [Plut.] Strom. fr. 4, ἀποφαίνεται δὲ καὶ περὶ θεῶν ὡς οὐδεμιᾶς ἡγεμονίας
ἐν αὐτοῖς οὔσης· οὐ γὰρ ὅσιον δεσπόζεσθαί τινα τῶν θεῶν, ἐπιδεῖσθαί τε
μηδενὸς αὐτῶν μηδένα μηδ' ὅλως, ἀκούειν δὲ καὶ ὁρᾶν καθόλου καὶ μὴ κατὰ μέρος.
[4] The fact that he speaks of the world as living and sentient makes
no difference. No Greek ever doubted that the world was in some sense
a ζῷον.
[5] Freudenthal, Die Theologie des Xenophanes (Breslau, 1886).

hard.[1]   Least of all can we admit that Xenophanes allowed the existence of subordinate or departmental gods ; for it was just the existence of such that he was chiefly concerned to deny.   At the same time, I cannot help thinking that Freudenthal was more nearly right than Wilamowitz, who says that Xenophanes " upheld the only real monotheism that has ever existed upon earth." [2]   Diels, I fancy, comes nearer the mark when he calls it a " somewhat narrow pantheism." [3]   But all these views would have surprised Xenophanes himself about equally.   He was really Goethe's *Weltkind*, with prophets to right and left of him, and he would have smiled if he had known that one day he was to be regarded as a theologian.

---

[1] Xenophanes calls his god " greatest among gods and men," but this is simply a case of " polar expression," to which parallels will be found in Wilamowitz's note to Euripides' *Herakles*, v. 1106.   Cf. especially the statement of Herakleitos (fr. 20) that " no one of gods or men " made the world.

[2] *Griechische Literatur*, p. 38.

[3] *Parmenides Lehrgedicht*, p. 9.

CHAPTER III

HERAKLEITOS OF EPHESOS

Life of
Hera-
kleitos.

63. HERAKLEITOS of Epheso, son of Bloson, is said to have " flourished " in Ol. LXIX. (504/3–501/0 B.C.) ;[1] that is to say, just in the middle of the reign of Dareios, with whom several traditions connected him.[2] It is more important, however, for our purpose to notice that, while Herakleitos refers to Pythagoras and Xenophanes by name and in the past tense (fr. 16), he is in turn alluded to by Parmenides (fr. 6). These references mark his place in the history of philosophy. Zeller held, indeed, that he could not have published his work till after 478 B.C., on the ground that the expulsion of Hermodoros, alluded to in fr. 114, could not have taken place before the downfall of Persian rule. If that were so, it might be hard to see how Parmenides could have known the views of Herakleitos at the time he wrote his poem ;[3] but there is no difficulty in supposing that the Ephesians may have sent one of their citizens into banishment when they were still paying tribute to the Great King. The spurious *Letters* of Herakleitos show that the expulsion of Hermodoros was believed to have taken place during the reign of

---

[1] Diog. ix. 1 (R. P. 29), no doubt from Apollodoros through some intermediate authority. The name Bloson is better attested than Blyson (see Diels, *Vors.* 12 A 1, *n.*), and is known from inscriptions as an Ionic name.

[2] Bernays, *Die heraklitischen Briefe*, pp. 13 *sqq.*

[3] For the date of Parmenides, see p. 169.

Dareios,[1] and it seems probable that the party led by him had enjoyed the confidence of the Persian government. His expulsion would mark the beginnings of the movement against Persian rule, rather than its successful issue.

Sotion quotes a statement that Herakleitos was a disciple of Xenophanes,[2] which is not probable ; for Xenophanes left Ionia before Herakleitos was born. More likely he was not a disciple of any one ; but it is clear that he was acquainted both with the Milesian cosmology and with the poems of Xenophanes. He also knew something of the theories taught by Pythagoras (fr. 17). Of his life we really know nothing, except, perhaps, that he belonged to the ancient royal house and resigned the nominal position of Basileus in favour of his brother.[3] The origin of the other statements bearing on it is quite transparent.[4]

64. We do not know the title of the work of Herakleitos [5] **His book.** —if, indeed, it had one—and it is not easy to form a clear idea of its contents. We are told that it was divided into three discourses : one dealing with the universe, one political,

---

[1] Bernays, *op. cit.* pp. 20 *sqq.* This is quite consistent with the Roman tradition that Hermodoros took part later in the legislation of the Twelve Tables at Rome (*Dig.* I, 2, 2, 4 ; Strabo, xiv. p. 642). There was a statue of him in the Comitium (Pliny, *H.N.* xxxiv. 21). The Romans were well aware that the Twelve Tables were framed on a Greek model; and, as Bernays said (*op. cit.* p. 85), the fact is attested as few things are in the early history of Rome.

[2] Sotion *ap.* Diog. ix. 5 (R. P. 29 c).

[3] Diog. ix. 6 (R. P. 31).

[4] Herakleitos said (fr. 68) that it was death to souls to become water ; and we are told accordingly that he died of dropsy. He said (fr. 114) that the Ephesians should leave their city to their children, and (fr. 79) that Time was a child playing draughts. We are therefore told that he refused to take any part in public life, and went to play with the children in the temple of Artemis. He said (fr. 85) that corpses were more fit to be cast out than dung ; and we are told that he covered himself with dung when attacked with dropsy. Lastly, he is said to have argued at great length with his doctors because of fr. 58. For these tales see Diog. ix. 3-5.

[5] The variety of titles enumerated in Diog. ix. 12 (R. P. 30 b) seems to show that none was authentically known. That of " Muses " comes from Plato, *Soph.* 242 d 7. The others are mere " mottoes " (Schuster) prefixed by Stoic editors (Diog. ix. 15 ; R. P. 30 c).

and one theological.[1] It is not to be supposed that this division is due to Herakleitos himself ; all we can infer is that the work fell naturally into these three parts when the Stoic commentators took their editions of it in hand.

The style of Herakleitos is proverbially obscure, and, at a later date, got him the nickname of " the Dark." [2] Now the fragments about the Delphic god and the Sibyl (frs. 11 and 12) seem to show that he was conscious of writing an oracular style, and we have to ask why he did so. In the first place, it was the manner of the time.[3] The stirring events of the age, and the influence of the religious revival, gave something of a prophetic tone to all the leaders of thought. Pindar and Aischylos have it too. It was also an age of great individualities, and these are apt to be solitary and disdainful. Herakleitos at least was so. If men cared to dig for the gold they might find it (fr. 8) ; if not, they must be content with straw (fr. 51). This seems to have been the view taken by Theophrastos, who said the headstrong temperament of Herakleitos sometimes led him into incompleteness and inconsistencies of statement.[4]

The fragments.
65. I give a version of the fragments according to the arrangement of Bywater's exemplary edition : [5]

(1) It is wise to hearken, not to me, but to my Word, and to confess that all things are one.[6] R. P. 40.

---

[1] Diog. ix. 5 (R. P. 30). Bywater followed this hint in his arrangement of the fragments. The three sections are 1-90, 91-97, 98-130.

[2] R. P. 30 a. The epithet ὁ σκοτεινός is of later date, but Timon of Phleious already called him αἰνικτής (fr. 43, Diels).

[3] See the valuable observations of Diels in the Introduction to his *Herakleitos von Ephesos*, pp. iv. *sqq.*

[4] Cf. Diog. ix. 6 (R. P. 31).

[5] In his edition, Diels has given up all attempt to arrange the fragments according to subject, and this makes his text unsuitable for our purpose. I think, too, that he overestimates the difficulty of an approximate arrangement, and makes too much of the view that the style of Herakleitos was "aphoristic." That it was so, is an important and valuable remark ; but it does not follow that Herakleitos wrote like Nietzsche. For a Greek, however prophetic in his tone, there must always be a distinction between an aphoristic and an incoherent style.

[6] Both Bywater and Diels accept Bergk's λόγου for δόγματος and Miller's εἶναι for εἰδέναι. Cf. Philo, *Leg. all.* iii. c 3, quoted in Bywater's note.

(2) Though this Word [1] is true evermore, yet men are as unable to understand it when they hear it for the first time as before they have heard it at all. For, though all things come to pass in accordance with this Word, men seem as if they had no experience of them, when they make trial of words and deeds such as I set forth, dividing each thing according to its kind and showing how it truly is. But other men know not what they are doing when awake, even as they forget what they do in sleep. R. P. 32.

(3) Fools when they do hear are like the deaf : of them does the saying bear witness that they are absent when present. R. P. 31 a.

(4) Eyes and ears are bad witnesses to men if they have souls that understand not their language. R. P. 42.

(5) The many do not take heed of such things as those they meet with, nor do they mark them when they are taught, though they think they do.

(6) Knowing not how to listen nor how to speak.

(7) If you do not expect the unexpected, you will not find it ; for it is hard to be sought out and difficult.[2]

(8) Those who seek for gold dig up much earth and find a little. R. P. 44 b.

(10) Nature loves to hide. R. P. 34 f.

(11) The lord whose is the oracle at Delphoi neither utters nor hides his meaning, but shows it by a sign. R. P. 30 a.

(12) And the Sibyl, with raving lips uttering things mirthless,

---

[1] The λόγος is primarily the discourse of Herakleitos himself ; though, as he is a prophet, we may call it his " Word." It can neither mean a discourse addressed to Herakleitos nor yet " reason." (Cf. Zeller, p. 630, n. 1 ; Eng. trans. ii. p. 7, n. 2.) A difficulty has been raised about the words ἐόντος ἀεί. How could Herakleitos say that his discourse had always existed ? The answer is that in Ionic ἐών means " true " when coupled with words like λόγος. Cf. Herod. i. 30, τῷ ἐόντι χρησάμενος λέγει ; and even Aristoph. Frogs, 1052, οὐκ ὄντα λόγον. It is only by taking the words in this way that we can understand Aristotle's hesitation as to the proper punctuation (Rhet. Γ, 5. 1407 b 15 ; R. P. 30 a). The Stoic interpretation given by Marcus Aurelius, iv. 46 (R. P. 32 b), must be rejected. In any case, the Johannine doctrine of the λόγος has nothing to do with Herakleitos or with anything at all in Greek philosophy, but comes from the Hebrew Wisdom literature. See Rendel Harris, " The Origin of the Prologue to St. John's Gospel," in The Expositor, 1916, pp. 147 sqq.

[2] I have departed from the punctuation of Bywater here, and supplied a fresh object to the verb as suggested by Gomperz (Arch. i. 100).

unbedizened, and unperfumed, reaches over a thousand years with her voice, thanks to the god in her. R. P. 30 a.

(13) The things that can be seen, heard, and learned are what I prize the most. R. P. 42.

(14) . . . bringing untrustworthy witnesses in support of disputed points.

(15) The eyes are more exact witnesses than the ears.[1] R. P. 42 c.

(16) The learning of many things teacheth not understanding, else would it have taught Hesiod and Pythagoras, and again Xenophanes and Hekataios. R. P. 31.

(17) Pythagoras, son of Mnesarchos, practised scientific inquiry beyond all other men, and making a selection of these writings, claimed for his own wisdom what was but a knowledge of many things and an imposture.[2] R. P. 31 a.

(18) Of all whose discourses I have heard, there is not one who attains to understanding that wisdom is apart from all. R. P. 32 b.

(19) Wisdom is one thing. It is to know the thought by which all things are steered through all things. R. P. 40.

(20) This world,[3] which is the same for all, no one of gods or men has made ; but it was ever, is now, and ever shall be an ever-living Fire, with measures of it kindling, and measures going out. R. P. 35.[4]

---

[1] Cf. Herod. i. 8.

[2] The best attested reading is ἐποιήσατο, not ἐποίησεν, and ἐποιήσατο ἑαυτοῦ means " claimed as his own." The words ἐκλεξάμενος ταύτας τὰς συγγραφάς have deen doubted since the time of Schleiermacher, and Diels now regards the whole fragment as spurious. This is because it was used to prove that Pythagoras wrote books (cf. Diels, Arch. iii. p. 451). As Bywater pointed out, however, the fragment itself only says that he read books. I would further suggest that the old-fashioned συγγραφάς is too good for a forger, and that the omission of the very thing to be proved would be remarkable. The last suggestion of a book by Pythagoras disappears with the reading ἐποιήσατο for ἐποίησεν. For the rendering given for κακοτεχνίη, compare its legal sense of " falsified evidence."

[3] The word κόσμος must mean " world " here, not merely " order " ; for only the world could be identified with fire. This use of the word is Pythagorean, and Herakleitos may quite well have known it.

[4] It is important to notice that μέτρα is internal accusative with ἁπτόμενον, " with its measures kindling and its measures going out." This interpretation, which I gave in the first edition, is now adopted by Diels (Vors.[3] 12 B 30 n.).

(21) The transformations of Fire are, first of all, sea ; and half of the sea is earth, half whirlwind.[1] . . . R. P. 35 b.

(22) All things are an exchange for Fire, and Fire for all things, even as wares for gold and gold for wares.   R. P. 35.

(23) It becomes liquid sea, and is measured by the same tale as before it became earth.[2]   R. P. 39.

(24) Fire is want and surfeit.   R. P. 36 a.

(25) Fire lives the death of air,[3] and air lives the death of fire ; water lives the death of earth, earth that of water.   R. P. 37.

(26) Fire in its advance will judge and convict [4] all things.   R. P. 36 a.

(27) How can one hide from that which never sets ?

(28) It is the thunderbolt that steers the course of all things.   R. P. 35 b.

(29) The sun will not overstep his measures ; if he does, the Erinyes, the handmaids of Justice, will find him out.   R. P. 39.

(30) The limit of dawn and evening is the Bear ; and opposite the Bear is the boundary of bright Zeus.[5]

(31) If there were no sun it would be night, for all the other stars could do.[6]

(32) The sun is new every day.

---

[1] On the word πρηστήρ, see below, p. 149, *n.* 1.

[2] The subject of fr. 23 is γῆ, as we see from Diog. ix. 9 (R. P. 36), πάλιν τε αὖ τὴν γῆν χεῖσθαι ; and Aet. i. 3, 11 (*Dox.* p. 284 a 1 ; b 5), ἔπειτα ἀναχαλωμένην τὴν γῆν ὑπὸ τοῦ πυρὸς χύσει (Dübner : φύσει, *libri*) ὕδωρ ἀποτελεῖσθαι. Herakleitos may have said γῆ θάλασσα διαχέεται, and Clement (*Strom.* v. p. 712) seems to imply this. The phrase μετρέεται εἰς τὸν αὐτὸν λόγον can only mean that the proportion of the measures remains constant. So Zeller (p. 690, *n.* 1), *zu derselben Grösse.* Diels (*Vors.* 12 B 31 *n.*) renders " nach demselben Wort (*Gesetz*)," but refers to Lucr. v. 257, which supports the other interpretation (*pro parte sua*).

[3] It is doubtful whether this fragment is quoted textually. It seems to imply the four elements of Empedokles.

[4] I understand ἐπελθόν of the πυρὸς ἔφοδος, for which see p. 151, *n.* 1. Diels has pointed out that καταλαμβάνειν is the old word for " to convict."

[5] Here it is clear that οὖρος=τέρματα, and therefore means " boundary," not " hill." Strabo, who quotes the fragment (i. 6, p. 3), is probably right in taking ἠοῦς καὶ ἑσπέρας as equivalent to ἀνατολῆς καὶ δύσεως and making the words refer to the " arctic " circle. As αἴθριος Ζεύς means the bright blue sky, it is impossible for its οὖρος to be the South Pole, as Diels suggests. It is more likely the horizon. I take the fragment as a protest against the Pythagorean theory of a southern hemisphere.

[6] We learn from Diog. ix. 10 (quoted below, p. 147) that Herakleitos explained why the sun was warmer and brighter than the moon, and this is doubtless a fragment of that passage.

(33) (Thales foretold an eclipse.)

(34) . . . the seasons that bring all things.

(35) Hesiod is most men's teacher. Men are sure he knew very many things, a man who did not know day or night ! They are one.[1] R. P. 39 b.

(36) God is day and night, winter and summer, war and peace, surfeit and hunger ; but he takes various shapes, just as fire,[2] when it is mingled with spices, is named according to the savour of each. R. P. 39 b.

(37) If all things were turned to smoke, the nostrils would distinguish them.

(38) Souls smell in Hades. R. P. 46 d.

(39) Cold things become warm, and what is warm cools ; what is wet dries, and the parched is moistened.

(40) It scatters and it gathers ; it advances and retires.

(41, 42) You cannot step twice into the same rivers ; for fresh waters are ever flowing in upon you. R. P. 33.

(43) Homer was wrong in saying : " Would that strife might perish from among gods and men ! " He did not see that he was praying for the destruction of the universe ; for, if his prayer were heard, all things would pass away.[3] . . . R. P. 34 d.

(44) War is the father of all and the king of all ; and some he has made gods and some men, some bond and some free. R. P. 34.

(45) Men do not know how what is at variance agrees with itself. It is an attunement of opposite tensions,[4] like that of the bow and the lyre. R. P. 34.

(46) It is the opposite which is good for us.[5]

(47) The hidden attunement is better than the open. R. P. 34.

(48) Let us not conjecture at random about the greatest things.

---

[1] Hesiod said Day was the child of Night (*Theog.* 124).

[2] Reading ὅκωσπερ πῦρ for ὅκωσπερ with Diels.

[3] *Il.* xviii. 107. I add οἰχήσεσθαι γὰρ πάντα from Simpl. *in Cat.* 412, 26. It must represent something that was in the original.

[4] I cannot believe Herakleitos said both παλίντονος and παλίντροπος ἁρμονίη, and I prefer Plutarch's παλίντονος (R. P. 34 b) to the παλίντροπος of Hippolytos. Diels thinks that the polemic of Parmenides favours παλίντροπος, but see below, p. 164, *n.* 1, and Chap. IV. p. 174, *n.* 3.

[5] This refers to the medical rule αἱ δ' ἰατρεῖαι διὰ τῶν ἐναντίων, *e.g.* βοηθεῖν τῷ θερμῷ ἐπὶ τὸ ψυχρόν.

(49) Men that love wisdom must be acquainted with very many things indeed.

(50) The straight and the crooked path of the fuller's comb is one and the same.

(51) Asses would rather have straw than gold. R. P. 31 a.

(51a) [1] Oxen are happy when they find bitter vetches to eat. R. P. 48 b.

(52) The sea is the purest and the impurest water. Fish can drink it, and it is good for them ; to men it is undrinkable and destructive. R. P. 47 c.

(53) Swine wash in the mire, and barnyard fowls in dust.

(54) . . . to delight in the mire.

(55) Every beast is driven to pasture with blows.[2]

(56) Same as 45.

(57) Good and ill are one. R. P. 47 c.

(58) Physicians who cut, burn, stab, and rack the sick, demand a fee for it which they do not deserve to get. R. P. 47 c.[3]

(59) Couples are things whole and things not whole, what is drawn together and what is drawn asunder, the harmonious and the discordant. The one is made up of all things, and all things issue from the one.[4]

(60) Men would not have known the name of justice if these things were not.[5]

(61) To God all things are fair and good and right, but men hold some things wrong and some right. R. P. 45.

(62) We must know that war is common to all and strife is justice, and that all things come into being and pass away (?) through strife.

(64) All the things we see when awake are death, even as all we see in slumber are sleep. R. P. 42 c.[6]

---

1 See Bywater in *Journ. Phil.* ix. p. 230.
2 On fr. 55 see Diels in *Berl. Sitzb.*, 1901, p. 188.
3 I now read ἐπαιτέονται with Bernays and Diels.
4 On fr. 59 see Diels in *Berl. Sitzb.*, 1901, p. 188. The reading συνάψιες seems to be well attested and gives an excellent sense. The alternative reading συλλάψιες is preferred by Hoffmann, *Gr. Dial.* iii. 240.
5 By " these things " he probably meant all kinds of injustice.
6 Diels supposes that fr. 64 went on ὁκόσα δὲ τεθνηκότες ζωή. " Life, Sleep, Death is the threefold ladder in psychology, as in physics Fire, Water, Earth."

(65) The wise is one only. It is unwilling and willing to be called by the name of Zeus. R. P. 40.

(66) The bow (βιός) is called life (βίος), but its work is death. R. P. 49 a.

(67) Mortals are immortals and immortals are mortals, the one living the others' death and dying the others' life. R. P. 46.

(68) For it is death to souls to become water, and death to water to become earth. But water comes from earth ; and from water, soul. R. P. 38.

(69) The way up and the way down is one and the same. R. P. 36 d.

(70) In the circumference of a circle the beginning and end are common.

(71) You will not find the boundaries of soul by travelling in any direction, so deep is the measure of it.[1] R. P. 41 d.

(72) It is pleasure to souls to become moist. R. P. 46 c.

(73) A man, when he gets drunk, is led by a beardless lad, tripping, knowing not where he steps, having his soul moist. R. P. 42.

(74-76) The dry soul is the wisest and best.[2] R. P. 42.

(77) Man kindles a light for himself in the night-time, when he has died but is alive. The sleeper, whose vision has been put out, lights up from the dead ; he that is awake lights up from the sleeping.[3]

---

[1] The words οὕτω βαθὺν λόγον ἔχει present no difficulty if we remember that λόγος means " measurement," as in fr. 23.

[2] This fragment is interesting because of the antiquity of the corruptions it has suffered. According to Stephanus, who is followed by Bywater, we should read : Αὔη ψυχὴ σοφωτάτη καὶ ἀρίστη, ξηρή being a mere gloss upon αὔη. When once ξηρή got into the text, αὔη became αὐγή, and we get the sentence, " the dry light is the wisest soul," whence the siccum lumen of Bacon. Now this reading is as old as Plutarch, who, in his Life of Romulus (c. 28), takes αὐγή to mean lightning, as it sometimes does, and supposes the idea to be that the wise soul bursts through the prison of the body like dry lightning (whatever that may be) through a cloud. (It should be added that Diels now holds that αὐγὴ ξηρὴ ψυχὴ σοφωτάτη καὶ ἀρίστη is the genuine reading.) Lastly, though Plutarch must have written αὐγή, the MSS. vary between αὔτη and αὐτή (cf. De def. or. 432 f. αὔτη γὰρ ξηρὰ ψυχὴ in the MSS.). The next stage is the corruption of the αὐγή into οὖ γῆ. This yields the sentiment that " where the earth is dry, the soul is wisest," and is as old as Philo (see Bywater's notes).

[3] I adopt the fuller text of Diels here. It is clear that Death, Sleep, Waking correspond to Earth, Water, Air in Herakleitos (cf. fr. 68). I think, however, that we must take ἅπτεται in the same sense all through the fragment, so I do not translate " is in contact with," as Diels does.

(78) And it is the same thing in us that is quick and dead, awake and asleep, young and old ; the former are shifted [1] and become the latter, and the latter in turn are shifted and become the former. R. P. 47.

(79) Time is a child playing draughts, the kingly power is a child's. R. P. 40 a.

(80) I have sought for myself. R. P. 48.

(81) We step and do not step into the same rivers ; we are and are not. R. P. 33 a.

(82) It is a weariness to labour for the same masters and be ruled by them.

(83) It rests by changing.

(84) Even the posset separates if it is not stirred.

(85) Corpses are more fit to be cast out than dung.

(86) When they are born, they wish to live and to meet with their dooms—or rather to rest—and they leave children behind them to meet with their dooms in turn.

(87-89) A man may be a grandfather in thirty years.

(90) Those who are asleep are fellow-workers (in what goes on in the world).

(91a) Thought is common to all.

(91b) Those who speak with understanding must hold fast to what is common to all as a city holds fast to its law, and even more strongly. For all human laws are fed by the one divine law. It prevails as much as it will, and suffices for all things with something to spare. R. P. 43.

(92) So we must follow the common,[2] yet though my Word is common, the many live as if they had a wisdom of their own. R. P. 44.

(93) They are estranged from that with which they have most constant intercourse.[3] R. P. 32 b.

(94) It is not meet to act and speak like men asleep.

---

[1] I understand μεταπεσόντα here as meaning "moved" from one γραμμή or division of the draught-board to another.

[2] Sext. Math. vii. 133, διὸ δεῖ ἔπεσθαι τῷ κοινῷ (so the MSS. : ξυνῷ Schleiermacher). ξυνὸς γὰρ ὁ κοινός. Bywater omits the words, but I think they must belong to Herakleitos. Diels adopts Bekker's suggestion to read διὸ δεῖ ἔπεσθαι τῷ ⟨ξυνῷ, τουτέστι τῷ⟩ κοινῷ. I now think also that, if we understand the term λόγος in the sense explained above (p. 133, n. 1), there is no reason to doubt the words which follow.

[3] The words λόγῳ τῷ τὰ ὅλα διοικοῦντι belong to Marcus Aurelius and not to Herakleitos.

(95) The waking have one common world, but the sleeping turn aside each into a world of his own.

(96) The way of man has no wisdom, but that of God has. R. P. 45.

(97) Man is called a baby by God, even as a child by a man. R. P. 45.

(98, 99) The wisest man is an ape compared to God, just as the most beautiful ape is ugly compared to man.

(100) The people must fight for its law as for its walls. R. P. 43 b.

(101) Greater deaths win greater portions.   R. P. 49 a.

(102) Gods and men honour those who are slain in battle. R. P. 49 a.

(103) Wantonness needs putting out, even more than a house on fire.   R. P. 49 a.

(104) It is not good for men to get all they wish to get.   It is sickness that makes health pleasant ; evil,[1] good ; hunger, plenty ; weariness, rest.   R. P. 48 b.

(105-107) It is hard to fight with one's heart's desire.[2] Whatever it wishes to get, it purchases at the cost of soul. R. P. 49 a.

(108, 109) It is best to hide folly ; but it is hard in times of relaxation, over our cups.

(110) And it is law, too, to obey the counsel of one.   R. P. 49 a.

(111) For what thought or wisdom have they ?   They follow the poets and take the crowd as their teacher, knowing not that there are many bad and few good.   For even the best of them choose one thing above all others, immortal glory among mortals, while most of them are glutted like beasts.[3]   R. P. 31 a.

(112) In Priene lived Bias, son of Teutamas, who is of more account than the rest. (He said, " Most men are bad.")

(113) One is ten thousand to me, if he be the best.   R. P. 31 a.

(114) The Ephesians would do well to hang themselves, every grown man of them, and leave the city to beardless lads ; for they have cast out Hermodoros, the best man among them,

---

[1] Adopting Heitz's κακὸν for καὶ with Diels.

[2] The word θυμός has its Homeric sense.   The gratification of desire implies the exchange of dry soul-fire (fr. 74) for moisture (fr. 72).   Aristotle misunderstood θυμός here as anger (*Eth. Nic.* B, 2. 1105 a 8).

[3] This seems to refer to the " three lives," Chap. II. § 45, p. 98.

saying, " We will have none who is best among us ; if there be any such, let him be so elsewhere and among others." [1]   R. P. 29 b.

(115) Dogs bark at every one they do not know.   R. P. 31 a.

(116) . . . (The wise man) is not known because of men's want of belief.

(117) The fool is fluttered at every word.   R. P. 44 b.

(118) The most esteemed of them knows but fancies,[2] and holds fast to them, yet of a truth justice shall overtake the artificers of lies and the false witnesses.

(119) Homer should be turned out of the lists and whipped, and Archilochos likewise.   R. P. 31.

(120) One day is like any other.

(121) Man's character is his fate.[3]

(122) There awaits men when they die such things as they look not for nor dream of.   R. P. 46 d.

(123) . . . [4] that they rise up and become the wakeful guardians of the quick and dead.   R. P. 46 d.

(124) Night-walkers, Magians, Bakchoi, Lenai, and the initiated . . .

(125) The mysteries practised among men are unholy mysteries.   R. P. 48.

(126) And they pray to these images, as if one were to talk with a man's house, knowing not what gods or heroes are. R. P. 49 a.

(127) For if it were not to Dionysos that they made a procession and sang the shameful phallic hymn, they would be acting most shamelessly.   But Hades is the same as Dionysos in whose honour they go mad and rave.   R. P. 49.

(129, 130) They vainly purify themselves by defiling themselves with blood, just as if one who had stepped into the mud were to wash his feet in mud.   Any man who marked him doing thus, would deem him mad.   R. P. 49 a.

---

[1] He went to Italy and took part in framing the Twelve Tables at Rome.   See p. 131, *n.* 1.

[2] Reading δοκέοντα with Schleiermacher (or δοκέοντ' ὦν with Diels). I also read γινώσκει, φυλάσσει with Diels, who quotes the combination φυλάσσουσι καὶ γινώσκουσι from Hippokrates.

[3] On the meaning of δαίμων here, see my edition of Aristotle's *Ethics*, pp. 1 *sq.*

[4] I have not ventured to include the words ἔνθα δ' ἐόντι at the beginning, as the text seems to me too uncertain.   See, however, Diels's note.

The doxo-
graphical
tradition.
66. Some of these fragments are far from clear, and there are probably not a few of which the meaning will never be recovered. We turn, then, to the doxographers for a clue ; but unfortunately they are less instructive with regard to Herakleitos than we have found them in other cases. Hippolytos, on whom we can generally rely for a fairly accurate account of what Theophrastos said, derived the material for his first four chapters, which treat of Thales, Pythagoras, Herakleitos, and Empedokles, not from the excellent epitome he afterwards used, but from a bio-graphical compendium,[1] mostly consisting of apocryphal anecdotes and apophthegms. It was based, further, on some writer of *Successions* who regarded Herakleitos as a Pythagorean. The link between him and the Pythagoreans was Hippasos, in whose system fire played an important part. Theophrastos, following Aristotle, had spoken of the two in the same sentence, and that was enough for the writers of *Successions*.[2] We are forced, then, to look to the more detailed of the two accounts of the opinions of Hera-kleitos given in Diogenes,[3] which goes back to the *Vetusta Placita*, and is, fortunately, pretty full and accurate.

Another difficulty we have to face is that most of the commentators on Herakleitos mentioned in Diogenes were Stoics.[4] Now, the Stoics held the Ephesian in peculiar veneration, and sought to interpret him as far as possible in accordance with their own system. Further, they were fond of " accommodating "[5] the views of earlier thinkers to their own, and this has had serious consequences. In

---

[1] See Diels, *Dox.* p. 145. We must distinguish *Ref.* i. and *Ref.* ix. as sources of information about Herakleitos. The latter book is an attempt to show that the Monarchian heresy of Noetos was derived from Herakleitos, and is a rich mine of Herakleitean fragments.

[2] Arist. *Met.* A, 3. 984 a 7 (R. P. 56 c) ; Theophr. *ap.* Simpl. *Phys.* 23, 33 (R. P. 36 c).

[3] For these double accounts see Note on Sources, § 15.

[4] Diog. ix. 15 (R. P. 30 c). Schleiermacher rightly insisted upon this.

[5] The word συνοικειοῦν is used of the Stoic method of interpretation by Philodemos (cf. *Dox.* 547 b, *n.*), and Cicero (*N.D.* i. 41) renders it by *accommodare.*

particular, the Stoic theories of the λόγος and the ἐκπύρωσις are constantly ascribed to Herakleitos, and the very fragments are adulterated with scraps of Stoic terminology.

67. Herakleitos looks down not only on the mass of men, but on all previous inquirers into nature. This must mean that he believed himself to have attained insight into some truth not hitherto recognised, though it was staring men in the face (fr. 93). To get at the central thing in his teaching, we must try then to find out what he was thinking of when he launched into those denunciations of human dulness and ignorance. The answer seems to be given in two fragments, 18 and 45. From them we gather that the truth hitherto ignored is that the many apparently independent and conflicting things we know are really one, and that, on the other hand, this one is also many. The " strife of opposites " is really an " attunement " (ἁρμονία). From this it follows that wisdom is not a knowledge of many things, but the perception of the underlying unity of the warring opposites. That this really was the fundamental thought of Herakleitos is stated by Philo. He says : " For that which is made up of both the opposites is one ; and, when the one is divided, the opposites are disclosed. Is not this just what the Greeks say their great and much belauded Herakleitos put in the forefront of his philosophy as summing it all up, and boasted of as a new discovery ? " [1]

The discovery of Herakleitos.

68. Anaximander had taught that the opposites were separated out from the Boundless, but passed away into it once more, so paying the penalty to one another for their unjust encroachments. It is here implied that there is something wrong in the war of opposites, and that the existence of the opposites is a breach in the unity of the One. The truth Herakleitos proclaimed was that the world is at once one and many, and that it is just the " opposite tension " of the opposites that constitutes the unity of the One. It is the same conclusion as that of Pythagoras, though it is

The One and the Many.

[1] Philo, *Rer. div. her.* 43 (R. P. 34 e).

put in another way. The use of the word ἁρμονίη suggests
that Herakleitos had come under the influence of his older
contemporary to some extent.

Plato clearly states that this was the central thought
of Herakleitos. In the *Sophist* (242 d), the Eleatic stranger,
after explaining how the Eleatics maintained that what we
call many is really one, proceeds :

But certain Ionian and (at a later date) certain Sicilian
Muses remarked that it was safest to unite these two things, and
to say that reality is both many and one, and is kept together by
Hate and Love. " For," say the more severe Muses, " in its
division it is always being brought together " (cf. fr. 59) ; while
the softer Muses relaxed the requirement that this should always
be so, and said that the All was alternately one and at peace
through the power of Aphrodite, and many and at war with itself
because of something they called Strife.

In this passage the Ionian Muses stand, of course, for
Herakleitos, and the Sicilian for Empedokles. According
to Plato, then, Herakleitos taught that reality was at once
many and one. This was not meant as a logical principle.[1]
The identity which Herakleitos explains as consisting in
difference is just that of the primary substance in all its
manifestations. This identity had been realised already
by the Milesians, but they had found a difficulty in the
difference. Anaximander had treated the strife of opposites
as an " injustice," and what Herakleitos set himself to

[1] This was the mistake of Lassalle's book. The source of his error
was Hegel's statement that there was no proposition of Herakleitos that
he had not taken up into his own logic (*Gesch. d. Phil.* i. 328). The
example which he cites is the statement that Being does not exist any
more than not-Being, for which he refers to Arist. *Met.* A, 4. This, however, is not there ascribed to Herakleitos, but to Leukippos or Demokritos, with whom it meant that space was as real as body (§ 175).
Aristotle does, indeed, tell us in the *Metaphysics* that " some " think
Herakleitos says that the same thing can be and not be ; but he adds
that it does not follow that a man thinks what he says (*Met.* Γ, 3. 1005 b 24).
This is explained by K, 5. 1062 a 31, where we are told that by being
questioned in a certain manner Herakleitos could be made to admit the
principle of contradiction ; as it was, he did not understand what he said.
In other words, he was unconscious of its logical bearing.

show was that, on the contrary, it was the highest justice (fr. 62).

69. All this made it necessary for him to seek out a new **Fire.** primary substance. He wanted not merely something from which opposites could be " separated out," but something which of its own nature would pass into everything else, while everything else would pass in turn into it. This he found in Fire, and it is easy to see why, if we consider the phenomenon of combustion. The quantity of fire in a flame burning steadily appears to remain the same, the flame seems to be what we call a " thing." And yet the substance of it is continually changing. It is always passing away in smoke, and its place is always being taken by fresh matter from the fuel that feeds it. This is just what we want. If we regard the world as an " ever-living fire " (fr. 20), we can understand how it is always becoming all things, while all things are always returning to it.[1]

70. This necessarily brings with it a certain way of **Flux.** looking at the change and movement of the world. Fire burns continuously and without interruption. It is always consuming fuel and always liberating smoke. Everything is either mounting upwards to serve as fuel, or sinking down-

---

[1] That the Fire of Herakleitos was something on the same level as the " Air " of Anaximenes is clearly implied in such passages as Arist. *Met.* A, 3. 984 a 5. In support of the view that something different from literal fire is meant, Plato, *Crat.* 413 b, is sometimes quoted ; but the context shows the passage will not bear this interpretation. Sokrates is discussing the derivation of δίκαιον from δια-ιόν, and certainly δίκη was a prominent Herakleitean conception, and a good deal that is here said may be the authentic doctrine of the school. He goes on to complain that when he asks what this is which " goes through " everything, he gets inconsistent answers. One says it is the sun. Another asks if there is no justice after sunset, and says it is simply fire. A third says it is not fire itself, but the heat which is in fire. A fourth identifies it with Mind. Now all we are entitled to infer from this is that different accounts were given in the Herakleitean school at a later date. The view that it was not fire itself, but Heat, which " passed through " all things, is related to the theory of Herakleitos as Hippo's Moisture is to the Water of Thales. It is quite likely, too, that some Herakleiteans attempted to fuse the system of Anaxagoras with their own, just as Diogenes of Apollonia tried to fuse it with that of Anaximenes. We shall see, indeed, that we still have a work in which this attempt is made (p. 150, *n.* 2).

wards after having nourished the flame. It follows that the whole of reality is like an ever-flowing stream, and that nothing is ever at rest for a moment. The substance of the things we see is in constant change. Even as we look at them, some of the stuff of which they are composed has already passed into something else, while fresh stuff has come into them from another source. This is usually summed up, appropriately enough, in the phrase " All things are flowing " (πάντα ῥεῖ), though this does not seem to be a quotation from Herakleitos. Plato, however, expresses the idea quite clearly. " Nothing ever is, everything is becoming " ; " All things are in motion like streams " ; " All things are passing, and nothing abides " ; " Herakleitos says somewhere that all things pass and naught abides ; and, comparing things to the current of a river, he says you cannot step twice into the same stream " (cf. fr. 41)—these are the terms in which he describes the system. And Aristotle says the same thing, " All things are in motion," " nothing steadfastly is." [1] Herakleitos held, in fact, that any given thing, however stable in appearance, was merely a section in the stream, and that the stuff composing it was never the same in any two consecutive moments. We shall see presently how he conceived the process to operate ; meanwhile we remark that this is not the most original feature of the system. The Milesians had held a similar view.

The Upward and Downward path. 71. Herakleitos appears to have worked out the details with reference to the theories of Anaximenes.[2] It is unlikely, however, that he explained the transformations of matter by means of rarefaction and condensation.[3] Theophrastos, it appears, suggested that he did ; but he allowed it was by no means clear. The passage from Diogenes we are about to quote has faithfully preserved this touch.[4] In the

[1] Plato, *Theaet.* 152 e 1 ; *Crat.* 401 d 5, 402 a 8 ; Arist. *Top.* A, 11. 104 b 22 ; *De caelo,* Γ, 1. 298 b 30 ; *Phys.* Θ, 3. 253 b 2.
[2] See above, Chap. I. § 29.
[3] See, however, the remark of Diels (*Dox.* p. 165) quoted R. P. 36 c.
[4] Diog. ix. 8, σαφῶς δ' οὐθὲν ἐκτίθεται.

fragments we find nothing about rarefaction and condensation. The expression used is " exchange " (fr. 22), a very good name for what happens when fire gives out smoke and takes in fuel instead.

It has been pointed out that, in default of Hippolytos, our best account of the Theophrastean doxography of Herakleitos is the fuller of the two accounts given in Laertios Diogenes. It is as follows :

His opinions on particular points are these :

He held that Fire was the element, and that all things were an exchange for fire, produced by condensation and rarefaction. But he explains nothing clearly. All things were produced in opposition, and all things were in flux like a river.

The all is finite and the world is one. It arises from fire, and is consumed again by fire alternately through all eternity in certain cycles. This happens according to fate. Of the opposites, that which leads to the becoming of the world is called War and Strife ; that which leads to the final conflagration is Concord and Peace.

He called change the upward and the downward path, and held that the world comes into being in virtue of this. When fire is condensed it becomes moist, and when compressed it turns to water ; water being congealed turns to earth, and this he calls the downward path. And, again, the earth is in turn liquefied, and from it water arises, and from that everything else ; for he refers almost everything to the evaporation from the sea. This is the path upwards. R. P. 36.

He held, too, that exhalations arose both from the sea and the land ; some bright and pure, others dark. Fire was nourished by the bright ones, and moisture by the others.

He does not make it clear what is the nature of that which surrounds the world. He held, however, that there were bowls in it with the concave sides turned towards us, in which the bright exhalations were collected and produced flames. These were the heavenly bodies.

The flame of the sun was the brightest and warmest ; for the other heavenly bodies were more distant from the earth ; and for that reason gave less light and heat. The moon, on the other hand, was nearer the earth ; but it moved through an impure region. The sun moved in a bright and unmixed region and at the same time was at just the right distance from us. That is why it gives more heat and light. The eclipses of the sun and moon were due to the turning of the bowls upwards, while the monthly phases of the moon were produced by a gradual turning of its bowl.

Day and night, months and seasons and years, rains and winds, and things like these, were due to the different exhalations. The bright exhalation, when ignited in the circle of the sun, produced day, and the preponderance of the opposite exhalations produced night. The increase of warmth proceeding from the bright exhalation produced summer, and the preponderance of moisture from the dark exhalation produced winter. He assigns the causes of other things in conformity with this.

As to the earth, he makes no clear statement about its nature, any more than he does about that of the bowls.

These, then, were his opinions. R. P. 39 b.

Now, if we can trust this passage, it is of the greatest value ; and that, upon the whole, we can trust it is shown by the fact that it follows the exact order of topics to which all the doxographies derived from the work of Theophrastos adhere. First we have the primary substance, then the world, then the heavenly bodies, and lastly, meteorological phenomena. We conclude, then, that it may be accepted with the exceptions, firstly, of the probably erroneous conjecture of Theophrastos as to rarefaction and condensation ; and secondly, of some pieces of Stoical interpretation which come from the *Vetusta Placita*.

Let us look at the details. The pure fire, we are told, is to be found chiefly in the sun. This, like the other heavenly bodies, is a trough or bowl, with the concave side turned towards us, in which the bright exhalations from the sea collect and burn. How does the fire of the sun pass into other forms ? If we look at the fragments which deal with the downward path, we find that the first transformation it undergoes is into sea, and we are further told that half of the sea is earth and half of it πρηστήρ (fr. 21). What is this πρηστήρ ? So far as I know, no one has yet proposed to take the word in the sense it usually bears elsewhere, that, namely, of hurricane accompanied by a fiery water-spout.[1] Yet surely this is just what is wanted. It is amply attested that Herakleitos explained the rise of the sea to fire by means of the bright evaporations ; and we want a similar meteorological explanation of the passing of fire back into sea. We want, in fact, something which will stand equally for the smoke produced by the burning of the sun and for the immediate stage between fire and water. What could serve the turn better than a fiery waterspout ? It sufficiently resembles smoke to be accounted for as the product of the sun's combustion, and it certainly comes down in the form of water. And this interpretation becomes practically certain when taken in connexion with the report of Aetios as to the Herakleitean theory of πρηστῆρες. They were due, we are told, " to the kindling and extinction of clouds." [2] In other words, the bright vapour, after kindling in the bowl of the sun and going out again, reappears as the dark fiery storm-cloud, and so passes once more into sea. At the next stage we find water continually passing into earth. We are already familiar with this idea (§ 10). Turning to the " upward path," we find that the earth is liquefied in the same proportion as the sea becomes earth, so that the sea is still " measured by the same tale " (fr. 23). Half of it is earth and half of it is πρηστήρ (fr. 21). This must mean that, at any given moment, half of the sea is taking the downward path, and has just been fiery storm-cloud, while half of it is going up, and has just been earth. In proportion as the sea is increased by rain, water passes

---

[1] This was written in 1890. In his *Herakleitos von Ephesos* (1901) Diels takes it as I did, rendering *Glutwind*.   Cf. Herod. vii. 42, and Lucretius vi. 424.   Seneca (*Q.N.* ii. 56) calls it *igneus turbo*.   The opinions of early philosophers on these phenomena are collected in Aetios iii. 3. The πρηστήρ of Anaximander (Chap. I. p. 68, *n.* 2) is a different thing. Greek sailors probably named the meteorological phenomena after the familiar bellows of the smith.

[2] Aet. iii. 3. 9, πρηστῆρας δὲ κατὰ νεφῶν ἐμπρήσεις καὶ σβέσεις (sc. Ἡράκλειτος ἀποφαίνεται γίγνεσθαι).

into earth ; in proportion as the sea is diminished by
evaporation, it is fed by the earth. Lastly, the ignition of
the bright vapour from the sea in the bowl of the sun
completes the circle of the " upward and downward path."

Measure
or
measure.

72. How is it that, in spite of this constant flux, things
appear relatively stable ? The answer of Herakleitos was
that it is owing to the observance of the " measures," in
virtue of which the aggregate bulk of each form of matter
in the long run remains the same, though its substance
is constantly changing. Certain " measures " of the
" ever-living fire " are always being kindled, while like
" measures " are always going out (fr. 20). All things
are " exchanged " for fire and fire for all things (fr. 22),
and this implies that for everything it takes, fire will give
as much. "The sun will not exceed his measures" (fr. 29).

And yet the " measures " are not absolutely fixed. We
gather from the passage of Diogenes quoted above that
Theophrastos spoke of an alternate preponderance of the
bright and dark exhalations, and Aristotle speaks of Herakleitos as explaining all things by evaporation.[1] In particular, the alternation of day and night, summer and winter,
were accounted for in this way. Now, in a passage of the
pseudo-Hippokratean treatise Περὶ διαίτης which is almost
certainly of Herakleitean origin,[2] we read of an " advance of

[1] Arist. De an. B, 2. 405 a 26, τὴν ἀναθυμίασιν ἐξ ἧς τἆλλα συνίστησιν.

[2] The presence of Herakleitean matter in this treatise was pointed out
by Gesner, but Bernays was the first to make any considerable use of it in
reconstructing the system.   The older literature of the subject has been in
the main superseded by Carl Fredrichs' *Hippokratische Untersuchungen*
(1899). He shows that (as I said already in the first edition) the work
belongs to the period of eclecticism and reaction briefly characterised in
§ 184, and he points out that c 3, which was formerly supposed to be
mainly Herakleitean, is strongly influenced by Empedokles and Anaxagoras.   I think, however, that he goes wrong in attributing the section to
a nameless " Physiker " of the school of Archelaos, or even to Archelaos
himself ; it is far more like what we should expect from the eclectic
Herakleiteans described by Plato in *Crat.* 413 c (see p. 145, *n.* 1). He is
certainly wrong in holding the doctrine of the balance of fire and water
not to be Herakleitean, and there is no justification for separating the
remark quoted in the text from its context because it happens to agree
almost verbally with the beginning of c 3.

fire and water " in connexion with day and night and the
courses of the sun and moon.[1] In fr. 26, again, we read of
fire " advancing," and all these things seem to be closely
connected. We must therefore try to see whether there is
anything in the remaining fragments that bears on the
subject.

73. In studying this alternate advance of fire and water, Man.
it will be convenient to start with the microcosm. We have
more definite information about the two exhalations in
man than about the analogous processes in the world at
large, and it would seem that Herakleitos himself explained
the world by man rather than man by the world. Aristotle
implies that soul is identical with the dry exhalation,[2] and
this is confirmed by the fragments. Man is made up of
three things, fire, water; and earth. But, just as in the
macrocosm fire is identified with the one wisdom, so in the
microcosm the fire alone is conscious. When it has left the
body, the remainder, the mere earth and water, is altogether
worthless (fr. 85). Of course, the fire which animates man
is subject to the " upward and downward path," just as
much as the fire of the world. The Περὶ διαίτης has preserved the obviously Herakleitean sentence : " All things
are passing, both human and divine, upwards and downwards by exchanges." [3] We are just as much in perpetual
flux as anything else in the world. We are and are not the
same for two consecutive instants (fr. 81). The fire in us is
perpetually becoming water, and the water earth ; but, as

---

[1] Περὶ διαίτης, i. 5. I read thus : ἡμέρη καὶ εὐφρόνη ἐπὶ τὸ μήκιστον καὶ
ἐλάχιστον · ἥλιος, σελήνη ἐπὶ τὸ μήκιστον καὶ ἐλάχιστον · πυρὸς ἔφοδος καὶ
ὕδατος. In any case, the sentence occurs between χωρεῖ δὲ πάντα καὶ θεῖά
καὶ ἀνθρώπινα ἄνω καὶ κάτω ἀμειβόμενα and πάντα ταὐτὰ καὶ οὐ τὰ αὐτά,
which are surely Herakleitean utterances.

[2] Arist. De an. A, 2. 405 a 25 (R. P. 38). Diels attributes to Herakleitos
himself the words καὶ ψυχαὶ δὲ ἀπὸ τῶν ὑγρῶν ἀναθυμιῶνται, which are
found in Areios Didymos after fr. 42. I can hardly believe, however,
that the word ἀναθυμίασις is Herakleitean. He seems rather to have
called the two exhalations καπνός and ἀήρ (cf. fr. 37).

[3] Περὶ διαίτης i. 5, χωρεῖ δὲ πάντα καὶ θεῖα καὶ ἀνθρώπινα ἄνω καὶ κάτω
ἀμειβόμενα.

the opposite process goes on simultaneously, we appear to remain the same.[1]

(a) Sleeping and waking.

74. This, however, is not all. Man is subject to a certain oscillation in his " measures " of fire and water, which gives rise to the alternations of sleeping and waking, life and death. The *locus classicus* on this is a passage of Sextus Empiricus, which reproduces the account given by Ainesidemos.[2]   It is as follows (R. P. 41) :

The natural philosopher is of opinion that what surrounds us [3] is rational and endowed with consciousness.   According to Herakleitos, when we draw in this divine reason by means of respiration, we become rational.   In sleep we forget, but at our waking we become conscious once more.   For in sleep, when the openings of the senses close, the mind which is in us is cut off from contact with that which surrounds us, and only our connexion with it by means of respiration is preserved as a sort of root (from which the rest may spring again) ; and, when it is thus separated, it loses the power of memory that it had before. When we awake again, however, it looks out through the openings of the senses, as if through windows, and coming together with the surrounding mind, it assumes the power of reason.   Just, then, as embers, when they are brought near the fire, change and become red-hot, and go out when they are taken away from it again, so does the portion of the surrounding mind which sojourns in our body become irrational when it is cut off, and so does it become of like nature to the whole when contact is established through the greatest number of openings.

---

[1] We seem to have a reference to this in Epicharmos, fr. 2, Diels (170 b, Kaibel) : " Look now at men too.   One grows and another passes away, and all are in change always.   What changes in its substance ($\kappa\alpha\tau\grave{\alpha}$ $\phi\acute{\upsilon}\sigma\iota\nu$) and never abides in the same spot, will already be something different from what has passed away.   So thou and I were different yesterday, and are now quite other people, and again we shall become others and even the same again, and so on in the same way."   This is said by a debtor who does not wish to pay.

[2] Sextus quotes " Ainesidemos according to Herakleitos."   Natorp holds (*Forschungen*, p. 78) that Ainesidemos really did combine Herakleiteanism with Skepticism.   Diels (*Dox.* pp. 210, 211), insists that he only gave an account of the theories of Herakleitos.   This controversy does not affect the use we make of the passage.

[3] Τὸ περιέχον ἡμᾶς, opposed to but parallel with τὸ περιέχον τὸν κόσμον.

In this passage there is clearly a large admixture of later ideas. In particular, the identification of " that which surrounds us " with the air cannot be Herakleitean ; for Herakleitos knew nothing of air except as a form of water (§ 27). The reference to the pores or openings of the senses is probably foreign to him also ; for the theory of pores is due to Alkmaion (§ 96). Lastly, the distinction between mind and body is far too sharply drawn. On the other hand, the important rôle assigned to respiration may very well be Herakleitean ; for we have met with it already in Anaximenes. And we can hardly doubt that the striking simile of the embers which glow when brought near the fire is genuine (cf. fr. 77). The true doctrine doubtless was, that sleep was produced by the encroachment of moist, dark exhalations from the water in the body, which cause the fire to burn low. In sleep, we lose contact with the fire in the world which is common to all, and retire to a world of our own (fr. 95). In a soul where the fire and water are evenly balanced, the equilibrium is restored in the morning by an equal advance of the bright exhalation.

75. But in no soul are the fire and water thus evenly balanced for long. One or the other acquires predominance, and the result in either case is death. Let us take each of these cases in turn. It is death, we know, to souls to become water (fr. 68) ; but that is what happens to souls which seek after pleasure. For pleasure is a moistening of the soul (fr. 72), as may be seen in the case of the drunken man, who has so moistened his soul that he does not know where he is going (fr. 73). Even in gentle relaxation over our cups, it is more difficult to hide folly than at other times (fr. 108). That is why we must quench wantonness (fr. 103) ; for whatever our heart's desire insists on it purchases at the price of life, that is, of the fire within us (fr. 105). Take now the other case. The dry soul, that which has least moisture, is the best (fr. 74) ; but the preponderance of fire causes death as much as that of water. It is a very different

(b) Life and death.

F

death, however, and wins " greater portions " for those who die it (fr. 101).

Further, just as summer and winter are one, and necessarily reproduce one another by their " opposite tension," so do life and death. They, too, are one, we are told ; and so are youth and age (fr. 78). It follows that the soul will be now living and now dead ; that it will only turn to fire or water, as the case may be, to recommence once more its unceasing upward and downward path. The soul that has died from excess of moisture sinks down to earth ; but from the earth comes water, and from water is once more exhaled a soul (fr. 68). So, too, we are told (fr. 67) that gods and men are really one. They live each others' life, and die each others' death. Those mortals that die the fiery death become immortal,[1] they become the guardians of the quick and the dead (fr. 123) ;[2] and those immortals become mortal in their turn. Everything is the death of something else (fr. 64). The living and the dead are always changing places (fr. 78), like the pieces on a child's draught-board (fr. 79), and this applies not only to the souls that have become water, but to those that have become fire and are now guardian spirits. The real weariness is continuance in the same state (fr. 82), and the real rest is change (fr. 83). Rest in any other sense is tantamount to dissolution (fr. 84),[3] So they too are born once more. Herakleitos estimated the duration of the cycle which preserves the balance of life

[1] The word is used for its paradoxical effect. Strictly speaking, they are all mortal from one point of view and immortal from another.

[2] Those who fall in battle apparently share the same lot (fr. 102). Rohde, *Psyche* (II.² pp. 148 *sqq.*), refused to admit that Herakleitos believed the soul survived death. Strictly speaking, it is no doubt an inconsistency ; but I believe, with Zeller and Diels, that it is one of a kind we may well admit. The first argument which Plato uses to establish the doctrine of immortality in the *Phaedo* is just the Herakleitean parallelism of life and death with sleeping and waking.

[3] These fragments are quoted by Plotinos, Iamblichos, and Noumenios in this connexion (R. P. 46 c), and it does not seem possible to hold, with Rohde, that they had no grounds for so interpreting them. They knew the context and we do not.

and death as thirty years, the shortest time in which a man may become a grandfather (frs. 87-89).[1]

76. Let us turn now to the world. Diogenes tells us that fire was kept up by the bright vapours from land and sea, and moisture by the dark.[2] What are these " dark " vapours which increase the moist element ? If we remember the " Air " of Anaximenes, we shall be inclined to regard them as darkness itself. We know that the idea of darkness as privation of light is not primitive. I suppose, then, that Herakleitos believed night and winter to be produced by the rise of darkness from earth and sea—he saw, of course, that the valleys were dark before the hill-tops—and that this darkness, being moist, so increased the watery element as to put out the sun's light. This, however, destroys the power of darkness itself. It can no longer rise upwards unless the sun gives it motion, and so it becomes possible for a fresh sun (fr. 32) to be kindled, and to nourish itself at the expense of the moist element for a time. But it can only be for a time. The sun, by burning up the bright vapour, deprives himself of nourishment, and the dark vapour once more gets the upper hand. It is in this sense that " day and night are one " (fr. 35). Each implies the other ; they are merely two sides of one process, in which alone their true ground of explanation is to be found (fr. 36).

Summer and winter were to be explained in the same way. We know that the "turnings back" of the sun were a subject of interest in those days, and it was natural for Herakleitos to see in its retreat to the south the advance of the moist element, caused by the heat of the sun itself.

The day and the year.

---

[1] Plut. *Def. orac.* 415 d, ἔτη τριάκοντα ποιοῦσι τὴν γενεὰν καθ' Ἡράκλειτον, ἐν ᾧ χρόνῳ γεννῶντα παρέχει τὸν ἐξ αὑτοῦ γεγεννημένον ὁ γεννήσας. Philo, fr. Harris, p. 20, δυνατὸν ἐν τριακοστῷ ἔτει αὖ τὸν ἄνθρωπον πάππον γενέσθαι κτλ. Censorinus, *De die nat.* 17. 2, " hoc enim tempus (triaginta annos) *genean* vocari Heraclitus auctor est, quia *orbis aetatis* in eo sit spatio : orbem autem vocat aetatis, dum natura ab sementi humana ad sementim revertitur." The words *orbis aetatis* seem to mean αἰῶνος κύκλος, " the circle of life." If so, we may compare the Orphic κύκλος γενέσεως.

[2] Diog. ix. 9 (R. P. 39 b).

This, however, diminishes the power of the sun to cause evaporation, and so it must return to the north that it may supply itself with nourishment. Such was, at any rate, the Stoic doctrine,[1] and that it comes from Herakleitos seems to be proved by its occurrence in the Περὶ διαίτης. The following passage is clearly Herakleitean :

And in turn each (fire and water) prevails and is prevailed over to the greatest and least degree that is possible. For neither can prevail altogether for the following reasons. If fire advances towards the utmost limit of the water, its nourishment fails it. It retires, then, to a place where it can get nourishment. And if water advances towards the utmost limit of the fire, movement fails it. At that point, then, it stands still ; and, when it has come to a stand, it has no longer power to resist, but is consumed as nourishment for the fire that falls upon it. For these reasons neither can prevail altogether. But if at any time either should be in any way overcome, then none of the things that exist would be as they are now. So long as things are as they are, fire and water will always be too, and neither will ever fail.[2]

The Great Year.

77. Herakleitos spoke also of a longer period, which is identified with the " Great Year," and is variously described as lasting 18,000 and 10,800 years.[3] We have no definite statement, however, of what process Herakleitos supposed

---

[1] Cf. Cic. N.D. iii. 37 : " Quid enim ? non eisdem vobis placet omnem ignem pastus indigere nec permanere ullo modo posse, nisi alitur : ali autem solem, lunam, reliqua astra aquis, alia dulcibus (from the earth), alia marinis ? eamque causam Cleanthes (fr. 29 Pearson; I. 501 v. Arnim) adfert cur se sol referat nec longius progrediatur solstitiali orbi itemque brumali, ne longius discedat a cibo."

[2] For the Greek text see below, p. 162, n. 3. Fredrichs allows that it is from the same source as that quoted above (p. 151, n. 1), and, as that comes from Περὶ διαίτης, i. 3, he denies the Herakleitean origin of this passage too. He has not taken account of the fact that it gives the Stoic doctrine, which raises a presumption in favour of its being Herakleitean. If I could agree with Fredrichs' theory, I should still say that the present passage was a Herakleitean interpolation in the Physiker rather than that the other was an interpolation from the Physiker in the Herakleitean section. See p. 150, n. 2.

[3] Aet. ii. 32. 3. Ἡράκλειτος ἐκ μυρίων ὀκτακισχιλίων ἐνιαυτῶν ἡλιακῶν (τὸν μέγαν ἐνιαυτὸν εἶναι). Censorinus, De die nat. 11, Heraclitus et Linus, Xᴅᴄᴄᴄ.

to take place in the Great Year. The period of 36,000 years
was Babylonian, and 18,000 years is just half that period, a
fact which may be connected with Herakleitos's way of
dividing all cycles into an " upward and downward path."
The Stoics, or some of them, held that the Great Year was
the period between one world-conflagration and the next.
They were careful, however, to make it a good deal longer
than Herakleitos did, and, in any case, we are not entitled
without more ado to credit him with the theory of a general
conflagration.[1] We must try first to interpret the Great
Year on the analogy of the shorter periods discussed already.

Now we have seen that a generation is the shortest time
in which a man can become a grandfather, it is the period of
the upward or downward path of the soul, and the most
natural interpretation of the longer period would surely be
that it represents the time taken by a " measure " of the
fire in the world to travel on the downward path to earth or
return to fire once more by the upward path. Plato implies
that such a parallelism between the periods of man and the
world was recognised,[2] and this receives a curious confirmation from a passage in Aristotle, which is usually supposed
to refer to the doctrine of a periodic conflagration. He is
discussing the question whether the " heavens," that is to
say, what he calls the " first heaven," is eternal or not, and
naturally enough, from his own point of view, he identifies
this with the Fire of Herakleitos. He quotes him along
with Empedokles as holding that the " heavens " are alternately as they are now and in some other state, one of
passing away ; and he goes on to point out that this is not

---

[1] For the Stoic doctrine, cf. Nemesios, *De nat. hom.* 38 (R. P. 503).
Adam (*Republic*, vol. ii. p. 303) allowed that no destruction of the world
or conflagration marked the end of Plato's year, but he declined to draw
what seems to me the natural inference that the connexion between the
two things belongs to a later age, and should not, therefore, be ascribed
to Herakleitos in the absence of any evidence that he did so connect them.

[2] This is certainly the general sense of the parallelism between the
periods of the ἀνθρώπειον and the θεῖον γεννητόν, however we may understand the details. See Adam, *Republic*, vol. ii. pp. 288 *sqq.*

really to say they pass away, any more than it would be to say that a man ceases to be, if we said that he turned from boy to man and then from man to boy again.[1]   It is surely clear that this is a reference to the parallel between the generation and the Great Year, and, if so, the ordinary interpretation of the passage must be wrong.   It is not, indeed, quite consistent with the theory to suppose that a " measure " of Fire could preserve its identity throughout the whole of its upward and downward path ; but that is exactly the inconsistency we have felt bound to recognise with regard to the continuance of individual souls.   Now, it will be noted that, while 18,000 is half 36,000, 10,800 is 360 × 30, which would make each generation a day in the Great Year, and this is in favour of the higher number.[2]

Did Herakleitos teach a general conflagration ?

78. Most writers ascribe to Herakleitos the doctrine of a periodical conflagration or ἐκπύρωσις, to use the Stoic term.[3]   That this is inconsistent with his general view is obvious, and is indeed admitted by Zeller, who adds to his paraphrase of the statement of Plato quoted above (p. 144) the words : " Herakleitos did not intend to retract this principle in the doctrine of a periodic change in the constitution of the world ; if the two doctrines are not compatible, it is a contradiction which he has not observed."   Now, it is quite likely that there were contradictions in the discourse of Herakleitos, but it is very unlikely that there was this particular contradiction.   In the first place, it is inconsistent with the central idea of his system, the thought that pos-

[1] Arist. De caelo, A, 10. 279 b 14, οἱ δ' ἐναλλὰξ ὁτὲ μὲν οὕτως ὁτὲ δὲ ἄλλως ἔχειν φθειρόμενον, . . . ὥσπερ Ἐμπεδοκλῆς ὁ Ἀκραγαντῖνος καὶ Ἡράκλειτος ὁ Ἐφέσιος.   Aristotle points out that this really amounts only to saying that it is eternal and changes its form, ὥσπερ εἴ τις ἐκ παιδὸς ἄνδρα γιγνόμενον καὶ ἐξ ἀνδρὸς παῖδα ὁτὲ μὲν φθείρεσθαι, ὁτὲ δ' εἶναι οἴοιτο (280 a 14).   The point of the reference to Empedokles will appear from De Gen. Corr. B, 6. 334 a 1 sqq.   What Aristotle finds fault with in both theories is that they do not regard the substance of the heavens as something outside the upward and downward motion of the elements.

[2] Cf. Tannery, Science hellène, p. 168.   Diels, accordingly, now reads μυρίων ὀκτακοσίων in Aetios (Vors. 12 A 13).

[3] Schleiermacher and Lassalle are notable exceptions.   Zeller, Diels, and Gomperz are all positive that Herakleitos believed in the ἐκπύρωσις.

sessed his whole mind (§ 67), and we can only admit the possibility of that, if the evidence for it should prove irresistible. In the second place, such an interpretation destroys the whole point of Plato's contrast between Herakleitos and Empedokles (§ 68), which is just that, while Herakleitos said the One was always many, and the Many always one, Empedokles said the All was many and one by turns. Zeller's interpretation obliges us, then, to suppose that Herakleitos flatly contradicted his own discovery without noticing it, and that Plato, in discussing this very discovery, was also blind to the contradiction.[1]

Nor is there anything in Aristotle to set against Plato's statement. We have seen that the passage in which he speaks of him along with Empedokles as holding that the heavens were alternately in one condition and in another refers not to the world, but to fire, which Aristotle identified with the substance of his own " first heaven."[2] It is also quite consistent with our interpretation when he says that all things at one time or another become fire. This need not mean that they all become fire at the same time, but may be merely a statement of the undoubted Herakleitean doctrine of the upward and downward path.[3]

The earliest statements to the effect that Herakleitos

---

[1] In his fifth edition (p. 699) Zeller seems to have felt this last difficulty; for he said there: " It is a contradiction which he, *and which probably Plato too (und den wahrscheinlich auch Plato)* has not observed." This seems to me still less arguable. Plato may or may not be mistaken; but he makes the perfectly definite statement that Herakleitos says ἀεί, while Empedokles says ἐν μέρει. The Ionian Muses are called συντονώτεραι and the Sicilian μαλακώτεραι just because the latter " lowered the pitch " (ἐχάλασαν) of the doctrine that this is always so (τὸ ἀεὶ ταῦτα οὕτως ἔχειν).

[2] See above, p. 158, *n.* 1.

[3] *Phys.* Γ 5, 205 a 3 (*Met.* K, 10. 1067 a 4), ὥσπερ Ἡράκλειτός φησιν ἅπαντα γίνεσθαί ποτε πῦρ. Zeller translates this *es werde alles dereinst zu Feuer werden*; but that would require γενήσεσθαι. Nor is there anything in his suggestion that ἅπαντα (" not merely πάντα ") implies that all things become fire at once. In Aristotle's day, there was no distinction of meaning between πᾶς and ἅπας. Of course, as Diels says, the present tense *might* be used of a " constant alternation of epochs " (*Vors.* 12 A 10 *n.*); but, for the purpose of Zeller's argument, we want something which not only *may* but *must* mean that.

taught the doctrine of a general conflagration are found in Stoic writers. The Christian apologists too were interested in the idea of a final conflagration, and reproduce the Stoic view. The curious thing, however, is that there was a difference of opinion on the subject even among the Stoics. In one place, Marcus Aurelius says : " So that all these things are taken up into the Reason of the universe, whether by a periodical conflagration or a renovation effected by eternal exchanges." [1] Indeed, there were some who said there was no general conflagration at all in Herakleitos. " I hear all that," Plutarch makes one of his personages say, " from many people, and I see the Stoic conflagration spreading over the poems of Hesiod, just as it does over the writings of Herakleitos and the verses of Orpheus." [2] We see from this that the question was debated, and we should therefore expect any statement of Herakleitos which could settle it to be quoted over and over again. It is highly significant that not a single quotation of the kind can be produced.[3]

On the contrary, the absence of anything to show that Herakleitos spoke of a general conflagration only becomes more patent when we turn to the few fragments which are supposed to prove it. The favourite is fr. 24, where we are

[1] Marcus Aurelius, x. 7, ὥστε καὶ ταῦτα ἀναληφθῆναι εἰς τὸν τοῦ ὅλου λόγον, εἴτε κατὰ περίοδον ἐκπυρουμένου, εἴτε ἀιδίοις ἀμοιβαῖς ἀνανεουμένου. The ἀμοιβαί are specifically Herakleitean, and the statement is the more remarkable as Marcus elsewhere follows the usual Stoic interpretation.

[2] Plut. De def. orac. 415 f., καὶ ὁ Κλεόμβροτος, 'Ακούω ταῦτ', ἔφη, πολλῶν καὶ ὁρῶ τὴν Στωικὴν ἐκπύρωσιν ὥσπερ τὰ Ἡρακλείτου καὶ 'Ορφέως ἐπινεμομένην ἔπη οὕτω καὶ τὰ Ἡσιόδου καὶ συνεξάπτουσαν. As Zeller admits (p. 693 n.), this proves that some opponents of the Stoic ἐκπύρωσις tried to withdraw the support of Herakleitos from it.

[3] This has been called a mere argumentum ex silentio ; but, in such cases, the argumentum ex silentio is stronger than any other. Positive statements may be misinterpreted ; but, when we know that a subject was keenly debated, and when we find that neither party can produce an unambiguous text in support of its view, the conclusion that none such existed becomes irresistible. The same remark applies to modern pronouncements on the subject. Diels briefly says that my view " is wrong " (ist irrig), but he does not adduce any fresh reason for saying so. The conclusion is that he knows of none.

told that Herakleitos said Fire was Want and Surfeit. That is just in his manner, and it has a perfectly intelligible meaning on our interpretation, which is further confirmed by fr. 36. The next is fr. 26, where we read that fire in its advance will judge and convict all things. There is nothing in this, however, to suggest that fire will judge all things at once rather than in turn, and, indeed, the phraseology reminds us of the advance of fire and water which we have seen reason for attributing to Herakleitos, but which is expressly said to be limited to a certain maximum.[1] These appear to be the only passages which the Stoics and the Christian apologists could discover, and, whether our interpretation of them is right or wrong, it is surely clear that they cannot bear the weight of their conclusion, and that there was nothing more definite to be found.

It is much easier to find fragments which are inconsistent with a general conflagration. The " measures " of fr. 20 and fr. 29 must be the same thing, and they must be interpreted in the light of fr. 23. If this be so, fr. 20, and more especially fr. 29, directly contradict the idea of a general conflagration. " The sun will not overstep his measures." [2] Secondly, the metaphor of " exchange," which is applied to the transformations of fire in fr. 22, points in the same direction. When gold is given in exchange for wares and wares for gold, the sum or " measure " of each remains constant, though they change owners. All the wares and gold do not come into the same hands. In the same way, when anything becomes fire, something of equal amount must cease to be fire, if the " exchange " is to be a just one ; and that it will be just, we are assured by the watchfulness of the Erinyes (fr. 29), who sees to it that the sun does not take more than he gives. Of course there is a certain variation, as we saw ; but it is strictly confined

---

[1] Περὶ διαίτης, i. 3, ἐν μέρει δὲ ἑκάτερον κρατεῖ καὶ κρατεῖται ἐς τὸ μήκιστον καὶ ἐλάχιστον ὡς ἀνυστόν.

[2] If any one doubts that this is really the meaning of the " measures," let him compare the use of the word by Diogenes of Apollonia, fr. 3.

within limits, and is compensated in the long run by a variation in the other direction. Thirdly, fr. 43, in which Herakleitos blames Homer for desiring the cessation of strife, is very conclusive. The cessation of strife would mean that all things should take the upward or downward path at the same time, and cease to "run in opposite directions." If they all took the upward path, we should have a general conflagration. Now, if Herakleitos had himself held this to be the appointment of fate, would he have been likely to upbraid Homer for desiring so necessary a consummation?[1] Fourthly, we note that in fr. 20 it is *this* world,[2] and not merely the "ever-living fire," which is said to be eternal; and it appears also that its eternity depends on the fact that it is always kindling and always going out in the same "measures," or that an encroachment in one direction is compensated by a subsequent encroachment in the other. Lastly, Lassalle's argument from the concluding sentence of the passage from the Περὶ διαίτης, quoted above, is really untouched by Zeller's objection, that it cannot be Herakleitean because it implies that all things are fire and water. It does not imply this, but only that *man*, like the heavenly bodies, oscillates between fire and water; and that is just what Herakleitos taught. Now, in this passage we read that neither fire nor water can prevail completely, and a very good reason is given for this, a reason too which is in striking agreement with the other views of Herakleitos.[3] And, indeed, it is not easy to see how, in

---

[1] This is just the argument which Plato uses in the *Phaedo* (72 c) to prove the necessity of ἀνταπόδοσις, and the whole series of arguments in that passage is distinctly Herakleitean in character.

[2] However we understand κόσμος here, the meaning is the same. Indeed, if we suppose with Bernays that it means "order," the argument will be all the stronger. In no sense of the word could a κόσμος survive the ἐκπύρωσις, and the Stoics accordingly said the κόσμος was φθαρτός, though Herakleitos had declared it to be everlasting.

[3] Περὶ διαίτης, i. 3 (see above, p. 150, *n.* 2), οὐδέτερον γὰρ κρατῆσαι παντελῶς δύναται διὰ τάδε · τὸ ⟨τε⟩ πῦρ ἐπεξιὸν ἐπὶ τὸ ἔσχατον τοῦ ὕδατος ἐπιλείπει ἡ τροφή · ἀποτρέπεται οὖν ὅθεν μέλλει τρέφεσθαι · τὸ ὕδωρ τε ἐπεξιὸν τοῦ πυρὸς ἐπὶ τὸ ἔσχατον, ἐπιλείπει ἡ κίνησις · ἵσταται οὖν ἐν τούτῳ, ὅταν δὲ στῇ, οὐκέτι

accordance with these views, the world could ever recover from a general conflagration if such a thing were to take place. The whole process depends on the fact that Surfeit is also Want, or, in other words, that an advance of fire increases the moist exhalation, while an advance of water deprives the fire of its power to cause evaporation. The conflagration, though it lasted but for a moment,[1] would destroy the opposite tension on which the rise of a new world depends, and then motion would become impossible.

79. We are now in a position to understand more clearly the law of strife or opposition which manifests itself in the "upward and downward path." At any given moment, each of the three aggregates, Fire, Water, and Earth, is made up of two equal portions—subject, of course, to the oscillation described above—one of which is taking the upward and the other the downward path. Now, it is just the fact that the two halves of everything are being "drawn in opposite directions," this "opposite tension," that "keeps things together," and maintains them in an equilibrium which can only be disturbed temporarily and within certain limits. It thus forms the "hidden attunement" of the universe (fr. 47), though, in another aspect of it, it is Strife. As to the "bow and the lyre" (fr. 45), I think that Campbell gave the best explanation of the simile. "As the arrow leaves the string," he said, "the hands are pulling opposite ways to each other, and to the different parts of the bow (cf. Plato, *Rep.* iv. 439); and the sweet note of the lyre is due to a similar tension and retention. The secret of

Strife and "harmony."

ἐγκρατές ἐστιν, ἀλλ' ἤδη τῷ ἐμπίπτοντι πυρὶ ἐς τὴν τροφὴν καταναλίσκεται· οὐδέτερον δὲ διὰ ταῦτα δύναται κρατῆσαι παντελῶς, εἰ δέ ποτε κρατηθείη καὶ ὁπότερον, οὐδὲν ἂν εἴη τῶν νῦν ἐόντων ὥσπερ ἔχει νῦν· οὕτω δὲ ἐχόντων ἀεὶ ἔσται τὰ αὐτὰ καὶ οὐδέτερον οὐδαμὰ ἐπιλείψει.

[1] In his note on fr. 66 (=26 Byw.) Diels seeks to minimise the difficulty of the ἐκπύρωσις by saying that it is only a little one, and can last but a moment; but the contradiction remains. Diels holds that Herakleitos was "dark only in form," and that "he himself was perfectly clear as to the sense and scope of his ideas" (*Herakleitos*, p. i.). To which I would add that he was probably called "the Dark" just because the Stoics sometimes found it hard to read their own ideas into his words.

the universe is the same." [1] War, then, is the father and king of all things, in the world as in human society (fr. 44) ; and Homer's wish that strife might cease was really a prayer for the destruction of the world (fr. 43).

We know from Philo that Herakleitos supported his theory by a multitude of examples ; and some of these can still be recovered. There is a remarkable agreement between a passage of this kind in the pseudo-Aristotelian Περὶ κόσμου and the Hippokratean Περὶ διαίτης. That the authors of both drew from the same source, namely, Herakleitos, is made practically certain by the fact that this agreement extends in part to the *Letters of Herakleitos*, which, though spurious, were certainly composed by some one who had access to the original work. The argument was that men themselves act just in the same way as Nature, and it is therefore surprising that they do not recognise the laws by which she works. The painter produces his harmonious effects by the contrast of colours, the musician by that of high and low notes. " If one were to make all things alike, there would be no delight in them." There are many similar examples, some of which must certainly come from Herakleitos ; but it is not easy to separate them from the later additions. [2]

---

[1] Campbell's *Theaetetus* (2nd ed.), p. 244. Bernays explained the phrase as referring to the *shape* of the bow and lyre, but this is much less likely. Wilamowitz's interpretation is based on Campbell's. " Es ist mit der Welt wie mit dem Bogen, den man auseinanderzieht, damit er zusammenschnellt, wie mit der Saite, die man ihrer Spannung entgegen- ziehen muss, damit sie klingt" (*Lesebuch*, ii. p. 129). Here we seem to feel the influence of the Pythagorean " tuned string."

[2] The sentence (Περὶ διαίτης, i. 5), καὶ τὰ μὲν πρήσσουσιν οὐκ οἴδασιν, ἃ δὲ οὐ πρήσσουσι δοκέουσιν εἰδέναι· καὶ τὰ μὲν ὁρέουσιν οὐ γινώσκουσιν, ἀλλ' ὅμως αὐτοῖσι πάντα γίνεται . . . καὶ ἃ βούλονται καὶ ἃ μὴ βούλονται, has the true Herakleitean ring. This, too, can hardly have had another author : " They trust to their eyes rather than to their understanding, though their eyes are not fit to judge even of the things that are seen. But I speak these things from understanding." These words are gro- tesque in the mouth of the medical compiler ; but we are accustomed to hear such things from the Ephesian. Other examples which may be Herakleitean are the image of the two men sawing wood—" one pushes, the other pulls "—and the illustration from the art of writing.

80. There are several Herakleitean fragments which
form a class by themselves, and are among the most striking
of the utterances that have come down to us.   These assert
in the most downright way the identity of various things
usually regarded as opposites.   The clue to their meaning
is to be found in the account already given of the assertion
that day and night are one.   We have seen that Herakleitos
meant, not that day was night or night was day, but that
they were two sides of the same process, namely, the oscillation of the " measures " of fire and water, and that neither
would be possible without the other.   Any explanation
that can be given of night will also be an explanation of
day, and *vice versa* ; for it will be an account of what is
common to both, and manifests itself now as one and now
as the other.   Now this is only a particular application of
the principle that the primary fire is one even in its division.
It itself is, even in its unity, both surfeit and want, war and
peace (fr. 36).   In other words, the " satiety " which makes
fire pass into other forms, which makes it seek " rest
in change " (fr. 83), and " hide itself " (fr. 10) in the
" hidden attunement " of opposition, is only one side of the
process.   The other is the " want " which leads it to con-
sume the bright vapour as fuel.   The upward path is nothing
without the downward (fr. 69).   If either were to cease, the
other would cease too, and the world would disappear ;
for it takes both to make an apparently stable reality.

All other utterances of the kind are to be explained in
the same way.   If there were no cold, there would be no
heat ; for a thing can only grow warm if, and in so far as,
it is already cold.   And the same thing applies to the opposition of wet and dry (fr. 39).   These, it will be observed, are
just the two primary oppositions of Anaximander, and
Herakleitos is showing that the war between them is really
peace, for it is the common element in them (fr. 62) which
appears as strife, and that very strife is justice, and not, as
Anaximander had taught, an injustice which they commit

one against the other, and which must be expiated by a reabsorption of both in their common ground.[1]

The most startling of these sayings is that which affirms that good and evil are the same (fr. 57). This does not mean that good is evil or that evil is good, but simply that they are the two inseparable halves of one and the same thing. A thing can become good only in so far as it is already evil, and evil only in so far as it is already good, and everything depends on the contrast. The illustration given in fr. 58 shows this clearly. Torture, one would say, was an evil, and yet it is made a good by the presence of another evil, namely, disease ; as is shown by the fact that surgeons expect a fee for inflicting it on their patients. Justice, on the other hand, which is a good, would be unknown were it not for injustice, which is an evil (fr. 60). And that is why it is not good for men to get everything they wish (fr. 104). Just as the cessation of strife in the world would mean its destruction, so the disappearance of hunger, disease, and weariness would mean the disappearance of satisfaction, health, and rest.

This leads to a theory of relativity which prepares the way for the doctrine of Protagoras, that " Man is the measure of all things." [2] Sea-water is good for fish and bad for men (fr. 52), and so with many other things. At the same time, Herakleitos is not a believer in absolute relativity. The process of the world is not merely a circle, but an " upward and downward path." At the upper end, where the two paths meet, we have the pure fire, in which, as there is no separation, there is no relativity. We are told that, while to man some things are evil and some things are good, all things are good to God (fr. 61). Now by God, or the

---

[1] Chap. I. § 16.

[2] Plato's exposition of the relativity of knowledge in the *Theaetetus* (152 d *sqq.*) can hardly go back to Herakleitos himself, but is meant to show how Herakleiteanism might give rise to such a doctrine. If the soul is a stream and things are a stream, then of course knowledge is relative. Perhaps the later Herakleiteans had worked out the theory in this direction.

" one wise," there is no doubt Herakleitos meant Fire.
There can hardly be any question that what he meant to
say was that in it the opposition and relativity universal in
the world disappear.   It is doubtless to this that frs. 96, 97,
and 98 refer.

81. Herakleitos speaks of " wisdom " or the " wise " in The Wise.
two senses.   We have seen already that he said wisdom was
" something apart from everything else " (fr. 18), meaning
by it the perception of the unity of the many ; and he also
applies the term to that unity itself regarded as the " thought
that directs the course of all things."   This is synonymous
with the pure fire which is not differentiated into two parts,
one taking the upward and the other the downward path.
That alone has wisdom ; the partial things we see have
not.   We ourselves are only wise in so far as we are fiery
(fr. 74).

82. With certain reservations, Herakleitos was prepared Theology.
to call the one Wisdom by the name of Zeus.   Such, at
least, appears to be the meaning of fr. 65.   What these
reservations were, it is easy to guess.   It is not, of course,
to be pictured in the form of a man.   In saying this, Herakleitos would only have been repeating what had already
been said by Xenophanes.   He agrees further with Xenophanes in holding that this " god," if it is to be called so,
is one ; but his polemic against popular religion was directed
rather against the rites and ceremonies themselves than
their mythological outgrowth.   He gives a list (fr. 124) of
some of the religious figures of his time, and the context in
which the fragment is quoted shows that he in some way
threatened them with the wrath to come.   He comments
on the absurdity of praying to images (fr. 126), and the
strange idea that blood-guiltiness can be washed out by
the shedding of blood (fr. 130).   He seems also to have said
that it was absurd to celebrate the worship of Dionysos
by cheerful and licentious ceremonies, while Hades was pro-
pitiated by gloomy rites (fr. 127).   According to the mystic

doctrine itself, the two were really one ; and the one Wisdom ought to be worshipped in its integrity.

83. The moral teaching of Herakleitos is summed up in the rule " Follow the common." The " common " upon which Herakleitos insists is, nevertheless, something very different from common sense, for which, indeed, he had the greatest possible contempt (fr. 111). It is, in fact, his strongest objection to " the many," that they live each in his own world (fr. 95), as if they had a private wisdom of their own (fr. 92) ; and public opinion is therefore just the opposite of " the common." The rule is really to be interpreted as a corollary of his anthropological and cosmological views. The first requirement is that we keep our souls dry, and thus assimilate them to the one Wisdom, which is fire. That is what is really " common," and the greatest fault is to act like men asleep (fr. 94), that is, by letting our souls grow moist, to cut ourselves off from the fire in the world.

Herakleitos prepared the way for the Stoic world-state by comparing " the common " to the laws of a city. And these are even more than a type of the divine law : they are imperfect embodiments of it. They cannot, however, exhaust it altogether ; for in all human affairs there is an element of relativity (fr. 91). " Man is a baby compared to God " (fr. 97). Such as they are, however, the city must fight for them as for its walls ; and, if it has the good fortune to possess a citizen with a dry soul, he is worth ten thousand (fr. 113) ; for in him alone is " the common " embodied.

CHAPTER IV

PARMENIDES OF ELEA

84. PARMENIDES, son of Pyres, was a citizen of Hyele, Elea, or
Velia, a colony founded in Oinotria by refugees from Phokaia
in 540–39 B.C.[1] Diogenes tells us that he " flourished " in
Ol. LXIX. (504–500 B.C.), and this was doubtless the date
given by Apollodoros.[2] On the other hand, Plato says that
Parmenides came to Athens in his sixty-fifth year, accompanied by Zeno, and conversed with Sokrates, who was then
quite young. Now Sokrates was just over seventy when
he was put to death in 399 B.C. ; and therefore, if we suppose
him to have been an *ephebos*, that is, from eighteen to twenty
years old, at the time of his interview with Parmenides, we
get 451–449 B.C. as the date of that event. It is quite
uncritical to prefer the estimate of Apollodoros to Plato's
express statement,[3] especially as Parmenides himself speaks
of visiting " all towns," [4] and we have independent evidence
of the visit of Zeno to Athens, where Perikles is said to have

---

[1] Diog. ix. 21 (R. P. 111). For the foundation of Elea, see Herod. i.
165 *sqq.* It was on the coast of Lucania, south of Poseidonia (Paestum).

[2] Diog. ix. 23 (R. P. 111). Cf. Diels, *Rhein. Mus.* xxxi. p. 34 ; and
Jacoby, pp. 231 *sqq.*

[3] Plato, *Parm.* 127 b (R. P. 111 d). Wilamowitz once said that there
were no anachronisms in Plato, though he now (*Platon*, vol. i. p. 507) regards
this statement as an "invention." I cannot agree. In the first place, we
have exact figures as to the ages of Parmenides and Zeno, which imply
that the latter was twenty-five years younger than the former, not forty
as Apollodoros said. In the second place, Plato refers to this meeting in
two other places (*Theaet.* 183 e 7 and *Soph.* 217 c 5), which do not seem
to be mere references to the dialogue entitled *Parmenides.*

[4] Cf. p. 172, *n.* 1.

" heard " him.[1] The date given by Apollodoros depends solely on that of the foundation of Elea (540 B.C.), which he had adopted as the *floruit* of Xenophanes. Parmenides is born in that year, just as Zeno is born in the year when Parmenides " flourished." I do not understand how any one can attach importance to such combinations.

We have seen (§ 55) that Aristotle mentions a statement which made Parmenides a disciple of Xenophanes ; but it is practically certain that the statement referred to is only Plato's humorous remark in the *Sophist*, which we have dealt with already.[2] Xenophanes tells us himself that, in his ninety-second year, he was still wandering up and down (fr. 8). At that time Parmenides would be well advanced in life. And we must not overlook the statement of Sotion, preserved by Diogenes, that, though Parmenides " heard " Xenophanes, he did not " follow " him. He was really the " associate " of a Pythagorean, Ameinias, son of Dio-chaitas, " a poor but noble man to whom he afterwards built a shrine as to a hero." It was Ameinias and not Xenophanes that " converted " Parmenides to the philo-sophic life.[3] This does not read like an invention. The shrine erected by Parmenides would still be there in later days, like the grave of Pythagoras at Metapontion, and would have a dedicatory inscription. It should also be mentioned that Strabo describes Parmenides and Zeno as Pythagoreans, and that Kebes talks of a " Parmenidean and Pythagorean way of life." [4] It is certain, moreover, that

---

[1] Plut. *Per.* 4, 3. See below, p. 311, *n.* 1.

[2] See above, Chap. II. p. 127, *n.* 2.

[3] Diog. ix. 21 (R. P. 111), reading Ἀμεινίᾳ Διοχαίτα with Diels (*Hermes*, xxxv. p. 197). Sotion, in his *Successions*, separated Parmenides from Xenophanes and associated him with the Pythagoreans (*Dox.* pp. 146, 148, 166). So Proclus *in Parm.* iv. 5 (Cousin), Ἐλεᾶται δ' ἄμφω (Parmenides and Zeno) καὶ οὐ τοῦτο μόνον, ἀλλὰ καὶ τοῦ Πυθαγορικοῦ διδασκαλείου μεταλαβόντε, καθάπερ που καὶ Νικόμαχος ἱστόρησεν. Presumably this comes from Timaios.

[4] Strabo, vi. 1, p. 252 (p. 171, *n.* 2) ; Ceb. *Tab.* 2 (R. P. 111 c). The statements of Strabo are of the greatest value ; for they are based upon historians (especially Timaios) now lost.

the opening of the poem of Parmenides is an allegorical description of his conversion from some form of error to what he held to be the truth, and that it is thrown into the form of an Orphic apocalypse.[1] That would be quite natural if he had been a Pythagorean in his early days, so we need not hesitate to accept the tradition that he had. As regards the relation of Parmenides to the Pythagorean system, we shall have something to say later. At present we need only note that, like most of the older philosophers, he took part in politics ; and Speusippos recorded that he legislated for his native city. Others add that the magistrates of Elea made the citizens swear every year to abide by the laws Parmenides had given them.[2]

85. Parmenides was the first philosopher to expound The poem. his system in metrical language. His predecessors, Anaximander, Anaximenes, and Herakleitos, wrote in prose, and the only Greeks who ever wrote philosophy in verse at all were just these two, Parmenides and Empedokles ; for Xenophanes was not a philosopher any more than Epicharmos. Empedokles copied Parmenides ; and he, no doubt, was influenced by the Orphics. But the thing was an innovation, and one that did not maintain itself.

The fragments of Parmenides are preserved for the most part by Simplicius, who fortunately inserted them in his commentary, because in his time the original work was already rare.[3] I follow the arrangement of Diels.

[1] We know too little of the apocalyptic poems of the sixth century B.C. to be sure of the details. All we can say is that Parmenides has taken the form of his poem from some such source. See Diels, " Über die poetischen Vorbilder des Parmenides " (*Berl. Sitzb.* 1896), and the Introduction to his *Parmenides Lehrgedicht*, pp. 9 *sqq.*

[2] Diog. ix. 23 (R. P. 111). Plut. *Adv. Col.* 1226 a, Παρμενίδης δὲ τὴν ἑαυτοῦ πατρίδα διεκόσμησε νόμοις ἀρίστοις, ὥστε τὰς ἀρχὰς καθ' ἕκαστον ἐνιαυτὸν ἐξορκοῦν τοὺς πολίτας ἐμμενεῖν τοῖς Παρμενίδου νόμοις. Strabo, vi. 1, p. 252, ('Ελέαν) ἐξ ἧς Παρμενίδης καὶ Ζήνων ἐγένοντο ἄνδρες Πυθαγόρειοι. δοκεῖ δέ μοι καὶ δι' ἐκείνους καὶ ἔτι πρότερον εὐνομηθῆναι. We can hardly doubt that this too comes from Timaios.

[3] Simpl. *Phys.* 144, 25 (R. P. 117). Simplicius, of course, had the library of the Academy at his command. Diels estimates that we have about nine-tenths of the 'Αλήθεια and about one-tenth of the Δόξα.

(1)

The car that bears me carried me as far as ever my heart
desired, when it had brought me and set me on the renowned way
of the goddess, which leads the man who knows through all the
towns.[1] On that way was I borne along; for on it did the wise
5 steeds carry me, drawing my car, and maidens showed the way.
And the axle, glowing in the socket—for it was urged round by
the whirling wheels at each end—gave forth a sound as of a pipe,
when the daughters of the Sun, hasting to convey me into the
light, threw back their veils from off their faces and left the
10 abode of Night.

There are the gates of the ways of Night and Day,[2] fitted
above with a lintel and below with a threshold of stone. They
themselves, high in the air, are closed by mighty doors, and
Avenging Justice keeps the keys that fit them. Her did the
15 maidens entreat with gentle words and cunningly persuade to
unfasten without demur the bolted bars from the gates. Then,
when the doors were thrown back, they disclosed a wide opening,
when their brazen posts fitted with rivets and nails swung back
one after the other. Straight through them, on the broad way,
20 did the maidens guide the horses and the car, and the goddess
greeted me kindly, and took my right hand in hers, and spake
to me these words :

Welcome, O youth, that comest to my abode on the car that
bears thee tended by immortal charioteers ! It is no ill chance,
25 but right and justice that has sent thee forth to travel on this
way. Far, indeed, does it lie from the beaten track of men !
Meet it is that thou shouldst learn all things, as well the unshaken
heart of well-rounded truth, as the opinions of mortals in which
is no true belief at all. Yet none the less shalt thou learn these
30 things also,—how passing right through all things one should
judge the things that seem to be.[3]

.   .   .   .

---

[1] The best MS. of Sextus, who quotes this passage, reads κατὰ πάντ'
ἄστη. Parmenides, then, was an itinerant philosopher, like the sophists
of the next generation, and this makes his visit to the Athens of Perikles
all the more natural.

[2] For these see Hesiod, *Theog.* 748.

[3] I read δοκιμῶσ' (*i.e.* δοκιμῶσαι) with Diels. I have left it ambiguous
in my rendering whether εἶναι is to be taken with δοκιμῶσαι or δοκοῦντα.

But do thou restrain thy thought from this way of inquiry, nor let habit by its much experience force thee to cast upon this way a wandering eye or sounding ear or tongue; but judge by 35 argument [1] the much disputed proof uttered by me. There is only one way left that can be spoken of. . . . R. P. 113.

THE WAY OF TRUTH

(2)

Look steadfastly with thy mind at things though afar as if they were at hand. Thou canst not cut off what is from holding fast to what is, neither scattering itself abroad in order nor coming together. R. P. 118 a.

(3)

It is all one to me where I begin; for I shall come back again there.

(4, 5)

Come now, I will tell thee—and do thou hearken to my saying and carry it away—the only two ways of search that can be thought of. The first, namely, that *It is*, and that it is impossible for it not to be, is the way of belief, for truth is its companion. The other, namely, that *It is not*, and that it must needs not be,—that, I tell thee, is a path that none can learn of at all. For thou canst not know what is not—that is impossible—nor utter it; for it is the same thing that can be thought and that can be.[2] R. P. 114.

---

[1] This is the earliest instance of λόγος in the sense of (dialectical) argument which Sokrates made familiar. He got it, of course, from the Eleatics. The Herakleitean use is quite different. (See p. 133, *n.* 1.)

[2] I still believe that Zeller's is the only possible interpretation of τὸ γὰρ αὐτὸ νοεῖν ἐστιν τε καὶ εἶναι (*denn dasselbe kann gedacht werden und sein*, p. 558, *n.* 1: Eng. trans. p. 584, *n.* 1). It is impossible to separate νοεῖν ἐστιν here from fr. 4, εἰσὶ νοῆσαι, " can be thought." No rendering is admissible which makes νοεῖν the subject of the sentence; for a bare infinitive is never so used. (Some grammars make ποιεῖν the subject in a sentence like δίκαιόν ἐστι τοῦτο ποιεῖν, but this is shown to be wrong by δίκαιός εἰμι τοῦτο ποιεῖν.) The use of the infinitive as a subject only became possible when the articular infinitive was developed (cf. Monro, *H. Gr.* §§ 233, 234, 242). The original dative meaning of the infinitive at once explains the usage (νοεῖν ἐστιν, " is for thinking," " can be thought," ἐστιν εἶναι, " is for being," " can be ").

(6)

It needs must be that what can be spoken and thought *is* ; for it is possible for it to be, and it is not possible for what is nothing to be.[1] This is what I bid thee ponder. I hold thee back from this first way of inquiry, and from this other also, 5 upon which mortals knowing naught wander two-faced ; for helplessness guides the wandering thought in their breasts, so that they are borne along stupefied like men deaf and blind. Undiscerning crowds, who hold that it is and is not the same and not the same,[2] and all things travel in opposite directions![3] R. P. 115.

(7)

For this shall never be proved, that the things that are not are ; and do thou restrain thy thought from this way of inquiry. R. P. 116.

(8)

One path only is left for us to speak of, namely, that *It is*. In this path are very many tokens that what is is uncreated and indestructible ; for it is complete,[4] immovable, and without end. Nor 5 was it ever, nor will it be ; for now *it is*, all at once, a continuous

---

[1] The construction here is the same as that explained in the last note. The words τὸ λέγειν τε νοεῖν τ' ἐόν mean "that which it is possible to speak of and think," and are correctly paraphrased by Simplicius (*Phys.* p. 86, 29, Diels), εἰ οὖν ὅπερ ἄν τις ἢ εἴπῃ ἢ νοήσῃ τὸ ὄν ἐστι. Then ἔστι γὰρ εἶναι means " it can be," and the last phrase should be construed οὐκ ἔστι μηδὲν.(εἶναι), " there is no room for nothing to be."

[2] I construe οἷς νενόμισται τὸ πέλειν τε καὶ οὐκ εἶναι ταὐτὸν καὶ οὐ ταὐτόν. The subject of the infinitives πέλειν καὶ οὐκ εἶναι is the *it*, which has to be supplied also with ἔστιν and οὐκ ἔστιν. This way of taking the words makes it unnecessary to believe that Parmenides said (τὸ) οὐκ εἶναι instead of (τὸ) μὴ εἶναι for " not-being." There is no difference between πέλειν and εἶναι except in rhythmical value.

[3] I take πάντων as neuter and understand παλίντροπος κέλευθος as equivalent to the ὁδὸς ἄνω κάτω of Herakleitos. I do not think it has anything to do with the παλίντονος (or παλίντροπος) ἁρμονίη. See Chap. III. p. 136, *n*. 4.

[4] I prefer to read ἔστι γὰρ οὐλομελές with Plutarch (*Adv. Col.* 1114 c). Proklos (*in Parm.* 1152, 24) also read οὐλομελές. Simplicius, who has μουνογενές here, calls the One of Parmenides ὁλομελές elsewhere (*Phys.* p. 137, 15). The reading of [Plut.] *Strom.* 5, μοῦνον μουνογενές, helps to explain the confusion. We have only to suppose that the letters μ, ν, γ were written above the line in the Academy copy of Parmenides by some one who had *Tim.* 31 b 3 in mind. Parmenides could not call what *is* " only-begotten," though the Pythagoreans might call the world so.

one. For what kind of origin for it wilt thou look for ? In what way and from what source could it have drawn its increase ? . . . I shall not let thee say nor think that it came from what is not ; for it can neither be thought nor uttered that anything is not. And, if it came from nothing, what need could have made it 10 arise later rather than sooner ? Therefore must it either be altogether or be not at all. Nor will the force of truth suffer aught to arise besides itself from that which is not. Wherefore, Justice doth not loose her fetters and let anything come into being or pass away, but holds it fast. Our judgment thereon 15 depends on this : " *Is it* or *is it not ?* " Surely it is adjudged, as it needs must be, that we are to set aside the one way as unthinkable and nameless (for it is no true way), and that the other path is real and true. How, then, can what *is* be going to be in the future ? Or how could it come into being ? If it came into 20 being, it is not ; nor is it if it is going to be in the future. Thus is becoming extinguished and passing away not to be heard of. R. P. 117.

Nor is it divisible, since it is all alike, and there is no more [1] of it in one place than in another, to hinder it from holding together, nor less of it, but everything is full of what is. Wherefore it is 25 wholly continuous ; for what is, is in contact with what is.

Moreover, it is immovable in the bonds of mighty chains, without beginning and without end ; since coming into being and passing away have been driven afar, and true belief has cast them away. It is the same, and it rests in the self-same place, abiding in itself. And thus it remaineth constant in its place ; 30 for hard necessity keeps it in the bonds of the limit that holds it fast on every side. Wherefore it is not permitted to what is to be infinite ; for it is in need of nothing ; while, if it were infinite, it would stand in need of everything.[2] R. P. 118.

---

[1] For the difficulties which have been felt about μᾶλλον here, see Diels's note. If the word is to be pressed, his interpretation is admissible ; but it seems to me that this is simply an instance of " polar expression." It is true that it is only the case of there being less of what is in one place than another that is important for the divisibility of the One ; but if there is less in one place, there is more in another *than in that place.* In any case, the reference to the Pythagorean " air " or " void " which makes reality discontinuous is plain.

[2] Simplicius certainly read μὴ ἐὸν δ' ἂν παντὸς ἐδεῖτο, which is metrically impossible. I have followed Bergk in deleting μή, and have interpreted with Zeller. So too Diels.

The thing that can be thought and that for the sake of which
35 the thought exists is the same ; [1] for you cannot find thought
without something that is, as to which it is uttered.[2]   And there
is not, and never shall be, anything besides what is, since fate
has chained it so as to be whole and immovable.   Wherefore all
these things are but names which mortals have given, believing
40 them to be true—coming into being and passing away, being
and not being, change of place and alteration of bright colour.
R. P. 119.

Since, then, it has a furthest limit, it is complete on every
side, like the mass of a rounded sphere, equally poised from the
45 centre in every direction ; for it cannot be greater or smaller in
one place than in another.   For there is no nothing that could
keep it from reaching out equally, nor can aught that is be more
here and less there than what is, since it is all inviolable.   For
the point from which it is equal in every direction tends equally
to the limits.   R. P. 120.

The Way of Belief

50   Here shall I close my trustworthy speech and thought about
the truth.   Henceforward learn the beliefs of mortals, giving ear
to the deceptive ordering of my words.

Mortals have made up their minds to name two forms, one
of which they should not name, and that is where they go astray
55 from the truth.   They have distinguished them as opposite in
form, and have assigned to them marks distinct from one another.
To the one they allot the fire of heaven, gentle, very light, in
every direction the same as itself, but not the same as the other.
The other is just the opposite to. it, dark night, a compact and
60 heavy body.   Of these I tell thee the whole arrangement as it
seems likely ; for so no thought of mortals will ever outstrip
thee.   R. P. 121.

(9)

Now that all things have been named light and night, and
the names which belong to the power of each have been assigned

---

[1] For the construction of ἔστι νοεῖν, see above, p. 173, *n.* 2.
[2] As Diels rightly points out, the Ionic φατίζειν is equivalent to
ὀνομάζειν.   The meaning, I think, is this.   We may name things as we
choose, but there can be no thought corresponding to a name that is not
the name of something real.

to these things and to those, everything is full at once of light and dark night, both equal, since neither has aught to do with the other.

(10, 11)

And thou shalt know the substance of the sky, and all the signs in the sky, and the resplendent works of the glowing sun's pure torch, and whence they arose. And thou shalt learn likewise of the wandering deeds of the round-faced moon, and of her substance. Thou shalt know, too, the heavens that surround 5 us, whence they arose, and how Necessity took them and bound them to keep the limits of the stars . . . how the earth, and the sun, and the moon, and the sky that is common to all, and the Milky Way, and the outermost Olympos, and the burning might of the stars arose. R. P. 123, 124. 10

(12)

The narrower bands were filled with unmixed fire, and those next them with night, and in the midst of these rushes their portion of fire. In the midst of these is the divinity that directs the course of all things ; for she is the beginner of all painful birth and all begetting, driving the female to the embrace of the 5 male, and the male to that of the female. R. P. 125.

(13)

First of all the gods she contrived Eros. R. P. 125.

(14)

Shining by night with borrowed light,[1] wandering round the earth.

(15)

Always looking to the beams of the sun.

(16)

For just as thought stands at any time to the mixture of its erring organs, so does it come to men ; for that which thinks

---

[1] Note the curious echo of *Il.* v. 214. Empedokles has it too (fr. 45). It appears to be a joke, made in the spirit of Xenophanes, when it was first discovered that the moon shone by reflected light. Anaxagoras may have introduced this view to the Athenians (§ 135), but these verses prove it was not originated by him.

is the same, namely, the substance of the limbs, in each and every man; for their thought is that of which there is more in them.[1] R. P. 128.

(17)

On the right boys; on the left girls.[2]

(19)

Thus, according to men's opinions, did things come into being, and thus they are now. In time they will grow up and pass away. To each of these things men have assigned a fixed name. R. P. 129 b.

"It is." 86. In the First Part of his poem, we find Parmenides chiefly interested to prove that *it is*; but it is not quite obvious at first sight what it is precisely that *is*. He says simply, *What is, is*. There can be no real doubt that this is what we call body. It is certainly regarded as spatially extended; for it is quite seriously spoken of as a sphere (fr. 8, 43). Moreover, Aristotle tells us that Parmenides believed in none but a sensible reality.[3] Parmenides does not say a word about "Being" anywhere,[4] and it is remark-

---

[1] This fragment of the theory of knowledge which was expounded in the second part of the poem of Parmenides must be taken in connexion with what we are told by Theophrastos in the "Fragment on Sensation" (*Dox.* p. 499; cf. p. 193). It appears from this that he said the character of men's thought depended upon the preponderance of the light or the dark element in their bodies. They are wise when the light element predominates, and foolish when the dark gets the upper hand.

[2] This is a fragment of Parmenides's embryology. Diels's fr. 18 is a re-translation of the Latin hexameters of Caelius Aurelianus quoted R. P. 127 a.

[3] Arist. *De caelo*, Γ, 1. 298 b 21, ἐκεῖνοι δὲ (οἱ περὶ Μέλισσόν τε καὶ Παρμενίδην) διὰ τὸ μηθὲν μὲν ἄλλο παρὰ τὴν τῶν αἰσθητῶν οὐσίαν ὑπολαμβάνειν εἶναι κτλ. So too Eudemos, in the first book of his Physics (*ap.* Simpl. *Phys.* p. 133, 25), said of Parmenides : τὸ μὲν οὖν κοινὸν οὐκ ἂν λέγοι. οὔτε γὰρ ἐζητεῖτό πω τὰ τοιαῦτα, ἀλλ' ὕστερον ἐκ τῶν λόγων προῆλθεν, οὔτε ἐπιδέχοιτο ἂν ἃ τῷ ὄντι ἐπιλέγει. πῶς γὰρ ἔσται τοῦτο "μέσσοθεν ἰσοπαλὲς" καὶ τὰ τοιαῦτα; τῷ δὲ οὐρανῷ (the world) σχεδὸν πάντες ἐφαρμόσουσιν οἱ τοιοῦτοι λόγοι. The Neoplatonists, of course, saw in the One the νοητὸς κόσμος, and Simplicius calls the sphere a "mythical figment." See especially Bäumker, "Die Einheit des Parmenideischen Seiendes" (*Jahrb. f. kl. Phil.*, 1886, pp. 541 sqq.), and *Das Problem der Materie*, pp. 50 sqq.

[4] We must not render τὸ ἰόν by "Being," *das Sein* or *l'être*. It is "what is," *das Seiende, ce qui est*. As to (τὸ) εἶναι it does not occur, and hardly could occur at this date.

able that he avoids the term " god," which was so freely
used by earlier and later thinkers. The assertion that *it is*
amounts just to this, that the universe is a *plenum* ; and
that there is no such thing as empty space, either inside
or outside the world. From this it follows that there can
be no such thing as motion. Instead of endowing the
One with an impulse to change, as Herakleitos had done,
and thus making it capable of explaining the world, Parmenides dismissed change as an illusion. He showed once
for all that if you take the One seriously you are bound
to deny everything else. All previous solutions of the
question, therefore, had missed the point. Anaximenes,
who thought to save the unity of the primary substance
by his theory of rarefaction and condensation, did not
observe that, by assuming there was less of what is in
one place than another, he virtually affirmed the existence
of what is not (fr. 8, 45). The Pythagorean explanation
implied that empty space or air existed outside the world,
and that it entered into it to separate the units (§ 53).
It, too, assumes the existence of what is not. Nor is the
theory of Herakleitos any more satisfactory ; for it is based
on the contradiction that fire both is and is not (fr. 6).

The allusion to Herakleitos in the verses last referred
to has been doubted, though upon insufficient grounds.
Zeller points out quite rightly that Herakleitos never says
Being and not-Being are the same (the old translation of
fr. 6, 8) ; and, were there nothing more than this, the reference might well seem doubtful. The statement, however,
that, according to the view in question, " all things travel in
opposite directions," can hardly be understood of anything
but the " upward and downward path " of Herakleitos
(§ 71). And, as we have seen, Parmenides does not attribute
the view that Being and not-Being are the same to the
philosopher whom he is attacking ; he only says that *it* is
and is not the same and not the same.[1] That is the natural

[1] See above, fr. 6, *n.* 2.

meaning of the words; and it furnishes a very accurate description of the theory of Herakleitos.

87. The great novelty in the poem of Parmenides is the method of argument. He first asks what is the common presupposition of all the views he has to deal with, and he finds that this is the existence of what is not. The next question is whether this can be thought, and the answer is that it cannot. If you think at all, you must think of something. Therefore there is no nothing. Only that can be which can be thought (fr. 5); for thought exists for the sake of what is (fr. 8, 34).

This method Parmenides carries out with the utmost rigour. He will not have us pretend that we think what we must admit to be unthinkable. It is true that if we resolve to allow nothing but what we can understand, we come into direct conflict with our senses, which present us with a world of change and decay. So much the worse for the senses, says Parmenides. That is the inevitable outcome of a corporeal monism, and this bold declaration of it ought to have destroyed that theory for ever. If Parmenides had lacked courage to work out the prevailing views of his time to their logical conclusion, and to accept that conclusion, however paradoxical it might appear, men might have gone on in the endless circle of opposition, rarefaction, and condensation, one and many, for ever. It was the thorough-going dialectic of Parmenides that made progress possible. Philosophy must now cease to be monistic or cease to be corporealist. It could not cease to be corporealist; for the incorporeal was still unknown. It therefore ceased to be monistic, and arrived ultimately at the atomic theory, which, so far as we know, is the last word of the view that the world is body in motion.[1]

[1] From the point of view we are now taking, it is doubtful if even Atomism can rightly be called Monism, since it implies the real existence of space. The most modern forms of Monism are not corporealist, since they replace body by energy as the ultimate reality.

88. Parmenides goes on to develop all the consequences **The** of the admission that *it is*.   It must be uncreated and inde- **results.** structible.   It cannot have arisen out of nothing ; for there is no such thing as nothing.   Nor can it have arisen from something ; for there is no room for anything but itself. What *is* cannot have beside it any empty space in which something else might arise ; for empty space is nothing, nothing cannot be thought, and therefore cannot exist. What *is* never came into being, nor is anything going to come into being in the future.   " Is it or is it not ? "   If it *is*, then it is now, all at once.

That this is a denial of the existence of empty space was well known to Plato.   He says Parmenides held " all things were one, and that the one remains at rest in itself, *having no place in which to move*." [1]   Aristotle is no less clear. He lays down that Parmenides was driven to take up the position that the One was immovable just because no one had yet imagined there was any reality other than the sensible. [2]

That which is, *is* ; and it cannot be more or less.   There is, therefore, as much of it in one place as in another, and the world is a continuous, indivisible *plenum*.   From this it follows at once that it must be immovable.   If it moved, it must move into an empty space, and there is no empty space.   It is hemmed in by *what is*, by the real, on every side.   For the same reason, it must be finite, and can have nothing beyond it.   It is complete in itself, and has no need to stretch out indefinitely into an empty space that does not exist.   Hence, too, it is spherical.   It is equally real in every direction, and the sphere is the only form that meets this condition.   Any other would *be* in one direction more than in another.

---

[1] Plato, *Theaet.* 180 e 3, ὡς ἕν τε πάντα ἐστὶ καὶ ἕστηκεν αὐτὸ ἐν αὑτῷ οὐκ ἔχον χώραν ἐν ᾗ κινεῖται.   This is explicitly stated by Melissos (fr. 7, p. 323), but Plato clearly meant to ascribe it to Parmenides as well.
[2] Arist. *De caelo*, I´, 1. 298 b 21, quoted above, p. 178, *n.* 3, and the other passages there quoted.

Par-
menides
the
father of
material-
ism.

89. To sum up. What *is*, is a finite, spherical, motion-less corporeal *plenum*, and there is nothing beyond it. The appearances of multiplicity and motion, empty space and time, are illusions. We see from this that the primary substance of which the early cosmologists were in search has now become a sort of " thing in itself." It never quite lost this character again. What appears later as the elements of Empedokles, the so-called " homoeomeries " of Anaxagoras and the atoms of Leukippos and Demokritos, is just the Parmenidean " being." Parmenides is not, as some have said, the " father of idealism " ; on the contrary, all materialism depends on his view of reality.

90. It is commonly held that, in the Second Part of his poem, Parmenides offered a dualistic theory of the origin of things as his own conjectural explanation of the sensible world, or that, as Gomperz says, " What he offered were the Opinions of Mortals ; and this description did not merely cover other people's opinions. It included his own as well, as far as they were not confined to the unassailable ground of an apparent philosophical necessity." [1] Now it is true that in one place Aristotle appears to countenance a view of this sort, but nevertheless it is an anachronism.[2] Nor is it really Aristotle's view. He was well aware that Parmenides did not admit the existence of " not-being " in any degree whatever ; but it was a natural way of speaking to call the cosmology of the Second Part of the poem that of Parmenides. His hearers would understand in what sense this was meant. At any rate, the Peripatetic tradition was that Parmenides, in the Second Part of the poem, meant to give the belief of " the many." This is how Theophrastos put the matter,

---

[1] *Greek Thinkers*, vol. i. pp. 180 *sqq.*

[2] *Met.* A, 5. 986 b 31 (R. P. 121 a). Aristotle's way of putting the matter is due to his interpretation of fr. 8, 54, which he took to mean that one of the two " forms " was to be identified with τὸ ὄν and the other with τὸ μὴ ὄν. Cf. *De gen. corr.* A, 3. 318 b 6, ὥσπερ Παρμενίδης λέγει δύο, τὸ ὄν καὶ τὸ μὴ ὄν εἶναι φάσκων. This last sentence shows clearly that when Aristotle says Παρμενίδης, he sometimes means what we should call " Parmenides."

and Alexander seems to have spoken of the cosmology as something which Parmenides himself regarded as wholly false.[1] The other view comes from the Neoplatonists, and especially Simplicius, who regarded the Way of Truth as an account of the intelligible world, and the Way of Opinion as a description of the sensible. It need hardly be said that this is almost as great an anachronism as the Kantian parallelism suggested by Gomperz.[2] Parmenides himself tells us in the most unequivocal language that there is no truth at all in the theory which he expounds, and that he gives it merely as the belief of " mortals." It was this that led Theophrastos to speak of it as the opinion of " the many."

His explanation however, though preferable to that of Simplicius, is not convincing either. " The many " are as far as possible from believing in an elaborate dualism such as Parmenides expounded, and it is a highly artificial hypothesis to assume that he wished to show how the popular view of the world could best be systematised. " The many " would hardly be convinced of their error by having their beliefs presented to them in a form they would certainly fail to recognise them in. This, indeed, seems the most incredible interpretation of all. It still, however, finds adherents, so it is necessary to point out that the beliefs in question are only called " the opinions of mortals " for the very simple reason that the speaker is a goddess. Further, we have to note that Parmenides forbids two ways of research, and we have seen that the second of these, which is also expressly ascribed to " mortals," must be the system of Herakleitos. We should expect, then, to find that the other way is also the system of some contemporary school,

[1] Theophr. *Phys. Op.* fr. 6 (*Dox.* p. 482 ; R. P. 121 a), κατὰ δόξαν δὲ τῶν πολλῶν εἰς τὸ γένεσιν ἀποδοῦναι τῶν φαινομένων δύο ποιῶν τὰς ἀρχάς. For Alexander, cf. Simpl. *Phys.* p. 38, 24, εἰ δὲ ψευδεῖς πάντη τοὺς λόγους οἴεται ἐκείνους (᾽Αλέξανδρος) κτλ.

[2] Simpl. *Phys.* p. 39, 10 (R. P. 121 b). Gomperz, *Greek Thinkers,* vol. i. p. 180.

and it seems hard to discover any of sufficient importance at this date except the Pythagorean. Now it is admitted by every one that there are Pythagorean ideas in the Second Part of the poem, and it is therefore to be presumed, in the absence of evidence to the contrary, that the whole of its cosmology comes from the same source. It does not appear that Parmenides said any more about Herakleitos than the words to which we have just referred, in which he forbids the second way of inquiry. He implies, indeed, that there are really only two ways that can be thought of, and that the attempt of Herakleitos to combine them was futile.[1] In any case, the Pythagoreans were far more serious opponents at that date in Italy, and it is certainly to them that we should expect Parmenides to define his attitude.

It is still not quite clear, however, why he should have thought it worth while to put into hexameters a view he believed to be false. Here it becomes important to remember that he had been a Pythagorean himself, and that the poem is a renunciation of his former beliefs. In the introductory verses, he tells us distinctly that he has passed from darkness into the light. In such cases men commonly feel the necessity of showing where their old views were wrong. The goddess tells him that he must learn of those beliefs also "how one ought to pass right through all things and judge the things that seem to be." We get a further hint in another place. He is to learn these beliefs, "and so no opinion of mortals will ever get the better of him" (fr. 8, 61). If we remember that the Pythagorean system at this time was handed down by oral tradition alone, we shall see what this may mean. Parmenides was founding a dissident school, and it was necessary for him to instruct his disciples in the system they might be called upon to oppose. In any case, they could not reject it intelligently without

---

[1] Cf. frs. 4 and 6, especially the words αἵπερ ὁδοὶ μοῦναι διζήσιός εἰσι νοῆσαι. The third way, that of Herakleitos, is only added as an afterthought—αὐτὰρ ἔπειτ᾽ ἀπὸ τῆς κτλ.

a knowledge of it, and this Parmenides had to supply himself.[1]

91. The view that the Second Part of the poem of Parmenides was a sketch of contemporary Pythagorean cosmology is, doubtless, incapable of rigorous demonstration, but it can be made extremely probable.   The entire history of Pythagoreanism up to the end of the fifth century B.C. is certainly conjectural ; but, if we find in Parmenides ideas wholly unconnected with his own view of the world, and if we find precisely the same ideas in later Pythagoreanism, the most natural inference will be that the later Pythagoreans derived these views from their predecessors, and that they formed part of the original stock-in-trade of the society.   This will be confirmed if we find that they are developments of certain features in the old Ionian cosmology. Pythagoras came from Samos, and it was not, so far as we can see, in his cosmological views that he chiefly displayed originality.   It has been pointed out (§ 53) that the idea of the world breathing came from Anaximenes, and we need not be surprised to find traces of Anaximander too.   Now, if we were confined to what Aristotle tells us on this subject, it would be hard to make out a case ; but his statements require, as usual, to be examined with care.   He says, first of all, that the two elements of Parmenides were the Warm and the Cold.[2]   In this he is so far justified by the fragments that, since the Fire of which Parmenides speaks is, of course, warm, the other " form," which has all the opposite qualities, must of necessity be cold.   Here, then, we have the traditional " opposites " of the Milesians.   Aristotle's identifica-

The dualist cosmology.

---

[1] I read χρῆν δοκιμῶσ' εἶναι in fr. 1, 32 with Diels.   The view that the opinions contained in the Second Part are those of others, and are not given as true in any sense whatsoever, is shared by Diels. The objections of Wilamowitz (Hermes, xxxiv. pp. 203 sqq.) do not appear to me cogent.   If we interpret him rightly, Parmenides never says that " this hypothetical explanation is . . . better than that of any one else."   What he does say is that it is untrue altogether.

[2] Met. A, 5. 986 b 34, θερμὸν καὶ ψυχρόν; Phys. A, 5. 188 a 20; De gen. corr. A, 3. 318 b 6 ; B, 3. 330 b 14.

G

tion of these with Fire and Earth is, however, misleading, though Theophrastos followed him in it.[1] Simplicius, who had the poem before him (§ 85), after mentioning Fire and Earth, at once adds " or rather Light and Darkness " ;[2] and this is suggestive. Lastly, Aristotle's identification of the dense element with " what is not," [3] the unreal of the First Part of the poem, is not easy to reconcile with the view that it is earth. On the other hand, if we suppose that the second of the two " forms," the one which should not have been " named," is the Pythagorean Air or Void, we get a very good explanation of Aristotle's identification of it with " what is not." We seem, then, to be justified in neglecting the identification of the dense element with earth for the present. At a later stage, we shall be able to see how it may have originated.[4] The further statement of Theophrastos, that the Warm was the efficient cause and the Cold the material or passive,[5] is not, of course, to be regarded as historical.

We have seen that Simplicius, with the poem of Parmenides before him, corrects Aristotle by substituting Light and Darkness for Fire and Earth, and he is amply borne out by the fragments he quotes. Parmenides himself calls one " form " Light, Flame, and Fire, and the other Night, and we have now to consider whether these can be identified with the Pythagorean Limit and Unlimited. We have seen good reason to believe (§ 58) that the idea of the world breathing belonged to the earliest form of Pythagoreanism, and there can be no difficulty in identifying this " boundless breath " with Darkness, which stands very well for the

[1] *Phys.* A, 5. 188 a 21, ταῦτα δὲ (θερμὸν καὶ ψυχρὸν) προσαγορεύει πῦρ καὶ γῆν ; *Met.* A, 5. 986 b 34, οἷον πῦρ καὶ γῆν λέγων. Cf. Theophr. *Phys. Op.* fr. 6 (*Dox.* p. 482 ; R. P. 121 a).

[2] *Phys.* p. 25, 15, ὡς Παρμενίδης ἐν τοῖς πρὸς δόξαν πῦρ καὶ γῆν (ἢ μᾶλλον φῶς καὶ σκότος). So already Plut. *Adv. Col.* 1114 b, τὸ λαμπρὸν καὶ σκοτεινόν.

[3] *Met.* A, 5. 986 b 35, τούτων δὲ κατὰ μὲν τὸ ὂν τὸ θερμὸν τάττει, θάτερον δὲ κατὰ τὸ μὴ ὄν. See above, p. 182, *n.* 2.

[4] See below, Chap. VII. § 147.

[5] Theophr. *Phys. Op.* fr. 6 (*Dox.* p. 482 ; R. P. 121 a), followed by the doxographers.

Unlimited. " Air " or mist was always regarded as the
dark element.[1] And that which gives definiteness to the
vague darkness is certainly light or fire, and this may
account for the prominence given to that element by
Hippasos.[2] We may probably conclude, then, that the
Pythagorean distinction between the Limit and the Unlimited, which we shall have to consider later (Chap. VII.),
made its first appearance in this crude form. If, on the
other hand, we identify darkness with the Limit, and light
with the Unlimited, as many critics do, we get into insuper-
able difficulties.

92. We must now look at the general cosmical view   The
expounded in the Second Part of the poem.   The fragments   heavenly
                                                              bodies.
are scanty, and the doxographical tradition hard to interpret ; but enough remains to show that here, too, we are
on Pythagorean ground.   Aetios says :

> Parmenides held that there were bands crossing one another [3]
> and encircling one another, formed of the rare and the dense
> element respectively, and that between these there were other
> mixed bands made up of light and darkness. That which
> surrounds them all was solid like a wall, and under it is a fiery
> band. That which is in the middle of all the bands is also solid,
> and surrounded in turn by a fiery band. The central circle
> of the mixed bands is the cause of movement and becoming to
> all the rest. He calls it " the goddess who directs their course,"
> "the Holder of Lots," and "Necessity."—Aet. ii. 7. 1 (R. P. 126).

93. Now it is quite unjustifiable to regard these " bands "   The
as spheres.   The word στέφαναι can mean " rims " or   στέφαναι.

---

[1] Note the identification of the dense element with " air " in [Plut.]
Strom. fr. 5 (*Dox.* p. 581), λέγει δὲ τὴν γῆν τοῦ πυκνοῦ καταρρυέντος ἀέρος
γεγονέναι. This is pure Anaximenes. For the identification of this
" air " with " mist and darkness," cf. Chap. I. § 27, and Chap. V. § 107.
It is to be observed further that Plato puts this last identification into
the mouth of a Pythagorean (*Tim.* 52 d).

[2] See above, p. 109.

[3] It seems most likely that ἐπαλλήλους here means " crossing one
another," as the Milky Way crosses the Zodiac. The term ἐπάλληλος is
opposed to παράλληλος.

" brims " or anything of that sort,[1] but it seems incredible
that it should be used of spheres. It does not appear,
either, that the solid circle which surrounds all the crowns is
to be regarded as spherical. The expression " like a wall "
would be highly inappropriate in that case.[2] We seem, then,
to be face to face with something like the " wheels " of
Anaximander, and it is highly probable that Pythagoras
adopted the theory from him. Nor is evidence lacking
that the Pythagoreans did regard the heavenly bodies in
this way. In Plato's Myth of Er, which is certainly Pythagorean in its general character, we do not hear of spheres,
but of the " lips " of concentric whorls fitted into one another
like a nest of boxes.[3] In the *Timaeus* there are no spheres
either, but bands or strips crossing each other at an angle.[4]
Lastly, in the Homeric *Hymn to Ares*, which seems to have
been composed under Pythagorean influence, the word
used for the orbit of the planet is ἄντυξ, which must mean
" rim."[5]

The fact is, there is no evidence that any one ever adopted
the theory of celestial spheres, till Aristotle turned the
geometrical construction which Eudoxos had set up as a
hypothesis " to save appearances " (σῴζειν τὰ φαινόμενα)

---

[1] As Diels points out, στεφάνη in Homer is used of a golden band in
the hair (Σ 597) or the brim of a helmet (Η 12). It may be added that it
was used technically of the figure contained between two concentric circles
(Proclus, *in Eucl. I.* p. 163, 12). It always means something annular.

[2] It must be remembered that τεῖχος is a city-wall or fortification,
and that Euripides uses στεφάνη for a city-wall (*Hec.* 910). Heath's
remark (p. 69) that " certainly Parmenides' All was spherical " is irrelevant.
We have nothing to do with his own views here.

[3] *Rep.* x. 616 d 5, καθάπερ οἱ κάδοι οἱ εἰς ἀλλήλους ἁρμόττοντες ; e 1,
κύκλους ἄνωθεν τὰ χείλη φαίνοντας (σφονδύλους).

[4] *Tim.* 36 b 6, ταύτην οὖν τὴν σύστασιν πᾶσαν διπλῆν κατὰ μῆκος σχίσας,
μέσην πρὸς μέσην ἑκατέραν ἀλλήλαις οἷον χεῖ (the letter X) προσβαλὼν
κατέκαμψεν εἰς ἓν κύκλῳ.

[5] *Hymn to Ares*, 6 :   πυραυγέα κύκλον ἑλίσσων
    αἰθέρος ἑπταπόροις ἐνὶ τείρεσιν, ἔνθα σε πῶλοι
    ζαφλεγέες τριτάτης ὑπὲρ ἄντυγος αἰὲν ἔχουσι.

So, in allusion to an essentially Pythagorean view, Proclus says to the
planet Venus (h. iv. 17) :

    εἴτε καὶ ἑπτὰ κύκλων ὑπὲρ ἄντυγας αἰθέρα ναίεις.

into real things.[1] At this date, spheres would not have served to explain anything that could not be explained more simply without them.

We are next told that these " bands " encircle one another or are folded over one another, and that they are made of the rare and the dense element. We also learn that between them are " mixed bands " made up of light and darkness. Now it is to be observed, in the first place, that light and darkness are exactly the same thing as the rare and the dense, and it looks as if there was some confusion here. It may be doubted whether these statements are based on anything else than fr. 12, which might certainly be interpreted to mean that between the bands of fire there were bands of night with a portion of fire in them. That may be right ; but I think it rather more natural to understand the passage as saying that the narrower circles are surrounded by wider circles of night, and that each has its portion of fire rushing in the midst of it. These last words would then be a simple repetition of the statement that the narrower circles are filled with unmixed fire,[2] and we should have a fairly exact description of the " wheels " of Anaximander.

94. " In the middle of those," says Parmenides, " is the goddess who steers the course of all things." Aetios explains this to mean in the middle of the " mixed bands," while Simplicius declares that it means in the middle of all the bands, that is to say, in the centre of the world.[3] It is not likely that either of them had anything better to go upon than the words of Parmenides himself, and these are ambiguous. Simplicius, as is clear from the language he

The goddess.

---

[1] On the concentric spheres of Eudoxos, see Heath, pp. 193 sqq.

[2] Such a repetition (παλινδρομία) is characteristic of all Greek style, but the repetition at the end of the period generally adds a new touch to the statement at the opening. The new touch is here given in the word ἵεται. I do not press this interpretation, but it seems to me much simpler than that of Diels, who has to take "night" as equivalent to "earth," since he identifies it with the στερεόν.

[3] Simpl. Phys. p. 34, 14 (R. P. 125 b).

uses, identified this goddess with the Pythagorean Hestia
or central fire, while Theophrastos could not do that, because
he knew and stated that Parmenides described the earth as
round and in the centre of the world.[1] In this very passage
we are told that what is in the middle of all the bands is
solid. The data furnished by Theophrastos, in fact, exclude
the identification of the goddess with the central fire altogether. We cannot say that what is in the middle of *all*
the bands is solid, and that under it there is again a fiery
band.[2] Nor does it seem fitting to relegate a goddess to the
middle of a solid spherical earth.

We are further told by Aetios that this goddess was called
Ananke and the " Holder of Lots." [3] We know already
that she " steers the course of all things," that is, that she
regulates the motions of the celestial bands. Simplicius
adds, unfortunately without quoting the actual words, that
she sends souls at one time from the light to the unseen
world, at another from the unseen world to the light.[4] It
would be difficult to describe more exactly what the goddess
does in the Myth of Er, and so here once more we seem to
be on Pythagorean ground. It is to be noticed further that
in fr. 10 we read how Ananke took the heavens and com-

---

[1] Diog. ix. 21, πρῶτος δ' αὐτὸς τὴν γῆν ἀπέφηνε σφαιροειδῆ καὶ ἐν
μέσῳ κεῖσθαι. Cf. viii. 48 (of Pythagoras), ἀλλὰ μὴν καὶ τὸν οὐρανὸν
πρῶτον ὀνομάσαι κόσμον καὶ τὴν γῆν στρογγύλην (cf. Plato, *Phaed.* 97 d), ὡς
δὲ Θεόφραστος, Παρμενίδην. This appears to justify us in ascribing the
doctrine of a spherical earth to Pythagoras (cf. p. 111).

[2] I do not discuss the interpretation of περὶ δ πάλιν πυρώδης which
Diels gave in *Parmenides Lehrgedicht*, p. 104, and which is adopted in
R. P. 162 a, as it is now virtually retracted. In the later editions of his
Vorsokratiker (18 A 37) he reads καὶ τὸ μεσαίτατον πασῶν (sc. τῶν στεφανῶν)
στερεόν, ⟨ὑφ' ᾧ⟩ πάλιν πυρώδης (sc. στεφάνη). That is a flat contradiction.

[3] R. P. 126, where Fülleborn's ingenious emendation κληδοῦχον for
κληροῦχον is tacitly adopted. This is based upon the view that Aetios (or
Theophrastos) was thinking of the goddess that keeps the keys in the
Proem (fr. 1, 14). I now think that the κλῆροι of the Myth of Er give
the true explanation.

[4] Simpl. *Phys.* p. 39, 19, καὶ τὰς ψυχὰς πέμπειν ποτὲ μὲν ἐκ τοῦ ἐμφανοῦς
εἰς τὸ ἀειδές (i.e. ἀιδές), ποτὲ δὲ ἀνάπαλίν φησιν. We should probably
connect this with the statement of Diog. ix. 22 (R. P. 127) that men arose
from the sun (reading ἡλίου with the MSS. for the conjecture ἰλύος).

pelled them to hold fast the fixed courses of the stars, and that in fr. 12 we are told that she is the beginner of all pairing and birth. Lastly, in fr. 13 we hear that she created Eros first of all the gods. So we shall find that in Empedokles it is an ancient oracle or decree of Ananke that causes the gods to fall and become incarnate in a cycle of births.[1]

We should be more certain of the place this goddess occupies in the universe if we could be sure where Ananke is in the Myth of Er. Without, however, raising that vexed question, we may lay down with some confidence that, according to Theophrastos, she occupied a position midway between the earth and the heavens. Whether we believe in the " mixed bands " or not makes no difference in this respect ; for the statement of Aetios that she was in the middle of the mixed bands undoubtedly implies that she was between earth and heaven. Now she is identified with one of the bands in a somewhat confused passage of Cicero,[2] and the whole theory of wheels or bands was probably suggested by the Milky Way. It seems to me, therefore, that we must think of the Milky Way as a band intermediate between those of the Sun and the Moon, and this agrees very well with the prominent way in which it is mentioned in fr. 11. It is better not to be too positive about the other details, though it is interesting to notice that according to some it was Pythagoras, and according to others Parmenides, who discovered the identity of the evening and morning star.[3]

---

[1] Empedokles, fr. 115.

[2] Cicero, De nat. d. i. 11, 28 : " Nam Parmenides quidem commenticium quiddam coronae simile efficit (στεφάνην appellat), continente ardore lucis orbem, qui cingat caelum, quem appellat deum." We may connect with this the statement of Aetios, ii. 20, 8, τὸν ἥλιον καὶ τὴν σελήνην ἐκ τοῦ γαλαξίου κύκλου ἀποκριθῆναι.

[3] Diog. ix. 23, καὶ δοκεῖ (Παρμενίδης) πρῶτος πεφωρακέναι τὸν αὐτὸν εἶναι Ἕσπερον καὶ Φωσφόρον, ὥς φησι Φαβωρῖνος ἐν πέμπτῳ Ἀπομνημονευμάτων· οἱ δὲ Πυθαγόραν. Cf. viii. 14 (of Pythagoras), πρῶτόν τε Ἕσπερον καὶ Φωσφόρον τὸν αὐτὸν εἰπεῖν, ὥς φησι Παρμενίδης. So Diels now reads with all the MSS. (the vulgate οἱ δέ φασι Παρμενίδην is due to Casaubon). It is not necessary to suppose that Parmenides made this statement explicitly in his poem ; there may have been an unmistakable allusion, as in Empedokles, fr. 129. In that case, we should have a

Besides all this, it is certain that Parmenides went on to describe how the other gods were born and how they fell, an idea which we know to be Orphic, and which may well have been Pythagorean. We shall come to it again in Empedokles. In Plato's *Symposium*, Agathon couples Parmenides with Hesiod as a narrator of ancient deeds of violence committed by the gods.[1] If Parmenides was expounding the Pythagorean theology, this is just what we should expect ; but it seems hopeless to explain it on any of the other theories which have been advanced on the purpose of the Way of Belief.[2] Such things belong to theological speculation, and not to the beliefs of "the many." Still less can we think it probable that Parmenides made up these stories himself to show what the popular view of the world really implied if properly formulated. We must ask, I think, that any theory shall account for what was evidently no inconsiderable portion of the poem.

Physio-logy.   95. In describing the views of his contemporaries, Parmenides was obliged, as we see from the fragments, to say a good deal about physiological matters. Like everything else, man was composed of the warm and the cold, and death was caused by the removal of the warm. Some curious views with regard to generation were also stated. In the first place, males came from the right side and females from the left. Women had more of the warm and men of the cold, a view we shall find Empedokles contradicting.[3] It is the proportion of the warm and cold in men that deter-

---

remarkable confirmation of the view that the Δόξα of Parmenides was Pythagorean. If, as Achilles says, the poet Ibykos of Rhegion had anticipated Parmenides in announcing this discovery, that is to be explained by the fact that Rhegion became for a time, as we shall see, the chief seat of the Pythagorean school.

[1] Plato, *Symp.* 195 c 1. It is implied that these παλαιὰ πράγματα were πολλὰ καὶ βίαια, including ἐκτομαί and δεσμοί. The Epicurean criticism of this is partially preserved in Philodemos, *De pietate*, p. 68, Gomperz ; and Cicero, *De nat. d.* i. 28 (*Dox.* p. 534 ; R. P. 126 b).

[2] For these theories, see § 90.

[3] For all this, see R. P. 127 a, with Arist. *De part. an.* B, 2. 648 a 28 ; *De gen. an.* Δ, 1. 765 b 19.

mines the character of their thought, so that even corpses, from which the warm has been removed, retain a perception of what is cold and dark.[1] These fragments of information do not tell us much when taken by themselves ; but they connect themselves in an interesting way with the history of medicine, and point to the fact that one of its leading schools stood in close relation with the Pythagorean Society. Even before the days of Pythagoras, we know that Kroton was famous for its doctors.[2] We also know the name of a very distinguished medical writer who lived at Kroton in the days between Pythagoras and Parmenides, and the few facts we are told about him enable us to regard the physiological views described by Parmenides not as isolated curiosities, but as landmarks by which we can trace the origin and growth of one of the most influential of medical theories, that which explains health as a balance of opposites.

96. Aristotle tells us that Alkmaion of Kroton[3] was a young man in the old age of Pythagoras. He does not actually say, as later writers do, that he was a Pythagorean, though he points out that he seems either to have derived his theory of opposites from the Pythagoreans or they theirs from him.[4] In any case, he was intimately connected with the society, as is proved by one of the scanty fragments of his book. It began as follows : " Alkmaion of Kroton, son of Peirithous, spoke these words to Brotinos and Leon and Bathyllos. As to things invisible and things mortal, the gods have certainty ; but, so far as men may infer . . ."[5]

Alkmaion of Kroton.

---

[1] Theophr. De sens. 3, 4 (R. P. 129).   [2] See p. 89, n. 2.

[3] On Alkmaion, see especially Wachtler, De Alcmaeone Crotoniata (Leipzig, 1896).

[4] Arist. Met. A, 5. 986 a 27 (R. P. 66). In a 30 Diels reads, with great probability, ἐγένετο τὴν ἡλικίαν ⟨κέος⟩ ἐπὶ γέροντι Πυθαγόρᾳ. Cf. Iambl. V. Pyth. 104, where Alkmaion is mentioned among the συγχρονίσαντες καὶ μαθητεύσαντες τῷ Πυθαγόρᾳ πρεσβύτῃ νέοι.

[5] Ἀλκμαίων Κροτωνιήτης τάδε ἔλεξε Πειρίθου υἱὸς Βροτίνῳ καὶ Λέοντι καὶ Βαθύλλῳ· περὶ τῶν ἀφανέων, περὶ τῶν θνητῶν, σαφήνειαν μὲν θεοὶ ἔχοντι, ὡς δὲ ἀνθρώποις τεκμαίρεσθαι καὶ τὰ ἑξῆς (fr. 1, Diels, Vors. 14 B 1). The fact that this is not written in conventional Doric is a strong proof of its genuineness.

The quotation unfortunately ends in this abrupt way, but we learn two things from it. In the first place, Alkmaion possessed that reserve which marks all the best Greek medical writers ; and in the second place, he dedicated his work to the heads of the Pythagorean Society.[1]

Alkmaion's importance really lies in the fact that he is the founder of empirical psychology.[2] He regarded the brain as the common sensorium, a view which Hippokrates and Plato adopted from him, though Empedokles, Aristotle, and the Stoics reverted to the more primitive view that the heart is the central organ of sense. There is no reason to doubt that he made this discovery by anatomical means. We have authority for saying that he practised dissection, and, though the nerves were not yet recognised as such, it was known that there were certain " passages " ($\pi \acute{o} \rho o \iota$) which might be prevented from communicating sensations to the brain by lesions.[3] He also distinguished between sensation and understanding, though we have no means of knowing where he drew the line between them. His theories of the special senses are of great interest. We find in him already, what is characteristic of Greek theories of vision as a whole, the attempt to combine the view of vision as a radiation proceeding from the eye with that which attributes it to an image reflected in the eye. He knew the importance of air for the sense of hearing, though he called it the void, a thoroughly Pythagorean touch. With regard to the other senses, our information is more

---

[1] Brotinos (or Brontinos) is variously described as the son-in-law or father-in-law of Pythagoras. Leon is one of the Metapontines in the catalogue of Iamblichos (Diels, *Vors.* 45 A), and Bathyllos is presumably the Poseidoniate Bathylaos also mentioned there.

[2] Everything bearing on the early history of this subject is brought together and discussed in Prof. Beare's *Greek Theories of Elementary Cognition*, to which I must refer the reader for all details.

[3] Theophr. *De sens.* 26 (Beare, p. 252, *n.* 1). Our authority for the dissections of Alkmaion is only Chalcidius, but he gets his information on such matters from far older sources. The $\pi \acute{o} \rho o \iota$ and the inference from lesions are vouched for by Theophrastos.

scanty, but sufficient to show that he treated the subject systematically.[1]

His astronomy seems very crude for one who stood in close relations with the Pythagoreans. We are told that he adopted Anaximenes' theory of the sun and Herakleitos's explanation of eclipses.[2] If, however, we were right in holding that the Second Part of the poem of Parmenides represents the view of Pythagoras, we see that he had not gone very far beyond the Milesians in such matters. His theory of the heavenly bodies was still " meteorological." It is all the more remarkable that Alkmaion is credited with the view that the planets have an orbital motion in the opposite direction to the diurnal revolution of the heavens. This view, which he may have learnt from Pythagoras, would naturally be suggested by the difficulties we noted in the system of Anaximander.[3] It doubtless stood in close connexion with his saying that soul was immortal because it resembled immortal things, and was always in motion like the heavenly bodies.[4] He seems, in fact, to be the author of the curious view Plato put into the mouth of the Pythagorean Timaios, that the soul has circles in it revolving just as the heavens and the planets do. This too seems to be the explanation of his further statement that man dies because he cannot join the beginning to the end.[5] The orbits of the heavenly bodies always come full circle, but the circles in the human head may fail to complete themselves.

Alkmaion's theory of health as " isonomy " is at once that which most clearly connects him with earlier inquirers

---

[1] The details will be found in Beare, pp. 11 sqq. (vision), pp. 93 sqq. (hearing), pp. 131 sqq. (smell), pp. 180 sqq. (touch), pp. 160 sqq. (taste).

[2] Aet. ii. 22, 4, πλατὺν εἶναι τὸν ἥλιον ; 29, 3, κατὰ τὴν τοῦ σκαφοειδοῦς στροφὴν καὶ τὰς περικλίσεις (ἐκλείπειν τὴν σελήνην).

[3] Aet. ii. 16, 2, (τῶν μαθηματικῶν τινες) τοὺς πλανήτας τοῖς ἀπλάνεσιν ἀπὸ δυσμῶν ἐπ' ἀνατολὰς ἀντιφέρεσθαι. τούτῳ δὲ συνομολογεῖ καὶ Ἀλκμαίων. For the difficulties in Anaximander's system see p. 69 sq.

[4] Arist. De an. A, 2. 405 a 30 (R. P. 66 c).

[5] Arist. Probl. 17, 3. 916 a 33, τοὺς ἀνθρώπους φησὶν Ἀλκμαίων διὰ τοῦτο ἀπόλλυσθαι, ὅτι οὐ δύνανται τὴν ἀρχὴν τῷ τέλει προσάψαι.

like Anaximander, and also that which had the greatest influence on the subsequent development of philosophy. He observed, to begin with, that " most things human were two," and by this he meant that man was made up of the hot and the cold, the moist and the dry, and the rest of the opposites.[1] Disease was just the " monarchy " of any one of these—the same thing that Anaximander had called " injustice "—while health was the establishment in the body of a free government with equal laws.[2] This was the leading doctrine of the Sicilian school of medicine, and we shall have to consider in the sequel its influence on the development of Pythagoreanism. Taken along with the theory of " pores," it is of the greatest importance for later science.

[1] Arist. *Met.* A, 5. 986 a 27 (R. P. 66).

[2] Aet. v. 30, 1, 'Αλκμαίων τῆς μὲν ὑγιείας εἶναι συνεκτικὴν τὴν ἰσονομίαν τῶν δυνάμεων, ὑγροῦ, ξηροῦ, ψυχροῦ, θερμοῦ, πικροῦ, γλυκέος, καὶ τῶν λοιπῶν, τὴν δ' ἐν αὐτοῖς μοναρχίαν νόσου ποιητικήν· φθοροποιὸν γὰρ ἑκατέρου μοναρχίαν.

CHAPTER V

EMPEDOKLES OF AKRAGAS

97. THE belief that all things are one was common to the Pluralism. early Ionians ; but now Parmenides has shown that, if this one thing really *is*, we must give up the idea that it can take different forms. The senses, which present to us a world of change and multiplicity, are deceitful. There seemed to be no escape from his arguments, and so we find that from this time onwards all the thinkers in whose hands philosophy made progress abandoned the monistic hypothesis. Those who still held by it adopted a critical attitude, and confined themselves to a defence of the theory of Parmenides against the new views. Others taught the doctrine of Herakleitos in an exaggerated form ; some continued to expound the systems of the early Milesians ; but the leading men are all pluralists. The corporealist hypothesis had proved unable to bear the weight of a monistic structure.

98. Empedokles was a citizen of Akragas in Sicily. He Date of Empe-
dokles. was the only native citizen of a Dorian state who plays an important part in the history of philosophy.[1] His father's name, according to the best accounts, was Meton.[2] His grandfather, also called Empedokles, had won a victory in the horse-race at Olympia in Ol. LXXI. (496–95 B.C.),[3] and

[1] See, however, Introd. § II (p. 3).

[2] Aet. i. 3, 20 (R. P. 164), Apollodoros *ap.* Diog. viii. 52 (R. P. 162). The details of the life of Empedokles are discussed, with a careful criticism of the sources, by Bidez, *La Biographie d'Empédocle* (Gand, 1894).

[3] For this we have the authority of Apollodoros (Diog. viii. 51, 52 : R. P. 162), who follows the *Olympic Victors* of Eratosthenes, who followed Aristotle. Herakleides, in his Περὶ νόσων (see below, p. 200, *n.* 5), spoke of

Apollodoros fixed the *floruit* of Empedokles himself in Ol. LXXXIV. 1 (444–43 B.C.). That is the date of the foundation of Thourioi ; and it appears from the quotation in Diogenes that the fifth-century biographer, Glaukos of Rhegion,[1] said Empedokles visited the new city shortly after its foundation. But we are not bound to believe that he was just forty years old at the time. That is the usual assumption of Apollodoros ; but there are reasons for thinking that his date is considerably too late.[2] It is more likely that Empedokles did not go to Thourioi till after his banishment from Akragas, and he may well have been more than forty years old when that happened. All, therefore, we can be said to know is, that his grandfather was still alive in 496 B.C. ; that he himself was active at Akragas after 472, the date of Theron's death ; and that he died later than 444.

Empe-
dokles
as a
politician.

99. Empedokles certainly played an important part in the political events which followed the death of Theron. The Sicilian historian Timaios seems to have treated these fully, and tells some stories which are obviously genuine traditions picked up about a hundred and fifty years after-

---

the elder Empedokles as a " breeder of horses " (R. P. 162 a) ; and Timaios mentioned him in his Fifteenth Book. Satyros confused him with his grandson.

[1] Glaukos wrote Περὶ τῶν ἀρχαίων ποιητῶν καὶ μουσικῶν, and is said to have been contemporary with Demokritos (Diog. ix. 38). Apollodoros adds (R. P. 162) that, according to Aristotle and Herakleides, Empedokles died at the age of sixty. It is to be observed, however, that the words ἔτι δ' Ἡρακλείδης are Sturz's conjecture, the MSS. having ἔτι δ' Ἡράκλειτον, and Diogenes certainly said (ix. 3) that Herakleitos lived sixty years. On the other hand, if the statement of Aristotle comes from the Περὶ ποιητῶν, it is not obvious why he should mention Herakleitos at all ; and Herakleides was one of the chief sources for the biography of Empedokles. The names are often confused.

[2] See Diels, " Empedokles und Gorgias," 2 (*Berl. Sitzb.*, 1884). Theophrastos said (*Dox.* p. 477, 17) that Empedokles was born " not long after Anaxagoras," *i.e.* not long after 500 B.C. (see below, § 120). As he was certainly later than Parmenides, this is a fresh ground for following Plato in making Parmenides some fifteen years older than Apollodoros does (see above, § 84). In general it should be noted that the epoch of Thourioi has misled Apollodoros in many cases. Almost every one who had anything to do with Thourioi (*e.g.* Herodotos, Protagoras) is said to have been born in 484 B.C.

wards. Like all popular traditions, however, they are a little confused. The picturesque incidents are remembered, but the essential parts of the story are dropped. Still, we may be thankful that the " collector of old wives' tales," [1] as his critics called him, has enabled us to measure the historical importance of Empedokles for ourselves by showing us how he was pictured by the great-grandchildren of his contemporaries.[2] All the tales are intended to show the strength of his democratic convictions, and we are told, in particular, that he broke up the assembly of the Thousand—perhaps some oligarchical association or club.[3] It may have been for this that he was offered the kingship, which Aristotle tells us he refused.[4] At any rate, we see that Empedokles was the great democratic leader at Akragas in those days, though we have no clear knowledge of what he did.

100. But there is another side to his public character which Timaios found it hard to reconcile with his political views. He claimed to be a god, and to receive the homage of his fellow-citizens in that capacity. The truth is, Empedokles was not a mere statesman ; he had a good deal of the " medicine-man " about him. According to Satyros,[5]

Empedokles as a religious teacher.

---

[1] He is called γραοσυλλέκτρια in Souidas, *s.v.*

[2] For instance Timaios (*ap*. Diog. viii. 64) said that once he was invited to sup with one of the magistrates. Supper was well advanced, but no wine was brought in. The rest of the company said nothing, but Empedokles was indignant, and insisted on its being served. The host, however, said he was waiting for the Sergeant of the Council. When that official arrived, he was appointed ruler of the feast. The host, of course, appointed him. Thereupon he began to give signs of an incipient tyranny. He ordered the company either to drink or have the wine poured over their heads. Empedokles said nothing, but next day he brought both of them before the court and had them put to death— both the man who asked him to supper and the ruler of the feast ! The story reminds us of an accusation of *incivisme* under the Terror.

[3] Diog. viii. 66, ὕστερον δ' ὁ Ἐμπεδοκλῆς καὶ τὸ τῶν χιλίων ἄθροισμα κατέλυσε συνεστὼς ἐπὶ ἔτη τρία. The word ἄθροισμα hardly suggests a legal council, and συνίστασθαι suggests a conspiracy.

[4] Diog. viii. 63. Aristotle probably mentioned this in his *Sophist.* Cf. Diog. viii. 57.

[5] Diog. viii. 59 (R. P. 162). Satyros probably followed Alkidamas. Diels suggests (*Emp. u. Gorg.* p. 358) that the φυσικός of Alkidamas was a dialogue in which Gorgias was the chief speaker.

Gorgias affirmed that he had been present when his master was performing sorceries. We can see what this means from the fragments of the *Purifications*. Empedokles was a preacher of the new religion which sought to secure release from the " wheel of birth " by purity and abstinence. Orphicism seems to have been strong at Akragas in the days of Theron, and there are even some verbal coincidences between the poems of Empedokles and the Orphicising Odes which Pindar addressed to that prince.[1] On the other hand, there is no reason to doubt the statement of Ammonios that fr. 134 refers to Apollo ; [2] and, if that is so, it points to his having been an adherent of the Ionic form of the mystic doctrine, as we have seen (§ 39) Pythagoras was. Further, Timaios already knew the story that Empedokles had been expelled from the Pythagorean Order for " stealing discourses," [3] and it is probable on the whole that fr. 129 refers to Pythagoras.[4] It seems most likely, then, that Empedokles preached a form of Pythagoreanism which was not considered orthodox by the heads of the Society. The actual marvels related of him seem to be mere developments of hints in his poems.[5]

101. Aristotle said that Empedokles was the inventor of Rhetoric ; [6] and Galen made him the founder of the Italian school of Medicine, which he puts on a level with those of

Rhetoric and medicine.

---

[1] See Bidez, p. 115, n. 1.
[2] See below, note *in loc.*
[3] Diog. viii. 54 (R. P. 162).   [4] See below, note *in loc.*
[5] Timaios told, for instance (*ap.* Diog. viii. 60), how he weakened the force of the etesian winds by hanging bags of asses' skins on the trees to catch them. In fr. 111 he says that knowledge of science as taught by him will enable his disciples to control the winds. We are also told how he brought back to life a woman who had been breathless and pulseless for thirty days. In fr. 111 he tells Pausanias that his teaching will enable him to bring the dead back from Hades. The story of the ἄπνους was given at length in the Περὶ νόσων of Herakleides of Pontos, and Diogenes says that it was related to Pausanias by Empedokles. That gives us a hint of the way in which these stories were worked up. Cf. the very similar anecdotes about Herakleitos, p. 131, n. 4.
[6] Diog. viii. 57 (R. P. 162 g).

Kos and Knidos.[1] Both these statements must be considered in connexion with his political and scientific activity. It is probable that Gorgias was his disciple, and also that the speeches, of which he must have made many, were marked by that euphuism which Gorgias introduced to Athens at a later date, and which gave rise to the idea of an artistic prose.[2] His influence on the development of medicine was, however, far more important, as it affected not only medicine itself, but, through it, the whole tendency of scientific thinking. It has been said that Empedokles had no successors,[3] and the remark is true if we confine ourselves strictly to philosophy ; but the medical school he founded was still living in the days of Plato, and had considerable influence on him, and still more on Aristotle.[4] Its fundamental doctrine was the identification of the four elements with the hot and the cold, the moist and the dry. It also held that we breathe through all the pores of the body, and that the act of respiration is closely connected with the motion of the blood. The heart, not the brain, was regarded as the organ of consciousness.[5] A more

---

[1] Galen, *Meth. Med.* i. 1, ἤριζον δ' αὐτοῖς (the schools of Kos and Knidos) . . . καὶ οἱ ἐκ τῆς Ἰταλίας ἰατροί, Φιλιστίων τε καὶ Ἐμπεδοκλῆς καὶ Παυσανίας καὶ οἱ τούτων ἑταῖροι. Philistion was the contemporary and friend of Plato ; Pausanias is the disciple to whom Empedokles addressed his poem.

[2] See Diels, " Empedokles und Gorgias " (*Berl. Sitzb.*, 1884, pp. 343 *sqq.*). The oldest authority for saying that Gorgias was a disciple of Empedokles is Satyros *ap.* Diog. viii. 58 (R. P. 162) ; but he seems to have derived his information from Alkidamas, who was the disciple of Gorgias himself. In Plato's *Meno* (76 c 4-8) the Empedoklean theory of effluvia and pores is ascribed to Gorgias.

[3] Diels (*Berl. Sitzb.*, 1884, p. 343).

[4] See M. Wellmann, *Fragmentsammlung der griechischen Ärtze*, vol. i. (Berlin, 1901). According to Wellmann, both Plato (in the *Timaeus*) and Diokles of Karystos depend upon Philistion. It is impossible to understand the history of philosophy from this point onwards without keeping the history of medicine constantly in view.

[5] For the four elements, cf. Anon. Lond. xx. 25 (Menon's *Iatrika*), Φιλιστίων δ' οἴεται ἐκ δ' ἰδεῶν συνεστάναι ἡμᾶς, τοῦτ' ἐστιν ἐκ δ' στοιχείων· πυρός, ἀέρος, ὕδατος, γῆς. εἶναι δὲ καὶ ἑκάστου δυνάμεις, τοῦ μὲν πυρὸς τὸ θερμόν, τοῦ δὲ ἀέρος τὸ ψυχρόν, τοῦ δὲ ὕδατος τὸ ὑγρόν, τῆς δὲ γῆς τὸ ξηρόν. For the theory of respiration, see Wellmann, pp. 82 *sqq.* ; and for the heart as the seat of consciousness, *ib.* pp. 15 *sqq.*

external characteristic of the medicine taught by the followers of Empedokles is that they still clung to ideas of a magical nature. A protest against this by a member of the Koan school has been preserved. He refers to them as "magicians and purifiers and charlatans and quacks, who profess to be very religious." [1]

Relation to predecessors. 102. In the biography of Empedokles, we hear nothing of his theory of nature. The only hints we get are some statements about his teachers. Alkidamas, who had good opportunities of knowing, made him a fellow-student of Zeno under Parmenides. Theophrastos too made him a follower and imitator of Parmenides. But the further statement that he had "heard" Pythagoras cannot be right. No doubt Alkidamas said "Pythagoreans." [2]

Some writers hold that certain parts of the system of Empedokles, in particular the theory of pores and effluvia (§ 118), were due to the influence of Leukippos. [3] We know, however, that Alkmaion (§ 96) spoke of "pores" in connexion with sensation, and it was more probably from him that Empedokles got the theory. Moreover, this is more in accordance with the history of certain other physiological views which are common to Alkmaion and the later Ionian philosophers. We can generally see that those reached Ionia through the medical school which Empedokles founded. [4]

Death. 103. We are told that Empedokles leapt into the crater of Etna that he might be deemed a god. This appears to be a malicious version [5] of a tale set on foot by his adherents

---

[1] Hippokr. Περὶ ἱερῆς νόσου, c 1, μάγοι τε καὶ καθάρται καὶ ἀγύρται καὶ ἀλαζόνες. The whole passage should be read. Cf. Wellmann, p. 29 *n.*

[2] Diog. viii. 54-56 (R. P. 162).

[3] Diels, *Verhandl. d. 35 Philologenversamml.* pp. 104 *sqq.*, Zeller, p. 767. It would be fatal to the main thesis of the next few chapters if it could be proved that Empedokles was influenced by Leukippos. I hope to show that Leukippos was influenced by the later Pythagorean doctrine (Chap. IX. § 171), which was in turn affected by Empedokles (Chap. VII. § 147).

[4] For πόροι in Alkmaion, cf. Arist. *De gen. an.* B, 6. 744 a 8 ; Theophr. *De sens.* 26; and for the way in which his embryological and other views were transmitted through Empedokles to the Ionian physicists, cf. Fredrich, *Hippokratische Untersuchungen*, pp. 126 *sqq.*

[5] R. P. 162 h. The story is always told with a hostile purpose.

that he had been snatched up to heaven in the night.[1] Both stories would easily get accepted ; for there was no local tradition. Empedokles did not die in Sicily, but in the Peloponnese, or, perhaps, at Thourioi. It is not at all unlikely that he visited Athens.[2] Plato represents Sokrates as familiar with his views in early life, and the elder Kritias adopted one of his characteristic theories.[3]

104. Empedokles was the second philosopher to expound his system in verse, if we leave the satirist Xenophanes out of account. He was also the last among the Greeks ; for the forged Pythagorean poems may be neglected. Lucretius imitates Empedokles in this, just as Empedokles imitated Parmenides. Of course, the poetical imagery creates a difficulty for the interpreter ; but it cannot be said that it is harder to extract the philosophical kernel from the verses of Empedokles than from the prose of Herakleitos. *Writings.*

105. We have more abundant remains of Empedokles than of any other early Greek philosopher. If we may trust our manuscripts of Diogenes and of Souidas, the librarians of Alexandria estimated the *Poem on Nature* and the *Purifications* together as 5000 verses, of which about *The remains.*

---

[1] R. P. *ib.* This was the story told by Herakleides of Pontos, at the end of his romance about the ἄπνους.

[2] Timaios refuted the common stories at some length (Diog. viii. 71 sqq. ; R. P. *ib.*). He was quite positive that Empedokles never returned to Sicily after he went to Olympia to have his poem recited to the Hellenes. The plan for the colonisation of Thourioi would, of course, be discussed at Olympia, and we know that Greeks from the Peloponnese and elsewhere joined it. He may very well have gone to Athens in connexion with this.

[3] See my edition of the *Phaedo,* 96 b 4 *n.*, and, for Kritias, Arist. *De anima,* 405 b 6. This is the Kritias who appears in Plato's *Timaeus,* and he is certainly not the Kritias who was one of the Thirty, but his grandfather. The Kritias of the *Timaeus* is a very old man, who remembers the events of his boyhood quite well, but forgets what happened the other day (*Tim.* 26 b). He also tells us that the poems of Solon were a novelty when he was a boy (*ib.* 21 b). It is hard to understand how he was ever supposed to be the oligarch, though Diels, Wilamowitz, and E. Meyer seem to have felt no difficulty in the identification. It is clear too that it must have been the grandfather who exchanged poetical compliments with Anakreon (Diels, *Vors.*[3] ii. p. 81 B 1). Kritias of the Thirty did not live to be an old man.

2000 belonged to the former work.[1] Diels gives about 350 verses and parts of verses from the cosmological poem, or not a fifth of the whole. It is important to remember that, even in this favourable instance, so much has been lost. The other poems ascribed to Empedokles by the Alexandrian scholars were probably not his.[2]

I give the remains as they are arranged by Diels :

(1)

And do thou give ear, Pausanias, son of Anchitos the wise !

(2)

For straitened are the powers that are spread over their bodily parts, and many are the woes that burst in on them and blunt the edge of their careful thoughts ! They behold but a brief span of a life that is no life,[3] and, doomed to swift death, are borne up and fly off like smoke. Each is convinced of that
5 alone which he had chanced upon as he is hurried every way, and idly boasts he has found the whole. So hardly can these things be seen by the eyes or heard by the ears of men, so hardly grasped by their mind ! Howbeit, thou, since thou hast found thy way hither, shalt learn no more than mortal mind hath power. R. P. 163.

(3)

. . . to keep within thy dumb heart.

---

[1] Diog. viii. 77 (R. P. 162) ; Souidas s.v. Ἐμπεδοκλῆς· καὶ ἔγραψε δι' ἐπῶν Περὶ φύσεως τῶν ὄντων βιβλία β', καὶ ἔστιν ἔπη ὡς δισχίλια. It hardly seems likely, however, that the Καθαρμοί extended to 3000 verses, so Diels proposes to read πάντα τρισχίλια for πεντακισχίλια in Diogenes. See Diels, " Über die Gedichte des Empedokles " (Berl. Sitzb., 1898, pp. 396 sqq.).

[2] Hieronymos of Rhodes declared (Diog. viii. 58) that he had met with forty-three tragedies by Empedokles ; but see Stein, pp. 5 sqq. The poem on the Persian Wars, which he also refers to (Diog. viii. 57), seems to have arisen from a corruption in the text of Arist. Probl. 929 b 16, where Bekker reads ἐν τοῖς Περσικοῖς. The same passage, however, is said to occur ἐν τοῖς φυσικοῖς, in Meteor. Δ, 4. 382 a 1, though there too E has Περσικοῖς.

[3] The MSS. of Sextus have ζωῇσι βίου. Diels reads ζωῆς ἰδίου. I still prefer Scaliger's ζωῆς ἀβίου. Cf. fr. 15, τὸ δὴ βίοτον καλέουσι.

(4)

But, O ye gods, turn aside from my tongue the madness of those men. Hallow my lips and make a pure stream flow from them! And thee, much-wooed, white-armed Virgin Muse, do I beseech that I may hear what is lawful for the children of a day! Speed me on my way from the abode of Holiness and drive 5 my willing car! Thee shall no garlands of glory and honour at the hands of mortals constrain to lift them from the ground, on condition of speaking in thy pride beyond that which is lawful and right, and so to gain a seat upon the heights of wisdom.

Go to now, consider with all thy powers in what way each thing is clear. Hold not thy sight in greater credit as compared 10 with thy hearing, nor value thy resounding ear above the clear instructions of thy tongue ; [1] and do not withhold thy confidence in any of thy other bodily parts by which there is an opening for understanding, but consider everything in the way it is clear. R. P. 163.

(5)

But it is all too much the way of low minds to disbelieve their betters. Do thou learn as the sure testimonies of my Muse bid thee, when my words have been divided [2] in thy heart.

(6)

Hear first the four roots of all things : shining Zeus, life-bringing Hera, Aidoneus and Nestis whose tear-drops are a well-spring to mortals. R. P. 164.[3]

(7)

. . . uncreated.

(8)

And I shall tell thee another thing. There is no substance [4] of

---

[1] The sense of taste, not speech.

[2] Clement's reading διατμηθέντος may perhaps stand if we take λόγοιο as " discourse," " argument " (cf. διαιρεῖν). Diels conjectures διασσηθέντος and renders " when their speech has penetrated the sieve of thy mind."

[3] The four " elements " are introduced under mythological names, for which see below, p. 229, *n.* 2.

[4] Plutarch (*Adv. Col.* 1112 a) says that φύσις here means " birth," as is shown by its opposition to death, and all interpreters (including myself) have hitherto followed him. On the other hand, the fragment clearly deals with θνητά, and Empedokles cannot have said that there was no death of *mortal* things. The θνητά are just perishable combinations of

any of all the things that perish, nor any cessation for them of baneful death. They are only a mingling and interchange of what has been mingled. Substance is but a name given to these things by men. R. P. 165.

(9)

But they (hold ?) that when Light and Air (chance ?) to have been mingled in the fashion of a man, or in the fashion of the race of wild beasts or of plants or birds, that that is to be born, and when these things have been separated once more, they call it (wrongly ?) woeful death. I follow the custom and call it so myself.[1]

(10)

Avenging death.

---

the four elements (cf. fr. 35, 11), and the point is that they are constantly coming into being and passing away. It is, therefore, impossible, as pointed out by Prof. Lovejoy (*Philosophical Review*, xviii. 371 sqq.), to take θανάτοιο τελευτή as equivalent to θάνατος here, and it may equally well mean "end of death." Now Aristotle, in a passage where he is carefully distinguishing the various senses of φύσις (*Met.* Δ, 4. 1015 a 1), quotes this very verse as an illustration of the meaning ἡ τῶν ὄντων οὐσία (see further in the Appendix). I understand the words ἐπὶ τοῖσδ' as equivalent to ἐπὶ τοῖς θνητοῖς, and I take the meaning of the fragment to be that temporary compounds or combinations like flesh, bone, etc., have no φύσις of their own. Only the four "immortal" elements have a φύσις which does not pass away. This interpretation is confirmed by the way Diogenes of Apollonia speaks in denying the ultimate reality of the "elements." He says (fr. 2) εἰ τούτων τι ἦν ἕτερον τοῦ ἑτέρου, ἕτερον ὂν τῇ ἰδίᾳ φύσει, *i.e.* he says the elements are θνητά.

[1] I understand this fragment to deal with the "elements," of which φῶς and αἰθήρ (Fire and Air) are taken as examples. These are not subject to birth and death, like the θνητά of fr. 8, and the application of the terms to them is as much a matter of convention as the application of the term φύσις to the perishable combinations which are subject to birth and death. The text is corrupt in Plutarch, and has two or three lacunae, but the usual reconstructions depart too far from the tradition. I suggest the following, which has at least the merit of not requiring the alteration of a single letter :

> οἱ δ', ὅτε μὲν κατὰ φῶτα μιγὲν φῶς αἰθέρι ⟨κύρσῃ⟩,
> ἢ κατὰ θηρῶν ἀγροτέρων γένος ἢ κατὰ θάμνων
> ἠὲ κατ' οἰωνῶν, τότε μὲν τὸ ν⟨έμουσι⟩ γενέσθαι·
> εὖτε δ' ἀποκρινθῶσι τάδ' αὖ, δυσδαίμονα πότμον
> ᾗ θέμις ⟨οὐ⟩ καλέουσι, νόμῳ δ' ἐπίφημι καὶ αὐτός.

I understand τάδε in the fourth verse as referring to the "elements" (*e.g.* Fire and Air), which cannot properly be said to be born or to die as their combinations do. I take it that Fire and Air are specially mentioned because the life of animate creatures depends on them. The earth and water would never of themselves produce a living being.

(11, 12)

Fools !—for they have no far-reaching thoughts—who deem
that what before was not comes into being, or that aught can
perish and be utterly destroyed.   For it cannot be that aught
can arise from what in no way is, and it is impossible and unheard
of that what *is* should perish ; for it will always *be*, wherever 5
one may keep putting it.   R. P. 165 a.

(13)

And in the All there is naught empty and naught too full.

(14)

In the All there is naught empty.   Whence, then, could
aught come to increase it ?

(15)

A man who is wise in such matters would never surmise in
his heart that as long as mortals live what they call their life, so
long they are, and suffer good and ill ; while before they were
formed and after they have been dissolved they are just nothing
at all.   R. P. 165 a.

(16)

For even as they (Strife and Love) were aforetime, so too
they shall be ; nor ever, methinks, will boundless time be
emptied of that pair.   R. P. 166 c.

(17)

I shall tell thee a twofold tale.   At one time it grew to be
one only out of many ; at another, it divided up to be many
instead of one.   There is a double becoming of perishable things
and a double passing away.   The coming together of all things
brings one generation into being and destroys it ; the other grows 5
up and is scattered as things become divided.   And these things
never cease continually changing places, at one time all uniting
in one through Love, at another each borne in different directions
by the repulsion of Strife.   Thus, as far as it is their nature to
grow into one out of many, and to become many once more 10
when the one is parted asunder, so far they come into being and
their life abides not.   But, inasmuch as they never cease changing

their places continually, so far they are ever immovable as they
go round the circle of existence.

. . . . . .

But come, hearken to my words, for it is learning that
15 increaseth wisdom. As I said before, when I declared the heads
of my discourse, I shall tell thee a twofold tale. At one time it
grew together to be one only out of many, at another it parted
asunder so as to be many instead of one ;—Fire and Water and
Earth and the mighty height of Air ; dread Strife, too, apart
20 from these, of equal weight to each, and Love in their midst,
equal in length and breadth. Her do thou contemplate with thy
mind, nor sit with dazed eyes. It is she that is known as being
implanted in the frame of mortals. It is she that makes them
have thoughts of love and work the works of peace. They call
25 her by the names of Joy and Aphrodite. Her has no mortal yet
marked moving round among them,[1] but do thou attend to the
undeceitful ordering of my discourse.

For all these are equal and alike in age, yet each has a different
prerogative and its own peculiar nature, but they gain the upper
30 hand in turn when the time comes round. And nothing comes
into being besides these, nor do they pass away ; for, if they had
been passing away continually, they would not be now, and what
could increase this All and whence could it come ? How, too,
could it perish, since no place is empty of these things ? There
35 are these alone ; but, running through one another, they become
now this, now that,[2] and like things evermore. R. P. 166.

(18)

Love.

(19)

Clinging Love.

(20)

This (the contest of Love and Strife) is manifest in the mass
of mortal limbs. At one time all the limbs that are the body's
portion are brought together by Love in blooming life's high
5 season ; at another, severed by cruel Strife, they wander each
alone by the breakers of life's sea. It is the same with plants

---

[1] Reading μετὰ τοῖσιν. I still think, however, that Knatz's palaeo-
graphically admirable conjecture μετὰ θεοῖσιν (i.e. among the elements)
deserves consideration.   [2] Keeping ἄλλοτε with Diels.

and the fish that make their homes in the waters, with the beasts
that have their lairs on the hills and the seabirds that sail on
wings.   R. P. 173 d.

(21)

Come now, look at the things that bear witness to my earlier
discourse, if so be that there was any shortcoming as to their
form in the earlier list.   Behold the sun, everywhere bright and
warm, and all the immortal things that are bathed in heat and
bright radiance.[1]   Behold the rain, everywhere dark and cold ; 5
and from the earth issue forth things close-pressed and solid.
When they are in strife all these are different in form and
separated ; but they come together in love, and are desired by
one another.

For out of these have sprung all things that were and are
and shall be—trees and men and women, beasts and birds and 10
the fishes that dwell in the waters, yea, and the gods that live
long lives and are exalted in honour.   R. P. 166 i.

For there are these alone ; but, running through one another,
they take different shapes—so much does mixture change them.
R. P. 166 g.

(22)

For all of these—sun, earth, sky, and sea—are at one with
all their parts that are cast far and wide from them in mortal
things.   And even so all things that are more adapted for
mixture are like to one another and united in love by Aphrodite. 5
Those things, again, that differ most in origin, mixture and the
forms imprinted on each, are most hostile, being altogether
unaccustomed to unite and very sorry by the bidding of Strife,
since it hath wrought their birth.

(23)

Just as when painters are elaborating temple-offerings, men
whom wisdom hath well taught their art,—they, when they
have taken pigments of many colours with their hands, mix
them in due proportion, more of some and less of others, and

---

[1] Reading ἄμβροτα δ’ ὅσσ’ ἴδει with Diels.   For the word ἴδος, cf. frs.
62, 5 ; 73, 2.   The reference is to the moon, etc., which are made of
solidified Air, and receive their light from the fiery hemisphere.   See
below, § 113.

5 from them produce shapes like unto all things, making trees and
men and women, beasts and birds and fishes that dwell in the
waters, yea, and gods, that live long lives, and are exalted in
honour,—so let not the error prevail over thy mind,[1] that there
is any other source of all the perishable creatures that appear in
10 countless numbers.   Know this for sure, for thou hast heard the
tale from a goddess.[2]

(24)

Stepping from summit to summit, not to travel only one
path of words to the end. . . .

(25)

What is right may well be said even twice.

(26)

For they prevail in turn as the circle comes round, and pass
into one another, and grow great in their appointed turn.   R. P.
166 c.

There are these alone ; but, running through one another,
they become men and the tribes of beasts.   At one time they
5 are all brought together into one order by Love ;   at another,
they are carried each in different directions by the repulsion of
Strife, till they grow once more into one and are wholly subdued.
Thus in so far as they are wont to grow into one out of many,
10 and again divided become more than one, so far they come
into being and their life is not lasting ;   but in so far as
they never cease changing continually, so far are they evermore, immovable in the circle.

(27)

There (in the sphere) are distinguished neither the swift limbs
of the sun, no, nor the shaggy earth in its might, nor the sea,
—so fast was the god bound in the close covering of Harmony,
spherical and round, rejoicing in his circular solitude.[3]   R. P. 167.

---

[1] Reading with Blass (*Jahrb. f. kl. Phil.*, 1883, p. 19) and Diels :

οὕτω μή σ' ἀπάτη φρένα καινύτω κτλ.

Cf. Hesychios : καινύτω· νικάτω.   This is practically what the MSS. of
Simplicius give, and Hesychios has many Empedoklean glosses.

[2] The " goddess " is, of course, the Muse.   Cf. fr. 5.

[3] The word μονίη, if it is right, cannot mean " rest," but only solitude.
There is no reason for altering περιγγέι, though Simplicius has περιγηθέι.

(27 a)

There is no discord and no unseemly strife in his limbs.

(28)

But he was equal on every side and quite without end, spherical and round, rejoicing in his circular solitude.

(29)

Two branches do not spring from his back, he has no feet, no swift knees, no fruitful parts ; but he was spherical and equal on every side.

(30, 31)

But when Strife was grown great in the limbs of the god and sprang forth to claim his prerogatives, in the fulness of the alternate time set for them by the mighty oath, . . . for all the limbs of the god in turn quaked. R. P. 167.

(32)

The joint binds two things.

(33)

Even as when fig juice rivets and binds white milk. . . .

(34)

Cementing [1] meal with water. . . .

(35, 36)

But now I shall retrace my steps over the paths of song that I have travelled before, drawing from my saying a new saying. When Strife was fallen to the lowest depth of the vortex, and Love had reached to the centre of the whirl, in it do all things come together so as to be one only ; not all at once, but coming together 5 at their will each from different quarters ; and, as they mingled, strife began to pass out to the furthest limit. Yet many things remained unmixed, alternating with the things that were

---

[1] The masculine κολλήσας shows that the subject cannot have been Φιλότης ; and Karsten was doubtless right in believing that Empedokles introduced the simile of a baker here. It is in his manner to take illustrations from human arts.

being mixed, namely, all that Strife not fallen yet retained ; for
10 it had not yet altogether retired perfectly from them to the
outermost boundaries of the circle. Some of it still remained
within, and some had passed out from the limbs of the All. But
in proportion as it kept rushing out, a soft, immortal stream of
blameless Love kept running in, and straightway those things
became mortal which had been immortal before, those things
15 were mixed that had before been unmixed, each changing its
path. And, as they mingled, countless tribes of mortal creatures
were scattered abroad endowed with all manner of forms, a
wonder to behold.[1] R. P. 169.

.   .   .   .

(37)

Earth increases its own mass, and Air swells the bulk of Air.

(38)

Come, I shall now tell thee first of all the beginning of the
sun,[2] and the sources from which have sprung all the things we
now behold, the earth and the billowy sea, the damp vapour
and the Titan air that binds his circle fast round all things.
R. P. 170 a.

(39)

If the depths of the earth and the vast air were infinite, a
foolish saying which has been vainly dropped from the lips of
many mortals, though they have seen but a little of the All. . . .[3]
R. P. 103 b.

(40)

The sharp-darting sun and the gentle moon.

(41)

But (the sunlight) is gathered together and circles round the
mighty heavens.

---

[1] We see clearly from this fragment how the ἀθάνατα (the elements)
are identified with the " unmixed," and the θνητά (the perishable combinations) with the " mixed."

[2] The MSS. of Clement have ἥλιον ἀρχήν, and the reading ἥλίου ἀρχήν
is a mere makeshift. Diels reads ἥλικά τ' ἀρχήν, " the first (elements)
equal in age."

[3] The lines are referred to Xenophanes by Aristotle, who quotes them
De caelo, B, 13. 294 a 21. See above, Chap. II. p. 125, n. 3.

(42)

And she cuts off his rays as he goes above her, and casts a shadow on as much of the earth as is the breadth of the pale-faced moon.[1]

(43)

Even so the sunbeam, having struck the broad and mighty circle of the moon, returns at once, running so as to reach the sky.

(44)

It flashes back to Olympos with untroubled countenance. R. P. 170 c.

(45, 46)

There circles round the earth a round borrowed light, as the nave of the wheel circles round the furthest (goal).[2]

(47)

For she gazes at the sacred circle of the lordly sun opposite.

(48)

It is the earth that makes night by coming before the lights.

(49)

. . . of solitary, blind-eyed night.

(50)

And Iris bringeth wind or mighty rain from the sea.

(51)

(Fire) swiftly rushing upwards . . .

(52)

And many fires burn beneath the earth. R. P. 171 a.

(53)

For so it (the air) chanced to be running at that time, though often otherwise. R. P. 171 a.

---

[1] I translate Diels's conjecture ἀπεστέγασεν . . . ἔστ' ἂν ἴῃ.
[2] See p. 177, n. 1.

(54)

But the air sank down upon the earth with its long roots.
R. P. 171 a.

(55)

Sea the sweat of the earth.   R. P. 170 b.

(56)

Salt was solidified by the impact of the sun's beams.

(57)

On it (the earth) many heads sprung up without necks and
arms wandered bare and bereft of shoulders. Eyes strayed up
and down in want of foreheads. R. P. 173 a.

(58)

Solitary limbs wandered seeking for union.

(59)

But, as divinity was mingled still further with divinity, these
things joined together as each might chance, and many other
things besides them continually arose.

(60)

Shambling creatures with countless hands.

(61)

Many creatures with faces and breasts looking in different
directions were born ; some, offspring of oxen with faces of men,
while others, again, arose as offspring of men with the heads of
oxen, and creatures in whom the nature of women and men was
5 mingled, furnished with sterile [1] parts. R. P. 173 b.

(62)

Come now, hear how the Fire as it was separated caused the
night-born shoots of men and tearful women to arise ; for my
tale is not off the point nor uninformed. Whole-natured forms
first arose from the earth, having a portion both of water and

---

[1] Reading στείροις with Diels.

fire.[1] These did the fire, desirous of reaching its like, send up, [5]
showing as yet neither the charming form of the limbs, nor yet
the voice and parts that are proper to men.   R. P. 173 c.

(63)

. . . But the substance of 'the child's) limbs is divided
between them, part of it in men's (and part in women's body).

(64)

And upon him came desire reminding him through sight.

(65)

. . . And it was poured out in the purified parts ; and when
it met with cold women arose from it.

(66)

The divided meadows of Aphrodite.

(67)

For in its warmer part the womb brings forth males, and
that is why men are dark and more manly and shaggy.

(68)

On the tenth day of the eighth month it turns to a white
putrefaction.[2]

(69)

Double bearing.[3]

(70)

Sheepskin.[4]

(71)

But if thy assurance of these things was in any way deficient
as to how, out of Water and Earth and Air and Fire mingled

---

[1] Retaining εἶδεος (i.e. ἴδεος), which is read in the MSS. of Simplicius.
Cf. above, p. 209, n. 1.
[2] That Empedokles regarded milk as putrefied blood is stated by
Aristotle (De gen. an. Δ, 8. 777 a 7). The word πύον means pus. There
may be a pun on πυός, " beestings," but that has its vowel long.
[3] Said of women in reference to births in the seventh and ninth
months.
[4] Of the membrane round the foetus.

together, arose the forms and colours of all those mortal things that have been fitted together by Aphrodite, and so are now come into being. . . .

(72)

How tall trees and the fishes in the sea . . .

(73)

And even as at that time Kypris, preparing warmth,[1] after she had moistened the Earth in water, gave it to swift fire to harden it. . . . R. P. 171.

(74)

Leading the songless tribe of fertile fish.

(75)

All of those which are dense within and rare without, having received a flaccidity of this kind at the hands of Kypris. . . .

(76)

This thou mayest see in the heavy-backed shell-fish that dwell in the sea, in sea-snails and the stony-skinned turtles. In them thou mayest see that the earthy part dwells on the uppermost surface of the skin.

(77-78)

It is moisture[2] that makes evergreen trees flourish with abundance of fruit the whole year round.

(79)

And so first of all tall olive trees bear eggs. . . .

(80)

Wherefore pomegranates are late-born and apples succulent.

(81)

Wine is the water from the bark, putrefied in the wood.

---

[1] Reading ἰδέα ποιπνύουσα with Diels.
[2] This seems clearly to be the meaning of ἠήρ here. Cf. fr. 100, v. 13, and p. 228, n. 2.

(82)

Hair and leaves, and thick feathers of birds, and the scales that grow on mighty limbs, are the same thing.

(83)

But the hair of hedgehogs is sharp-pointed and bristles on their backs.

(84)

And even as when a man thinking to sally forth through a stormy night, gets him ready a lantern, a flame of blazing fire, fastening to it horn plates to keep out all manner of winds, and they scatter the blast of the winds that blow, but the light leaping out through them, shines across the threshold with unfailing 5 beams, as much of it as is finer ;[1] even so did she (Love) then entrap the elemental fire, the round pupil, confined within membranes and delicate tissues, which are pierced through and through with wondrous passages. They keep out the deep water that surrounds the pupil, but they let through the fire, as 10 much of it as is finer.   R. P. 177 b.

(85)

But the gentle flame (of the eye) has but a scanty portion of earth.

(86)

Out of these divine Aphrodite fashioned unwearying eyes.

(87)

Aphrodite fitting these together with rivets of love.

(88)

One vision is produced by both the eyes.

(89)

Know that effluences flow from all things that have come into being.   R. P. 166 h.

---

[1] See Beare, p. 16, *n.* 1, where Plato, *Tim.* 45 b 4 (τοῦ πυρὸς ὅσον τὸ μὲν κάειν οὐκ ἔσχεν, τὸ δὲ παρέχειν φῶς ἥμερον), is aptly quoted.

H

(90)

So sweet lays hold of sweet, and bitter rushes to bitter ; acid comes to acid, and warm couples with warm.

(91)

Water fits better into wine, but it will not (mingle) with oil. R. P. 166 h.

(92)

Copper mixed with tin.

(93)

The bloom of scarlet dye mingles with the grey linen.[1]

(94)

And the black colour at the bottom of a river arises from the shadow.   The same is seen in hollow caves.

(95)

Since they (the eyes) first grew together in the hands of Kypris.

(96)

The kindly earth received in its broad funnels two parts of gleaming Nestis out of the eight, and four of Hephaistos.   So arose white bones divinely fitted together by the cement of proportion.   R. P. 175.

(97)

The spine (was broken).

(98)

And the earth, anchoring in the perfect harbours of Aphrodite, meets with these in nearly equal proportions, with Hephaistos and Water and gleaming Air—either a little more of it, or less

---

[1] On this fragment see Clara E. Millerd, *On the Interpretation of Empedocles*, p. 38, *n.* 3.

of them and more of it. From these did blood arise and the manifold forms of flesh. R. P. 175 c.

(99)

The bell . . . the fleshy sprout (of the ear).[1]

(100)

Thus [2] do all things draw breath and breathe it out again. All have bloodless tubes of flesh extended over the surface of their bodies; and at the mouths of these the outermost surface of the skin is perforated all over with pores closely packed together, so as to keep in the blood while a free passage is cut 5 for the air to pass through. Then, when the thin blood recedes from these, the bubbling air rushes in with an impetuous surge; and when the blood runs back it is breathed out again. Just as when a girl, playing with a water-clock of shining brass, puts the 10 orifice of the pipe upon her comely hand, and dips the water-clock into the yielding mass of silvery water—the stream does not then flow into the vessel, but the bulk of the air [3] inside, pressing upon the close-packed perforations, keeps it out till she uncovers the compressed stream; but then air escapes and an equal 15 volume of water runs in,—just in the same way, when water occupies the depths of the brazen vessel and the opening and passage is stopped up by the human hand, the air outside, striving to get in, holds the water back at the gates of the ill-sounding neck, pressing upon its surface, till she lets go with her hand. 20 Then, on the contrary, just in the opposite way to what happened before, the wind rushes in and an equal volume of water runs out

---

[1] On fr. 99, see Beare, p. 96, n. 1.

[2] This passage is quoted by Aristotle (De respir, 473 b 9), who makes the curious mistake of taking ῥινῶν for the genitive of ῥίς instead of ῥινός. The locus classicus on the klepsydra is Probl. 914 b 9 sqq. (where read αὐλοῦ for ἄλλου, b 12). It was a metal vessel with a narrow neck (αὐλός) at the top and with a sort of strainer (ἠθμός) pierced with holes (τρήματα, τρυπήματα) at the bottom. The passage in the Problems just referred to attributes this theory of the phenomenon to Anaxagoras, and we shall see that he also made use of the experiment (§ 131).

[3] The MSS. of Aristotle have ἀέρος here, though the air is called αἰθήρ in four other verses of the fragment (vv. 5, 7, 18, 24). It is easier to suppose that Aristotle made a slip in this one verse than that Empedokles should use ἀήρ in a sense he elsewhere avoids (p. 228, n. 2), and this suspicion is confirmed by the form ἀέρος instead of ἠέρος. I think, therefore, that Stein was right in reading αἰθέρος.

to make room.[1] Even so, when the thin blood that surges through the limbs rushes backwards to the interior, straightway 25 the stream of air comes in with a rushing swell ; but when the blood runs back the air breathes out again in equal quantity.

(101)

(The dog) with its nostrils tracking out the fragments of the beast's limbs, and the breath from their feet that they leave in the soft grass.[2]

(102)

Thus all things have their share of breath and smell.

(103, 104)

Thus have all things thought by fortune's will. . . . And inasmuch as the rarest things came together in their fall.

(105)

(The heart), dwelling in the sea of blood that runs in opposite directions, where chiefly is what men call thought ; for the blood round the heart is the thought of men. R. P. 178 a.

(106)

For the wisdom of men grows according to what is before them. R. P. 177.

(107)

For out of these are all things formed and fitted together, and by these do men think and feel pleasure and pain. R. P. 178.

---

[1] This seems to be the experiment described in *Probl.* 914 b 26, ἐὰν γάρ τις αὐτῆς (τῆς κλεψύδρας) αὐτὴν τὴν κωδίαν ἐμπλήσας ὕδατος, ἐπιλαβὼν τὸν αὐλόν, καταστρέψῃ ἐπὶ τὸν αὐλόν, οὐ φέρεται τὸ ὕδωρ διὰ τοῦ αὐλοῦ ἐπὶ στόμα. ἀνοιχθέντος δὲ τοῦ στόματος, οὐκ εὐθὺς ἐκρεῖ κατὰ τὸν αὐλόν, ἀλλὰ μικροτέρῳ ὕστερον, ὡς οὐκ ὂν ἐπὶ τῷ στόματι τοῦ αὐλοῦ, ἀλλ᾿ ὕστερον διὰ τούτου φερόμενον ἀνοιχθέντος. The epithet δυσηχέος is best explained as a reference to the ἐρυγμός or " belching " referred to at 915 a 7. Any one can produce this effect with a water-bottle. If it were not for this epithet, it would be tempting to read ἠθμοῖο for ἰσθμοῖο, and that is actually the reading of a few MSS.

[2] On fr. 101, see Beare, p. 135, *n.* 2.

(108)

And just so far as they grow to be different, so far do different thoughts ever present themselves to their minds (in dreams).[1] R. P. 177 a.

(109)

For it is with earth that we see Earth, and Water with water ; by air we see bright Air, by fire destroying Fire.   By love do we see Love, and Hate by grievous hate.   R. P. 176.

(110)

For if, supported on thy steadfast mind, thou wilt contemplate these things with good intent and faultless care, then shalt thou have all these things in abundance throughout thy life, and thou shalt gain many others from them.   For these things grow of themselves into thy heart, where is each man's true 5 nature.   But if thou strivest after things of another kind, as it is the way with men that ten thousand sorry matters blunt their careful thoughts, soon will these things desert thee when the time comes round ; for they long to return once more to their own kind ; for know that all things have wisdom and a share of 10 thought.

(111)

And thou shalt learn all the drugs that are a defence against ills and old age ; since for thee alone will I accomplish all this. Thou shalt arrest the violence of the weariless winds that arise to sweep the earth and waste the fields ; and again, when thou so desirest, thou shalt bring back their blasts in return.   Thou 5 shalt cause for men a seasonable drought after the dark rains, and again thou shalt change the summer drought for streams that feed the trees as they pour down from the sky.   Thou shalt bring back from Hades the life of a dead man.

PURIFICATIONS

(112)

Friends, that inhabit the great town looking down on the yellow rock of Akragas, up by the citadel, busy in goodly works, harbours of honour for the stranger, men unskilled in meanness,

---

[1] That this refers to dreams, we learn from Simpl. *De an.* p. 202, 30.

all hail. I go about among you an immortal god, no mortal
5 now, honoured among all as is meet, crowned with fillets and
flowery garlands. Straightway, whenever I enter with these in
my train, both men and women, into the flourishing towns, is
reverence done me ; they go after me in countless throngs,
10 asking of me what is the way to gain ; some desiring oracles,
while some, who for many a weary day have been pierced by the
grievous pangs of all manner of sickness, beg to hear from me
the word of healing. R. P. 162 f.

(113)

But why do I harp on these things, as if it were any great
matter that I should surpass mortal, perishable men ?

(114)

Friends, I know indeed that truth is in the words I shall
utter, but it is hard for men, and jealous are they of the assault
of belief on their souls.

(115)

There is an oracle of Necessity, an ancient ordinance of the
gods,[1] eternal and sealed fast by broad oaths, that whenever one
of the daemons, whose portion is length of days, has sinfully
polluted his hands with blood,[2] or followed strife and forsworn
5 himself, he must wander thrice ten thousand seasons from the
abodes of the blessed, being born throughout the time in all
manners of mortal forms, changing one toilsome path of life for
another. For the mighty Air drives him into the Sea, and the
10 Sea spews him forth on the dry Earth ; Earth tosses him into
the beams of the blazing Sun, and he flings him back to the eddies
of Air. One takes him from the other, and all reject him. One
of these I now am, an exile and a wanderer from the gods, for
that I put my trust in insensate strife. R. P. 181.

(116)

Charis loathes intolerable Necessity.

---

[1] Necessity is an Orphic personage, and Gorgias, the disciple of
Empedokles, says θεῶν βουλεύμασιν καὶ ἀνάγκης ψηφίσμασιν (Hel. 6).

[2] I retain φόνῳ in v. 3 (so too Diels). The first word of v. 4 has been
lost. Diels suggests Νείκεϊ, which may well be right, and takes ἁμαρτήσας
as equivalent to ὁμαρτήσας. I have translated accordingly.

(117)

For I have been ere now a boy and a girl, a bush and a bird
and a dumb fish in the sea. R. P. 182.

(118)

I wept and I wailed when I saw the unfamiliar land. R. P.
182.

(119)

From what honour, from what a height of bliss have I fallen
to go about among mortals here on earth.

(120)

We have come under this roofed-in cave.[1]

(121)

. . . the joyless land, where are Death and Wrath and troops
of Dooms besides ; and parching Plagues and Rottennesses and
Floods roam in darkness over the meadow of Ate.

(122, 123)

There were [2] Chthonie and far-sighted Heliope, bloody
Discord and gentle-visaged Harmony, Kallisto and Aischre,
Speed and Tarrying, lovely Truth and dark-haired Uncertainty,
Birth and Decay, Sleep and Waking, Movement and Immobility,
crowned Majesty and Meanness, Silence and Voice. R. P. 182 a. 5

(124)

Alas, O wretched race of mortals, sore unblessed : such are
the strifes and groanings from which ye have been born !

(125)

From living creatures he made them dead, changing their
forms.

---

[1] According to Porphyry (De antro Nymph. 8), these words were
spoken by the " powers " who conduct the soul into the world (ψυχοπομποὶ
δυνάμεις). The " cave " is not originally Platonic but Orphic.

[2] This passage is closely modelled on the Catalogue of Nymphs in Iliad
xviii. 39 sqq. Chthonie is found already in Pherekydes (Diog. i. 119).

(126)

(The goddess) clothing them with a strange garment of flesh.[1]

(127)

Among beasts they[2] become lions that make their lair on the hills and their couch on the ground ; and laurels among trees with goodly foliage. R. P. 181 b.

(128)

Nor had they[3] any Ares for a god nor Kydoimos, no nor King Zeus nor Kronos nor Poseidon, but Kypris the Queen. . . . Her did they propitiate with holy gifts, with painted figures[4] and perfumes of cunning fragrancy, with offerings of
5 pure myrrh and sweet-smelling frankincense, casting on the ground libations of brown honey. And the altar did not reek with pure bull's blood, but this was held in the greatest abomination among men, to eat the goodly limbs after tearing out the life. R. P. 184.

(129)

And there was among them a man of rare knowledge, most skilled in all manner of wise works, a man who had won the utmost wealth of wisdom ; for whensoever he strained with all his mind, he easily saw everything of all the things that are, in
5 ten, yea, twenty lifetimes of men.[5]

---

[1] I have retained ἀλλόγνωτι, though it is a little hard to interpret. On the history of the Orphic *chiton* in gnostic imagery see Bernays, *Theophr. Schr. n.* 9. It was identified with the coat of skins made by God for Adam. Cf. also Shakespeare's " muddy vesture of decay."

[2] This is the best μετοίκησις (Ael. *Nat. an.* xii. 7).

[3] The dwellers in the Golden Age.

[4] The MSS. of Porphyry have γραπτοῖς τε ζώοισι. The emendation of Bernays (adopted in R. P.) does not convince me. I venture to suggest μακτοῖς, on the strength of the story related by Favorinus (*ap.* Diog. viii. 53) as to the bloodless sacrifice offered by Empedokles at Olympia.

[5] These lines were already referred to Pythagoras by Timaios (Diog. viii. 54). As we are told (Diog. *ib.*) that some referred the verses to Parmenides, it is clear that no name was given.

(130)

For all things were tame and gentle to man, both beasts and birds, and friendly feelings were kindled everywhere. R. P. 184 a.

(131)

If ever, as regards the things of a day, immortal Muse, thou didst deign to take thought for my endeavour, then stand by me once more as I pray to thee, O Kalliopeia, as I utter a pure discourse concerning the blessed gods. R. P. 179.

(132)

Blessed is the man who has gained the riches of divine wisdom ; wretched he who has a dim opinion of the gods in his heart. R. P. 179.

(133)

It is not possible for us to set God before our eyes, or to lay hold of him with our hands, which is the broadest way of persuasion that leads into the heart of man.

(134)

For he is not furnished with a human head on his body, two branches do not sprout from his shoulders, he has no feet, no swift knees, nor hairy parts ; but he is only a sacred and unutterable mind flashing through the whole world with rapid thoughts. R. P. 180.

(135)

(This is not lawful for some and unlawful for others ;) but the law for all extends everywhere, through the wide-ruling air and the infinite light of heaven. R. P. 183.

(136)

Will ye not cease from this ill-sounding slaughter ? See ye n t that ye are devouring one another in the thoughtlessness of your hearts ? R. P. 184 b.

(137)

And the father lifts up his own son in a changed form and slays him with a prayer. Infatuated fool ! And they run up to the sacrificers, begging mercy, while he, deaf to their cries, slaughters them in his halls and gets ready the evil feast. In

5 like manner does the son seize his father, and children their mother, tear out their life and eat the kindred flesh.   R. P. 184 b.

(138)

Draining their life with bronze.[1]

(139)

Ah, woe is me that the pitiless day of death did not destroy me ere ever I wrought evil deeds of devouring with my lips ! R. P. 184 b.

(140)

Abstain wholly from laurel leaves.

(141)

Wretches, utter wretches, keep your hands from beans !

(142)

Him will the roofed palace of aigis-bearing Zeus never rejoice, nor yet the house of . . .

(143)

Wash your hands, cutting the water from the five springs in the unyielding bronze   R. P. 184 c.

(144)

Fast from wickedness !   R. P. 184 c.

(145)

Therefore are ye distraught by grievous wickednesses, and will not unburden your souls of wretched sorrows.

(146, 147)

But, at the last, they appear among mortal men as prophets, song-writers, physicians, and princes ; and thence they rise up as gods exalted in honour, sharing the hearth of the other gods and the same table, free from human woes, safe from destiny, 5 and incapable of hurt.   R. P. 181 c.

(148)

. . . Earth that envelops the man.

---

[1] On frs. 138 and 143 see Vahlen on Arist. *Poet.* 21. 1457 b 13, and Diels in *Hermes*, xv. p. 173.

106. At the very outset of his poem, Empedokles speaks angrily of those who professed to have found the whole (fr. 2) ; he even calls this " madness " (fr. 4). No doubt he is thinking of Parmenides. His own position is not, however, sceptical. He only deprecates the attempt to construct a theory of the universe off-hand instead of trying to understand each thing we come across " in the way in which it is clear " (fr. 4). And this means that we must not, like Parmenides, reject the assistance of the senses. We soon discover, however, that Empedokles too sets up a system which is to explain everything, though that system is no longer a monistic one.

It is often said that this system was an attempt to mediate between Parmenides and Herakleitos. It is not easy, however, to find any trace of Herakleitean doctrine in it, and it would be truer to say that it aimed at mediating between Eleaticism and the senses. Empedokles repeats, almost in the same words, the Eleatic argument for the sole reality and indestructibility of " what *is* " (frs. 11-15) ; and his idea of the " Sphere " seems to be derived from the Parmenidean description of reality.[1] Parmenides had held that what underlies the illusory world of the senses was a corporeal, spherical, continuous, eternal, and immovable *plenum*, and it is from this Empedokles starts. Given the sphere of Parmenides, he seems to have said, how are we to get from it to the world we know ? How are we to introduce motion into the immovable *plenum* ? Now Parmenides need not have denied the possibility of motion within the Sphere, though he was bound to deny all motion of the Sphere itself ; but such an admission would not have served to explain anything. If any part of the Sphere were to move, the room of the displaced body must at once be taken by other body, for there is no empty space. This, however, would be of precisely the same kind as the body it had displaced ; for all " that *is* " is one. . The result of

[1] Cf. Emp. frs. 27, 28, with Parm. fr. 8.

the motion would be precisely the same as that of rest ; it could account for no change. But is this assumption of perfect homogeneity in the Sphere really necessary ? Evidently not ; it is simply the old unreasoned feeling that existence must be one. Nevertheless, we cannot regard the numberless forms of being the senses present us with as ultimate realities. They have no φύσις of their own, and are always passing away (fr. 8), so the only solution is to assume a limited number of ultimate forms of reality. We may then apply all that Parmenides says of *What is* to each one of these, and ·the transitory forms of existence we know may be explained by their mingling and separation. The conception of " elements " (στοιχεῖα), to use a later term,[1] was found, and the required formula follows at once. So far as concerns particular things, it is true, as our senses tell us, that they come into being and pass away ; but, if we have regard to the ultimate elements of which they are composed, we shall say with Parmenides that " what *is* " is uncreated and indestructible (fr. 17). The elements are immortal, just as the single φύσις of the Milesians was " ageless and deathless."

The "four roots." 107. The " four roots " of all things (fr. 6) which Empedokles assumed—Fire, Air, Earth, and Water—seem to have been arrived at by making each of the traditional " opposites "—hot and cold, wet and dry—into a *thing* which is real in the full Parmenidean sense of the word. It is to be noticed, however, that he does not call Air ἀήρ, but αἰθήρ,[2] and this must be because he wished to avoid

[1] For the history of the term στοιχεῖον see Diels, *Elementum*. Eudemos said (*ap.* Simpl. *Phys.* p. 7, 13) that Plato was the first to use it, but he probably got it from the Pythagoreans. The original term was μορφή or ἰδέα.

[2] In fr. 17, v. 18 Diels reads ἠέρος ἄπλετον ὕψος with Sextus and Simplicius. Plutarch, however, has αἰθέρος, and it is obvious that this was more likely to be corrupted into ἠέρος than *vice versa* in an enumeration of the elements. In frag. 38, v. 3, which is not an enumeration of elements, ὑγρὸς ἀήρ (*i.e.* the misty lower air) is distinguished from Τιτὰν αἰθήρ (*i.e.* the bright blue sky) in the traditional way. In fr. 78 the reference is clearly to moisture. On fr. 100, 13, see p. 219, *n.* 3. These

confusion with what had hitherto been meant by the former word. He had, in fact, made the discovery that atmospheric air is a distinct corporeal substance, and is not to be identified with empty space on the one hand or rarefied mist on the other. Water is not liquid air, but something quite different.[1] This truth Empedokles demonstrated by means of the *klepsydra*, and we still possess the verses in which he applied his discovery to the explanation of respiration and the motion of the blood (fr. 100). Aristotle laughs at those who try to show there is no empty space by shutting up air in water-clocks and torturing wineskins. They only prove, he says, that air is a thing.[2] That, however, is exactly what Empedokles intended to prove, and it was one of the most important discoveries in the history of science. It will be convenient for us to translate the αἰθήρ of Empedokles by " air " ; but we must be careful in that case not to render the word ἀήρ in the same way. Anaxagoras seems to have been the first to use it of atmospheric air.

Empedokles also called the " four roots " by the names of certain divinities—" shining Zeus, life-bringing Hera, Aidoneus, and Nestis " (fr. 6)—though there is some doubt as to how these names are to be apportioned among the elements. Nestis is said to have been a Sicilian water-goddess, and the description of her shows that she stands for Water ; but there is a conflict of opinion as to the other three. This, however, need not detain us.[3] We are

---

are the only passages in which Empedokles seems to speak of ἀήρ in the sense of atmospheric air. [1] Cf. Chap. I. § 27.

[2] Arist. *Phys.* Δ, 6, 213 a 22 (R. P. 159). Aristotle only mentions Anaxagoras by name in this passage ; but he speaks in the plural, and we know from fr. 100 that the *klepsydra* experiment was used by Empedokles.

[3] In antiquity the Homeric Allegorists made Hera Earth and Aidoneus Air, a view which has found its way into Aetios from Poseidonios. It arose as follows. The Homeric- Allegorists were not interested in the science of Empedokles, and did not see that his αἰθήρ was quite a different thing from Homer's ἀήρ. Now this is the dark element, and night is a form of it, so it would naturally be identified with Aidoneus. Again, Empedokles calls Hera φερέσβιος, and that is an epithet of Earth in

already prepared to find that Empedokles called the elements gods ; for all the early thinkers had spoken in this way of whatever they regarded as the primary substance. We must only remember that the word is not used in its religious sense. Empedokles did not pray or sacrifice to the elements.

Empedokles regarded the " roots of all things " as eternal. Nothing can come from nothing or pass away into nothing (fr. 12) ; what is *is*, and there is no room for coming into being and passing away (fr. 8). Further, Aristotle tells us, he taught that they were unchangeable.[1] This Empedokles expressed by saying that " they are always alike." Again, the four elements are all " equal," a statement which seemed strange to Aristotle,[2] but was quite intelligible in the days of Empedokles. Above all, the four elements are ultimate. All other bodies might be divided till you came to the elements ; but Empedokles could give no further account of these without saying (as he did not) that there is an element of which Fire and the rest are in turn composed.[3]

Hesiod and the Homeric Hymns. Another view identified Hera with Air, which is the theory of Plato's *Cratylus*, and Aidoneus with Earth. The Homeric Allegorists further identified Zeus with Fire, a view to which they were doubtless led by the use of the word $\alpha\iota\theta\eta\rho$. Now $\alpha\iota\theta\eta\rho$ certainly means Fire in Anaxagoras, as we shall see, but there is no doubt that in Empedokles it meant Air. It seems likely, then, that Knatz is right (" Empedoclea " in *Schedae Philologicae Hermanno Usenero oblatae*, 1891, pp. 1 *sqq.*) in holding that the bright Air of Empedokles was Zeus. This leaves Aidoneus to stand for Fire ; and nothing could have been more natural for a Sicilian poet, with the volcanoes and hot springs of his native island in mind, than this identification. He refers to the fires that burn beneath the Earth himself (fr. 52). If that is so, we shall have to agree with the Homeric Allegorists that Hera is Earth ; and surely $\phi\epsilon\rho\epsilon\sigma\beta\iota\sigma\varsigma$ "Hρα can be none other than " Mother Earth." The epithet seems only to be used of earth and corn.

[1] Arist. *De gen. corr.* B, 1. 329 b 1. [2] *Ibid.* B, 6. 333 a 16.

[3] *Ibid.* A, 8. 325 b 19 (R. P. 164 e). This was so completely misunderstood by later writers that they attribute to Empedokles the doctrine of $\sigma\tau\omicron\iota\chi\epsilon\hat{\iota}\alpha$ $\pi\rho\grave{o}$ $\tau\hat{\omega}\nu$ $\sigma\tau\omicron\iota\chi\epsilon\hat{\iota}\omega\nu$ (Aet. i. 13, 1 ; 17, 3). The criticism of the Pythagoreans and Plato had made the hypothesis of elements almost unintelligible to Aristotle, and *a fortiori* to his successors. As Plato put it (*Tim.* 48 b 8), they were " not even syllables," let alone " letters " ($\sigma\tau\omicron\iota\chi\epsilon\hat{\iota}\alpha$). That is why Aristotle calls them $\tau\grave{\alpha}$ $\kappa\alpha\lambda\omicron\acute{\upsilon}\mu\epsilon\nu\alpha$ $\sigma\tau\omicron\iota\chi\epsilon\hat{\iota}\alpha$ (Diels, *Elementum*, p. 25).

The " four roots " are given as an exhaustive enumeration of the elements (fr. 23 *sub fin.*) ; for they account for all the qualities presented by the world to the senses.   When we find, as we do, that the school of medicine which regarded Empedokles as its founder identified the four elements with the " opposites," the hot and the cold, the moist and the dry, which formed the theoretical foundation of its system,[1] we see at once how the theory is related to previous views of reality.   We must remember that the conception of quality had not yet been formed.   Anaximander had no doubt regarded his " opposites " as things ; though, before the time of Parmenides, no one had fully realised how much was implied in saying that anything is a thing.   That is the stage we have now reached.   There is still no conception of quality, but there is a clear apprehension of what is involved in saying a thing *is*.

Aristotle twice [2] makes the statement that, though Empedokles assumes four elements, he treats them as two, opposing Fire to all the rest.   This, he says, we can see for ourselves from his poem.   So far as the general theory goes, it is impossible to see anything of the sort ; but, when we come to the origin of the world (§ 112), we shall find that Fire plays a leading part, and this may be what Aristotle meant.   It is also true that in the biology (§§ 114-116) Fire fulfils a unique function, while the other three act more or less in the same way.   But we must remember that it has no pre-eminence over the rest : all are equal.

108. The Eleatic criticism had made it necessary to explain motion.[3]   Empedokles starts, we have seen, from an original state of the " four roots," which only differs from the Sphere of Parmenides in so far as it is a mixture, not a homogeneous and continuous mass.   It is this that makes change and motion possible ; but, were there nothing outside the Sphere which could enter in, like the Pythagorean " Air,"   *Strife and Love.*

[1] Philistion put the matter in this way. See p. 201, *n.* 5.
[2] Arist. *Met.* A, 4. 985 a 31 ; *De gen. corr.* B, 3. 330 b 19 (R. P. 164 e).
[3] Cf. Introd. § VIII.

to separate the elements, nothing could ever arise from it. Empedokles accordingly assumed the existence of such a substance, and he gave it the name of Strife. But the effect of this would be to separate all the elements in the Sphere completely, and then nothing more could possibly happen ; something else was needed to bring the elements together again. This Empedokles found in Love, which he regarded as the same impulse to union that is implanted in human bodies (fr. 17, 22 sqq.). He looks at it, in fact, from a physiological point of view, as was natural for the founder of a medical school. No mortal had yet marked, he says, that the very same Love men know in their bodies had a place among the elements.

The Love and Strife of Empedokles are no incorporeal forces. They are active, indeed, but they are still corporeal. At the time, this was inevitable ; nothing incorporeal had yet been dreamt of, Naturally, Aristotle is puzzled by this characteristic of what he regarded as efficient causes. " The Love of Empedokles," he says,[1] " is both an efficient cause, for it brings things together, and a material cause, for it is a part of the mixture." And Theophrastos expressed the same idea by saying [2] that Empedokles sometimes gave an efficient power to Love and Strife, and sometimes put them on a level with the other four. The fragments leave no room for doubt that they were thought of as spatial and corporeal. All the six are called " equal." Love is said to be " equal in length and breadth " to the others, and Strife is described as equal to each of them in weight (fr. 17).

The function of Love is to produce union ; that of Strife, to break it up again. Aristotle, however, rightly points out that in another sense it is Love that divides and Strife that unites. When the Sphere is broken up by Strife, the result is that all the Fire, for instance, which was contained in it comes together and becomes one ; and again, when the

<hr />

[1] Arist. *Met.* A, 10. 1075 b 3.
[2] Theophr. *Phys. Op.* fr. 3 (*Dox.* p. 477 ; R. P. 166 b).

elements are brought together once more by Love, the mass of each is divided. In another place, he says that, while Strife is assumed as the cause of destruction, and does, in fact, destroy the Sphere, it really gives birth to everything else in so doing.[1] It follows that we must carefully distinguish between the Love of Empedokles and that " attraction of like for like " to which he also attributed an important part in the formation of the world. The latter is not an element distinct from the others ; it depends on the proper nature of each element, and is only able to take effect when Strife divides the Sphere. Love, on the contrary, produces an attraction of *unlikes*.

109. But, when Strife has separated the elements, what *Mixture and separation.* determines the direction of their motion ? Empedokles seems to have given no further explanation than that each was " running " in a certain direction (fr. 53). Plato severely condemns this in the *Laws*,[2] on the ground that no room is thus left for design. Aristotle also blames him for giving no account of the Chance to which he ascribed so much importance. Nor is the Necessity, of which he also spoke, further explained.[3] Strife enters into the Sphere at a certain time in virtue of Necessity, or " the mighty oath " (fr. 30) ; but we are told no more about that.

The expression used by Empedokles to describe the movement of the elements is that they " run through each other " (fr. 17, 34). Aristotle tells us [4] that he explained mixture in general by " the symmetry of pores." And this is the true explanation of the " attraction of like for like." The " pores " of like bodies are, of course, much the same size, and these bodies can therefore mingle easily. On the other hand, a finer body will " run through " a coarse one without becoming mixed, and a coarse body will not be

---

[1] *Met.* A, 4. 985 a 21 ; Γ, 4. 1000 a 24 ; b 9 (R. P. 166 i).
[2] Plato, *Laws*, x. 889 b. The reference is not to Empedokles exclusively, but the language shows that Plato is thinking mainly of him.
[3] Arist. *De gen. corr.* B, 6. 334 a 1 ; *Phys.* Θ, 1. 252 a 5 (R. P. 166 k).
[4] Arist. *De gen. corr.* A, 8. 324 b 34 (R. P. 166 h).

able to enter the pores of a finer one at all.   As Aristotle says, this really implies something like the atomic theory ; but there is no evidence that Empedokles himself was conscious of that.   Another question raised by Aristotle is even more instructive.   Are the pores, he asks, empty or full ?   If empty, what becomes of the denial of the void ?   If full, why need we assume pores at all ? [1] These questions Empedokles would have found it hard to answer.

The four periods.

110. It will be clear from what has been said that we must distinguish four periods in the cycle.   First we have the Sphere, in which all the elements are mixed together by Love.   Secondly, there is the period when Love is passing out and Strife coming in, when, therefore, the elements are partially separated and partially combined.   Thirdly comes the complete separation of the elements, when Love is outside the world, and Strife has given free play to the attraction of like for like.   Lastly, we have the period when Love is bringing the elements together again, and Strife is passing out.   This brings us back to the Sphere, and the cycle begins afresh.   Now a world such as ours can exist only in the second and fourth of these periods.   It seems to be generally supposed that we are in the fourth period ; [2] I hope to show that we are in the second, that when Strife is gaining the upper hand.

Our world the work of Strife.

111. That a world of perishable things ($\theta\nu\eta\tau\acute{a}$) arises both in the second and fourth period is distinctly stated by Empedokles (fr. 17), and it is inconceivable that he had not made up his mind which of these worlds is ours.   Aristotle is clearly of opinion that in our world Strife is increasing. In one place, he says that Empedokles " holds that the world is in a similar condition now in the period of Strife

---

[1] Arist. *De gen. corr.* A, 8. 326 b 6.

[2] This is the view of Zeller (pp. 785 *sqq.*), but he admits that the external testimony, especially that of Aristotle, is wholly in favour of the other.   His difficulty is with the fragments, and if it can be shown that these can be interpreted in accordance with Aristotle's statements, the question is settled.

as formerly in that of Love."[1] In another, he tells us that Empedokles omits the generation of things in the period of Love, just because it is unnatural to represent this world, in which the elements are separate, as arising from things in a state of separation.[2] This remark can only mean that Empedokles assumed the increase of Strife, or, in other words, that he represented the course of evolution as the disintegration of the Sphere, not as the coming together of things from a state of separation.[3] That is what we should expect, if we are right in supposing that the problem he set himself to solve was the origin of this world from the Sphere of Parmenides, and it is also in harmony with the tendency of such speculations to represent the world as getting worse rather than better. We have only to consider, then, whether the details of the system bear out this general view.

112. To begin with the Sphere, in which the " four roots of all things " are mixed together, we note that it is called a god in the fragments just as the elements are, and that Aristotle more than once refers to it in the same way.[4] We

Formation of the world by Strife.

---

[1] Arist. *De gen. corr.* B, 6. 334 a 6, τὸν κόσμον ὁμοίως ἔχειν φησὶν ἐπί τε τοῦ νείκους νῦν καὶ πρότερον ἐπὶ τῆς φιλίας. Miss Millerd (*Interpretation of Empedocles*, p. 45) adds Theophrastos, *De sensu* § 20, συμβαίνει δὲ καὶ ἐπὶ τῆς Φιλίας ὅλως μὴ εἶναι αἴσθησιν ἢ ἧττον διὰ τὸ συγκρίνεσθαι τότε καὶ μὴ ἀπορρεῖν. Here ἐπὶ τῆς Φιλίας and τότε imply the antithesis ἐπὶ τοῦ Νείκους and νῦν.

[2] Arist. *De caelo*, Γ, 2. 301 a 14, ἐκ διεστώτων δὲ καὶ κινουμένων οὐκ εὔλογον ποιεῖν τὴν γένεσιν. διὸ καὶ Ἐμπεδοκλῆς παραλείπει τὴν ἐπὶ τῆς φιλότητος· οὐ γὰρ ἂν ἠδύνατο συστῆσαι τὸν οὐρανὸν ἐκ κεχωρισμένων μὲν κατασκευάζων, σύγκρισιν δὲ ποιῶν διὰ τὴν φιλότητα· ἐκ διακεκριμένων γὰρ συνέστηκεν ὁ κόσμος τῶν στοιχείων (" our world consists of the elements in a state of separation "), ὥστ᾽ ἀναγκαῖον γενέσθαι ἐξ ἑνὸς καὶ συγκεκριμένου.

[3] It need not mean that Empedokles said nothing about the world of Love at all ; for he obviously says something of both worlds in fr. 17. It is enough to suppose that, having described both in general terms, he went on to treat the world of Strife in detail.

[4] Arist. *De gen. corr.* B, 6. 333 b 21 (R. P. 168 e) ; *Met.* B, 4. 1000 a 28 (R. P. 166 i). Cf. Simpl. *Phys.* p. 1124, 1 (R. P. 167 b). In other places Aristotle speaks of it as " the One." Cf. *De gen. corr.* A, 1. 315 a 7 (R. P. 168 e) ; *Met.* B, 4. 1000 a 29 (R. P. 166 i) ; A, 4. 985 a 28 (R. P. *ib.*). This involves a slight Aristotelian " development." It is not the same thing to say, as Empedokles does, that all things come together " into one," and to say that they come together " into the One." The latter expression suggests that they lose their identity in the Sphere, and thus become something like Aristotle's " matter." As has been pointed out

must remember that Love itself is a part of this mixture,[1] while Strife surrounds or encompasses it on every side just as the Boundless encompasses the world in earlier systems. Strife, however, is not boundless, but equal in bulk to each of the four roots and to Love.

At the appointed time, Strife begins to enter into the Sphere and Love to go out of it (frs. 30, 31). The fragments by themselves throw little light on this ; but Aetios and the Plutarchean *Stromateis* have between them preserved a very fair tradition of what Theophrastos said on the point.

Empedokles held that Air was first separated out and secondly Fire. Next came Earth, from which, highly compressed as it was by the impetus of its revolution, Water gushed forth. From the water Mist was produced by evaporation. The heavens were formed out of the Air and the sun out of the Fire, while terrestrial things were condensed from the other elements. Aet. ii. 6. 3 (*Dox.* p. 334 ; R. P. 170).

Empedokles held that the Air when separated off from the original mixture of the elements was spread round in a circle. After the Air, Fire running outwards, and not finding any other place, ran up under the solid that surrounded the Air.[2] There were two hemispheres, revolving round the earth, the one altogether composed of fire, the other of a mixture of air and a little fire. The latter he supposed to be the Night. The origin of their motion he derived from the fact of fire preponderating in one hemisphere owing to its accumulation there. Ps.-Plut. *Strom.* fr. 10 (*Dox.* p. 582 ; R. P. 170 a).

(p. 230, *n.* 3), it is hard for Aristotle to grasp the conception of irreducible elements ; but there can be no doubt that in the Sphere, as in their separation, the elements remain " what they are " for Empedokles. As Aristotle also knows quite well, the Sphere is a mixture. Compare the difficulties about the " One " of Anaximander discussed in Chap. 1. § 15.

[1] This accounts for Aristotle's statement, which he makes once positively (*Met.* B, 1. 996 a 7) and once very doubtfully (*Met.* B, 4. 1001 a 12), that Love was the substratum of the One in just the same sense as the Fire of Herakleitos, the Air of Anaximenes, or the Water of Thales. He thinks that all the elements become merged in Love, and so lose their identity. In this case, it is in Love he recognises his own " matter."

[2] For the phrase τοῦ περὶ τὸν ἀέρα πάγου cf. Περὶ διαίτης, i. 10, 1, πρὸς τὸν περιέχοντα πάγον. Et. M. s.v. βηλός . . . τὸν ἀνωτάτω πάγον καὶ περιέχοντα τὸν πάντα ἀέρα.

The first of the elements to be separated out by Strife then, was Air, which took the outermost position surrounding the world (cf. fr. 38). We must not, however, take the statement that it surrounded the world " in a circle " too strictly. It appears that Empedokles regarded the heavens as shaped like an egg.[1] Here, probably, we have a trace of Orphic ideas. At any rate, the outer circle of the Air became solidified or frozen, and we thus get a crystalline vault as the boundary of the world. We note that it was Fire which solidified the Air and turned it to ice. Fire in general had a solidifying power.[2]

In its upward rush Fire displaced a portion of the Air in the upper half of the concave sphere formed by the frozen sky. This air then sunk downwards, carrying with it a small portion of the fire. In this way, two hemispheres were produced : one, consisting entirely of fire, the diurnal hemisphere ; the other, the nocturnal, consisting of air with a little fire.

The accumulation of Fire in the upper hemisphere disturbs the equilibrium of the heavens and causes them to revolve ; and this revolution not only produces the alternation of day and night, but by its rapidity keeps the heavens and the earth in their places. This was illustrated, Aristotle tells us, by the simile of a cup of water whirled round at the end of a string.[3] This experimental illustration is much in the manner of Empedokles. It has nothing to do with " centrifugal force," but is intended to show that rapid motion may counteract a tendency to fall.

113. It will be observed that day and night have been explained without reference to the sun. Day is the light

The sun, moon, stars, and earth.

---

[1] Aet. ii. 31, 4 (*Dox.* p. 363).   [2] Aet. ii. 11, 2 (R. P. 170 c).

[3] Arist. *De caelo*, B, 1. 284 a 24 ; 13. 295 a 16 (R. P. 170 b). Plato, *Phaed.* 99 b 6, διὸ ὁ μέν τις δίνην περιτιθεὶς τῇ γῇ ὑπὸ τοῦ οὐρανοῦ μένειν δὴ ποιεῖ τὴν γῆν. The experiment with τὸ ἐν τοῖς κυάθοις ὕδωρ which κύκλῳ τοῦ κυάθου φερομένου πολλάκις κάτω τοῦ χαλκοῦ γινόμενον ὅμως οὐ φέρεται κάτω, reminds us of that with the *klepsydra* in fr. 100. The point is that the φορά of the δίνη overcomes the οἰκεία ῥοπή by its velocity.

of the fiery diurnal hemisphere, while night is the shadow thrown by the earth when the fiery hemisphere is on the other side of it (fr. 48). What, then, is the sun ? The Plutarchean *Stromateis* [1] again give us the answer : " The sun is not fire in substance, but a reflexion of fire like that which comes from water." Plutarch himself makes one of his personages say : " You laugh at Empedokles for saying that the sun is a product of the earth, arising from the reflexion of the light of heaven, and once more ' flashes back to Olympos with untroubled countenance.' " [2] Aetios says : [3] " Empedokles held that there were two suns : one, the archetype, the fire in one hemisphere of the world, filling the whole hemisphere always stationed opposite its own reflexion ; the other, the visible sun, its reflexion in the other hemisphere, that which is filled with air mingled with fire, produced by the reflexion of the earth, which is round, on the crystalline sun, and carried round by the motion of the fiery hemisphere. Or, to sum it up shortly, the sun is a reflexion of the terrestrial fire."

These passages, and especially the last, are by no means clear.[4] The reflexion we call the sun cannot be in the hemisphere opposite the fiery one ; for that is the nocturnal hemisphere. We must say rather that the light of the fiery hemisphere is reflected by the earth on to the fiery hemisphere itself in one concentrated flash. It follows that the appearance which we call the sun is the same size as the earth. We may perhaps explain the origin of this view as follows.

[1] [Plut.] *Strom.* fr. 10 (*Dox.* p. 582, 11 ; R. P. 170 c).

[2] Plut. *De Pyth. or.* 400 b (R. P. 170 c). I keep the MS. reading περὶ γῆν with Diels.

[3] Aet. ii. 20, 13 (*Dox.* p. 350), Ἐμπεδοκλῆς δύο ἡλίους· τὸν μὲν ἀρχέτυπον, πῦρ ὃν ἐν τῷ ἑτέρῳ ἡμισφαιρίῳ τοῦ κόσμου, πεπληρωκὸς τὸ ἡμισφαίριον, αἰεὶ κατ᾽ ἀντικρὺ τῇ ἀνταυγείᾳ ἑαυτοῦ τεταγμένον· τὸν δὲ φαινόμενον, ἀνταύγειαν ἐν τῷ ἑτέρῳ ἡμισφαιρίῳ τῷ τοῦ ἀέρος τοῦ θερμομιγοῦς πεπληρωμένῳ, ἀπὸ κυκλοτεροῦς τῆς γῆς κατ᾽ ἀνάκλασιν γιγνομένην εἰς τὸν ἥλιον τὸν κρυσταλλοειδῆ, συμπεριελκομένην δὲ τῇ κινήσει τοῦ πυρίνου. ὡς δὲ βραχέως εἰρῆσθαι συντεμόντα, ἀνταύγειαν εἶναι τοῦ περὶ τὴν γῆν πυρὸς τὸν ἥλιον.

[4] I strongly suspect that the confusion is due to a somewhat captious criticism by Theophrastos (see below, p. 298, *n.* 1). It would be like him to point out that the theory implied "two suns."

It had just been discovered that the moon shone by reflected light, and there is always a tendency to give any novel theory a wider application than it really admits of. In the early part of the fifth century B.C., men saw reflected light everywhere ; some of the Pythagoreans held a similar view (§ 150).

It was probably in this connexion that Empedokles announced that light takes some time to travel, though its speed is so great as to escape our perception.[1]

" The moon was composed of air cut off by the fire ; it was frozen just like hail, and had its light from the sun." It is, in other words, a disc of frozen air, of the same substance as the solid sky which surrounds the heavens. Diogenes says that Empedokles taught it was smaller than the sun, and Aetios tells us it was only half as distant from the earth.[2]

Empedokles did not explain the fixed stars by reflected light, nor even the planets. They were made out of the fire which the air carried with it when forced beneath the earth by the upward rush of fire at the first separation. The fixed stars were attached to the frozen air ; the planets moved freely.[3]

Empedokles was acquainted (fr. 42) with the true theory of solar eclipses, which, along with that of the moon's light, was the great discovery of this period. He also knew (fr. 48) that night is the conical shadow of the earth, and not a sort of exhalation.

Wind was explained from the opposite motions of the fiery and airy hemispheres. Rain was caused by the compression of the Air, which forced any water there might be in it out of its pores in the form of drops. Lightning was fire forced out from the clouds in much the same way.[4]

[1] Arist. De sensu, 6. 446 a 28 ; De an. B, 7. 418 b 20.
[2] [Plut.] Strom. fr. 10 (Dox. p. 582, 12 ; R. P. 170 c) ; Diog. viii. 77 ; Aet. ii. 31, 1 (cf. Dox. p. 63). [3] Aet. ii. 13, 2 and 11 (Dox. pp. 341 sqq.).
[4] Aet. iii. 3, 7 ; Arist. Meteor. B, 9. 369 b 12, with Alexander's commentary.

The earth was at first mixed with water, but the increasing compression caused by the velocity of its revolution made the water gush forth, so that the sea is " the sweat of the earth," a phrase to which Aristotle objects as a mere poetical metaphor. The saltness of the sea was explained by this analogy.[1] It is taken for granted that the earth shares in the rotation of the vortex (δίνη).

Organic combinations.

114. Empedokles went on to show how the four elements, mingled in different proportions, gave rise to perishable things, such as bones, flesh, and the like. These, of course, are the work of Love ; but this in no way contradicts the view taken above as to the period to which this world belongs. Love is by no means banished from the world yet, though one day it will be. At present, it is still able to form combinations of elements ; but, just because Strife is ever increasing, they are all perishable. The important part played by proportion (λόγος) here is no doubt due to Pythagorean influence.

The possibility of organic combinations depends on the fact that there is still water in the earth, and even fire (fr. 52). The warm springs of Sicily were a proof of this, not to speak of Etna. These springs Empedokles appears to have explained by one of his characteristic images, drawn this time from the heating of warm baths.[2] His similes are nearly all drawn from human inventions and manufactures.

Plants.

115. Plants and animals were formed from the four elements under the influence of Love and Strife. The fragments which deal with trees and plants are 77-81 ; and these, taken along with certain Aristotelian statements and the doxographical tradition, enable us to make out pretty

---

[1] Arist. Meteor. B, 3. 357 a 24 ; Aet. iii. 16, 3 (R. P. 170 b). Cf. the clear reference in Arist. Meteor. B, 1. 353 b 11.

[2] Seneca, Q. Nat. iii. 24, " facere solemus dracones et miliaria et complures formas in quibus aere tenui fistulas struimus per declive circumdatas, ut saepe eundem ignem ambiens aqua per tantum fluat spatii quantum efficiendo calori sat est. frigida itaque intrat, effluit calida. idem sub terra Empedocles existimat fieri."

fully what the theory was. The text of Aetios is very corrupt here; but it may, perhaps, be rendered as follows :

Empedokles says trees were the first living creatures to grow up out of the earth, before the sun was spread out, and before day and night were distinguished ; from the symmetry of their mixture, they contain the proportion of male and female ; they grow, rising up owing to the heat which is in the earth, so that they are parts of the earth just as embryos are parts of the uterus; fruits are excretions of the water and fire in plants, and those which have a deficiency of moisture shed their leaves when that is evaporated by the summer heat, while those which have more moisture remain evergreen, as in the case of the laurel, the olive, and the palm ; the differences in taste are due to variations in the particles contained in the earth and to the plants drawing different particles from it, as in the case of vines : for it is not the difference of the vines that makes wine good, but that of the soil which nourishes them. Aet. v. 26, 4 (R. P. 172).

Aristotle finds fault with Empedokles for explaining the double growth of plants, upwards and downwards, by the opposite natural motions of the earth and fire contained in them.[1] For " natural motions " we must, of course, substitute the attraction of like for like (§ 109). Theophrastos says much the same thing.[2] The growth of plants, then, is to be regarded as an incident in the separation of the elements by Strife. Some of the fire still beneath the earth (fr. 52) meeting in its upward course with earth, still moist with water and " running " down so as to " reach its own kind," unites with it, under the influence of the Love still left in the world, to form a temporary combination, which we call a tree or a plant.

At the beginning of the pseudo-Aristotelian *Treatise on Plants*,[3] we are told that Empedokles attributed desire, sensation, and the capacity for pleasure and pain to plants, and he rightly saw that the two sexes are combined in them.

---

[1] Arist. *De an.* B, 4. 415 b 28.
[2] Theophr. *De causis plantarum*, i. 12, 5.
[3] [Arist.] *De plantis*, A, 1. 815 a 15.

This is mentioned by Aetios, and discussed in the pseudo-Aristotelian treatise. If we may so far trust that Byzantine translation from a Latin version of the Arabic,[1] we get a hint as to the reason. Plants, we are there told, came into being " in an imperfect state of the world,"[2] in fact, at a time when Strife had not so far prevailed as to differentiate the sexes. We shall see that the same thing applies to the original race of animals. It is strange that Empedokles never observed the actual process of generation in plants, but simply said they spontaneously " bore eggs " (fr. 79), that is to say, fruit.

Evolution of animals.

116. The fragments which deal with the evolution of animals (57-62) must be understood in the light of the statement (fr. 17) that there is a double coming into being and a double passing away of mortal things. The four stages are accurately distinguished in a passage of Aetios,[3] and we shall see that there is evidence for referring two of them to the second period of the world's history and two to the fourth.

The first stage is that in which the various parts of animals arise separately. It is that of heads without necks, arms without shoulders, and eyes without foreheads (fr. 57). It is clear that this must be the first stage in what we have called the fourth period of the world's history, that in which Love is coming in and Strife passing out. Aristotle distinctly refers it to the period of Love, by which, as we have seen, he means the period when Love is increasing.[4] It is in accordance with this that he also says these scattered members were subsequently put together by Love.[5]

[1] Alfred the Englishman translated the Arabic version into Latin in the reign of Henry III. It was retranslated from this version into Greek at the Renaissance by a Greek resident in Italy.
[2] A, 2. 817 b 35, " mundo . . . diminuto et non perfecto in complemento suo " (Alfred).   [3] Aet. v. 19, 5 (R. P. 173).
[4] Arist. De caelo, Γ, 2. 300 b 29 (R. P. 173 a). Cf. De gen. an. A, 18. 722 b 19, where fr. 57 is introduced by the words καθάπερ Ἐμπεδοκλῆς γεννᾷ ἐπὶ τῆς Φιλότητος: So Simplicius, De caelo, p. 587, 18, says μουνομελῆ ἔτι τὰ γυῖα ἀπὸ τῆς τοῦ Νείκους διακρίσεως ὄντα ἐπλανᾶτο.
[5] Arist. De an. Γ, 6. 430 a 30 (R. P. 173 a).

The second stage is that in which the scattered limbs are united. At first, they were combined in all possible ways (fr. 59). There were oxen with human heads, creatures with double faces and double breasts, and all manner of monsters (fr. 61). Those of them that were fitted to survive did so, while the rest perished. That is how the evolution of animals took place in the period of Love.[1]

The third stage belongs to the period when the unity of the Sphere is being destroyed by Strife. It is, therefore, the first stage in the evolution of our world. It begins with " whole-natured forms " in which there is not any distinction of sex or species.[2] They are composed of earth and water, and are produced by the upward motion of fire seeking to reach its like.

In the fourth stage, the sexes and species have been separated, and new animals no longer arise from the elements, but are produced by generation.

In both these processes of evolution, Empedokles was guided by the idea of the survival of the fittest. Aristotle severely criticises this. " We may suppose," he says, " that all things have fallen out accidentally just as they would have done if they had been produced for some end. Certain things have been preserved because they had spontaneously acquired a fitting structure, while those which were not so put together have perished and are perishing, as Empedokles says of the oxen with human faces." [3] This, according to Aristotle, leaves too much to chance. One curious instance has been preserved. Vertebration was explained by saying that an early invertebrate animal tried to turn round and broke its back in so

---

[1] This is well put by Simplicius, De caelo, p. 587, 20. It is ὅτε τοῦ Νείκους ἐπεκράτει λοιπὸν ἡ Φιλότης . . . ἐπὶ τῆς Φιλότητος οὖν ὁ Ἐμπεδοκλῆς ἐκεῖνα εἶπεν, οὐχ ὡς ἐπικρατούσης ἤδη τῆς Φιλότητος, ἀλλ' ὡς μελλούσης ἐπικρατεῖν. In Phys. p. 371, 33, he says the oxen with human heads were κατὰ τὴν τῆς Φιλίας ἀρχήν.

[2] Cf. Plato, Symp. 189 e.

[3] Arist. Phys. B, 8. 198 b 29 (R. P. 173 a).

doing. This was a favourable variation and so survived.[1]
It should be noted that it clearly belongs to the period of
Strife, and not, like the oxen with human heads, to that
of Love. The survival of the fittest was the law of
evolution in both periods.

Physio-
logy.

117. The distinction of the sexes was a result of the
differentiation brought about by Strife. Empedokles differed from the theory given by Parmenides in his Second
Part (§ 95) in holding that the warm element preponderated
in the male sex, and that males were conceived in the warmer
part of the uterus (fr. 65). The foetus was formed partly
from the male and partly from the female semen (fr. 63) :
and it was just the fact that the substance of a new being's
body was divided between the male and the female that
produced desire when the two were brought together by
sight (fr. 64). A certain symmetry of the pores in the male
and female semen is necessary for procreation, and from
its absence Empedokles explained the sterility of mules.
The children resemble that parent who contributed most to
their formation. The influence of statues and pictures was
also noted, however, as modifying the appearance of the
offspring. Twins and triplets were due to a superabundance
and division of the semen.[2]

Empedokles held that the foetus was enveloped in a
membrane, and that its formation began on the thirty-sixth
day and was complete on the forty-ninth. The heart was
formed first, the nails and such things last. Respiration
did not begin till the time of birth, when the fluids round
the foetus were withdrawn. Birth took place in the ninth
or seventh month, because the day had been originally nine
months long, and afterwards seven. Milk arises on the
tenth day of the eighth month (fr. 68).[3]

Death was the final separation by Strife of the fire and

[1] Arist. *De part. an.* A, 1. 640 a 19.
[2] Aet. v. 10, 1 ; 11, 1 ; 12, 2 ; 14, 2. Cf. Fredrich, *Hippokratische
Untersuchungen*, pp. 126 *sqq.*
[3] Aet. v. 15, 3 ; 21, 1 (*Dox.* p. 190).

earth in the body, each of which had all along been striving
to " reach its own kind." Sleep was a temporary separation
to a certain extent of the fiery element.[1] At death the
animal is resolved into its elements, which either enter into
fresh combinations, or are permanently united with " their
own kind." There can be no question here of an immortal
soul.

Even in life, we may see the attraction of like to like
operating in animals just as it did in the upward and downward growth of plants. Hair is the same thing as foliage
(fr. 82) ; and, generally speaking, the fiery part of animals
tends upwards and the earthy downwards, though there
are exceptions, as may be seen in the case of certain shell-
fish (fr. 76), where the earthy part is above. These exceptions are only possible because there is still a great deal of
Love in the world. We also see the attraction of like for
like in the habits of different species of animals. Those
that have most fire in them fly up into the air ; those in
which earth preponderates take to the earth, as did the dog
which always sat upon a tile.[2] Aquatic animals are those
in which water predominates. This does not, however,
apply to fishes, which are very fiery, and take to the water
to cool themselves.[3]

Empedokles paid great attention to respiration, and his
explanation of it has been preserved in a continuous form
(fr. 100). We breathe, he held, through all the pores of the
skin, not merely through the organs of respiration. The
cause of the alternate inspiration and expiration of breath
was the movement of the blood from the heart to the surface
of the body and back again, which was explained by the
klepsydra.

The nutrition and growth of animals is, of course, to be
explained from the attraction of like to like. Each part

[1] Aet. v. 25, 4 (Dox. p. 437).
[2] Aet. v. 19, 5 (Dox. p. 431). Cf. Eth. Eud. H, I. 1235 a 11.
[3] Arist. De respir. 14. 477 a 32 ; Theophr. De causis plant. i. 21.

of the body has pores into which the appropriate food will fit. Pleasure and pain were derived from the absence or presence of like elements, that is, of nourishment which would fit the pores. Tears and sweat arose from a disturbance which curdled the blood ; they were, so to say, the whey of the blood.[1]

Perception.

118. For the theory of perception held by Empedokles we have the original words of Theophrastos :

Empedokles speaks in the same way of all the senses, and says that perception is due to the " effluences " fitting into the passages of each sense. And that is why one cannot judge the objects of another ; for the passages of some of them are too wide and those of others too narrow for the sensible object, so that the latter either hold their course right through without touching or cannot enter at all. R. P. 177 b.

He tries, too, to explain the nature of sight. He says that the interior of the eye consists of fire, while round about it is earth and air,[2] through which its rarity enables the fire to pass like the light in lanterns (fr. 84). The passages of the fire and water are arranged alternately ; through those of the fire we perceive light objects, through those of the water, dark ; each class of objects fits into each class of passages, and the colours are carried to the sight by effluence. R. P. ib.

But eyes are not all composed in the same way ; some are composed of like elements and some of opposite ; some have the fire in the centre and some on the outside. That is why some animals are keen-sighted by day and others by night. Those which have less fire are keen-sighted in the daytime, for the fire within is brought up to an equality by that without ; those which have less of the opposite (i.e. water), by night, for then their deficiency is supplemented. But, in the opposite case, each will behave in the opposite manner. Those eyes in which fire predominates will be dazzled in the daytime, since the fire being still further increased will stop up and occupy the pores of the water. Those in which water predominates will, he says, suffer

---

[1] Nutrition, Aet. v. 27, 1 ; pleasure and pain, Aet. iv. 9, 15 ; v. 28, 1 ; tears and sweat, v. 22, 1.

[2] That is, watery vapour, not the elemental air or αἰθήρ (§ 107). It is identical with the " water " mentioned below. It is unnecessary, therefore, to insert καὶ ὕδωρ after πῦρ with Karsten and Diels.

the same at night, for the fire will be obstructed by the water.
And this goes on till the water is separated off by the air, for in
each case it is the opposite which is a remedy. The best tempered
and the most excellent vision is one composed of both in
equal proportions. This is practically what he says about
sight.

Hearing, he holds, is produced by sound outside, when the
air moved by the voice sounds inside the ear ; for the sense of
hearing is a sort of bell sounding inside the ear, which he calls a
" fleshy sprout." When the air is set in motion it strikes upon
the solid parts and produces a sound.[1] Smell, he holds, arises
from respiration, and that is why those smell most keenly whose
breath has the most violent motion, and why most smell comes
from subtle and light bodies.[2] As to touch and taste, he does
not lay down how nor by means of what they arise, except that
he gives us an explanation applicable to all, that sensation is
produced by adaptation to the pores. Pleasure is produced by
what is like in its elements and their mixture ; pain, by what is
opposite. R. P. *ib.*

And he gives a precisely similar account of thought and
ignorance. Thought arises from what is like and ignorance from
what is unlike, thus implying that thought is the same, or nearly
the same, as perception. For after enumerating how we know
each thing by means of itself, he adds, " for all things are
fashioned and fitted together out of these, and it is by these men
think and feel pleasure and pain " (fr. 107). And for this
reason we think chiefly with our blood, for in it of all parts
of the body all the elements are most completely mingled.
R. P. 178.

All, then, in whom the mixture is equal or nearly so, and in
whom the elements are neither at too great intervals nor too
small or too large, are the wisest and have the most exact perceptions ; and those who come next to them are wise in proportion. Those who are in the opposite condition are the most
foolish. Those whose elements are separated by intervals and
rare are dull and laborious ; those in whom they are closely
packed and broken into minute particles are impulsive, they
attempt many things and finish few because of the rapidity with
which their blood moves. Those who have a well-proportioned

---

[1] Beare, p. 96, *n.* I.   [2] *Ibid.* p. 133.

mixture in some one part of their bodies will be clever in that
respect. That is why some are good orators and some good
artificers. The latter have a good mixture in their hands,
and the former in their tongues, and so with all other special
capacities. R. P. *ib.*

Perception, then, is due to the meeting of an element in
us with the same element outside. This takes place when
the pores of the organ of sense are neither too large nor too
small for the " effluences " which all things are constantly
giving off (fr. 89). Smell was explained by respiration.
The breath drew in along with it the small particles which
fit into the pores. Empedokles proved this by the example
of people with a cold in their head,[1] who cannot smell, just
because they have a difficulty in breathing. We also see
from fr. 101 that the scent of dogs was referred to in support
of the theory. Empedokles seems to have given no detailed
account of smell, and did not refer to touch at all.[2] Hearing
was explained by the motion of the air which struck upon the
cartilage inside the ear and made it swing and sound like
a bell.[3]

The theory of vision [4] is more complicated ; and, as
Plato makes his Timaios adopt most of it, it is of great
importance in the history of philosophy. The eye was conceived, as by Alkmaion (§ 96),[5] to be composed of fire and
water. Just as in a lantern the flame is protected from the
wind by horn (fr. 84), so the fire in the iris is protected from
the water which surrounds it in the pupil by membranes
with very fine pores, so that, while the fire can pass out,
the water cannot get in. Sight is produced by the fire inside
the eye going forth to meet the object.

Empedokles was aware, too, that " effluences," as he
called them, came from things to the eyes as well ; for he
defined colours as " effluences from forms (or ' things ')

---

[1] Aet. iv. 17, 2 (*Dox.* p. 407).   Beare, p. 133.
[2] Beare, pp. 161-3, 180-81.   [3] *Ibid.* pp. 95 *sqq.*
[4] *Ibid.* pp. 14 *sqq.*   [5] Theophr. *De sens.* 26.

fitting into the pores and perceived." [1] It is not quite clear how these two accounts of vision were reconciled, or how far we are entitled to credit Empedokles with the theory of Plato's *Timaeus*. The statements quoted seem to imply something very like it. [2]

Theophrastos tells us that Empedokles made no distinction between thought and perception, a remark already made by Aristotle. [3] The chief seat of perception was the blood, in which the four elements are most evenly mixed, and especially the blood near the heart (fr. 105). [4] This does not, however, exclude the idea that other parts of the body may perceive also ; indeed, Empedokles held that all things have their share of thought (fr. 103). But the blood was specially sensitive because of its finer mixture. [5] From this it naturally follows that Empedokles adopted the view, already maintained in the Second Part of the poem of Parmenides (fr. 16), that our knowledge varies with the varying constitution of our bodies (fr. 106).

119. The theoretical theology of Empedokles reminds us of Xenophanes, his practical religious teaching of Pythagoras and the Orphics. We are told in the earlier part of the poem that certain " gods " are composed of the elements ; and that therefore though they " live long lives " they must pass away (fr. 21). The elements and the Sphere are also called gods, but that is in quite another sense of the word, and the elements do not pass away.

If we turn to the religious teaching of the *Purifications*,

Theology and religion.

---

[1] The definition is quoted from Gorgias in Plato, *Men.* 76 d 4. All our MSS. have ἀπορροαὶ σχημάτων, but Ven. T has in the margin γρ. χρημάτων, which may well be an old tradition. The Ionic for "things" is χρήματα. See Diels, *Empedokles und Gorgias*, p. 439.

[2] See Beare, *Elementary Cognition*, p. 18.

[3] Arist. *De an.* Γ, 3. 427 a 21.

[4] R. P. 178 a. This was the characteristic doctrine of the Sicilian school, from whom it passed to Aristotle and the Stoics. Plato and Hippokrates, on the other hand, adopted the view of Alkmaion (§ 97) that the brain was the seat of consciousness. At a later date, Philistion of Syracuse, Plato's friend, substituted the ψυχικὸν πνεῦμα ("animal spirits") which circulated along with the blood.   [5] Beare, p. 253.

I

we find that everything turns on the doctrine of trans-migration. On the general significance of this enough has been said above (§ 42) ; the details given by Empedokles are peculiar. According to a decree of Necessity, " daemons " who have sinned are forced to wander from their home in heaven for three times ten thousand seasons (fr. 115). He himself is such an exiled divinity, and has fallen from his high estate because he put his trust in raving Strife. The four elements toss him from one to the other with loathing ; and so he has not only been a human being and a plant, but even a fish. The only way to purify oneself from the taint of original sin is by the cultivation of ceremonial holiness, by purifications, and abstinence from animal flesh. For the animals are our kinsmen (fr. 137), and it is parricide to lay hands on them. In all this there are certain points of contact with the cosmology. We have the " mighty oath " (fr. 115 ; cf. fr. 30), the four elements, Hate as the source of original sin, and Kypris as queen in the Golden Age (fr. 128). But these points are not funda-mental, and the cosmological system of Empedokles leaves no room for an immortal soul, which is presupposed by the *Purifications*. All through this period, there seems to have been a gulf between men's religious beliefs, if they had any, and their cosmological views. The few points of contact we have mentioned may have been enough to hide this from Empedokles himself.

CHAPTER VI

ANAXAGORAS OF KLAZOMENAI

120. ALL that Apollodoros tells us with regard to the date Date. of Anaxagoras seems to rest on the authority of Demetrios Phalereus, who said of him, in his *Register of Archons*, that he "began to be a philosopher" at Athens at the age of twenty, in the archonship of Kallias or Kalliades (480–79 B.C.).[1] This date was probably derived from a calculation based on the philosopher's age at the time of his trial, which Demetrios had every opportunity of learning from sources no longer extant. Apollodoros inferred that Anaxagoras was born in Ol. LXX. (500–496 B.C.), and he adds that he died at the age of seventy-two in Ol. LXXXVIII. I (428–27 B.C.).[2] He doubtless thought it natural that he should not survive Perikles, and that he should die the year Plato was born.[3] We have a further statement, of doubtful origin, but probably due also to Demetrios, that Anaxagoras lived at Athens for thirty years. If it is correct, we get from about 480 to 450 B.C. as the time he lived there.

There can be no doubt that these dates are very nearly right. Aristotle tells us [4] that Anaxagoras was older than Empedokles, who was probably born before 490 B.C. (§ 98) ;

---

[1] Diog. ii. 7 (R. P. 148). For the variation in the archon's name, see Jacoby, p. 244, *n.* 1, and for the chronology generally, see A. E. Taylor in *Classical Quarterly*, xi. 81 *sqq.*, whose arguments appear to me convincing.

[2] We must read ὀγδοηκοστῆς with Scaliger to make the figures come right.   [3] On the statements of Apollodoros, see Jacoby, pp. 244 *sqq.*

[4] Arist. *Met.* A, 3. 984 a 11 (R. P. 150 a).

and Theophrastos said [1] that Empedokles was born " not long after Anaxagoras." Demokritos, too, said that he himself was a young man in the old age of Anaxagoras, and he must have been born about 460 B.C.[2]

Early life.   121. Anaxagoras was from Klazomenai, and Theophrastos tells us that his father's name was Hegesiboulos.[3] The tradition was that he neglected his possessions to follow science.[4] It is certain, at any rate, that already in the fourth century he was regarded as the type of the man who leads the " theoretic life." [5] Of course the story of his contempt for worldly goods was seized on later by the historical novelist and tricked out with the usual apophthegms. These do not concern us here.

One incident belonging to the early manhood of Anaxagoras is recorded, namely, the fall of a huge meteoric stone into the Aigospotamos in 468–67 B.C.[6] Our authorities tell us he predicted this phenomenon, which is plainly absurd. But we shall see reason to believe that it may have occasioned one of his most striking departures from the earlier cosmology, and led to his adoption of the very view for which he was condemned at Athens. At all events, the fall of the stone made a profound impression at the time, and it was still shown to tourists in the days of Pliny and Plutarch.[7]

[1] *Phys. Op.* fr. 3 (*Dox.* p. 477), *ap.* Simpl. *Phys.* p. 25, 19 (R. P. 162 e).

[2] Diog. ix. 41 (R. P. 187). On the date of Demokritos, see Chap. IX. § 171.

[3] *Phys. Op.* fr. 4 (*Dox.* p. 478), repeated by the doxographers.

[4] Plato, *Hipp. ma.* 283 a, τοὐναντίον γὰρ Ἀναξαγόρᾳ φασὶ συμβῆναι ἢ ὑμῖν· καταλειφθέντων γὰρ αὐτῷ πολλῶν χρημάτων καταμελῆσαι καὶ ἀπολέσαι πάντα· οὕτως αὐτὸν ἀνόητα σοφίζεσθαι. Cf. Plut. *Per.* 16.

[5] Arist. *Eth. Nic.* K, 9. 1179 a 13. Cf. *Eth. Eud.* A, 4. 1215 b 6 and 15, 1216 a 10.

[6] Diog. ii. 10 (R. P. 149 a). Pliny, *N.H.* ii. 149, gives the date as Ol. LXXVIII. 2 ; and Eusebios gives it under Ol. LXXVIII. 3. But cf. *Marm. Par.* 57, ἀφ' οὗ ἐν Αἰγὸς ποταμοῖς ὁ λίθος ἔπεσε . . . ἔτη HHII, ἄρχοντος Ἀθήνησι Θεαγενίδου, which is 468–67 B.C. The text of Diog. ii. 11 is corrupt. For suggested restorations, see Jacoby, p. 244, n. 2; and Diels, *Vors.* 46 A 1.

[7] Pliny, *loc. cit.*, " qui lapis etiam nunc ostenditur magnitudine vehis colore adusto." Cf. Plut. *Lys.* 12, καὶ δείκνυται . . . ἔτι νῦν.

122. The doxographers speak of Anaxagoras as the pupil Relation to the Ionic school.
of Anaximenes.[1] This can hardly be correct; Anaximenes
most probably died before Anaxagoras was born. But it is
not enough to say that the statement arose from the fact
that the name of Anaxagoras followed that of Anaximenes
in the *Successions*. We have its original source in a fragment
of Theophrastos himself, which states that Anaxagoras had
been " an associate of the philosophy of Anaximenes." [2]
Now this expression has a very distinct meaning if we accept
the view as to " schools " of science set forth in the Introduction (§ XIV.). It means that the old Ionic school survived the destruction of Miletos in 494 B.C., and continued
to flourish in the other cities of Asia. It means, further,
that it produced no man of distinction after its third great
representative, and that " the philosophy of Anaximenes "
was still taught by whoever was now at the head of the
society.

At this point, then, it may be well to indicate briefly the
conclusions we shall come to in the next few chapters with
regard to the development of philosophy during the first
half of the fifth century B.C. We shall find that, while the
old Ionic school was still capable of training great men, it
was now powerless to keep them. Anaxagoras went his own
way ; Melissos and Leukippos, though they still retained
enough of the old views to bear witness to the source of their
inspiration, were too strongly influenced by the Eleatic
dialectic to remain content with the theories of Anaximenes.
It was left to second-rate minds like Diogenes to champion
the orthodox system, while third-rate minds like Hippon

---

[1] Cicero, *De nat. d.* i. 26 (after Philodemos), " Anaxagoras qui accepit
ab Anaximene disciplinam (*i.e.* διήκουσε) ; Diog. i. 13 (R. P. 4) and ii. 6 ;
Strabo, xiv. p. 645, Κλαζομένιος δ' ἦν ἀνὴρ ἐπιφανὴς Ἀναξαγόρας ὁ φυσικός,
Ἀναξιμένους ὁμιλητής ; Euseb. *P.E.* p. 504 ; [Galen] *Hist. Phil.* 3 ;
Augustine, *De civ. Dei*, viii. 2.

[2] *Phys. Op.* fr. 4 (*Dox.* p. 478), Ἀναξαγόρας μὲν γὰρ Ἡγησιβούλου
Κλαζομένιος κοινωνήσας τῆς Ἀναξιμένους φιλοσοφίας κτλ. In his fifth edition
(p. 973, *n.* 2) Zeller adopts the view given in the text, and confirms it
by comparing the very similar statement as to Leukippos, κοινωνήσας
Παρμενίδῃ τῆς φιλοσοφίας. See below, Chap. IX. § 172.

of Samos went back to the cruder theory of Thales. The details of this anticipatory sketch will become clearer as we go on ; for the present, it is only necessary to call the reader's attention to the fact that the old Ionic Philosophy now forms a sort of background to our story, just as Orphic and Pythagorean religious ideas have done in the preceding chapters.

Anaxagoras at Athens.

123. Anaxagoras was the first philosopher to take up his abode at Athens. We are not informed what brought him there in the year of Salamis. He was, however, a Persian subject ; for Klazomenai had been reduced after the suppression of the Ionian Revolt, and it seems likely enough that he was in the Persian army.[1]

Anaxagoras is said to have been the teacher of Perikles, and the fact is placed beyond the reach of doubt by the testimony of Plato. In the *Phaedrus* [2] he makes Sokrates say : " For all arts that are great, there is need of talk and discussion on the parts of natural science that deal with things on high ; for that seems to be the source which inspires high-mindedness and effectiveness in every direction. Perikles added this very acquirement to his original gifts. He fell in, it seems, with Anaxagoras, who was a scientific man ; and, satiating himself with the theory of things on high, and having attained to a knowledge of the true nature of mind and intellect, which was just what the discourses of Anaxagoras were mainly about, he drew from that source whatever was of a nature to further him in the art of speech." This clearly means that Perikles associated with Anaxagoras before he became a prominent politician. So too Isokrates says that Perikles was the pupil of two " sophists," Anaxa-

[1] That might explain the charge of " Medism " which was perhaps brought against him at his trial (§ 124). It is also, perhaps, significant that Apollodoros (and probably Demetrios of Phaleron) spoke of him as twenty years old κατὰ τὴν Ξέρξου διάβασιν, which means, of course, the crossing of the Hellespont, and would hardly be relevant if Anaxagoras had not been with Xerxes then. It is certainly difficult to see what else could bring a young Klazomenian to Athens at that date.

[2] 270 a (R. P. 148 c).

goras and Damon.[1]   There can be no doubt that the teaching
of Damon belongs to the youth of Perikles,[2] and it is to be
inferred that the same is true of that of Anaxagoras.
A more difficult question is the alleged relation of
Euripides to Anaxagoras. The oldest authority for it is
Alexander of Aitolia, poet and librarian, who lived at the
court of Ptolemy Philadelphos (c. 280 B.C.).   He referred to
Euripides as the " nursling of brave Anaxagoras." [3] The
famous fragment on the blessedness of the scientific life
might just as well refer to any other cosmologist as to Anaxagoras, and indeed suggests more naturally a thinker of a
more primitive type.[4]   On the other hand, it is likely enough
that Anaxagoras did not develop his system all at once,
and he doubtless began by teaching that of Anaximenes.
Besides there is one fragment which distinctly expounds the
central thought of Anaxagoras, and could hardly be referred
to any one else.[5]

124. It is clear that, if we adopt the chronology of The trial.
Demetrios of Phaleron, the trial of Anaxagoras must be
placed early in the political career of Perikles.[6]   That is
the tradition preserved by Satyros, who says that the

---

[1] Isokrates, Περὶ ἀντιδόσεως, 235, Περικλῆς δὲ δυοῖν (σοφισταῖν) ἐγένετο
μαθητής, 'Αναξαγόρου τε τοῦ Κλαζομενίου καὶ Δάμωνος.
[2] Damon (or Damonides) must have been politically active about
460 B.C. (Meyer, Gesch. des Altert. iii. 567 ; Wilamowitz, Aristoteles und
Athen, i. 134), so that he must have been born about 500 B.C.   He was
ostracised before 443 B.C. according to Meyer, and an ostrakon with
the name of Damon son of Damonides has been found (Brückner, Arch.
Anz., 1914, p. 95).   If we suppose that he was ostracised in 445 and returned in 435, his subsequent relations with Sokrates are quite natural.
Plato can hardly have known him personally.   On the whole subject,
see Rosenberg in Neue Jahrb. xxxv. p. 205 sqq.
[3] Gell. xv. 20, " Alexander autem Aetolus hos de Euripide versus
composuit " ; ὁ δ' 'Αναξαγόρου τρόφιμος χαιοῦ (so Valckenaer for ἀρχαίου)
κτλ.   [4] See Introd. p. 10, n. 3.   [5] R. P. 150 b.
[6] The trial of Anaxagoras is generally referred to the period just before
the Peloponnesian War.   That is how it was represented by Ephoros
(reproduced by Diod. xii. 38), and the same account is followed by
Plutarch (V. Per. 32).   The pragmatic character of the chronology of
Ephoros is, however, sufficiently established, and we cannot infer anything from it.   Sotion, who made Kleon the accuser, must also have
assumed a late date for the trial.

accuser was Thoukydides, son of Melesias, and that the
charge was impiety and Medism.¹ As Thoukydides was
ostracised in 443 B.C., that would make it probable that the
trial of Anaxagoras took place about 450 B.C., and would
bring it into connexion with the ostracism of the other
teacher of Perikles, Damon.² If that is so, we understand
at once why Plato never makes Sokrates meet with
Anaxagoras. He had handed his school over to Archelaos
before Sokrates was old enough to take an interest in
scientific theories.³ We do learn from Plato, however,
what the charge of impiety was based on. It was that
Anaxagoras taught the sun was a red-hot stone, and
the moon earth,⁴ and we shall see that he certainly did
hold these views (§ 133). For the rest, the most likely
account is that he was got out of prison and sent away
by Perikles.⁵ We know that such things were possible at
Athens.

Driven from his adopted home, Anaxagoras naturally
went back to Ionia, where at least he would be free to teach
what he pleased. He settled at Lampsakos, a colony of
Miletos, and we shall see reason to believe that he founded
a school there. If so, he must have lived at Lampsakos for
some time before his death.⁶ The Lampsakenes erected an
altar to his memory in their market-place, dedicated to

¹ Diog. ii. 12, Σάτυρος δ' ἐν τοῖς Βίοις ὑπὸ Θουκυδίδου φησὶν εἰσαχθῆναι τὴν
δίκην, ἀντιπολιτευομένου τῷ Περικλεῖ· καὶ οὐ μόνον ἀσεβείας ἀλλὰ καὶ μηδισμοῦ·
καὶ ἀπόντα καταδικασθῆναι θανάτῳ.

² This would be in complete agreement with the statement that
Anaxagoras lived thirty years at Athens (p. 251). For the ostracism of
Damon, see p. 255, n. 2.

³ The well-known passage of the *Phaedo* (97 b 8 *sqq.*) distinctly
implies that Anaxagoras had left Athens when Sokrates was still quite
young. He hears of his doctrine only at second-hand (from Archelaos ?)
and he at once procures the book of Anaxagoras and reads it. If Anaxagoras had still been at Athens, it would have been a simple matter for
Sokrates to seek him out and question him, and it would have made an
excellent subject for a Platonic dialogue. The fact that Plato does make
Sokrates meet Parmenides and Zeno and does not make him meet Anaxagoras is clearly significant. ⁴ *Apol.* 26 d.

⁵ Plut. *Nic.* 23 (R. P. 148 c). Cf. *Per.* 32 (R. P. 148).

⁶ See the account of Archelaos in Chap. X. § 191.

Mind and Truth ; and the anniversary of his death was long
kept as a holiday for school-children, it was said at his own
request.[1]

125. Diogenes includes Anaxagoras in his list of philo- Writings.
sophers who left only a single book, and he has also preserved
the accepted criticism of it, namely, that it was written " in
a lofty and agreeable style." [2]   There is no evidence of any
weight to set against this testimony, which comes ultimately
from the librarians of Alexandria.[3]   The story that Anaxagoras wrote a treatise on perspective as applied to scene-
painting is most improbable ; [4] and the statement that he
composed a work dealing with the quadrature of the circle
is a misunderstanding of an expression in Plutarch.[5]   We
learn from the passage in the *Apology*, referred to above,
that the works of Anaxagoras could be bought at Athens
for a drachma ; and that the book was of some length may
be gathered from the way in which Plato makes Sokrates
go on to speak of it.[6]   In the sixth century A.D. Simplicius
had access to a copy, doubtless in the library of the Academy;
and it is to him we owe the preservation of all our fragments,
with one or two very doubtful exceptions.   Unfortunately
his quotations seem to be confined to the First Book, that
dealing with general principles, so that we are left somewhat
in the dark as to the treatment of details.

[1] The oldest authority for the honours paid to Anaxagoras is Alkidamas,
the pupil of Gorgias, who said these were still kept up in his own time.
Arist. *Rhet.* B, 23. 1398 b 15.

[2] Diog. i. 16 ; ii. 6 (R. P. 5 ; 153).

[3] Schaubach (*An. Claz. Fragm.* p. 57) fabricated a work entitled τὸ
πρὸς Λεχίνεον out of the pseudo-Aristotelian *De plantis*, 817 a 27.   But the
Latin version of Alfred, which is the original of the Greek, has simply *et
ideo dicit lechineon* ; and this seems to be due to failure to make out the
Arabic text from which the Latin was derived.   Cf. Meyer, *Gesch. d.
Bot.* i. 60.

[4] Vitruvius, vii. pr. 11.   A forger, seeking to decorate his production
with a great name, would think at once of the philosopher who was said
to have taught Euripides.

[5] Plut. *De exilio*, 607 f.   The words merely mean that he used to
draw figures relating to the quadrature of the circle on the prison floor.

[6] *Apol.* 26 d-e.   The expression βιβλία perhaps implies that it filled
more than one roll.

126. I give the fragments according to the text and arrangement of Diels :

(1) All things were together, infinite both in number and in smallness ; for the small too was infinite. And, when all things were together, none of them could be distinguished for their smallness. For air and aether prevailed over all things, being both of them infinite ; for amongst all things these are the greatest both in quantity and size.[1]   R. P. 151.

(2) For air and aether are separated off from the mass that surrounds the world, and the surrounding mass is infinite in quantity.   R. P. *ib.*

(3) Nor is there a least of what is small, but there is always a smaller ; for it cannot be that what is should cease to be by being cut.[2]   But there is also always something greater than what is great, and it is equal to the small in amount, and, compared with itself, each thing is both great and small.   R. P. 159 a.

(4) And since these things are so, we must suppose that there are contained many things and of all sorts in the things that are uniting, seeds of all things, with all sorts of shapes and colours and savours (R. P. *ib.*), and that men have been formed in them, and the other animals that have life, and that these men have inhabited cities and cultivated fields as with us ; and that they have a sun and a moon and the rest as with us ; and that their earth brings forth for them many things of all kinds of which they gather the best together into their dwellings, and use them (R. P. 160 b).   Thus much have I said with regard to separating off, to show that it will not be only with us that things are separated off, but elsewhere too.

But before they were separated off, when all things were together, not even was any colour distinguishable ; for the mixture of all things prevented it—of the moist and the dry, and the warm and the cold, and the light and the dark, and of much earth that was in it, and of a multitude of innumerable seeds in no way like each other. For none of the other things

---

[1] Simplicius tells us this was at the beginning of Book I. The sentence quoted by Diog. ii. 6 (R. P. 153) is not a fragment of Anaxagoras, but a summary, like the πάντα ῥεῖ ascribed to Herakleitos (Chap. III. p. 146).

[2] Zeller's τομῇ still seems to me a convincing correction of the MS. τὸ μή, which Diels retains.

either is like any other. And these things being so, we must hold that all things are in the whole. R. P. 151.[1]

(5) And those things having been thus decided, we must know that all of them are neither more nor less ; for it is not possible for them to be more than all, and all are always equal. R. P. 151.

(6) And since the portions of the great and of the small are equal in amount, for this reason, too, all things will be in everything ; nor is it possible for them to be apart, but all things have a portion of everything. Since it is impossible for there to be a least thing, they cannot be separated, nor come to be by themselves ; but they must be now, just as they were in the beginning, all together. And in all things many things are contained, and an equal number both in the greater and in the smaller of the things that are separated off.

(7) . . . So that we cannot know the number of the things that are separated off, either in word or deed.

(8) The things that are in one world are not divided nor cut off from one another with a hatchet, neither the warm from the cold nor the cold from the warm. R. P. 155 e.

(9) . . . as these things revolve and are separated off by the force and swiftness. And the swiftness makes the force. Their swiftness is not like the swiftness of any of the things that are now among men, but in every way many times as swift.

(10) How can hair come from what is not hair, or flesh from what is not flesh ? R. P. 155, f, *n.* 1.

(11) In everything there is a portion of everything except Nous, and there are some things in which there is Nous also. R. P. 160 b.

(12) All other things partake in a portion of everything, while Nous is infinite and self-ruled, and is mixed with nothing, but is alone, itself by itself. For if it were not by itself, but were mixed with anything else, it would partake in all things if it were mixed with any ; for in everything there is a portion of everything, as has been said by me in what goes before, and the things mixed with it would hinder it, so that it would have power over nothing in the same way that it has now being alone by itself. For it is the thinnest of all things and the purest, and it has all

---

[1] I had already pointed out in the first edition that Simplicius quotes this three times as a continuous fragment, and that we are not entitled to break it up. Diels now prints it as a single passage.

knowledge about everything and the greatest strength ; and Nous has power over all things, both greater and smaller, that have life. And Nous had power over the whole revolution, so that it began to revolve in the beginning. And it began to revolve first from a small beginning ; but the revolution now extends over a larger space, and will extend over a larger still. And all the things that are mingled together and separated off and distinguished are all known by Nous. And Nous set in order all things that were to be, and all things that were and are not now and that are, and this revolution in which now revolve the stars and the sun and the moon, and the air and the aether that are separated off. And this revolution caused the separating off, and the rare is separated off from the dense, the warm from the cold, the light from the dark, and the dry from the moist. And there are many portions in many things. But no thing is altogether separated off nor distinguished from anything else except Nous. And all Nous is alike, both the greater and the smaller ; while nothing else is like anything else, but each single thing is and was most manifestly those things of which it has most in it. R. P. 155.

(13) And when Nous began to move things, separating off took place from all that was moved, and so much as Nous set in motion was all separated. And as things were set in motion and separated, the revolution caused them to be separated much more.

(14) And Nous, which ever is, is certainly there, where everything else is, in the surrounding mass, and in what has been united with it and separated off from it.[1]

(15) The dense and the moist and the cold and the dark came together where the earth is now, while the rare and the warm and the dry (and the bright) went out towards the further part of the aether.[2] R. P. 156.

(16) From these as they are separated off earth is solidified ; for from mists water is separated off, and from water earth. From the earth stones are solidified by the cold, and these rush outwards more than water. R. P. 156.

(17) The Hellenes follow a wrong usage in speaking of coming

---

[1] Simplicius gives fr. 14 thus (p. 157, 5) : ὁ δὲ νοῦς ὅσα ἐστί τε κάρτα καὶ νῦν ἐστιν. Diels now reads ὁ δὲ νοῦς, ὃς ἀ⟨εί⟩ ἐστι, τὸ κάρτα καὶ νῦν ἐστιν. The correspondence of ἀεί . . . καὶ νῦν is strongly in favour of this.

[2] On the text of fr. 15, see R. P. 156 a. I have followed Schorn in adding καὶ τὸ λαμπρόν from Hippolytos.

into being and passing away ; for nothing comes into being or passes away, but there is mingling and separation of things that are. So they would be right to call coming into being mixture, and passing away separation. R. P. 150.

(18) It is the sun that puts brightness into the moon.

(19) We call rainbow the reflexion of the sun in the clouds. Now it is a sign of storm ; for the water that flows round the cloud causes wind or pours down in rain.

(20) With the rise of the Dogstar (?) men begin the harvest ; with its setting they begin to till the fields. It is hidden for forty days and nights.

(21) From the weakness of our senses we are not able to judge the truth.

(21a) What appears is a vision of the unseen.

(21b) (We can make use of the lower animals) because we use our own experience and memory and wisdom and art.

(22) What is called " birds' milk " is the white of the egg.

127. The system of Anaxagoras, like that of Empedokles, aimed at reconciling the Eleatic doctrine that corporeal substance is unchangeable with the existence of a world which everywhere presents the appearance of coming into being and passing away. The conclusions of Parmenides are frankly accepted and restated. Nothing can be added to all things ; for there cannot be more than all, and all is always equal (fr. 5). Nor can anything pass away. What men commonly call coming into being and passing away is really mixture and separation (fr. 17).

It is in every way probable that Anaxagoras derived his theory of mixture from his younger contemporary, whose poem may have been published before his own treatise.[1] In any case, we have seen that the opinions of the latter were known at Athens before the middle of the fifth century. We have seen how Empedokles sought to save the world of

Anaxa-
goras and
his pre-
decessors.

---

[1] I do not now think, however, that this is the meaning of the words τοῖs ἔργοιs ὕστεροs in Arist. Met. A, 3. 984 a 12 (R. P. 150 a). At any rate Theophrastos did not take them so ; for he imitates the passage in speaking of Plato (Dox. 484, 19), of whom he says Τούτοιs ἐπιγενόμενοs Πλάτων τῇ μὲν δόξῃ καὶ τῇ δυνάμει πρότεροs, τοῖs δὲ χρόνοιs ὕστεροs. It seems that he understood the Aristotelian formula as " inferior in his achievements."

appearance by maintaining that the opposites—hot and cold, moist and dry—were *things*, each one of which was real in the Parmenidean sense. Anaxagoras regarded this as inadequate. Everything changes into everything else,[1] the things of which the world is made are not " cut off with a hatchet " (fr. 8) in this way. On the contrary, the true formula must be : *There is a portion of everything in everything* (fr. 11).

" Everything in everything."

128. A part of the argument by which Anaxagoras sought to prove this point has been preserved in a corrupt form by Aetios, and Diels has recovered some of the original words from the scholiast on St. Gregory Nazianzene. " We use a simple nourishment," he said, " when we eat the fruit of Demeter or drink water. But how can hair be made of what is not hair, or flesh of what is not flesh ? " (fr. 10).[2] That is just the sort of question the early Milesians must have asked, only the physiological interest has now definitely replaced the meteorological. We shall find a similar train of reasoning in Diogenes of Apollonia (fr. 2).

The statement that there is a portion of everything in everything, is not to be understood as referring simply to the original mixture of things before the formation of the worlds (fr. 1). On the contrary, even now " all things are together," and everything, however small and however great, has an equal number of " portions " (fr. 6). A smaller particle of matter could only contain a smaller number of portions, if one of those portions ceased to be ; but if anything *is*, in the full Parmenidean sense, it is impossible that mere division should make it cease to be (fr. 3). Matter is infinitely divisible ; for there is no least thing, any more than there is a greatest. But however great or small a body may be, it contains just the same number of " portions," that is, a portion of everything.

The portions.

129. What are these " things " of which everything

[1] Arist. *Phys.* A, 4. 187 b 1 (R. P. 155 a).
[2] Act. i. 3, 5 (*Dox.* p. 279). See R. P. 155 f and *n.* 1. I read καρπὸν with Usener.

contains a portion ? It once was usual to represent the theory of Anaxagoras as if he had said that wheat, for instance, contained small particles of flesh, blood, bones, and the like ; but we have just seen that matter is infinitely divisible (fr. 3), and that there are as many " portions " in the smallest particle as in the greatest (fr. 6). That is fatal to the old view. However far we carry division, we can never reach anything " unmixed," so there can be no such thing as a particle of simple nature, however minute.

This difficulty can only be solved in one way.[1] In fr. 8 the examples given of things which are not " cut off from one another with a hatchet " are the hot and the cold ; and elsewhere (frs. 4, 15), mention is made of the other traditional " opposites." Aristotle says that, if we suppose the first principles to be infinite, they may either be one in kind, as with Demokritos, or opposite.[2] Simplicius, following Porphyry and Themistios, refers the latter view to Anaxagoras ;[3] and Aristotle himself implies that the opposites of Anaxagoras had as much right to be called first principles as the " homoeomeries."[4]

It is of those opposites, then, and not of the different forms of matter; that everything contains a portion. Every

[1] See Tannery, *Science hellène*, pp. 283 sqq. I still think that Tannery's interpretation is substantially right, though his statement of it requires some modification. It is, no doubt, difficult for us to think of the hot and cold, dry and wet as " things " (χρήματα) ; but we must remember that, even when the notion of quality (ποιότης) had been defined, this way of thinking survived. Galen (*De nat. fac.* i. 2, 4) is still quite clear on the point that it is the *qualities* which are eternal. He says οἱ δέ τινες εἶναι μὲν ἐν αὐτῇ (τῇ ὑποκειμένῃ οὐσίᾳ) βούλονται τὰς ποιότητας, ἀμεταβλήτους δὲ καὶ ἀτρέπτους ἐξ αἰῶνος, καὶ τὰς φαινομένας ταύτας ἀλλοιώσεις τῇ διακρίσει τε καὶ συγκρίσει γίγνεσθαί φασιν ὡς Ἀναξαγόρας.

[2] Arist. *Phys.* Α, 2. 184 b 21, ἢ οὕτως ὥσπερ Δημόκριτος, τὸ γένος ἕν, σχήματι δὲ ἢ εἴδει διαφερούσας, ἢ καὶ ἐναντίας.

[3] *Phys.* p. 44, 1. He goes on to refer to θερμότητας . . . καὶ ψυχρότητας ξηρότητάς τε καὶ ὑγρότητας μανότητάς τε καὶ πυκνότητας καὶ τὰς ἄλλας κατὰ ποιότητα ἐναντιότητας. He observes, however, that Alexander rejected this interpretation and took διαφερούσας ἢ καὶ ἐναντίας closely together as both referring to Demokritos.

[4] *Phys.* Α, 4. 187 a 25, τὸν μὲν (Ἀναξαγόραν) ἄπειρα ποιεῖν τά τε ὁμοιομερῆ καὶ τἀναντία. Aristotle's own theory only differs from this in so far as he makes ὕλη prior to the ἐναντία.

particle, however large or however small, contains every one of those opposite qualities. That which is hot is also to a certain extent cold. Even snow, Anaxagoras affirmed, was black ; [1] that is, even the white contains a certain portion of the opposite quality. It·is enough to indicate the connexion of this with the views of Herakleitos (§ 80).[2]

Seeds. 130. The difference, then, between the theory of Anaxagoras and that of Empedokles is this. Empedokles had taught that, if you divide the various things which make up this world, and in particular the parts of the body, such as flesh, bones, and the like, far enough, you come to the four " roots " or elements, which are, accordingly, the ultimate reality. Anaxagoras held that, however far you may divide any of these things—and they are infinitely divisible—you never come to a part so small that it does not contain portions of all the opposites. On the other hand, everything can pass into everything else just because the " seeds," as he called them, of each form of matter contain a portion of everything, that is, of all the opposites, though in different proportions. If we are to use the word " element " at all, it is these seeds that are the elements in the system of Anaxagoras.

Aristotle expresses this by saying that Anaxagoras regards the ὁμοιομερῆ as στοιχεῖα.[3] We have seen that the term στοιχεῖον is of later date than Anaxagoras, and it

[1] Sext. *Pyrrh.* i. 33 (R. P. 161 b).

[2] The connexion was already noted by the eclectic Herakleitean to whom I attribute Περὶ διαίτης, i. 3-4 (see above, Chap. III. p. 150, *n.* 2). Cf. the words ἔχει δὲ ἀπ' ἀλλήλων τὸ μὲν πῦρ ἀπὸ τοῦ ὕδατος τὸ ὑγρόν· ἔνι γὰρ ἐν πυρὶ ὑγρότης· τὸ δὲ ὕδωρ ἀπὸ τοῦ πυρὸς τὸ ξηρόν· ἔνι γὰρ καὶ ἐν ὕδατι ξηρόν.

[3] Arist. *De gen. corr.* A, 1, 314 a 18, ὁ μὲν γὰρ (Anaxagoras) τὰ ὁμοιομερῆ στοιχεῖα τίθησιν, οἷον ὀστοῦν καὶ σάρκα καὶ μυελόν, καὶ τῶν ἄλλων ὧν ἑκάστῳ συνώνυμον τὸ μέρος ἐστίν. This was, of course, repeated by Theophrastos and the doxographers ; but it is to be noted that Aetios, supposing as he does that Anaxagoras himself used the term, gives it an entirely wrong meaning. He says that the ὁμοιομέρειαι were so called from the likeness of the particles of the τροφή to those of the body (*Dox.* 279 a 21 ; R. P. 155 f). Lucretius, i. 830 *sqq.* (R. P. 150 a) has a similar account of the matter, derived from Epicurean sources. Obviously, it cannot be reconciled with what Aristotle says.

is natural to suppose that the word ὁμοιομερῆ is also only Aristotle's name for the " seeds." In his own system, the ὁμοιομερῆ are intermediate between the elements (στοιχεῖα), of which they are composed, and the organs (ὄργανα), which are composed of them. The heart cannot be divided into hearts, but the parts of flesh are flesh. That being so, Aristotle's statement is quite intelligible from his own point of view, but there is no reason for supposing that Anaxagoras expressed himself in that particular way. All we are entitled to infer is that he said the " seeds," which he substituted for the " roots " of Empedokles, were not the opposites in a state of separation, but each contained a portion of them all. If Anaxagoras had used the term " homoeomeries " himself, it would be very strange that Simplicius should quote no fragment containing it.

The difference between the two systems may also be regarded from another point of view. Anaxagoras was not obliged by his theory to regard the elements of Empedokles as primary, a view to which there were obvious objections, especially in the case of earth. He explained them in quite another way. Though everything has a portion of everything in it, things appear to be that of which there is most in them (fr. 12 *sub fin.*). We may say, then, that Air is that in which there is most cold, Fire that in which there is most heat, and so on, without giving up the view that there is a portion of cold in the fire and a portion of heat in the air.[1] The great masses which Empedokles had taken for elements are really vast collections of all manner of " seeds." Each of them is, in fact, a πανσπερμία.[2]

---

[1] Cf. above, p. 263.

[2] Arist. *De gen. corr.* A, I. 314 a 29. The word πανσπερμία was used by Demokritos (Arist. *De an.* A, 2. 404 a 8 ; R. P. 200), and it occurs in the Περὶ διαίτης (*loc. cit.*). It seems natural to suppose that it was used by Anaxagoras himself, as he used the term σπέρματα. Much difficulty has been caused by the apparent inclusion of Water and Fire among the ὁμοιομερῆ in Arist. *Met.* A, 3. 984 a 11 (R. P. 150 a). Bonitz understands the words καθάπερ ὕδωρ ἢ πῦρ to mean " as we have just seen that Fire and Water do in the system of Empedokles." In any case, καθάπερ goes closely with οὕτω, and the general sense is that Anaxagoras applies

131. From all this it follows that, when "all things were together," and when the different seeds of things were mixed together in infinitely small particles (fr. 1), the appearance presented would be that of one of what had hitherto been regarded as the primary substances. As a matter of fact, they did present the appearance of " air and aether " ; for the qualities (things) which belong to these —*i.e.* the hot and the cold, prevail in quantity over all other things in the universe, and everything is most obviously that of which it has most in it (fr. 12 *sub fin.*). Here, then, Anaxagoras attaches himself to Anaximenes. The primary condition of things, before the formation of the worlds, is much the same in both ; only, with Anaxagoras, the original mass is no longer the primary substance, but a mixture of innumerable seeds divided into infinitely small parts.

This mass is infinite, like the air of Anaximenes, and it supports itself, since there is nothing surrounding it.[1] Further, the " seeds " of all things which it contains are infinite in number (fr. 1). But, as the innumerable seeds may be divided into those in which the portions of cold, moist, dense, and dark prevail, and those which have most of the warm, dry, rare, and light in them, we may say that the original mass was a mixture of infinite Air and of infinite Fire. The seeds of Air, of course, contain " portions " of the " things " that predominate in Fire, and *vice versa* ; but we regard everything as being that of which it has most in it. Lastly, there is no void in this mixture, an addition to the theory made necessary by the arguments of Parmenides. It is, however, worthy of note that Anaxagoras added an experimental proof of this to the purely dialectical one of the Eleatics. He used the *klepsydra*

---

to the ὁμοιομερῆ what is really true of the στοιχεῖα. It would be better to delete the comma after πῦρ and add one after φησι, for συγκρίσει καὶ διακρίσει μόνον is explanatory of οὕτω . . . καθάπερ. In the next sentence, I read ἁπλῶς for ἄλλως with Zeller (*Arch.* ii. 261). See also Arist. *De caelo*, Γ, 3. 302 b 1 (R. P. 150 a), where the matter is very clearly put.

[1] Arist. *Phys.* Γ, 5. 205 b 1 (R. P. 154 a).

experiment as Empedokles had done (fr. 100), and also showed the corporeal nature of air by means of inflated skins.[1]

132. Like Empedokles, Anaxagoras required some Nous. external cause to produce motion in the mixture. Body, Parmenides had shown, would never move itself, as the Milesians had assumed. Anaxagoras called the cause of motion by the name of Nous. It was this which made Aristotle say that he " stood out like a sober man from the random talkers that had preceded him," [2] and he has often been credited with the introduction of the spiritual into philosophy. The disappointment expressed by Sokrates in the *Phaedo* as to the way in which Anaxagoras worked out the theory should, however, make us pause to reflect before accepting too exalted a view of it. Plato [3] makes Sokrates say : " I once heard a man reading a book, as he said, of Anaxagoras, and saying it was Mind that ordered the world and was the cause of all things. I was delighted to hear of this cause, and I thought he really was right. . . . But my extravagant expectations were all dashed to the ground when I went on and found that the man made no use of Mind at all. He ascribed no causal power whatever to it in the ordering of things, but to airs, and aethers, and waters, and a host of other strange things." Aristotle, of course with this passage in mind, says : [4] " Anaxagoras uses Mind as a *deus ex machina* to account for the formation of the world ; and whenever he is at a loss to explain why anything necessarily is, he drags it in. But in other cases he makes anything rather than Mind the cause." These utterances may well suggest that the Nous of Anaxagoras was something on the same level as the Love and Strife of Empedokles,

[1] *Phys.* Z, 6. 213 a 22 (R. P. 159). We have a full discussion of the experiments with the *klepsydra* in *Probl.* 914 b 9 *sqq.*, a passage which we have already used to illustrate Empedokles, fr. 100. See above, p. 219, *n.* 2.

[2] Arist. *Met.* A, 3. 984 b 15 (R. P. 152).

[3] Plato, *Phaed.* 97 b 8 (R. P. 155 d).

[4] Arist. *Met.* A, 4. 985 a 18 (R. P. 155 d).

and this will be confirmed when we look at what he has to say about it.

In the first place, Nous is unmixed (fr. 12), and does not, like other things, contain a portion of everything. This would hardly be worth saying of an immaterial mind ; no one would suppose that to be hot or cold. The result of its being unmixed is that it " has power over " everything, that is to say, in the language of Anaxagoras, it causes things to move.[1] Herakleitos had said as much of Fire, and Empedokles of Strife. Further, it is the " thinnest " of all things, so that it can penetrate everywhere, and it would be meaningless to say that the immaterial is " thinner " than the material. It is true that Nous also " knows all things " ; but so, perhaps, did the Fire of Herakleitos,[2] and certainly the Air of Diogenes.[3] Zeller holds, indeed, that Anaxagoras meant to speak of something incorporeal ; but he admits that he did not succeed in doing so,[4] and that is historically the important point. Nous is certainly imagined as occupying space ; for we hear of greater and smaller parts of it (fr. 12).

The truth probably is that Anaxagoras substituted Nous for the Love and Strife of Empedokles, because he wished to retain the old Ionic doctrine of a substance that " knows " all things, and to identify that with the new theory of a substance that " moves " all things. Perhaps, too, it was his increased interest in physiological as distinguished from purely cosmological matters that led him to speak of Mind rather than Soul. The former word certainly suggests to the Greek an intimate connexion with the living body which

---

[1] Arist. *Phys.* Θ, 5. 256 b 24, διὸ καὶ Ἀναξαγόρας ὀρθῶς λέγει, τὸν νοῦν ἀπαθῆ φάσκων καὶ ἀμιγῆ εἶναι, ἐπειδήπερ κινήσεως ἀρχὴν αὐτὸν ποιεῖ εἶναι· οὕτω γὰρ ἂν μόνως κινοίη ἀκίνητος ὢν καὶ κρατοίη ἀμιγὴς ὤν. This is only quoted for the meaning of κρατεῖν. Of course, the words ἀκίνητος ὤν are not meant to be historical, and still less is the interpretation in *De an.* Γ, 4. 429 a 1 ³. Diogenes of Apollonia (fr. 5) couples ὑπὸ τούτου πάντα κυβερνᾶσθαι (the old Milesian word) with πάντων κρατεῖν.
[2] If we retain the MS. εἰδέναι in fr. 1. In any case, the name τὸ σοφόν implies as much.   [3] See fr. 3, 5.   [4] Zeller, p. 993.

the latter does not. But, in any case, the originality of Anaxagoras lies far more in the theory of substance than in that of Nous.

133. The formation of a world starts with a rotatory motion which Nous imparts to a portion of the mixed mass in which " all things are together " (fr. 13), and this rotatory motion gradually extends over a wider and wider space. Its rapidity (fr. 9) produced a separation of the rare and the dense, the cold and the hot, the dark and the light, the moist and the dry (fr. 15). This separation produces two great masses, the one consisting mostly of the rare, hot, light, and dry, called the " Aether " ; the other, in which the opposite qualities predominate, called " Air " (fr. 1). Of these the Aether or Fire [1] took the outside while the Air occupied the centre (fr. 15).

The next stage is the separation of the air into clouds, water, earth, and stones (fr. 16). In this Anaxagoras follows Anaximenes closely. In his account of the origin of the heavenly bodies, however, he showed himself more original. We read at the end of fr. 16 that stones "rush outwards more than water," and we learn from the doxographers that the heavenly bodies were explained as stones torn from the earth by the rapidity of its rotation and made red-hot by the speed of their own motion.[2] Perhaps the fall of the meteoric stone at Aigospotamoi had something to do with the origin of this theory. It will also be observed that it necessarily implies the rotation of the flat earth along with the " eddy " ($\delta i\nu\eta$).

134. That Anaxagoras adopted the ordinary Ionian theory of innumerable worlds is clear from fr. 4, which we have no right to regard as other than continuous.[3] The

---

[1] Note that Anaxagoras says " air " where Empedokles said " aether," and that "aether" is with him equivalent to fire. Cf. Arist. De caelo, Γ, 3. 302 b 4, τὸ γὰρ πῦρ καὶ τὸν αἰθέρα προσαγορεύει ταὐτό and ib. A, 3. 270 b 24, Ἀναξαγόρας δὲ καταχρῆται τῷ ὀνόματι τούτῳ οὐ καλῶς· ὀνομάζει γὰρ αἰθέρα ἀντὶ πυρός.

[2] Aet. ii. 13, 3 (Dox. p. 341 ; R. P. 157 c).

[3] See above, p. 259, n. 1.

words " that it was not only with us that things were separated off, but elsewhere too " can only mean that Nous has caused a rotatory movement in more parts of the boundless mixture than one. Aetios certainly includes Anaxagoras among those who held there was only one world [1]; but this testimony cannot be considered of the same weight as that of the fragments. Zeller's reference of the words to the moon is very improbable. Is it likely that any one would say that the inhabitants of the moon " have a sun and moon as with us " ? [2]

Cos-
mology.

135. The cosmology of Anaxagoras is clearly based upon that of Anaximenes, as will be seen from a comparison of the following passage of Hippolytos [3] with the quotations given in Chap. I. (§ 29) :

(3) The earth is flat in shape, and remains suspended because of its size and because there is no vacuum.[4] For this reason the air is very strong, and supports the earth which is borne up by it.

(4) Of the moisture on the surface of the earth, the sea arose from the waters in the earth (for when these were evaporated the remainder turned salt),[5] and from the rivers which flow into it.

(5) Rivers take their being both from the rains and from the waters in the earth ; for the earth is hollow and has waters in its cavities. And the Nile rises in summer owing to the water that comes down from the snows in Ethiopia.[6]

---

[1] Aet. ii. 1, 3 (*Dox.* p. 327).

[2] Further, it can be proved that this passage (fr. 4) occurred quite near the beginning of the work. Cf. Simpl. *Phys.* p. 34, 28 μετ' ὀλίγα τῆς ἀρχῆς τοῦ πρώτου Περὶ φύσεως, p. 156, 1, καὶ μετ' ὀλίγα (after fr. 2), which itself occurred, μετ' ὀλίγον (after fr. 1), which was the beginning of the book. A reference to other " worlds " would be quite in place here, but not a reference to the moon.

[3] *Ref.* i. 8, 3 (*Dox.* p. 562).

[4] This is an addition to the older view occasioned by the Eleatic denial of the void.

[5] The text is corrupt here, but the general sense can be got from Aet. iii. 16. 2.

[6] The MS. reading is ἐν τοῖς ἄρκτοις, for which Diels adopts Fredrichs' ἐν τοῖς ἀνταρκτικοῖς. I have thought it safer to translate the ἐν τῇ Αἰθιοπίᾳ of Aetios (iv. 1, 3). This view is mentioned by Herodotos (ii. 22). Seneca (*N.Q.* iv. 2, 17) points out that it was adopted by Aischylos (*Suppl.* 559, fr. 300, Nauck), Sophokles (fr. 797), and Euripides (*Hel.* 3, fr. 228), who would naturally take their opinions from Anaxagoras.

(6) The sun and the moon and all the stars are fiery stones carried round by the rotation of the aether. Under the stars are the sun and moon, and also certain bodies which revolve with them, but are invisible to us.

(7) We do not feel the beat of the stars because of the greatness of their distance from the earth ; and, further, they are not so warm as the sun, because they occupy a colder region. The moon is below the sun, and nearer us.

(8) The sun surpasses the Peloponnesos in size. The moon has not a light of her own, but gets it from the sun. The course of the stars goes under the earth.

(9) The moon is eclipsed by the earth screening the sun's light from it, and sometimes, too, by the bodies below the moon coming before it. The sun is eclipsed at the new moon, when the moon screens it from us. Both the sun and the moon turn back in their courses owing to the repulsion of the air. The moon turns back frequently, because it cannot prevail over the cold.

(10) Anaxagoras was the first to determine what concerns the eclipses and the illumination of the sun and moon. And he said the moon was of earth, and had plains and ravines in it. The Milky Way was the reflexion of the light of the stars that were not illuminated by the sun. Shooting stars were sparks, as it were, which leapt out owing to the motion of the heavenly vault.

(11) Winds arose when the air was rarefied by the sun, and when things were burned and made their way to the vault of heaven and were carried off. Thunder and lightning were produced by heat striking upon clouds.

(12) Earthquakes were caused by the air above striking on that beneath tl e earth ; for the movement of the latter caused the earth which floats on it to rock.

All this confirms the statement of Theophrastos, that Anaxagoras had belonged to the school of Anaximenes. The flat earth floating on the air, the dark bodies below the ᵥmoon, the explanation of the solstices and the " turnings back " of the moon by the resistance of air, the explanations of wind and of thunder and lightning, are all derived from the Milesian.

As to the moon's light and the cause of eclipses, it was natural that Anaxagoras should be credited at Athens with these discoveries. On the other hand, it seems very unlikely that they were made by a believer in a flat earth, and there is sufficient evidence that they are really Pythagorean.[1]

Biology.

136. "There is a portion of everything in everything except Nous, and there are some things in which there is Nous also " (fr. 11). In these words Anaxagoras laid down the distinction between animate and inanimate things. He tells us that it is the same Nous that "has power over," that is, sets in motion, all things that have life, both the greater and the smaller (fr. 12). The Nous in living creatures is the same in all (fr. 12), and from this it followed that the different grades of intelligence we observe in the animal and vegetable worlds depend entirely on the structure of the body. The Nous was the same, but it had more opportunities in one body than another. Man was the wisest of animals, not because he had a better sort of Nous, but because he had hands.[2] This is in accordance with the previous development of thought upon the subject. Parmenides, in his Second Part (fr. 16), had already made the thought of men depend on the constitution of their limbs.

As all Nous is the same, we are not surprised to find that plants were regarded as living creatures. If we may trust the pseudo-Aristotelian *Treatise on Plants*[3] so far, Anaxagoras argued that they must feel pleasure and pain in connexion with their growth and with the fall of their leaves. Plutarch says[4] that he called plants "animals fixed in the earth."

Both plants and animals originated in the first instance from the πανσπερμία. Plants arose when the seeds of

---

[1] See p. 177, *n.* 1.
[2] Arist. *De part. an.* Δ, 10. 687 a 7 (R. P. 160 b).
[3] [Arist.] *De plant.* A, 1. 815 a 15 (R. P. 160).
[4] Plut. *Q.N.* 1 (R. P. 160), ζῷον . . . ἐγγεῖον.

them which the air contained were brought down by the rain-water,[1] and animals originated in a similar way.[2] Like Anaximander, Anaxagoras held that animals first arose in the moist element.[3]

137. In these scanty notices we seem to see traces of a polemical attitude towards Empedokles, and the same may be observed in what we are told of the theory of perception adopted by Anaxagoras, especially in the view that perception is of contraries.[4] The account which Theophrastos gives of this [5] is as follows :

Perception.

But Anaxagoras says that perception is produced by opposites ; for like things cannot be effected by like. He attempts to give a detailed enumeration of the particular senses. We see by means of the image in the pupil ; but no image is cast upon what is of the same colour, but only on what is different. With most living creatures things are of a different colour to the pupil by day, though with some this is so by night, and these are accordingly keen-sighted at that time. Speaking generally, however, night is more of the same colour with the eyes than day. And an image is cast on the pupil by day, because light is a concomitant cause of the image, and because the prevailing colour casts an image more readily upon its opposite.[6]

It is in the same way that touch and taste discern their objects. That which is just as warm or just as cold as we are neither warms us nor cools us by its contact ; and, in the same way, we do not apprehend the sweet and the sour by means of themselves. We know cold by warm, fresh by salt, and sweet by sour, in virtue of our deficiency in each ; for all these are in us to begin with. And we smell and hear in the same manner ; the former by means of the accompanying respiration, the latter by the sound penetrating to the brain, for the bone which surrounds this is hollow, and it is upon it that the sound falls.[7]

And all sensation implies pain, a view which would seem to be the consequence of the first assumption, for all unlike things

---

[1] Theophr. *Hist. Plant.* iii. 1, 4 (R. P. 160).
[2] Irenaeus, *Adv. Haer.* ii. 14, 2 (R. P. 160 a).
[3] Hipp. *Ref.* i. 8, 12 (*Dox.* p. 563).
[4] Beare, p. 37.   [5] Theophr. *De sensu,* 27 *sqq.* (*Dox.* p. 507).
[6] Beare, p. 38.   [7] Beare, p. 208.

produce pain by their contact. And this pain is made percept-
ible by the long continuance or by the excess of a sensation.
Brilliant colours and excessive noises produce pain, and we cannot
dwell long on the same things. The larger animals are the more
sensitive, and, generally, sensation is proportionate to the size
of the organs of sense. Those animals which have large, pure,
and bright eyes, see large objects and from a great distance, and
contrariwise.[1]

And it is the same with hearing. Large animals can hear
great and distant sounds, while less sounds pass unperceived ;
small animals perceive small sounds and those near at hand.[2]
It is the same too with smell. Rarefied air has more smell ;
for, when air is heated and rarefied, it smells. A large animal
when it breathes draws in the condensed air along with the
rarefied, while a small one draws in the rarefied by itself ; so
the large one perceives more. For smell is better perceived when
it is near than when it is far by reason of its being more condensed, while when dispersed it is weak. But, roughly speaking,
large animals do not perceive a rarefied smell, nor small animals
a condensed one.[3]

This theory marks in some respects an advance on that
of Empedokles. It was a happy thought of Anaxagoras to
make sensation depend upon irritation by opposites, and to
connect it with pain. Many modern theories are based upon
a similar idea.

That Anaxagoras regarded the senses as incapable of
reaching the truth of things is shown by the fragments
preserved by Sextus. But we must not, for all that, turn
him into a sceptic. The saying preserved by Aristotle [4]
that " things are as we suppose them to be," has no value
at all as evidence. It comes from some collection of apophthegms, not from the treatise of Anaxagoras himself ; and
it had, as likely as not, a moral application. He did say
(fr. 21) that " the weakness of our senses prevents our
discerning the truth," but this meant simply that we do
not see the " portions " of everything which are in every-

---

[1] Beare, p. 209. [2] Ibid. p. 103.
[3] Ibid. p. 137. [4] Met. Δ, 5. 1009 b 25 (R. P. 161 a).

thing ; for instance, the portions of black which are in the white. Our senses simply show us the portions that prevail. He also said that the things which are seen give us the power of seeing the invisible, which is the very opposite of scepticism (fr. 21*a*).

CHAPTER VII

THE PYTHAGOREANS

The
Pytha-
gorean
school.

138. After losing their supremacy in the Achaian cities, the Pythagoreans concentrated themselves at Rhegion ; but the school founded there did not maintain itself for long, and only Archytas stayed behind in Italy. Philolaos and Lysis, the latter of whom had escaped as a young man from the massacre of Kroton, had already found their way to Thebes.[1] We know from Plato that Philolaos was there towards the close of the fifth century, and Lysis was afterwards the teacher of Epameinondas.[2] Some of the Pythagoreans, however, were able to return to Italy later. Philolaos certainly did so, and Plato implies that he had left Thebes some time before 399 B.C., the year Sokrates was put to death. In the fourth century, the chief seat of the school is the Dorian city of Taras, and we find the Pythagoreans heading the opposition to Dionysios of Syracuse. It is to this period that the activity of Archytas belongs. He was the friend of Plato, and almost realised the ideal of the philosopher king. He ruled Taras for years, and Aristoxenos tells us that he was never defeated in the field of battle.[3]

[1] Iambl. *V. Pyth.* 251. The ultimate authority for all this is Timaios. There is no need to alter the MS. reading Ἀρχύτου to Ἀρχίππου (as Diels does after Beckmann). We are dealing with a later generation, and the sentence opens with οἱ δὲ λοιποὶ τῶν Πυθαγορείων, *i.e.* those other than Archippos and Lysis, who have been dealt with in the preceding section.

[2] For Philolaos, see Plato, *Phaed.* 61 d 7 ; e 7 ; and for Lysis, Aristoxenos in Iambl. *V. Pyth.* 250 (R. P. 59 b).

[3] Diog. viii. 79-83 (R. P. 61). Aristoxenos himself came from Taras. The story of Damon and Phintias (told by Aristoxenos) belongs to this time.

He was also the inventor of mathematical mechanics.   At
the same time, Pythagoreanism had taken root in the East.
Lysis remained at Thebes, where Simmias and Kebes had
heard Philolaos, while the remnant of the Pythagorean school
of Rhegion settled at Phleious.   Aristoxenos was personally
acquainted with the last generation of this school, and
mentioned by name Xenophilos the Chalkidian from Thrace,
with Phanton, Echekrates, Diokles, and Polymnastos of
Phleious.   They were all, he said, disciples of Philolaos and
Eurytos,[1] and we learn from Plato that Simmias and Kebes
of Thebes and Echekrates of Phleious were also associates of
Sokrates.[2]   Xenophilos was the teacher of Aristoxenos, and
lived in perfect health at Athens to the age of a hundred
and five.[3]

139. This generation of the school really belongs, how- Philolaos.
ever, to a later period ; it is with Philolaos we have now to
deal.   The facts we know about his teaching from external
sources are few in number.   The doxographers, indeed,
ascribe to him an elaborate theory of the planetary system,
but Aristotle never mentions his name in connexion with
that.   He gives it as the theory of " the Pythagoreans " or
of " some Pythagoreans." [4]   It seems natural to suppose,
however, that the Pythagorean elements of Plato's *Phaedo*
and *Gorgias* come mainly from Philolaos.   Plato makes
Sokrates express surprise that Simmias and Kebes had not
learnt from him why it is unlawful for a man to take his
life,[5] and it seems to be implied that the Pythagoreans at
Thebes used the word " philosopher " in the special sense of

---

[1] Diog. viii. 46 (R. P. 62).

[2] The whole *mise en scène* of the *Phaedo* presupposes this, and it is
quite incredible that Plato should have misrepresented the matter.
Simmias and Kebes were a little younger than Plato and he could hardly
have ventured to introduce them as disciples of Sokrates if they had not
in fact been so.   Xenophon too (*Mem.* i. 2. 48) includes Simmias and Kebes
in his list of genuine disciples of Sokrates, and in another place (iii. 11, 7)
he tells us that they had been attracted from Thebes by Sokrates and
never left his side.

[3] See Aristoxenos *ap.* Val. Max. viii. 13, ext. 3 ; and Souidas *s.v.*

[4] See below, §§ 150-152.   [5] Plato, *Phaed.* 61 d 6.

a man who is seeking to find a way of release from the burden of this life.[1] It is probable that Philolaos spoke of the body (σῶμα) as the tomb (σῆμα) of the soul.[2] We seem to be justified, then, in holding that he taught the old Pythagorean religious doctrine in some form, and that he laid special stress on knowledge as a means of release. That is the impression we get from Plato, who is far the best authority we have.

We know further that Philolaos wrote on " numbers " ; for Speusippos followed him in the account he gave of the Pythagorean theories on that subject.[3] It is probable that he busied himself mainly with arithmetic, and we can hardly doubt that his geometry was of the primitive type described in an earlier chapter. Eurytos was his disciple, and we have seen (§ 47) that his views were still very crude.

We also know now that Philolaos wrote on medicine,[4] and that, while apparently influenced by the theories of the Sicilian school, he opposed them from the Pythagorean standpoint. In particular, he said that our bodies were composed only of the warm, and did not participate in the

[1] This appears to follow from the remark of Simmias in *Phaed.* 64 b. The whole passage would be pointless if the words φιλόσοφος, φιλοσοφεῖν, φιλοσοφία had not in some way become familiar to the ordinary Theban of the fifth century.   Now Herakleides Pontikos made Pythagoras invent the word, and expound it in a conversation with Leon, tyrant of Sikyon *or Phleious*. Cf. Diog. i. 12 (R. P. 3), viii. 8 ; Cic. *Tusc.* v. 3. 8. Cf. also the remark of Alkidamas quoted by Arist. *Rhet.* B, 23. 1398 b 18, Θήβησιν ἅμα οἱ προστάται φιλόσοφοι ἐγένοντο καὶ εὐδαιμόνησεν ἡ πόλις.

[2] For reasons which will appear, I do not attach importance in this connexion to Philolaos, fr. 14 Diels=23 Mullach (R. P. 89), but it does seem likely that the μυθολογῶν κομψὸς ἀνήρ of *Gorg.* 493 a 5 (R. P. 89 b) is responsible for the whole theory there given. He is certainly, in any case, the author of the τετρημένος πίθος, which implies the same general view.   Now he is called ἴσως Σικελός τις ἢ 'Ιταλικός, which means he was an Italian ; for the Σικελός τις is merely an allusion to the Σικελὸς κομψὸς ἀνὴρ ποτὶ τὰν ματέρ' ἔφα of Timokreon. We do not know of any Italian from whom Sokrates could have learnt these views except Philolaos or one of his associates.

[3] See above, Chap. II. p. 102, *n.* 2.

[4] It is a good illustration of the defective character of our tradition (Introd. p. 26) that this was quite unknown till the publication of the extracts from Menon's *Iatrika* contained in the Anonymus Londinensis. See Diels in *Hermes,* xxviii. pp. 417 *sqq.*

cold. It was only after birth that the cold was introduced by respiration. The connexion of this with the old Pythagorean theory is clear. Just as the Fire in the macrocosm draws in and limits the cold dark breath which surrounds the world (§ 53), so do our bodies inhale cold breath from outside. Philolaos made bile, blood, and phlegm the causes of disease ; and, in accordance with this theory, he had to deny that the phlegm was cold, as the Sicilian school held. Its etymology proved it to be warm. We shall see that it was probably this preoccupation with the medicine of the Sicilian school that gave rise to some of the most striking developments of later Pythagoreanism.

140. Such, so far as I can judge, was the historical Philolaos, though he is usually represented in a very different light and has even been called a predecessor of Copernicus. To understand this, we must turn our attention to the story of a literary conspiracy. *Plato and the Pythagoreans.*

We have seen that there are one or two references to Philolaos in Plato,[1] but these hardly suggest that he played an important part in the development of Pythagorean science. The most elaborate account we have of this is put by Plato into the mouth of Timaios the Lokrian, of whom we know no more than he has chosen to tell us. It is clear at least that he is supposed to have visited Athens when Sokrates was still in the prime of life,[2] and that he must have been practically a contemporary of Philolaos. It hardly seems likely that Plato should have given him the credit of discoveries which were really due to his better-known contemporary. However, Plato had many enemies and detractors, and Aristoxenos was one of them. We know he made the extraordinary statement that most of the *Republic* was to be found in a work by Protagoras,[3] and he

---

[1] See p. 276, *n.* 2, and p. 278, *n.* 2.

[2] This follows at once from the fact that he is represented as conversing with the elder Kritias (p. 203, *n.* 3), who is very aged, and with Hermokrates, who is quite young.

[3] Diog. iii. 37. For similar charges, cf. Zeller, *Plato*, p. 429, *n.* 7.

seems also to be the original source of the story that Plato
bought "three Pythagorean books" from Philolaos and
copied the *Timaeus* out of them. According to this, the
"three books" had come into the possession of Philolaos ;
and, as he had fallen into great poverty, Dion was able to
buy them from him, or from his relatives, at Plato's request,
for a hundred *minae*.[1] It is certain, at any rate, that this
story was already current in the third century ; for the
sillographer Timon of Phleious addresses Plato thus : " And
of thee too, Plato, did the desire of discipleship lay hold.
For many pieces of silver thou didst get in exchange a small
book, and starting from it didst learn to write *Timaeus*." [2]
Hermippos, the pupil of Kallimachos, said that " some
writer " said Plato himself bought the books from the
relatives of Philolaos for forty Alexandrian *minae* and
copied the *Timaeus* out of it ; while Satyros, the Arist-
archean, says he got it through Dion for a hundred *minae*.[3]
There is no suggestion in any of these accounts that the book
was by Philolaos himself ; they imply rather that what
Plato bought was either a book by Pythagoras, or at any
rate authentic notes of his teaching, which had come into
the hands of Philolaos. In later times, it was generally
supposed that the forgery entitled *The Soul of the World*,
which goes by the name of Timaios the Lokrian, was meant ; [4]
but it has now been proved that this cannot have existed
earlier than the first century A.D. Moreover, it is plain that
it is based on Plato's *Timaeus* itself, and that it was written
in order to bolster up the story of Plato's plagiarism. It
does not, however, fulfil the most important requirement,
that of being in three books, which is always an essential
feature of that story.[5]

[1] Iambl. *V. Pyth.* 199. Diels is clearly right in ascribing the story to
Aristoxenos (*Arch.* iii. p. 461, *n.* 26).

[2] Timon, fr. 54 (Diels), *ap.* Gell. iii. 17 (R. P. 60 a).

[3] For Hermippos and Satyros, see Diog. iii. 9 ; viii. 84, 85.

[4] So Iambl. *in Nicom.* p. 105, 11 ; Proclus, *in Tim.* p. 1, Diehl.

[5] They are τὰ θρυλούμενα τρία βιβλία (Iambl. *V. Pyth.* 199), τὰ διαβόητα
τρία βιβλία (Diog. viii. 15).

Not one of the writers just mentioned professes to have seen these famous " three books " ; [1] but at a later date there were at least two works which claimed to represent them. Diels has shown how a treatise in three sections, entitled Παιδευτικόν, πολιτικόν, φυσικόν, was composed in the Ionic dialect and attributed to Pythagoras. It was largely based on the Πυθαγορικαὶ ἀποφάσεις of Aristoxenos, but its date is uncertain.[2] In the first century B.C., Demetrios Magnes professes to quote the opening words of the work published by Philolaos.[3] These, however, are in Doric. Demetrios does not actually say this work was written by Philolaos himself, though it is no doubt the same from which a number of extracts are preserved under his name in Stobaios and later writers. If it professed to be by Philolaos, that was not quite in accordance with the original story ; but it is easy to see how his name may have become attached to it. We are told that the other book which passed under the name of Pythagoras was really by Lysis.[4] Boeckh has shown that the work ascribed to Philolaos probably consisted of three books also, and Proclus referred to it as the *Bakchai*,[5] a fanciful Alexandrian title which recalls the " Muses " of Herodotos. Two of the extracts in Stobaios bear it. It must surely be confessed that the whole story is very suspicious.

141. Boeckh argued that all the fragments preserved under the name of Philolaos were genuine ; but no one will now go so far as that. The lengthy extract on the soul is given up even by those who maintain the genuineness of the The " Fragments of Philolaos."

[1] As Bywater said (*J. Phil.* i. p. 29), the history of this work "reads like the history, not so much of a book, as of a literary *ignis fatuus* floating before the minds of imaginative writers."
[2] Diels, " Ein gefälschtes Pythagorasbuch " (*Arch.* iii. pp. 451 *sqq.*).
[3] Djog. viii. 85 (R. P. 63 b). Diels reads πρῶτον ἐκδοῦναι τῶν Πυθαγορικῶν ⟨βιβλία καὶ ἐπιγράψαι Περὶ⟩ Φύσεως.
[4] Diog. viii. 7.
[5] Proclus, *in Eucl.* p. 22, 15 (Friedlein). Cf. Boeckh, *Philolaos*, pp. 36 *sqq.* Boeckh refers to a sculptured group of *three* Bakchai, whom he supposes to be Ino, Agaue, and Autonoe.

K

rest.[1] It cannot be said that this position is plausible. Boeckh saw there was no ground for supposing that there ever was more than a single work, and he drew the conclusion that we must accept all the remains as genuine or reject all as spurious.[2] As, however, many scholars still maintain the genuineness of most of the fragments, we cannot ignore them altogether. Arguments based on their doctrine would, it is true, present the appearance of a vicious circle at this stage, but there are two serious objections to the fragments, which may be mentioned at once.

In the first place, we must ask whether it is likely that Philolaos should have written in Doric ? Ionic was the dialect of science and philosophy till the time of the Peloponnesian War, and there is no reason to suppose the early Pythagoreans used any other.[3] Pythagoras was himself an Ionian, and it is not likely that in his time the Achaian states in which he founded his Order had adopted the Dorian dialect.[4] Alkmaion of Kroton seems to have written in Ionic.[5] Diels says that Philolaos and then Archytas were the first Pythagoreans to use the dialect of their homes ;[6] but Philolaos can hardly be said to have had a home, and it is hard to see why an Achaian refugee at Thebes should

---

[1] The passage is given in R. P. 68. For a full discussion of this and the other fragments, see Bywater, " On the Fragments attributed to Philolaus the Pythagorean " (*J. Phil.* i. pp. 21 *sqq.*).

[2] Boeckh, *Philolaos*, p. 38. Diels (*Vors.* p. 246) distinguishes the *Bakchai* from the three books Περὶ φύσιος (*ib.* p. 239). As, however, he identifies the latter with the " three books " bought from Philolaos, and regards it as genuine, this does not seriously affect the argument.

[3] See Diels in *Arch.* iii. pp. 460 *sqq.*

[4] On the Achaian dialect, see O. Hoffmann in Collitz and Bechtel, *Dialekt-Inschriften*, vol. ii. p. 151. How slowly Doric penetrated into the Chalkidian states may be seen from the mixed dialect of the inscription of Mikythos of Rhegion (*Dial.-Inschr.* iii. 2, p. 498), which is later than 468–67 B.C. There is no reason to suppose that the Achaian dialect of Kroton was less tenacious of life. We can see from Herodotos that there was a strong prejudice against the Dorians there.

[5] The scanty fragments contain one Doric (or Achaian ?) form, ἔχοντι (fr. 1), but Alkmaion calls himself Κροτωνιήτης, which is very significant; for Κροτωνιάτας is the Achaian as well as the Doric form.   [6] *Arch.* iii. p. 460.

write in Doric.[1] Nor did Archytas write in the Laconian dialect of Taras, but in what may be called " common Doric," and he is a generation later than Philolaos, which makes a great difference. In the time of Philolaos and later, Ionic was still used even by the citizens of Dorian states for scientific purposes. The Syracusan historian Antiochos wrote in Ionic, and so did the medical writers of Dorian Kos and Knidos. The forged work of Pythagoras, which some ascribed to Lysis, was in Ionic ; and so was the book on the *Akousmata* attributed to Androkydes,[2] which shows that, even in Alexandrian times, it was believed that Ionic was the proper dialect for Pythagorean writings.

In the second place, there can be no doubt that one of the fragments refers to the five regular solids, four of which are identified with the elements of Empedokles.[3] Now Plato tells us in the *Republic* that stereometry had not been adequately investigated at the time that dialogue is supposed to take place,[4] and we have express testimony that the five " Platonic figures," as they were called, were discovered in the Academy. In the Scholia to Euclid we read that the Pythagoreans only knew the cube, the pyramid (tetrahedron), and the dodecahedron, while the octahedron and

---

[1] He is distinctly called a Krotoniate in the extracts from Menon's Ἰατρικά (cf. Diog. viii. 84). It is true that Aristoxenos called him and Eurytos Tarentines (Diog. viii. 46), but this only means that he settled at Taras after leaving Thebes. These variations are common in the case of migratory philosophers. Eurytos is also called a Krotoniate and a Metapontine (Iambl. *V. Pyth.* 148, 266). Cf. also p. 330, *n.* 1 on Leukippos, and p. 351, *n.* 1 on Hippon.

[2] For Androkydes, see Diels, *Vors.* p. 281. As Diels points out (*Arch.* iii. p. 461), even Lucian has sufficient sense of style to make Pythagoras speak Ionic.

[3] Cf. fr. 12=20 M. (R. P. 79), which I read as it stands in the MS. of Stobaios, but bracketing an obvious adscript or dittography, καὶ τὰ ἐν τᾷ σφαίρᾳ σώματα πέντε ἐντί [τὰ ἐν τᾷ σφαίρᾳ], πῦρ, ὕδωρ καὶ γᾶ καὶ ἀήρ, καὶ ὁ τᾶς σφαίρας ὁλκὰς πέμπτον. In any case, we are not justified in reading τὰ μὲν τᾶς σφαίρας σώματα with Diels. For the identification of the four elements with four of the regular solids, cf. §.147, and for the description of the fifth, the dodecahedron, cf. § 148.

[4] Plato, *Rep.* 528 b.

the icosahedron were discovered by Theaitetos.[1]   This sufficiently justifies us in regarding the " fragments of Philolaos "
with suspicion, and all the more so as Aristotle does not
appear to have seen the work from which these fragments
come.[2]

The
Problem.

142. We must look, then, for other evidence.   From
what has been said, it will be clear that it is above all from
Plato we can learn to regard Pythagoreanism sympatheti-
cally.   Aristotle was out of sympathy with Pythagorean
ways of thinking, but he took great pains to understand
them.   This was because they played so great a part in the
philosophy of Plato and his successors, and he had to make
the relation of the two doctrines as clear as he could to
himself and his disciples.   What we have to do, then, is
to interpret what Aristotle tells us in the spirit of Plato,
and then to consider how the doctrine we thus arrive at is
related to the systems which preceded it.   It is a delicate
operation, no doubt, but it has been made much safer by
recent discoveries in the early history of mathematics and
medicine.

[1] Heiberg's Euclid, vol. v. p. 654, 1, ἐν τούτῳ τῷ βιβλίῳ, τουτέστι
τῷ ιγ΄, γράφεται τὰ λεγόμενα Πλάτωνος ἒ σχήματα, ἃ αὐτοῦ μὲν οὐκ ἔστιν,
τρία δὲ τῶν προειρημένων ἒ σχημάτων τῶν Πυθαγορείων ἐστίν, ὅ τε κύβος
καὶ ἡ πυραμὶς καὶ τὸ δωδεκάεδρον, Θεαιτήτου δὲ τό τε ὀκτάεδρον καὶ τὸ
εἰκοσάεδρον.   It is no objection to this that, as Newbold points out (Arch.
xix. p. 204), the inscription of the dodecahedron is more difficult than that
of the octahedron and icosahedron.   We have no right to reject the definite
testimony quoted above (no doubt from Eudemos) on grounds of a priori
probability.   As a matter of fact, there are Celtic and Etruscan dodeca-
hedra of considerable antiquity in the Louvre and elsewhere (G. Loria,
Scienze esatte, p. 39), and the fact is significant in view of the connexion
between Pythagoreanism and the North which has been suggested.

[2] Philolaos is quoted only once in the Aristotelian corpus, in Eth. Eud.
B, 8. 1225 a 33 ἀλλ' ὥσπερ Φιλόλαος ἔφη εἶναί τινας λόγους κρείττους ἡμῶν,
which looks like an apophthegm.   His name is not even mentioned anywhere else, and this would be inconceivable if Aristotle had ever seen
a work of his which expounded the Pythagorean system.   He must have
known the importance of Philolaos from Plato's Phaedo, and would certainly
have got hold of his book if it had existed.   It should be added that
Tannery held the musical theory of our fragments to be too advanced for
Philolaos.   It must, he argued, be later than Plato and Archytas (Rev. de
Phil. xxviii. pp. 233 sqq.).   His opinion on such a point is naturally of
the greatest weight.

Zeller has cleared the ground by eliminating the Platonic elements which have crept into later accounts of the system. These are of two kinds. First of all, we have genuine Academic formulae, such as the identification of the Limit and the Unlimited with the One and the Indeterminate Dyad ; [1] and secondly, there is the Neoplatonic doctrine which represents the opposition between them as one between God and Matter.[2] It is not necessary to repeat Zeller's arguments here, as no one will now attribute the doctrine in that form to the Pythagoreans.

This simplifies the problem, but it is still very difficult. According to Aristotle, the Pythagoreans said *Things are numbers*, though that is not the doctrine of the fragments of " Philolaos." According to them, things *have* number, which makes them knowable, while their real essence is something unknowable.[3] We have seen reason for believing that Pythagoras himself said *Things are numbers* (§ 52), and there is no doubt as to what his followers meant by the formula ; for Aristotle · says they used it in a cosmological sense. The world, according to them, was made of numbers in the same sense as others had said it was made of " four roots " or " innumerable seeds." It will not do to dismiss this as mysticism. The Pythagoreans of the fifth century were scientific men, and must have meant something quite definite. We shall, no doubt, have to say that they used the words *Things are numbers* in a somewhat non-natural sense, but there is no difficulty in that. The Pythagoreans had a great veneration for the actual words of the Master (αὐτὸς ἔφα) ; but such veneration is often

---

[1] Aristotle says distinctly (*Met.* A, 6. 987 b 25) that " to set up a dyad instead of the unlimited regarded as one, and to make the unlimited consist of the great and small, is distinctive of Plato."

[2] Zeller, p. 369 *sqq.* (Eng. trans. p. 397 *sqq.*).

[3] For the doctrine of " Philolaos," cf. fr. 1 (R. P. 64) ; and for the unknowable ἐστὼ τῶν πραγμάτων, see fr. 3 (R. P. 67). It has a suspicious resemblance to the later ὕλη, which Aristotle would hardly have failed to note. He is always on the look-out for anticipations of ὕλη.

accompanied by a singular licence of interpretation. We shall start, then, from what Aristotle tells us about the numbers.

143. In the first place, Aristotle is quite clear that Pythagoreanism was intended to be a cosmological system like the others. " Though the Pythagoreans," he tells us, " made use of less obvious first principles and elements than the rest, seeing that they did not derive them from sensible objects, yet all their discussions and studies had reference to nature alone. They describe the origin of the heavens, and they observe the phenomena of its parts, all that happens to it and all it does." [1] They apply their first principles entirely to these things, " agreeing apparently with the other natural philosophers in holding that reality was just what could be perceived by the senses, and is contained within the compass of the heavens," [2] though " the first principles and causes they made use of were really adequate to explain realities of a higher order than the sensible." [3]

The doctrine is more precisely stated by Aristotle to be that the elements of numbers are the elements of things, and that therefore things are numbers.[4] He is equally positive that these " things " are sensible things,[5] and indeed that they are bodies,[6] the bodies of which the world is con-

---

[1] Arist. *Met.* A, 8. 989 b 29 (R. P. 92 a).

[2] Arist. *Met.* A, 8. 990 a 3, ὁμολογοῦντες τοῖς ἄλλοις φυσιολόγοις ὅτι τό γ' ὂν τοῦτ' ἐστὶν ὅσον αἰσθητόν ἐστι καὶ περιείληφεν ὁ καλούμενος οὐρανός.

[3] *Met. ib.* 990 a 5, τὰς δ' αἰτίας καὶ τὰς ἀρχάς, ὥσπερ εἴπομεν, ἱκανὰς λέγουσιν ἐπαναβῆναι καὶ ἐπὶ τὰ ἀνωτέρω τῶν ὄντων, καὶ μᾶλλον ἢ τοῖς περὶ φύσεως λόγοις ἁρμοττούσας.

[4] *Met.* A, 5. 986 a 1, τὰ τῶν ἀριθμῶν στοιχεῖα τῶν ὄντων στοιχεῖα πάντων ὑπέλαβον εἶναι; N, 3. 1090 a 22, εἶναι μὲν ἀριθμοὺς ἐποίησαν τὰ ὄντα, οὐ χωριστοὺς δέ, ἀλλ' ἐξ ἀριθμῶν τὰ ὄντα.

[5] *Met.* M, 6. 1080 b 2, ὡς ἐκ τῶν ἀριθμῶν ἐνυπαρχόντων ὄντα τὰ αἰσθητά; *ib.* 1080 b 17, ἐκ τούτου (τοῦ μαθηματικοῦ ἀριθμοῦ) τὰς αἰσθητὰς οὐσίας συνεστάναι φασίν.

[6] *Met.* M, 8. 1083 b 11, τὰ σώματα ἐξ ἀριθμῶν εἶναι συγκείμενα ; *ib.* b 17, ἐκεῖνοι δὲ τὸν ἀριθμὸν τὰ ὄντα λέγουσιν· τὰ γοῦν θεωρήματα προσάπτουσι τοῖς σώμασιν ὡς ἐξ ἐκείνων ὄντων τῶν ἀριθμῶν ; N, 3. 1090 a 32, κατὰ μέντοι τὸ ποιεῖν ἐξ ἀριθμῶν τὰ φυσικὰ σώματα, ἐκ μὴ ἐχόντων βάρος μηδὲ κουφότητα ἔχοντα κουφότητα καὶ βάρος.

structed.[1] This construction of the world out of numbers was a real process in time, which the Pythagoreans described in detail.[2]

Further, the numbers were intended to be mathematical numbers, though they were not separated from the things of sense.[3] On the other hand, they were not mere predicates of something else, but had an independent reality of their own. "They did not hold that the limited and the unlimited and the one were certain other substances, such as fire, water, or anything else of that sort; but that the unlimited itself and the one itself were the reality of the things of which they are predicated, and that is why they said that number was the reality of everything."[4] Accordingly the numbers are, in Aristotle's own language, not only the formal, but also the material, cause of things.[5]

Lastly, Aristotle notes that the point in which the Pythagoreans agreed with Plato was in giving numbers an independent reality of their own; while Plato differed from the Pythagoreans in holding that this reality was distinguishable from that of sensible things.[6] Let us consider these statements in detail.

The elements of numbers.

144. Aristotle speaks of certain "elements" (*στοιχεῖα*) of numbers, which were also the elements of things. That is clearly the key to the problem, if we can discover what it means. Primarily, the "elements of number" are the Odd and the Even, but that does not seem to help us much. We find, however, that the Odd and Even were identified with the Limit and the Unlimited, which we have seen reason to regard as the original principles of the Pythagorean cosmo-

[1] *Met.* A, 5. 986 a 2, *τὸν ὅλον οὐρανὸν ἁρμονίαν εἶναι καὶ ἀριθμόν*; A, 8. 990 a 21, *τὸν ἀριθμὸν τοῦτον ἐξ οὗ συνέστηκεν ὁ κόσμος*; M, 6. 1080 b 18, *τὸν γὰρ ὅλον οὐρανὸν κατασκευάζουσιν ἐξ ἀριθμῶν*; *De caelo*, Γ, 1. 300 a 15, *τοῖς ἐξ ἀριθμῶν συνιστᾶσι τὸν οὐρανόν· ἔνιοι γὰρ τὴν φύσιν ἐξ ἀριθμῶν συνιστᾶσιν, ὥσπερ τῶν Πυθαγορείων τινές.*

[2] *Met.* N, 3. 1091 a 18, *κοσμοποιοῦσι καὶ φυσικῶς βούλονται λέγειν.*

[3] *Met.* M, 6. 1080 b 16; N, 3. 1090 a 20.

[4] Arist. *Met.* A, 5. 987 a 15.

[5] *Met. ib.* 986 a 15 (R. P. 66).

[6] *Met.* A, 6. 987 b 27, *ὁ μὲν (Πλάτων) τοὺς ἀριθμοὺς παρὰ τὰ αἰσθητά, οἱ δ' (οἱ Πυθαγόρειοι) ἀριθμοὺς εἶναί φασιν αὐτὰ τὰ αἰσθητά.*

logy (§ 53). Aristotle tells us that it is the Even which gives
things their unlimited character when it is contained in
them and limited by the Odd,[1] and the commentators are
at one in understanding this to mean that the Even is in
some way the cause of infinite divisibility. They get into
difficulties, however, when they try to show how this can
be. Simplicius has preserved an explanation, in all probability Alexander's, to the effect that they called the even
number unlimited " because every even is divided into
equal parts, and what is divided into equal parts is unlimited
in respect of bipartition ; for division into equals and halves
goes on *ad infinitum*. But, when the odd is added, it limits
it ; for it prevents its division into equal parts." [2] Now it
is plain that we must not impute to the Pythagoreans the
view that even numbers can be halved indefinitely. They
must have known that the even numbers 6 and 10 can only
be halved once. The explanation is rather to be found in a
fragment of Aristoxenos, where we read that " even numbers
are those which are divided into equal parts, while odd
numbers are divided into unequal parts and have a middle
term." [3] This is still further elucidated by a passage which is
quoted in Stobaios and ultimately goes back to Poseidonios.
It runs : " When the odd is divided into two equal parts,
a unit is left over in the middle ; but when the even is so
divided, an empty field is left, without a master and without
a number, showing that it is defective and incomplete." [4]

[1] *Met.* A, 5. 986 a 17 (R. P. 66) ; *Phys.* Γ, 4. 203 a 10 (R. P. 66 a).

[2] Simpl. *Phys.* p. 455, 20 (R. P. 66 a). I owe the passages which I
have used in illustration of this subject to W. A. Heidel, " Πέρας and ἄπειρον
in the Pythagorean Philosophy " (*Arch.* xiv. pp. 384 *sqq.*). The general
principle of my interpretation is the same as his, though I think that,
by bringing the passage into connexion with the numerical figures, I have
avoided the necessity of regarding the words ἡ γὰρ εἰς ἴσα καὶ ἡμίση διαίρεσις
ἐπ' ἄπειρον as " an attempted elucidation added by Simplicius."

[3] Aristoxenos, fr. 81, *ap.* Stob. i. p. 20, 1, ἐκ τῶν Ἀριστοξένου Περὶ
ἀριθμητικῆς. . . τῶν δὲ ἀριθμῶν ἄρτιοι μέν εἰσιν οἱ εἰς ἴσα διαιρούμενοι, περισσοὶ
δὲ οἱ εἰς ἄνισα καὶ μέσον ἔχοντες.

[4] [Plut.] *ap.* Stob. i. p. 22, 19, καὶ μὴν εἰς δύο διαιρουμένων ἴσα τοῦ μὲν
περισσοῦ μονὰς ἐν μέσῳ περίεστι τοῦ δὲ ἀρτίου κενὴ λείπεται χώρα καὶ ἀδέσποτος
καὶ ἀνάριθμος, ὡς ἂν ἐνδεοῦς καὶ ἀτελοῦς ὄντος.

Again, Plutarch says : " In the division of numbers, the even, when parted in any direction, leaves as it were within itself . . . a field ; but, when the same thing is done to the odd, there is always a middle left over from the division." [1] It is clear that all these passages refer to the same thing, and that can hardly be anything else than the "terms" or dots with which we are already familiar (§ 47). The division must fall between these ; for, if it meets with an indivisible unit, it is at once arrested.

145. Now there can be no doubt that by his Unlimited Pythagoras meant something spatially extended ; for he identified it with air, night, or the void. We are prepared, then, to find that his followers also thought of the Unlimited as extended. Aristotle certainly regarded it so. He argues that, if the Unlimited is itself a reality, and not merely the predicate of some other reality, then every part of it must be unlimited too, just as every part of air is air.[2] The same thing is implied in his statement that the Pythagorean Unlimited was outside the heavens.[3] Further than this, it is not safe to go. Philolaos and his followers cannot have regarded the Unlimited as Air ; for, as we shall see, they adopted the theory of Empedokles as to that " element," and accounted for it otherwise. One of them, Xouthos, argued that rarefaction and condensation implied the void ; without it the universe would overflow.[4] We do not know, however, whether he was earlier than the Atomists or not.

The numbers spatial.

---

[1] Plut. *De E apud Delphos*, 388 a, ταῖς γὰρ εἰς ἴσα τομαῖς τῶν ἀριθμῶν, ὁ μὲν ἄρτιος πάντῃ διϊστάμενος ὑπολείπει τινὰ δεκτικὴν ἀρχὴν οἷον ἐν ἑαυτῷ καὶ χώραν, ἐν δὲ τῷ περιττῷ ταὐτὸ παθόντι μέσον ἀεὶ περίεστι τῆς νεμήσεως γόνιμον. The words which I have omitted in translating refer to the further identification of Odd and Even with Male and Female. The passages quoted by Heidel might be added to. Cf., for instance, what Nikomachos says (p. 13, 10, Höche), ἔστι δὲ ἄρτιον μὲν ὃ οἷόν τε εἰς δύο ἴσα διαιρεθῆναι μονάδος μέσον μὴ παρεμπιπτούσης, περιττὸν δὲ τὸ μὴ δυνάμενον εἰς δύο ἴσα μερισθῆναι διὰ τὴν προειρημένην τῆς μονάδος μεσιτείαν. He significantly adds that this definition is ἐκ τῆς δημώδους ὑπολήψεως.

[2] Arist. *Phys.* Γ, 4. 204 a 20 *sqq.*, especially a 26, ἀλλὰ μὴν ὥσπερ ἀέρος ἀὴρ μέρος, οὕτω καὶ ἄπειρον ἀπείρου, εἴ γε οὐσία ἐστὶ καὶ ἀρχή.

[3] See Chap. II. § 53.   [4] Ar. *Phys.* Δ, 9. 216 b 25, κυμανεῖ τὸ ὅλον.

It is enough to say that the Pythagoreans meant by the Unlimited the *res extensa*.

As the Unlimited is spatial, the Limit must be spatial too, and we should expect to find that the point, the line, and the surface were regarded as forms of the Limit. That was the later doctrine ; but the characteristic feature of Pythagoreanism is just that the point was not regarded as a limit, but as the first product of the Limit and the Unlimited, and was identified with the arithmetical unit instead of with zero. According to this view, then, the point has one dimension, the line two, the surface three, and the solid four.[1] In other words, the Pythagorean points have magnitude, their lines breadth, and their surfaces thickness. The whole theory, in short, turns on the definition of the point as a unit " having position " (μονὰς θέσιν ἔχουσα).[2] It was out of such elements that it seemed possible to construct a world.

The numbers as magnitudes.

146. This way of regarding the point, the line, and the surface is closely bound up with the practice of representing numbers by dots arranged in symmetrical patterns, which we have seen reason for attributing to the Pythagoreans (§ 47). Geometry had already made considerable advances, but the old view of quantity as a sum of units had not been revised, and so the point was identified with 1 instead of with 0. That is the answer to Zeller's contention that to regard the Pythagorean numbers as spatial is to ignore the fact that the doctrine was originally arithmetical rather than geometrical. Our interpretation takes full account of that

[1] Cf. Speusippos in the extract preserved in the *Theologumena arithmetica*, p. 61 (Diels, *Vors.* 32 A 13), τὸ μὴν γὰρ ā στιγμή, τὰ δὲ β̄ γραμμή, τὰ δὲ ȳ τρίγωνον, τὰ δὲ δ̄ πυραμίς. We know that Speusippos is following Philolaos here. Arist. *Met.* Z, 11. 1036 b 12, καὶ ἀνάγουσι πάντα εἰς τοὺς ἀριθμούς, καὶ γραμμῆς τὸν λόγον τὸν τῶν δύο εἶναί φασιν. The matter is clearly put by Proclus *in Eucl. I.* p. 97, 19, τὸ μὲν σημεῖον ἀνάλογον τίθενται μονάδι, τὴν δὲ γραμμὴν δυάδι, τὴν δὲ ἐπιφάνειαν τῇ τριάδι καὶ τὸ στερεὸν τῇ τετράδι. καίτοι γε ὡς διαστατὰ λαμβάνοντες μοναδικὴν μὲν εὑρήσομεν τὴν γραμμήν, δυαδικὴν δὲ τὴν ἐπιφάνειαν, τριαδικὸν δὲ τὸ στερεόν.
[2] The identification of the point with the unit is referred to by Aristotle, *Phys.* E, 3. 227 a 27.

fact, and indeed makes the peculiarities of the whole system depend on it. Aristotle is very decided as to the Pythagorean points having magnitude. " They construct the whole world out of numbers," he tells us, " but they suppose the units have magnitude. As to how the first unit with magnitude arose, they appear to be at a loss." [1] Zeller holds that this is only an inference of Aristotle's,[2] and he is probably right in this sense, that the Pythagoreans never felt the need of saying in so many words that points had magnitude. It does seem probable, however, that they called them ὄγκοι.[3]

Zeller, moreover, allows, and indeed insists, that in the Pythagorean cosmology the numbers were spatial, but he raises difficulties about the other parts of the system. There are other things, such as the Soul and Justice and Opportunity, which are said to be numbers, and which cannot be regarded as constructed of points, lines, and surfaces.[4] Now it appears to me that this is just the meaning of a passage in which Aristotle criticises the Pythagoreans. They held, he says, that in one part of the world Opinion prevailed, while a little above it or below it were to be found Injustice or Separation or Mixture, each of which was, according to them, a number. But in the very same regions of the heavens were to be found things having magnitude which were also numbers. How can this be, since Justice has no magnitude ? [5] This means surely that the Pythagoreans

---

[1] Arist. Met. M, 6. 1080 b 18 sqq., 1083 b 8 sqq. ; De caelo, Γ, 1. 300 a 16 (R. P. 76 a). [2] Zeller, p. 381.
[3] Zeno in his fourth argument about motion, which, we shall see (§ 163), was directed against the Pythagoreans, used ὄγκοι for points. Aetios, i. 3, 19 (R. P. 76 b), says that Ekphantos of Syracuse was the first of the Pythagoreans to say that their units were corporeal. Cf. also the use of ὄγκοι in Plato, Parm. 164 d, and Galen, Hist. Phil. 18 (Dox. p. 610), Ἡρα- κλείδης δὲ ὁ Ποντικὸς καὶ ᾿Ασκληπιάδης ὁ Βιθυνὸς ἀνάρμους ὄγκους τὰς ἀρχὰς ὑπο- τίθενται τῶν ὅλων. [4] Zeller, p. 381.
[5] Arist. Met. A, 8. 990 a 22 (R. P. 81 e). I read and interpret thus : " For, seeing that, according to them, Opinion and Opportunity are in a given part of the world, and a little above or below them Injustice and Separation and Mixture,—in proof of which they allege that each of these is a number,—and seeing that it is also the case (reading συμβαίνῃ with

had failed to give any clear account of the relation between these more or less fanciful analogies and their geometrical construction of the universe.

The numbers and the elements.

147. We seem to see further that what distinguished the Pythagoreanism of this period from its earlier form was that it sought to adapt itself to the new theory of " elements." This is what makes it necessary to take up the consideration of the system once more in connexion with the pluralists. When the Pythagoreans returned to Southern Italy, they would find views prevalent there which demanded a partial reconstruction of their own system. We do not know that Empedokles founded a philosophical society, but there can be no doubt of his influence on the medical school of these regions ; and we also know now that Philolaos played a part in the history of medicine.[1] This gives us the clue to what formerly seemed obscure. The tradition is that the Pythagoreans explained the elements as built up of geometrical figures, a theory we can study for ourselves in the more developed form it attained in Plato's *Timaeus*.[2] If they were to retain their position as the leaders of medical study in Italy, they were bound to account for the elements.

Bonitz) that there is already in that part of the world a number of composite magnitudes (*i.e.* composed of the Limit and the Unlimited), because those affections (of number) are attached to their respective regions ;— (seeing that they hold these two things), the question arises whether the number which we are to understand each of these things (Opinion, etc.) to be is the same as the number in the world (*i.e.* the cosmological number) or a different one." I cannot doubt that these are the extended numbers which are composed (συνίσταται) of the elements of number, the limited and the unlimited, or, as Aristotle here says, the " affections of number," the odd and the even. Zeller's view that " celestial bodies " are meant comes near this, but the application is too narrow. Nor is it the number (πλῆθος) of those bodies that is in question, but their magnitude (μέγεθος). For other views of the passage see Zeller, p. 391, *n.* 1.

[1] All this has been put in its true light by the publication of the extract from Menon's Ἰατρικά, on which see p. 278, *n.* 4.

[2] In Aet. ii. 6, 5 (R. P. 80) the theory is ascribed to Pythagoras, which is an anachronism, as the mention of " elements " shows it must be later than Empedokles. In his extract from the same source, Achilles says οἱ Πυθαγόρειοι, which doubtless represents Theophrastos better.

We must not take it for granted, however, that the Pythagorean construction of the elements was exactly the same as that we find in Plato's *Timaeus*. As we have seen, there is good reason for believing they only knew three of the regular solids, the cube, the pyramid (tetrahedron), and the dodecahedron.[1] Now Plato makes Timaios start from fire and earth,[2] and in the construction of the elements he proceeds in such a way that the octahedron and the icosahedron can easily be transformed into pyramids, while the cube and the dodecahedron cannot. From this it follows that, while air and water pass readily into fire, earth cannot do so,[3] and the dodecahedron is reserved for another purpose, which we shall consider presently. This would exactly suit the Pythagorean system ; for it would leave room for a dualism of the kind outlined in the Second Part of the poem of Parmenides. We know that Hippasos made Fire the first principle, and we see from the *Timaeus* how it would be possible to represent air and water as forms of fire. The other element is, however, earth, not air, as we have seen reason to believe that it was in early Pythagoreanism. That would be a natural result of the discovery of atmospheric air by Empedokles and of his general theory of the elements. It would also explain the puzzling fact, which we had to leave unexplained above, that Aristotle identifies the two " forms " spoken of by Parmenides with Fire and Earth.[4]

148. The most interesting point in the theory is, however, the use made of the dodecahedron. It was identified, we are told, with the " sphere of the universe," or, as it is put

The dodeca-hedron.

---

[1] See above, p. 283.   [2] Plato, *Tim.* 31 b 5.

[3] Plato, *Tim.* 54 c 4. It is to be observed that in *Tim.* 48 b 5 Plato says of the construction of the elements οὐδείς πω γένεσιν αὐτῶν μεμήνυκεν, which implies that there is some novelty in the theory as Timaios states it. If we read the passage in the light of what has been said in § 141, we shall be inclined to believe that Plato is making Timaios work out the Pythagorean doctrine on the lines of the discovery of Theaitetos.

[4] See above, Chap. IV. p. 186.

in the Philolaic fragment, with the " hull of the sphere." [1] Whatever we may think of the authenticity of the fragments, there is no reason to doubt that this is a genuine Pythagorean expression, and it must be taken in close connexion with the word " keel " applied to the central fire.[2] The structure of the world was compared to the building of a ship, an idea of which there are other traces.[3] The key to what we are told of the dodecahedron is also given by Plato. In the *Phaedo*, which must have been written before the doctrine of the regular solids was fully established, we read that the " true earth," if looked at from above, is " many-coloured like the balls that are made of twelve pieces of leather." [4] In the *Timaeus* the same thing is referred to in these words : " Further, as there is still one construction left, the fifth, God made use of it for the universe when he painted it." [5] The point is that the dodecahedron approaches more nearly to the sphere than any other of the regular solids. The twelve pieces of leather used to make a ball would all be regular pentagons ; and, if the material were not flexible

---

[1] Aet. ii. 6, 5 (R. P. 80) ; " Philolaos," fr. 12 (=: 20 M. ; R. P. 79). On the ὁλκάς, see Gundermann in *Rhein. Mus.* 1904, pp. 145 *sqq.* In the Pythagorean myth of Plato's *Politicus*, the world is regarded as a ship, of which God is the κυβερνήτης (272 e *sqq.*). The πόντος τῆς ἀνομοιότητος (273 d) is just the ἄπειρον.

[2] Aet. ii. 4, 15, ὅπερ τρόπεως δίκην προϋπεβάλετο τῇ τοῦ παντὸς ⟨σφαίρᾳ⟩ ὁ δημιουργὸς θεός.

[3] Cf. the ὑποζώματα of Plato, *Rep.* 616 c 3. As ὕλη generally means " timber " for shipbuilding (when it does not mean firewood), I suggest that we should look in this direction for an explanation of the technical use of the word in later philosophy. Cf. Plato, *Phileb.* 54 c 1, γενέσεως . . . ἕνεκα . . . πᾶσαν ὕλην παρατίθεσθαι πᾶσιν, which is part of the answer to the question πότερα πλοίων ναυπηγίαν ἕνεκα φῇς γίγνεσθαι μᾶλλον ἢ πλοῖα ἕνεκα ναυπηγίας ; (*ib.* b 2) ; *Tim.* 69 a 6, οἷα τέκτοσιν ἡμῖν ὕλη παράκειται.

[4] Plato, *Phaed.* 110 b 6, ὥσπερ οἱ δωδεκάσκυτοι σφαῖραι, the meaning of which phrase is quite correctly explained by Plutarch, *Plat. q.* 1003 b, καὶ γὰρ μάλιστα τῷ πλήθει τῶν στοιχείων ἀμβλύτητι δὲ τῶν γωνιῶν τὴν εὐθύτητα διαφυγὸν εὐκαμπές ἐστι [τὸ δωδεκάεδρον], καὶ τῇ περιτάσει ὥσπερ αἱ δωδεκάσκυτοι σφαῖραι κυκλοτερὲς γίγνεται καὶ περιληπτικόν.

[5] Plato, *Tim.* 55 c 4. Neither this passage nor the last can refer to the Zodiac, which would be described by a dodecagon, not a dodecahedron. What is implied is the division of the heavens into twelve pentagonal fields, in which the constellations were placed. For the history of such methods see Newbold in *Arch.* xix. pp. 198 *sqq.*

like leather, we should have a dodecahedron instead of a sphere. That proves that the dodecahedron was well known before Theaitetos, and we may infer that it was regarded as forming the " timbers " on which the spherical hulk of the heavens was built.

The tradition confirms in an interesting way the importance of the dodecahedron in the Pythagorean system. According to one account, Hippasos was drowned at sea for revealing " the sphere formed out of the twelve pentagons." [1] The Pythagorean construction of the dodecahedron we may partially infer from the fact that they adopted the pentagram or *pentalpha* as their symbol. The use of this figure in later magic is well known ; and Paracelsus still employed it as a symbol of health, which is exactly what the Pythagoreans called it. [2]

149. The view that the soul is a " harmony," or rather an attunement, is intimately connected with the theory of the four elements. It cannot have belonged to the earliest form of Pythagoreanism ; for, as shown in Plato's *Phaedo*, it is quite inconsistent with the idea that the soul can exist independently of the body. It is the very opposite of the belief that " any soul can enter any body." [3] On the other hand, we are told in the *Phaedo* that it was accepted by Simmias and Kebes, who had heard Philolaos at Thebes, and by Echekrates of Phleious, who was the disciple of Philolaos and Eurytos. [4] The account of the doctrine given by Plato is quite in accordance with the view that it was of medical origin. Simmias says : " Our body being, as it were, strung and held together by the warm and the cold, the dry and the

The Soul a "harmony."

---

[1] Iambl. *V. Pyth.* 247. Cf. above, Chap. II. p. 106, *n.* 1.

[2] See Gow, *Short History of Greek Mathematics*, p. 151, and the passages there referred to, adding Schol. Luc. p. 234, 21, Rabe, τὸ πεντάγραμμον] ὅτι τὸ ἐν τῇ συνηθείᾳ λεγόμενον πεντάλφα σύμβολον ἦν πρὸς ἀλλήλους Πυθαγορείων ἀναγνωριστικὸν καὶ τούτῳ ἐν ταῖς ἐπιστολαῖς ἐχρῶντο. The Pythagoreans may quite well have known the method given by Euclid iv. 11 of dividing a line in extreme and mean ratio, the so-called " golden section."

[3] Arist. *De an.* A, 3. 407 b 20 (R. P. 86 c).

[4] Plato, *Phaed.* 85 e *sqq.* ; and for Echekrates, *ib.* 88 d.

moist, and things of that sort, our soul is a sort of temperament and attunement of these, when they are mingled with
one another well and in due proportion. If, then, our soul
is an attunement, it is clear that, when the body has been
relaxed or strung up out of measure by diseases and other
ills, the soul must necessarily perish at once." [1] This is
clearly an application of the theory of Alkmaion (§ 96), and
is in accordance with the views of the Sicilian school. It
completes the evidence that the Pythagoreanism of the
end of the fifth century was an adaptation of the old doctrine
to the new principles introduced by Empedokles.

It is further to be observed that, if the soul is regarded
as an attunement in the Pythagorean sense, we should expect
it to contain the three intervals then recognised, the fourth,
the fifth and the octave, and this makes it extremely
probable that Poseidonios was right in saying that the
doctrine of the tripartite soul, as we know it from the
Republic of Plato, was really Pythagorean. It is quite
inconsistent with Plato's own view of the soul, but agrees
admirably with that just explained.[2]

The
central
fire.

150. The planetary system which Aristotle attributes to
" the Pythagoreans " and Aetios to Philolaos is sufficiently
remarkable.[3] The earth is no longer in the middle of the
world ; its place is taken by a central fire, which is not to

---

[1] Plato, *Phaed.* 86 b 7–c 5.

[2] See J. L. Stocks, *Plato and the Tripartite Soul* (*Mind N.S.*, No. 94,
1915, pp. 207 *sqq.*). Plato himself points to the connexion in *Rep.*
443 d, 5 συναρμόσαντα τρία ὄντα, ὥσπερ ὅρους τρεῖς ἁρμονίας ἀτεχνῶς, νεάτης
τε καὶ ὑπάτης καὶ μέσης, καὶ εἰ ἄλλα ἄττα μεταξὺ τυγχάνει ὄντα (*i.e.* the
movable notes). Now there is good ground for believing that the statement of Aristides Quintilianus (ii. 2) that the θυμικόν is intermediate
between the λογικόν and the ἄλογον comes from the musician Damon (Deiters,
De Aristidis Quint. fontibus, 1870), the teacher of Perikles (p. 255, *n.* 2), to
whom the Platonic Sokrates refers as his authority on musical matters, but
who must have died when Plato was quite young. Moreover, Poseidonios
(ap. Galen, *De Hipp. et Plat.* pp. 425 and 478) attributed the doctrine of the
tripartite soul to Pythagoras, αὐτοῦ μὲν τοῦ Πυθαγόρου συγγράμματος οὐδενὸς
εἰς ἡμᾶς διασῳζομένου, τεκμαιρόμενος δὲ ἐξ ὧν ἔνιοι τῶν μαθητῶν αὐτοῦ γεγράφασιν.

[3] For the authorities see R. P. 81-83. The attribution of the theory
to Philolaos is perhaps due to Poseidonios. The " three books " were
doubtless, in existence by his time.

be identified with the sun. Round this fire revolve ten
bodies. First comes the *Antichthon* or Counter-earth, and
next the earth, which thus becomes one of the planets. After
the earth comes the moon, then the sun, the planets, and
the heaven of the fixed stars. We do not see the central
fire and the *antichthon* because the side of the earth on
which we live is always turned away from them. This is to
be explained by the analogy of the moon, which always
presents the same face to us, so that men living on the other
side of it would never see the earth. This implies, of course,
from our point of view, that these bodies rotate on their
axes in the same time as they revolve round the central
fire,[1] and that the antichthon revolves round the central fire
in the same time as the earth, so that it is always in opposition to it.[2]

It is not easy to accept the statement of Aetios that this
system was taught by Philolaos. Aristotle nowhere mentions him in connexion with it, and in the *Phaedo* Sokrates
gives a description of the earth and its position in the world
which is entirely opposed to it, but is accepted without demur
by Simmias the disciple of Philolaos.[3] It is undoubtedly
a Pythagorean theory, however, and marks a noticeable
advance on the Ionian views current at Athens. It is clear
too that Sokrates states it as something of a novelty that the
earth does not require the support of air or anything of the
sort to keep it in its place. Even Anaxagoras had not been
able to shake himself free of that idea, and Demokritos still

[1] Plato makes Timaios attribute an axial rotation to the heavenly bodies,
which must be of this kind (*Tim.* 40 a 7). The rotation of the moon upon
its axis takes the same time as its revolution round the earth; but it comes
to the same thing if we say that it does not rotate at all relatively to its
orbit, and that is how the Greeks put it. It would be quite natural for
the Pythagoreans to extend this to all the heavenly bodies. This led
ultimately to Aristotle's view that they were all fixed (ἐνδεδεμένα) in
corporeal spheres.

[2] This seems more natural than to suppose the earth and counter-
earth to be always in conjunction. Cf. Aet. iii. 11, 3, τὴν οἰκουμένην γῆν
ἐξ ἐναντίας κειμένην καὶ περιφερομένην τῇ ἀντίχθονι.

[3] Plato, *Phaed.* 108 e 4 *sqq.* Simmias assents to the geocentric theory
in the emphatic words καὶ ὀρθῶς γε.

held it along with the theory of a flat earth. The natural inference from the *Phaedo* would certainly be that the theory of a spherical earth, kept in the middle of the world by its equilibrium, was that of Philolaos himself. If so, the doctrine of the central fire would belong to a later generation.

It seems probable that the theory of the earth's revolution round the central fire really originated in the account of the sun's light given by Empedokles. The two things are brought into close connexion by Aetios, who says that Empedokles believed in two suns, while " Philolaos " believed in two or even in three. His words are obscure, but they seem to justify us in holding that Theophrastos regarded the theories as akin.[1] We saw that Empedokles gave two inconsistent explanations of the alternation of day and night (§ 113), and it may well have seemed that the solution of the difficulty was to make the sun shine by reflected light from a central fire. Such a theory would, in fact, be the natural issue of recent discoveries as to the moon's light and the cause of its eclipses, if these were extended to the sun, as they would almost inevitably be.

The central fire received a number of mythological names, such as the " hearth of the world," the " house," or " watch-tower " of Zeus, and " the mother of the gods." [2] That was in the. manner of the school, but it must not blind

---

[1] Aet. ii. 20, 13 (Chap. VI. p. 238, *n.* 3) compared with *ib.* 12 Φιλόλαος ὁ Πυθαγόρειος ὑαλοειδῆ τὸν ἥλιον, δεχόμενον μὲν τοῦ ἐν τῷ κόσμῳ πυρὸς τὴν ἀνταύγειαν, διηθοῦντα δὲ πρὸς ἡμᾶς τό φῶς, ὥστε τρόπον τινὰ διττοὺς ἡλίους γίγνεσθαι, τό τε ἐν τῷ οὐρανῷ πυρῶδες καὶ τὸ ἀπ' αὐτοῦ πυροειδὲς κατὰ τὸ ἐσοπτροειδές· εἰ μή τις καὶ τρίτον λέξει τὴν ἀπὸ τοῦ ἐνόπτρου κατ' ἀνάκλασιν διασπειρομένην πρὸς ἡμᾶς αὐγήν. This is not, of course, a statement of any doctrine held by " Philolaos," but a rather captious criticism such as we often find in Theophrastos. Moreover, it is pretty clear that it is inaccurately reported. The phrase τὸ ἐν τῷ κόσμῳ πῦρ, if used by Theophrastos, must surely mean the central fire, and τὸ ἐν τῷ οὐρανῷ πυρῶδες must be the same thing, as it very well may, seeing that Aetios tells us himself (ii. 7. 7, R. P. 81) that " Philolaos " used the term οὐρανός of the sublunary region. It is true that Achilles says τὸ πυρῶδες καὶ διαυγὲς λαμβάνοντα ἄνωθεν ἀπὸ τοῦ ἀερίου πυρός, but his authority is not sufficiently great to outweigh the other considerations.

[2] Aet. i. 7, 7 (R. P. 81). Proclus *in Tim.* p. 106, 22 (R. P. 83 e).

us to the fact that we are dealing with a scientific hypothesis. It was a great thing to see that the phenomena could best be " saved " by a central luminary, and that the earth must therefore be a revolving sphere like the other planets.[1] Indeed, we are tempted to say that the identification of the central fire with the sun was a detail in comparison. It is probable, at any rate, that this theory started the train of thought which made it possible for Aristarchos of Samos to reach the heliocentric hypothesis,[2] and it was certainly Aristotle's successful reassertion of the geocentric theory which made it necessary for Copernicus to discover the truth afresh. We have his own word for it that he started from what he had read about the Pythagoreans.[3]

In the form in which it was now stated, however, the theory raised almost as many difficulties as it solved, and it did not maintain itself for long. It is clear from Aristotle that its critics raised the objection that it failed to " save the phenomena " inasmuch as the assumed revolution of the earth would produce parallaxes too great to be negligible, and that the Pythagoreans gave some reason for the belief that they were negligible. Aristotle has no clear account of the arguments on either side, but it may be pointed out that the earth was probably supposed to be far smaller than it is, and there is no reason why its orbit should have been thought to have an appreciably greater diameter than we now know the earth itself to have.[4]

[1] Aristotle expresses this by saying that the Pythagoreans held τὴν . . . γῆν ἐν τῶν ἄστρων οὖσαν κύκλῳ φερομένην περὶ τὸ μέσον νύκτα τε καὶ ἡμέραν ποιεῖν (De caelo, B, 13. 293 a 23).

[2] I do not discuss here the claims of Herakleides to be the real author of the heliocentric hypothesis.

[3] In a letter to Pope Paul III., Copernicus quotes Plut. Plac. iii. 13, 2–3 (R. P. 83 a) and adds Inde igitur occasionem nactus, coepi et ego de terrae mobilitate cogitare.

[4] Cf. Ar. De caelo, B, 13. 293 b 25 ἐπεὶ γὰρ οὐκ ἔστιν ἡ γῆ κέντρον, ἀλλ' ἀπέχει τὸ ἡμισφαίριον αὐτῆς ὅλον, οὐθὲν κωλύειν οἴονται τὰ φαινόμενα συμβαίνειν ὁμοίως μὴ κατοικοῦσιν ἡμῖν ἐπὶ τοῦ κέντρου, ὥσπερ κἂν εἰ ἐπὶ τοῦ μέσου ἦν ἡ γῆ· οὐθὲν γὰρ οὐδὲ νῦν ποιεῖν ἐπίδηλον τὴν ἡμισεῖαν ἀπέχοντας ἡμᾶς διάμετρον. (Of course the words τὸ ἡμισφαίριον αὐτῆς ὅλον refer to Aristotle's own theory of celestial spheres ; he really means the radius of its orbit.)

A truer view of the earth's dimensions would naturally suggest that the alternation of night and day was due to the earth's rotation on its own axis, and in that case the earth could once more be regarded as in the centre. It does not appear that Aristotle knew of any one who had held this view, but Theophrastos seems to have attributed it to Hiketas and Ekphantos of Syracuse, of whom we know very little otherwise.[1] Apparently they regarded the heaven of the fixed stars as stationary, a thing Aristotle would almost have been bound to mention if he had ever heard of it, since his own system turns entirely on the diurnal revolution.

Both theories, that of the earth's revolution round a central fire and that of its rotation on its own axis, had the effect of making the revolution of the fixed stars, to which the Pythagoreans certainly adhered, very difficult to account for. They must either be stationary or their motion must be something quite different from the diurnal

---

Now it is inconceivable that any one should have argued that, since the geocentric parallax is negligible, parallax in general is negligible. On the other hand, the geocentric Pythagorean (the real Philolaos ?), whose views are expounded by Sokrates in the *Phaedo*, appears to have made a special point of saying that the earth was πάμμεγα (109 a 9), and that would make the theory of the central fire very difficult to defend. If Philolaos was one of the Pythagoreans who held that the radius of the moon's orbit is only three times that of the earth's (Plut. *De an. procr.* 1028 b), he cannot have used the argument quoted by Aristotle.

[1] Aet. iii. 13, 3 Ἡρακλείδης ὁ Ποντικὸς καὶ Ἔκφαντος ὁ Πυθαγόρειος κινοῦσι μὲν τὴν γῆν· οὐ μήν γε μεταβατικῶς, ἀλλὰ τρεπτικῶς [l. στρεπτικῶς] τρόχου δίκην ἐνηξονισμένην, ἀπὸ δυσμῶν ἐπ᾽ ἀνατολὰς περὶ τὸ ἴδιον αὐτῆς κέντρον. Cicero attributes the same doctrine to Hiketas (*Acad. pr.* ii. 39), but makes nonsense of it by saying that he made the sun and moon stationary as well as the fixed stars. Tannery regarded Hiketas and Ekphantos as fictitious personages from a dialogue of Herakleides, but it seems clear that Theophrastos recognised their existence. It may be added that the idea of the earth's rotation was no novelty. The Milesians probably (§ 21) and Anaxagoras certainly (p. 269) held this view of their flat earth. All that was new was the application of it to a sphere. If we could be sure that the geocentric Pythagoreans who made the earth rotate placed the central fire in the interior of the earth, that would prove them to be later in date than the system of "Philolaos." Simplicius appears to say this (*De caelo*, p. 512 9 *sqq.*), and he may be quoting from Aristotle's lost work on the Pythagoreans. The point, however, is doubtful.

revolution.[1] It was probably this that led to the abandonment of the theory.

In discussing the views of those who hold the earth to be in motion, Aristotle only mentions one theory as alternative to that of its revolution round the central fire, and he says that it is that of the *Timaeus*. According to this the earth is not one of the planets but " at the centre," while at the same time it has some kind of motion relatively to the axis of the universe.[2] Now this motion can hardly be an axial rotation, as was held by Grote ;[3] for the whole cosmology of the *Timaeus* implies that the alternation of day and night is due to the diurnal revolution of the heavens.[4] The fact that the earth is referred to a little later as "the guardian and artificer of night and day "[5] proves nothing to the contrary, since night is in any case the conical shadow of the earth, which is thus the cause of the alternation of day and night. So far, Boeckh and his followers appear to be in the right.

[1] The various possibilities are enumerated by Sir T. L. Heath (*Aristarchus*, p. 103). Only two are worth noting. The universe as a whole might share in the rotation of the ἀπλανές, while the sun, moon and planets had independent revolutions in addition to that of the universe. Or the rotation of the ἀπλανές might be so slow as to be imperceptible, in which case its motion, "though it is not the precession of the equinoxes, is something very like it " (Heath, *loc. cit.*).

[2] Arist. *De caelo*, B, 13. 293 b 5, ἔνιοι δὲ καὶ κειμένην ἐπὶ τοῦ κέντρου [τὴν γῆν] φασὶν αὐτὴν ἴλλεσθαι καὶ κινεῖσθαι περὶ τὸν διὰ παντὸς τεταμένον πόλον, ὥσπερ ἐν τῷ Τιμαίῳ γέγραπται. The text and interpretation of this passage are guaranteed by the reference in the next chapter (296 a 25) οἱ δ' ἐπὶ τοῦ μέσου θέντες ἴλλεσθαι καὶ κινεῖσθαί φασι περὶ τὸν πόλον μέσον. All attempts to show that this refers to something else are futile. We cannot, therefore, with Alexander, regard καὶ κινεῖσθαι as an interpolation in the first passage, even though it is omitted in some MSS. there. The omission is probably due to Alexander's authority. Moreover, when read in its context, it is quite clear that the passage gives one of two alternative theories of the earth's motion, and that this motion, like the revolution round the central fire, is a motion of translation (φορά), and not an axial rotation.

[3] *Plato's Doctrine respecting the Rotation of the Earth* (1860).

[4] Plato, *Tim.* 39 c 1, νὺξ μὲν οὖν ἡμέρα τε γέγονεν οὕτως καὶ διὰ ταῦτα, ἡ τῆς μιᾶς καὶ φρονιμωτάτης κυκλήσεως περίοδος. This refers to the revolution of the "circle of the Same," *i.e.* the equatorial circle, and is quite unambiguous.

[5] Plato, *Tim.* 40 c 1 [γῆν] φύλακα καὶ δημιουργὸν νυκτός τε καὶ ἡμέρας ἐμηχανήσατο. On this cf. Heath, *Aristarchus*, p. 178.

When, however, Boeckh goes on to argue that the word ἰλλομένην in the *Timaeus* does not refer to motion at all, but that it means " globed " or " packed " round, it is quite impossible for me to follow him. Apart from all philological considerations, this interpretation makes nonsense of Aristotle's line of argument. He says [1] that, if the earth is in motion, whether " outside the centre " or " at the centre," that cannot be a " natural motion " ; for, if it were, it would be shared by every particle of earth, and we see that the natural motion of every clod of earth is " down," *i.e.* towards the centre. He also says that, if the earth is in motion, whether " outside the centre " or " at the centre," it must have two motions like everything else but the " first sphere," and therefore there would be excursions in latitude (πάροδοι) and " turnings back " (τροπαί) of the fixed stars, which there are not. It is clear, then, that Aristotle regarded the second theory of the earth's movement as involving a motion of translation equally with the first, and that he supposed it to be the theory of Plato's *Timaeus*. It is impossible to believe that he can have been mistaken on such a point.[2]

When we turn to the passage in the *Timaeus* itself, we find that, when the text is correctly established, it completely corroborates Aristotle's statement that a motion of translation is involved,[3] and that Boeckh's rendering is inadmissible

---

[1] Arist. *De caelo*, B, 14. 296 a 29 *sqq.* The use of the word ὑπολειπόμενα of the apparent motion of the planets from west to east is an interesting survival of the old Ionian view (p. 70). The idea that the earth must have two motions, if it has any, is based on nothing more than the analogy of the planets (Heath, *Aristarchus*, p. 241).

[2] Aristotle must have been a member of the Academy when the *Timaeus* was published, and we know that the interpretation of that dialogue was one of the chief occupations of the Academy after Plato's death. If he had misrepresented the doctrine by introducing a motion of translation, Alexander and Simplicius would surely have been able to appeal to an authoritative protest by Krantor or another. The view which Boeckh finds in the *Timaeus* is precisely Aristotle's own, and it is impossible to believe that he could have failed to recognise the fact or that he should have misrepresented it deliberately.

[3] The best attested reading in *Tim.* is γῆν δὲ τροφὸν μὲν ἡμετέραν, ἰλλομένην δὲ τὴν περὶ τὸν διὰ παντὸς πόλον τεταμένον. The article τὴν

on grammatical and lexicological grounds.[1] We have therefore to ask what motion of translation is compatible with the
statement that the earth is " at the centre," and there seems
to be nothing left but a motion up and down (to speak loosely)
on the axis of the universe itself. Now the only clearly
attested meaning of the rare word ἴλλομαι is just that of
motion to and fro, backwards and forwards.[2] It may be
added that a motion of this kind was familiar to the Pythagoreans, if we may judge from the description of the waters
in the earth given by Sokrates in the *Phaedo* on the authority
of some unnamed cosmologist.[3]

What was this motion intended to explain? It is
impossible to be certain, but it is clear that the motions of
the circles of the Same and the Other, *i.e.* the equator and
the ecliptic, are inadequate to " save the appearances." So
far as they go, all the planets should either move in the

---

is in Par. A and also in the Palatine excerpts, and it is difficult to suppose
that any one would interpolate it. On the other hand, it might easily be
dropped, as its meaning is not at once obvious. It is to be explained, of
course, like τὴν ἐπὶ θάνατον or Xenophon's προελ ηλυθότος . . . τὴν πρὸς τὰ
φρούρια, and implies a *path* of some kind, and therefore a movement of
translation.

[1] In the first place, the meaning *globatam*, " packed," " massed " would
have to be expressed by a perfect participle and not a present, and we
find accordingly that Simplicius is obliged to paraphrase it by the
perfect participle, δεδεμένη or δεδεσμημένη. Sir T. L. Heath's " wound "
(*Aristarchus*, p. 177) ought also to be " winding." In the second place,
though Par. A has εἰλλομένην, the weight of authority distinctly favours
ἰλλομένην, the reading of Aristotle, Proclus and others. The verbs εἴλλω
(εἴλλω), εἰλῶ and ἴλλω are constantly confused in MSS. It is not, I think,
possible to regard ἴλλω as etymologically connected with the other verbs.
It seems rather to go with ἰλλός and ἰλλαίνω, which are both used in
Hippokrates. For its meaning, see below, *n*. 2.

[2] Cf. Soph. *Ant*. 340 ἰλλομένων ἀρότρων ἔτος εἰς ἔτος, clearly of the
ploughs going backwards and forwards in the furrows. Simplicius
makes a point of the fact that Apollonios Rhodios used ἰλλόμενος in the
sense of "shut in," "bound," εἰργόμενος (cf. Heath, *Aristarchus*, p. 175,
n. 6). That, however, cannot weigh against the probability that the scribes,
or even Apollonios himself, merely fell into the common confusion. Unless
we can get rid of the article τὴν and the testimony of Aristotle, we must
have a verb of motion.

[3] Cf. Plato, *Phaed*. 111 e 4, where we are told that there is an αἰώρα in
the earth, which causes the waters to move up and down in Tartaros,
which is a chasm extending from pole to pole. See my notes *in loc*.

ecliptic or remain at an invariable distance from it, and this is far from being the case. Some explanation is required of their excursions in latitude, *i.e.* their alternate approaches to the ecliptic and departures from it. We have seen (p. 63) that Anaximander already busied himself with the " turnings back " of the moon. Moreover, the direct and retrograde movements of the planets are clearly referred to in the *Timaeus* a few lines below.[1] We are not bound to show in detail that a motion of the kind suggested would account for these apparent irregularities ; it is enough if it can be made probable that the fifth-century Pythagoreans thought it could. It may have seemed worth while to them to explain the phenomena by a regular motion of the earth rather than by any waywardness in the planets ; and, if so, they were at least on the right track.

To avoid misunderstanding, I would add that I do not suppose Plato himself was satisfied with the theory which he thought it appropriate for a Pythagorean of an earlier generation to propound. The idea that Plato expounded his own personal views in a dialogue obviously supposed to take place before he was born, is one which, to me at least, is quite incredible. We know, moreover, from the unimpeachable authority of Theophrastos, who was a member of the Academy in Plato's later years, that he had then abandoned the geocentric hypothesis, though we have no information as to

---

[1] Proclus, in his commentary, explains the προχωρήσεις and ἐπανα-κυκλήσεις of *Tim.* 20 c as equivalent to προποδισμοί and ὑποποδισμοί. In a *corrigendum* prefixed to his *Aristarchus*, Sir T. L. Heath disputes this interpretation, and compares the application of the term ἐπανακυκλούμενον to the planet Mars in *Rep.* 617 b, which he understands to refer merely to its " circular revolution in a sense contrary to that of the fixed stars." It is to be observed, however, that Theon of Smyrna in quoting this passage has the words μάλιστα τῶν ἄλλων after ἐπανακυκλούμενον, which gives excellent sense if retrogradation is meant. In fact Mars has a greater arc of retrogradation than the other planets (Duhem, *Système du monde*, vol. i. p. 61). As I failed to note this in my text of the *Republic*, I should like to make amends by giving two reasons for believing that Theon has preserved Plato's own words. In the first place he is apparently quoting from Derkyllides, who first established the text of Plato from which ours is derived. In the second place μάλιστα τῶν ἄλλων is exactly fifteen letters, the normal length of omissions in the Platonic text.

what he supposed to be in the centre of our system.¹ It
seems clear too from the *Laws* that he must have attributed
an axial rotation to the earth.²

151. The existence of the *antichthon* was also a hypothesis   The
antichthon.
intended to account for the phenomena of eclipses. In one
place, indeed, Aristotle says the Pythagoreans invented it in
order to bring the number of revolving bodies up to ten ; ³
but that is a mere sally, and Aristotle really knew better.
In his work on the Pythagoreans, he said that eclipses of the
moon were caused sometimes by the intervention of the earth
and sometimes by that of the *antichthon* ; and the same
statement was made by Philip of Opous, a very competent
authority on the matter.⁴ Indeed, Aristotle shows in another
passage how the theory originated. He tells us that some
thought there might be a considerable number of bodies
revolving round the centre, though invisible to us because of
the intervention of the earth, and that they accounted in
this way for there being more eclipses of the moon than of
the sun.⁵ This is mentioned in close connexion with the
antichthon, so Aristotle clearly regarded the two hypotheses
as of the same nature. The history of the theory seems to
be this. Anaximenes had assumed the existence of dark

¹ Plut. *Plat. quaest*, 1006 c (cf. *V. Numae*, c. 11). It is important to
remember that Theophrastos was a member of the Academy in Plato's
last years.
² In the passage referred to (822 a 4 *sqq.*) he maintains that the planets
have a simple circular motion, and says that this is a view which he had not
heard in his youth nor long before. That must imply the rotation of the
earth on its axis in twenty-four hours, since it is a denial of the Pythagorean
theory that the planetary motions are composite. It does not follow that
we must find this view in the *Timaeus*, which only professes to give the
opinions of a fifth-century Pythagorean.
³ Arist. *Met.* A, 5. 986 a 3 (R. P. 83 b).
⁴ Aet. ii. 29, 4, τῶν Πυθαγορείων τινὲς κατὰ τὴν Ἀριστοτέλειον ἱστορίαν
καὶ τὴν Φιλίππου τοῦ Ὀπουντίου ἀπόφασιν ἀνταυγείᾳ καὶ ἀντιφράξει τοτὲ
μὲν τῆς γῆς, τοτὲ δὲ τῆς ἀντίχθονος (ἐκλείπειν τὴν σελήνην).
⁵ Arist. *De caelo*, B, 13. 293 b 21, ἐνίοις δὲ δοκεῖ καὶ πλείω σώματα
τοιαῦτα ἐνδέχεσθαι φέρεσθαι περὶ τὸ μέσον ἡμῖν ἄδηλα διὰ τὴν ἐπιπρόσθησιν
τῆς γῆς. διὸ καὶ τὰς τῆς σελήνης ἐκλείψεις πλείους ἢ τὰς τοῦ ἡλίου γίγνεσθαι
φασιν· τῶν γὰρ φερομένων ἕκαστον ἀντιφράττειν αὐτήν, ἀλλ' οὐ μόνον τὴν
γῆν

planets to account for lunar eclipses (§ 29), and Anaxagoras had revived that view (§ 135). Certain Pythagoreans [1] had placed these dark planets between the earth and the central fire in order to account for their invisibility, and the next stage was to reduce them to a single body. Here again we see how the Pythagoreans tried to simplify the hypotheses of their predecessors.

152. We have seen (§ 54) that the doctrine commonly, but incorrectly, known as the " harmony of the spheres " may have originated with Pythagoras, but its elaboration must belong to a later generation, and the extraordinary variations in our accounts of it must be due to the conflicting theories of the planetary motions which were rife at the end of the fifth and the beginning of the fourth centuries B.C. We have the express testimony of Aristotle that the Pythagoreans whose doctrine he knew believed that the heavenly bodies produced musical notes in their courses. Further, the pitch of the notes was determined by the velocities of these bodies, and these in turn by their distances, which were in the same ratios as the consonant intervals of the octave. Aristotle distinctly implies that the heaven of the fixed stars takes part in the celestial symphony ; for he mentions " the sun, the moon, and the stars, so great in magnitude and in number as they are," a phrase which cannot refer solely or chiefly to the five planets.[2] We are also told that the slower bodies give out a deep note and the swifter a high note, and the prevailing tradition gives the high note of the octave to

---

[1] It is not expressly stated that they were Pythagoreans, but it is natural to suppose so. So, at least, Alexander thought (Simpl. De caelo, p. 515, 25).

[2] Arist. De caelo, B, 9. 290 b, 12 sqq. (R. P. 82). Cf. Alexander, In met. p. 39, 24 (from Aristotle's work on the Pythagoreans) τῶν γὰρ σωμάτων τῶν περὶ τὸ μέσον φερομένων ἐν ἀναλογίᾳ τὰς ἀποστάσεις ἐχόντων . . . ποιούντων δὲ καὶ ψόφον ἐν τῷ κινεῖσθαι τῶν μὲν βραδυτέρων βαρύν, τῶν δὲ ταχυτέρων ὀξύν. There are all sorts of difficulties in detail. We can hardly attribute the identification of the seven planets (including sun and moon) with the strings of the heptachord to the Pythagoreans of this date ; for Mercury and Venus have the same mean angular velocity as the Sun, and we must take in the heaven of the fixed stars.

the heaven of the fixed stars, which revolves in twenty-four hours. Saturn, of course, comes next ; for, though it has a slow motion of its own in a contrary direction, that is " mastered " (κρατεῖται) by the diurnal revolution. The other view, which gives the highest note to the Moon and the lowest to the fixed stars, is probably due to the theory which substituted an axial rotation of the earth for the diurnal revolution of the heavens.[1]

153. We have still to consider a view, which Aristotle sometimes attributes to the Pythagoreans, that things were " like numbers." He does not appear to regard this as inconsistent with the doctrine that things *are* numbers, though it is hard to see how he could reconcile the two.[2] There is no doubt, however, that Aristoxenos represented the Pythagoreans as teaching that things were *like* numbers,[3] and there are other traces of an attempt to make out that this was the original doctrine. A letter was produced,

Things likenesses of numbers.

[1] For the various systems, see Boeckh, *Kleine Schriften*, vol. iii. pp. 169 *sqq.*, and Carl v. Jan, " Die Harmonie der Sphären " (*Philol.* 1893, pp. 13 *sqq.*). There is a sufficient account of them in Heath's *Aristarchus*, pp. 107 *sqq.*, where the distinction between absolute and relative velocity is clearly stated, a distinction which is not appreciated in Adam's note on *Rep.* 617 b (vol. ii. p. 452), with the result that, while the heaven of the fixed stars is rightly regarded as the νήτη (the highest note), the Moon comes next instead of Saturn—an impossible arrangement. The later view is represented by the " bass of Heaven's deep Organ " in the " ninefold harmony " of Milton's *Hymn on the Nativity* (xiii.). At the beginning of the Fifth Act of the *Merchant of Venice*, Shakespeare makes Lorenzo expound the doctrine in a truly Pythagorean fashion. According to him, the " harmony " in the soul ought to correspond with that of the heavenly bodies (" *such* harmony is in immortal souls "), but the " muddy vesture of decay " prevents their complete correspondence. The *Timaeus* states a similar view, and in the *Book of Homage to Shakespeare* (pp. 58 *sqq.*) I have tried to show how the theories of the *Timaeus* may have reached Shakespeare. There is no force in Martin's observation that the sounding of all the notes of an octave at once would not produce a harmony. There is no question of harmony in the modern sense, but only of attunement (ἁρμονία) to a perfect scale.

[2] Cf. especially *Met.* A, 6. 787, b 10 (R. P. 65 d). It is not quite the same thing when he says, as in A, 5. 985 b 23 *sqq.* (R. P. *ib.*), that they perceived many likenesses in things to numbers. That refers to the numerical analogies of Justice, Opportunity, etc.

[3] Aristoxenos *ap.* Stob. i. pr. 6 (p. 20), Πυθαγόρας . . . πάντα τὰ πράγματα ἀπεικάζων τοῖς ἀριθμοῖς.

purporting to be by Theano, the wife of Pythagoras, in
which she says that she hears many of the Hellenes think
Pythagoras said things were made *of* number, whereas he
really said they were made *according to* number.[1]

When this view is uppermost in his mind, Aristotle seems
to find only a verbal difference between Plato and the
Pythagoreans. The metaphor of " participation " was
merely substituted for that of " imitation." This is not
the place to discuss the meaning of the so-called " theory of
ideas " ; but it must be pointed out that Aristotle's ascription of the doctrine of " imitation " to the Pythagoreans is
abundantly justified by the *Phaedo*. When Simmias is asked
whether he accepts the doctrine, he asks for no explanation
of it, but replies at once and emphatically that he does. The
view that the equal itself is alone real, and that what we call
equal things are imperfect imitations of it, is quite familiar
to him,[2] and he is finally convinced of the immortality of the
soul just because Sokrates makes him see that the theory of
forms implies it.

It is also to be observed that Sokrates does not introduce
the theory as a novelty. The reality of the " ideas " is the
sort of reality " we are always talking about," and they are
explained in a peculiar vocabulary which is represented as
that of a school. The technical terms are introduced by such
formulas as " we say." [3] Whose theory is it ? It is usually
supposed to be Plato's own, though some call it his " early
theory of ideas," and say that he modified it profoundly in
later life. But there are serious difficulties in this view.

---

[1] Stob. *Ecl.* i. p. 125, 19 (R. P. 65 d).

[2] Plato, *Phaed.* 74 a *sqq.*

[3] Cf. especially the words ὃ θρυλοῦμεν ἀεί (76 d 8). The phrases αὐτὸ ὃ
ἔστιν, αὐτὸ καθ' αὐτό, and the like are assumed to be familiar. " We "
define reality by means of question and answer, in the course of which " we "
give an account of its being (ἧς λόγον δίδομεν τοῦ εἶναι, 78 d 1, where
λόγον . . . τοῦ εἶναι is equivalent to λόγον τῆς οὐσίας). When we have done
this, " we " set the seal or stamp of αὐτὸ ὃ ἔστιν upon it (75 d 2). Technical terminology implies a school. As Diels puts it (*Elementum*, p. 20),
it is in a school that " the simile concentrates into a metaphor, and the
metaphor condenses into a term."

Plato is very careful to tell us that he was not present at the conversation recorded in the *Phaedo*. Did any philosopher ever propound a new theory of his own by representing it as already familiar to a number of distinguished living contemporaries ? [1] It is not easy to believe that. It would be rash, on the other hand, to ascribe the origin of the theory to Sokrates, and there seems nothing for it but to suppose that the doctrine of " forms " (εἴδη, ἰδέαι) originally took shape in Pythagorean circles, though it was further developed by Sokrates. There is nothing startling in this. It is a historical fact that Simmias and Kebes were not only Pythagoreans but disciples of Sokrates, and there were, no doubt, more " friends of the ideas " [2] than we generally recognise. It is certain, in any case, that the use of the words εἴδη and ἰδέαι to express ultimate realities is pre-Platonic, and it seems most natural to regard it as of Pythagorean origin.

We have really exceeded the limits of this work by tracing the history of Pythagoreanism down to a point where it becomes practically indistinguishable from the theories which Plato puts into the mouth of Sokrates ; but it was necessary to do so in order to put the statements of our authorities in their true light. Aristoxenos is not likely to have been mistaken with regard to the opinions of the men he had known personally, and Aristotle's statements must have had some foundation.

[1] In the *Parmenides* Plato makes Sokrates expound the theory at a date which is carefully marked as at least twenty years before his own birth.

[2] Plato, *Soph.* 248 a 4. Proclus says (*In Parm.* iv. p. 149, Cousin) ἦν μὲν γὰρ καὶ παρὰ τοῖς Πυθαγορείοις ἡ περὶ τῶν εἰδῶν θεωρία, καὶ δηλοῖ καὶ αὐτὸς ἐν Σοφιστῇ τῶν εἰδῶν φίλους προσαγορεύων τοὺς ἐν Ἰταλίᾳ σοφούς, ἀλλ' ὅ γε μάλιστα πρεσβεύσας καὶ διαρρήδην ὑποθέμενος τὰ εἴδη Σωκράτης ἐστίν. This is not in itself authoritative ; but it is the only statement on the subject that has come down to us, and Proclus (who had the tradition of the Academy at his command) does not appear to have heard of any other interpretation of the phrase. In a later passage (v. p. 4, Cousin) he says it was natural for Parmenides to ask Sokrates whether he had thought of the theory for himself, since he might have heard a report of it.

CHAPTER VIII

THE YOUNGER ELEATICS

Relation
to pre-
decessors. 154. THE systems we have just been studying were all fundamentally pluralist, and they were so because Parmenides had shown that, if we take a corporeal monism seriously, we must ascribe to reality a number of predicates inconsistent with our experience of a world which everywhere displays multiplicity, motion, and change (§ 97). The four " roots " of Empedokles and the innumerable " seeds " of Anaxagoras were both of them conscious attempts to solve the problem Parmenides had raised (§§ 106, 127). There is no evidence indeed, that the Pythagoreans were directly influenced by Parmenides, but it has been shown (§ 147) how the later form of their system was based on the theory of Empedokles. Now it was just this prevailing pluralism that Zeno criticised from the Eleatic standpoint ; and his arguments were especially directed against Pythagoreanism. Melissos, too, criticises Pythagoreanism ; but he tries to find a common ground with his adversaries by maintaining the old Ionian thesis that reality is infinite.

I. ZENO OF ELEA

Life. 155. According to Apollodoros,[1] Zeno flourished in Ol. LXXIX. (464–460 B.C.). This date is arrived at by making him forty years younger than Parmenides, which is

---

[1] Diog. ix. 29 (R. P. 130 a). Apollodoros is not expressly referred to for Zeno's date ; but, as he is quoted for his father's name (ix. 25 ; R. P. 130), there can be no doubt that he is also the source of the *floruit*.

in direct conflict with the testimony of Plato. We have seen already (§ 84) that the meeting of Parmenides and Zeno with the young Sokrates cannot well have occurred before 449 B.C., and Plato tells us that Zeno was at that time " nearly forty years old." [1] He must, then, have been born about 489 B.C., some twenty-five years after Parmenides. He was the son of Teleutagoras, and the statement of Apollodoros that he had been adopted by Parmenides is only a misunderstanding of an expression of Plato's *Sophist*.[2] He was, Plato further tells us,[3] tall and of a graceful appearance.

Like Parmenides, Zeno played a part in the politics of his native city. Strabo, no doubt on the authority of Timaios, ascribes to him some share of the credit for the good government of Elea, and says that he was a Pythagorean.[4] This statement can easily be explained. Parmenides, we have seen, was originally a Pythagorean, and the school of Elea was naturally regarded as a mere branch of the larger society. We hear also that Zeno conspired against a tyrant, whose name is differently given, and the story of his courage under torture is often repeated, though with varying details.[5]

156. Diogenes speaks of Zeno's " books," and Souidas Writings. gives some titles which probably come from the Alexandrian librarians through Hesychios of Miletos.[6] In the *Parmenides* Plato makes Zeno say that the work by which he is best known was written in his youth and published against his will.[7] As he is supposed to be forty years old at the time of

---

[1] Plato, *Parm.* 127 b (R. P. 111 d). The visit of Zeno to Athens is confirmed by Plut. *Per.* 4 (R. P. 130 e), where we are told that Perikles " heard " him as well as Anaxagoras. It is also alluded to in *Alc. I.* 119 a, where we are told that Pythodoros, son of Isolochos, and Kallias, son of Kalliades, each paid him 100 minae for instruction.

[2] Plato, *Soph.* 241 d (R. P. 130 a).
[3] Plato, *Parm.*, *loc. cit.*   [4] Strabo, vi. p. 252 (R. P. 111 c).
[5] Diog. ix. 26, 27, and the other passages referred to in R. P. 130 c. The original of the account given in the tenth book of Diodoros is doubtless Timaios.   [6] Diog. ix. 26 (R. P. 130) ; Souidas *s.v.* (R. P. 130 d).
[7] Plato, *Parm.* 128 d 6 (R. P. 130 d).

the dialogue, this must mean that the book was written before 460 B.C., and it is very possible that he wrote others after it.[1] If he wrote a work against the " philosophers," as Souidas says, that must mean the Pythagoreans, who, as we have seen, made use of the term in a sense of their own.[2] The *Disputations* ("Ερίδες) and the *Treatise on Nature* may, or may not, be the same as the book described in Plato's *Parmenides*.

It is not likely that Zeno wrote dialogues, though certain references in Aristotle have been supposed to imply this. In the *Physics*[3] we hear of an argument of Zeno's, that any part of a heap of millet makes a sound, and Simplicius illustrates this by quoting a passage from a dialogue between Zeno and Protagoras.[4] If our chronology is right, it is quite possible that they may have met ; but it is most unlikely that Zeno should have made himself a personage in a dialogue of his own. That was a later fashion. In another place Aristotle refers to a passage where " the answerer and Zeno the questioner " occurred,[5] a reference which is most easily to be understood in the same way. Alkidamas seems to have written a dialogue in which Gorgias figured,[6] and the exposition of Zeno's arguments in dialogue form must always have been a tempting exercise.

Plato gives us a clear idea of what Zeno's youthful work was like. It contained more than one " discourse," and

[1] The most remarkable title given by Souidas is Ἐξήγησις τῶν Ἐμπεδοκλέους. Of course Zeno did not write a commentary on Empedokles, but Diels points out (*Berl. Sitzb.*, 1884, p. 359) that polemics against philosophers were sometimes called ἐξηγήσεις. Cf. the Ἡρακλείτου ἐξηγήσεις of Herakleides Pontikos and especially his Πρὸς τὸν Δημόκριτον ἐξηγήσεις (Diog. v. 88).

[2] See above, p. 278, *n.* 1. It hardly seems likely that a later writer would make Zeno argue πρὸς τοὺς φιλοσόφους, and the title given to the book at Alexandria must be based on something contained in it.

[3] Arist. *Phys.* H, 5. 250 a 20 (R. P. 131 a).

[4] Simpl. *Phys.* p. 1108, 18 (R. P. 131). If this is what Aristotle refers to, it is hardly safe to attribute the κεγχρίτης λόγος to Zeno himself. The existence of this dialogue is another indication of Zeno's visit to Athens at an age when he could converse with Protagoras, which agrees very well with Plato's representation of the matter.

[5] Arist. *Soph. El.* 170 b 22 (R. P. 130 b).   [6] Chap. V. p. 199, *n.* 5.

these discourses were subdivided into sections, each dealing with some one presupposition of his adversaries.[1] We owe the preservation of Zeno's arguments on the one and many to Simplicius.[2] Those relating to motion have been preserved by Aristotle ;[3] but he has restated them in his own language.

157. Aristotle in his *Sophist*[4] called Zeno the inventor **Dialectic.** of dialectic, and that, no doubt, is substantially true, though the beginnings at least of this method of arguing were contemporary with the foundation of the Eleatic school.   Plato[5] gives us a spirited account of the style and purpose of Zeno's book, which he puts into his own mouth :

In reality, this writing is a sort of reinforcement for the argument of Parmenides against those who try to turn it into ridicule on the ground that, if reality is one, the argument becomes involved in many absurdities and contradictions. This writing argues against those who uphold a Many, and gives them back as good and better than they gave ; its aim is to show that their assumption of multiplicity will be involved in still more absurdities than the assumption of unity, if it is sufficiently worked out.

The method of Zeno was, in fact, to take one of his adversaries' fundamental postulates and deduce from it two contradictory conclusions.[6] This is what Aristotle meant

---

[1] Plato, *Parm.* 127 d. Plato speaks of the first ὑπόθεσις of the first λόγος, which shows that the book was really divided into separate sections. Proclus (*in loc.*) says there were forty of these λόγοι altogether.

[2] Simplicius expressly says in one place (p. 140, 30 ; R. P. 133) that he is quoting κατὰ λέξιν. I see no reason to doubt this, as the Academy would certainly have a copy of the work. In that case, the use of the Attic dialect by Zeno is significant.

[3] Arist. *Phys.* Z, 9. 239 b 9 *sqq.*   [4] Cf. Diog. ix. 25 (R. P. 130).

[5] Plato, *Parm.* 128 c (R. P. 130 d). If historians of philosophy had started from this careful statement of Plato's, instead of from Aristotle's loose references, they would not have failed to understand his arguments, as they all did before Tannery.

[6] The technical terms used in Plato's *Parmenides* seem to be as old as Zeno himself. The ὑπόθεσις is the provisional assumption of the truth of a certain statement, and takes the form εἰ πολλά ἐστι or the like. The word does not mean the assumption of something as a foundation, but the setting before one's self of a statement as a problem to be solved (Ionic

L

by calling him the inventor of dialectic, which is just the art of arguing, not from true premisses, but from premisses admitted by the other side. The theory of Parmenides had led to conclusions which contradicted the evidence of the senses, and Zeno's object was not to bring fresh proofs of the theory itself, but simply to show that his opponents' view led to contradictions of a precisely similar nature.

Zeno and Pythagoreanism.
158. That Zeno's dialectic was mainly directed against the Pythagoreans is certainly suggested by Plato's statement, that it was addressed to the adversaries of Parmenides, who held that things were " a many." [1] Zeller holds, indeed, that it was merely the popular form of the belief that things are many that Zeno set himself to confute ; [2] but it is surely not true that ordinary people believe things to be " a many " in the sense required. Plato tells us that the premisses of Zeno's arguments were the beliefs of the adversaries of Parmenides, and the postulate from which all his contradictions are derived is the view that space, and therefore body, is made up of a number of discrete units, which is just the Pythagorean doctrine. We know from Plato that Zeno's book was the work of his youth.[3] It follows that he must have written it in Italy, and the Pythagoreans are the only people who can have criticised the views of Parmenides there and at that date.[4]

It will be noted how much clearer the historical position of Zeno becomes if we follow Plato in assigning him to a later date than is usual. We have first Parmenides, then the

ὑποθέσθαι, Attic προθέσθαι). If the conclusions (τὰ συμβαίνοντα) which necessarily follow from the ὑπόθεσις are impossible, the ὑπόθεσις is " destroyed " (cf. Plato, Rep. 533 c 8, τὰς ὑποθέσεις ἀναιροῦσα). The author of the Περὶ ἀρχαίης ἰατρικῆς (c. 1) knows the word ὑπόθεσις in a similar sense.

[1] The view that Zeno's arguments were directed against Pythagoreanism has been maintained in recent times by Tannery (Science hellène, pp. 249 sqq.), and Bäumker (Das Problem der Materie, pp. 60 sqq.).

[2] Zeller, p. 589 (Eng. trans. p. 612).　　　[3] Parm., loc. cit.

[4] Empedokles has been suggested. He was about the same age as Zeno, indeed (§ 98), and he seems to criticise Parmenides (§ 106), but the arguments of Zeno have no special applicability to his theories. Anaxagoras is still less likely.

pluralists, and then the criticism of Zeno. ₍This, at any rate,
seems to have been the view Aristotle took of the historical
development.[1]

159. The polemic of Zeno is clearly directed in the first What is
the unit?
instance against a certain view of the unit. Eudemos, in his
Physics,[2] quoted from him the saying that " if any one could
tell him what the unit was, he would be able to say what
things are." The commentary of Alexander on this, preserved by Simplicius, is quite satisfactory. " As Eudemos
relates," he says, " Zeno the disciple of Parmenides tried to
show that it was impossible that things could be a many,
seeing that there was no unit in things, whereas ' many '
means a number of units." [3] Here we have a clear reference
to the Pythagorean view that everything may be reduced to
a sum of units, which is what Zeno denied.

160. The fragments of Zeno himself also show that this The
Frag-
ments.
was his line of argument. I give them according to the
arrangement of Diels.

(1)

If what is had no magnitude, it would not even be. . . .
But, if it is, each one must have a certain magnitude and a certain
thickness, and must be at a certain distance from another, and the
same may be said of what is in front of it ; for it, too, will have
magnitude, and something will be in front of it.[4] It is all the
same to say this once and to say it always ; for no such part of it

---

[1] Arist. *Phys.* A, 3. 187 a 1 (R. P. 134 b). See below, § 173.

[2] Simpl. *Phys.* p. 138, 32 (R. P. 134 a).

[3] Simpl. *Phys.* p. 99, 13, ὡς γὰρ ἱστορεῖ, φησίν ('Αλέξανδρος), Εὔδημος,
Ζήνων ὁ Παρμενίδου γνώριμος ἐπειρᾶτο δεικνύναι ὅτι μὴ οἷόν τε τὰ ὄντα πολλὰ
εἶναι τῷ μηδὲν εἶναι ἐν τοῖς οὖσιν ἕν, τὰ δὲ πολλὰ πλῆθος εἶναι ἐνάδων.
This is the meaning of the statement that Zeno ἀνῄρει τὸ ἕν which
is not Alexander's (as implied in R. P. 134 a), but goes back to
no less an authority than Eudemos. It must be read in connexion
with the words τὴν γὰρ στιγμὴν ὡς τὸ ἕν λέγει (Simpl. *Phys.* p. 99, 11).

[4] I formerly rendered " the same may be said of what surpasses it in
smallness ; for it too will have magnitude, and something will surpass it in
smallness." This is Tannery's rendering, but I now agree with Diels in
thinking that ἀπέχειν refers to μέγεθος and προέχειν to πάχος. Zeno is
showing that the Pythagorean point must have three dimensions.

will be the last, nor will one thing not be as compared with another.[1] So, if things are a many, they must be both small and great, so small as not to have any magnitude at all, and so great as to be infinite. R. P. 134.

(2)

For if it were added to any other thing it would not make it any larger ; for nothing can gain in magnitude by the addition of what has no magnitude, and thus it follows at once that what was added was nothing.[2] But if, when this is taken away from another thing, that thing is no less ; and again, if, when it is added to another thing, that does not increase, it is plain that what was added was nothing, and what was taken away was nothing. R. P. 132.

(3)

If things are a many, they must be just as many as they are, and neither more nor less. Now, if they are as many as they are, they will be finite in number.

If things are a many, they will be infinite in number ; for there will always be other things between them, and others again between these. And so things are infinite in number. R. P. 133.[3]

The unit.   161. If we hold that the unit has no magnitude—and this is required by what Aristotle calls the argument from dichotomy,[4]—then everything must be infinitely small. Nothing made up of units without magnitude can itself have any magnitude. On the other hand, if we insist that the units of which things are built up are something and not nothing, we must hold that everything is infinitely great.

[1] Reading, with Diels and the MSS., οὔτε ἕτερον πρὸς ἕτερον οὐκ ἔσται. Gomperz's conjecture (adopted in R. P.) seems to me arbitrary.

[2] Zeller marks a lacuna here. Zeno must certainly have shown that the subtraction of a point does not make a thing less ; but he may have done so before the beginning of our present fragment.

[3] This is what Aristotle calls " the argument from dichotomy " (Phys. A, 3. 187 a 1 ; R. P. 134 b). If a line is made up of points, we ought to be able to answer the question, " How many points are there in a given line ? " On the other hand, you can always divide a line or any part of it into two halves ; so that, if a line is made up of points, there will always be more of them than any number you assign.   [4] See last note.

The line is infinitely divisible ; and, according to this view, it will be made up of an infinite number of units, each cf which has some magnitude.

That this argument refers to points is proved by an instructive passage from Aristotle's *Metaphysics*.[1]   We read there—

If the unit is indivisible, it will, according to the proposition of Zeno, be nothing.   That which neither makes anything larger by its addition to it, nor smaller by its subtraction from it, is not, he says, a real thing at all ; for clearly what is real must be a magnitude.   And, if it is a magnitude, it is corporeal ; for that is corporeal which is in every dimension.   The other things, *i.e.* the plane and the line, if added in one way will make things larger, added in another they will produce no effect ; but the point and the unit cannot make things larger in any way.

From all this it seems impossible to draw any other conclusion than that the " one " against which Zeno argued was the " one " of which a number constitute a " many," and that is just the Pythagorean unit.

162. Aristotle refers to an argument which seems to be Space. directed against the Pythagorean doctrine of space,[2] and Simplicius quotes it in this form : [3]

If there is space, it will be in something ; for all that is is in something, and what is in something is in space.   So space will be in space, and this goes on *ad infinitum*, therefore there is no space.   R. P. 135.

What Zeno is really arguing against here is the attempt to distinguish space from the body that occupies it.   If we insist that body must be *in* space, then we must go on to ask what space itself is in.   This is a " reinforcement " of the Parmenidean denial of the void.   Possibly the argument that

[1] Arist. *Met.* B, 4. 1001 b 7.
[2] Arist. *Phys.* Δ, 1. 209 a 23 ; 3. 210 b 22 (R. P. 135 a).
[3] Simpl. *Phys.* p. 562, 3 (R. P. 135).   The version of Eudemos is given in Simpl. *Phys.* p. 563, 26, ἀξιοῖ γὰρ πᾶν τὸ ὂν ποῦ εἶναι· εἰ δὲ ὁ τόπος τῶν ὄντων, ποῦ ἂν εἴη; οὐκοῦν ἐν ἄλλῳ τόπῳ κἀκεῖνος δὴ ἐν ἄλλῳ καὶ οὕτως εἰς τὸ πρόσω.

everything must be " in " something, or must have something beyond it, had been used against the Parmenidean theory of a finite sphere with nothing outside it.

Motion.   163. Zeno's arguments on the subject of motion have been preserved by Aristotle himself. The system of Parmenides made all motion impossible, and his successors had been driven to abandon the monistic hypothesis in order to avoid this very consequence. Zeno does not bring any fresh proofs of the impossibility of motion ; all he does is to show that a pluralist theory, such as the Pythagorean, is just as unable to explain it as was that of Parmenides. Looked at in this way, Zeno's arguments are no mere quibbles, but mark a great advance in the conception of quantity. They are as follows :

(1) You cannot cross a race-course.[1] You cannot traverse an infinite number of points in a finite time. You must traverse the half of any given distance before you traverse the whole, and the half of that again before you can traverse it. This goes on *ad infinitum*, so that there are an infinite number of points in any given space, and you cannot touch an infinite number one by one in a finite time.[2]

(2) Achilles will never overtake the tortoise. He must first reach the place from which the tortoise started. By that time the tortoise will have got some way ahead. Achilles must then make up that, and again the tortoise will be ahead. He is always coming nearer, but he never makes up to it.[3]

The " hypothesis " of the second argument is the same as that of the first, namely, that the line is a series of points ; but the reasoning is complicated by the introduction of another moving object. The difference, accordingly, is not a half every time, but diminishes in a constant ratio. Again, the first argument shows that, on this hypothesis, no moving object can ever traverse any distance at all, however fast it

[1] Arist. *Top.* Θ, 8. 160 b 8, Ζήνωνος (λόγος), ὅτι οὐκ ἐνδέχεται κινεῖσθαι οὐδὲ τὸ στάδιον διελθεῖν.
[2] Arist. *Phys.* Z, 9, 239 b 11 (R. P. 136). Cf. Z, 2. 233 a 11 ; a 21 (R. P. 136 a).
[3] Arist. *Phys.* Z, 9. 239 b 14 (R. P. 137).

may move ; the second emphasises the fact that, however slowly it moves, it will traverse an infinite distance.[1]

(3) The arrow in flight is at rest. For, if everything is at rest when it occupies a space equal to itself, and what is in flight at any given moment always occupies a space equal to itself, it cannot move.[2]

Here a further complication is introduced. The moving object itself has length, and its successive positions are not points but lines. The first two arguments are intended to destroy the hypothesis that a line consists of an infinite number of indivisibles ; this argument and the next deal with the hypothesis that it consists of a finite [3] number of indivisibles.

(4) Half the time may be equal to double the time. Let us suppose three rows of bodies,[4] one of which (A) is at rest while the other two (B, C) are moving with equal velocity in opposite directions (Fig. 1). By the time they are all in the same part of the course, B will have passed twice as many of the bodies in C as in A (Fig. 2).

FIG. 1.

```
A        •  •  •  •
B   •  •  •  •    →
C   ←       •  •  •  •
```

FIG. 2.

```
A  •  •  •  •
B  •  •  •  •
C  •  •  •  •
```

Therefore the time which it takes to pass C is twice as long as the time it takes to pass A. But the time which B and C take

---

[1] As Mr. Jourdain puts it (*Mind*, 1916, p. 42), " the first argument shows that motion can never *begin* ; the second argument shows that the slower moves as fast as the faster," on the hypothesis that a line is infinitely divisible into its constituent points.

[2] *Phys.* Z, 9, 239 b 30 (R. P. 138) ; *ib.* 239 b 5 (R. P. 138 a). The latter passage is corrupt, though the meaning is plain. I have translated Zeller's version of it : εἰ γάρ, φησίν, ἠρεμεῖ πᾶν ὅταν ᾖ κατὰ τὸ ἴσον, ἔστι δ' ἀεὶ τὸ φερόμενον ἐν τῷ νῦν κατὰ τὸ ἴσον, ἀκίνητον κ.τ.λ. Of course ἀεί means " at any time," not " always," and κατὰ τὸ ἴσον is, literally, " on a level with a space equal (to itself)." For other readings, see Zeller, p. 598, *n.* 3 ; and Diels, *Vors.* 19 A 27.

[3] See Jourdain (*loc. cit.*).

[4] The word is ὄγκοι ; cf. Chap. VII. p. 291, *n.* 3. The name is very appropriate for the Pythagorean units, which Zeno had shown to have length, breadth, and thickness (fr. 1).

to reach the position of A is the same. Therefore double the time is equal to the half.[1]

According to Aristotle, the paralogism here depends on the assumption that an equal magnitude moving with equal velocity must move for an equal time, whether the magnitude with which it is equal is at rest or in motion. That is certainly so, but we are not to suppose that this assumption is Zeno's own. The fourth argument is, in fact, related to the third just as the second is to the first. The Achilles adds a second moving point to the single moving point of the first argument ; this argument adds a second moving line to the single moving line of the arrow in flight. The lines, however, are represented as a series of units, which is just how the Pythagoreans represented them ; and it is quite true that, if lines are a sum of discrete units, and time is similarly a series of discrete moments, there is no other measure of motion possible than the number of units which each unit passes.

This argument, like the others, is intended to bring out the absurd conclusions which follow from the assumption that all quantity is discrete, and what Zeno has really done is to establish the conception of continuous quantity by a *reductio ad absurdum* of the other hypothesis. If we remember that Parmenides had asserted the one to be continuous (fr. 8, 25), we shall see how accurate is the account of Zeno's method which Plato puts into the mouth of Sokrates.

II. Melissos of Samos

Life.   164. In his Life of Perikles, Plutarch tells us, on the authority of Aristotle, that the philosopher Melissos, son of Ithagenes, was the Samian general who defeated the Athenian

[1] Arist. *Phys.* Z, 9. 239 b 33 (R. P. 139). I have had to express the argument in my own way, as it is not fully given by any of the authorities. The figure is practically Alexander's (Simpl. *Phys.* p. 1016, 14), except that he represents the ὄγκοι by letters instead of dots. The conclusion is plainly stated by Aristotle (*loc. cit.*), συμβαίνειν οἴεται ἴσον εἶναι χρόνον τῷ διπλασίῳ τὸν ἥμισυν, and, however we explain the reasoning, it must be so represented as to lead to the conclusion that, as Mr. Jourdain puts it (*loc. cit.*), " a body travels twice as fast as it does."

fleet in 441/0 B.C. ; [1] and it was no doubt for this reason that
Apollodoros fixed his *floruit* in Ol. LXXXIV. (444–41 B.C.).[2]
Beyond this, we really know nothing about his life. He is
said to have been, like Zeno, a disciple of Parmenides ; [3] but,
as he was a Samian, it is possible that he was originally a
member of the Ionic school, and we shall see that certain
features of his doctrine tend to bear out this view. On
the other hand, he was certainly convinced by the Eleatic
dialectic, and renounced the Ionic doctrine in so far as it
was inconsistent with that. We note here the effect of
the increased facility of intercourse between East and
West, which was secured by the supremacy of Athens.

165. The fragments which we have come from Simplicius, The Frag-
and are given, with the exception of the first, from the text ments.
of Diels.[4]

(1a) If nothing is, what can be said of it as of something
real ? [5]

(1) What was was ever, and ever shall be. For, if it had
come into being, it needs must have been nothing before it came

---

[1] Plut. *Per.* 26 (R. P. 141 b), from Aristotle's Σαμίων πολιτεία.

[2] Diog. ix. 24 (R. P. 141). It is possible, of course, that Apollodoros
meant the first and not the fourth year of the Olympiad. That is his
usual era, the foundation of Thourioi. But, on the whole, it is more
likely that he meant the fourth ; for the date of the ναυαρχία would be
given with precision. See Jacoby, p. 270.

[3] Diog. ix. 24 (R. P. 141).

[4] It is no longer necessary to discuss the passages which used to appear
as frs. 1-5 of Melissos, as it has been proved by A. Pabst that they are
merely a paraphrase of the genuine fragments (*De Melissi Samii fragmentis*,
Bonn, 1889). Almost simultaneously I had independently come to the
same conclusion (see the first edition, § 138). Zeller and Diels have both
accepted Pabst's demonstration, and the supposed fragments have been
relegated to the notes in the last edition of R. P. I still believe, however,
that the fragment which I have numbered 1a is genuine. See next
note.

[5] This fragment is from the beginning of the paraphrase which was
so long mistaken for the words of Melissos (Simpl. *Phys.* p. 103, 18 ; R. P.
142 a), and Diels has removed it along with the rest. I believe it to
be genuine because Simplicius, who had access to the original, introduces
it by the words ἄρχεται τοῦ συγγράμματος οὕτως, and because it is thoroughly
Eleatic in character. It is quite natural that the first words of the book
should be prefixed to the paraphrase.

into being. Now, if it were nothing, in no wise could anything have arisen out of nothing. R. P. 142.

(2) Since, then, it has not come into being, and since it is, was ever, and ever shall be, it has no beginning or end, but is without limit. For, if it had come into being, it would have had a beginning (for it would have begun to come into being at some time or other) and an end (for it would have ceased to come into being at some time or other) ; but, if it neither began nor ended, and ever was and ever shall be, it has no beginning or end ; for it is not possible for anything to be ever without all being. R. P. 143.

(3) Further, just as it ever is, so it must ever be infinite in magnitude. R. P. 143.

(4) But nothing which has a beginning or end is either eternal or infinite. R. P. 143.

(5) If it were not one, it would be bounded by something else. R. P. 144 a.

(6) For if it is (infinite), it must be one ; for if it were two, it could not be infinite ; for then they would be bounded by one another.[1] R. P. 144.

(6a) (And, since it is one, it is alike throughout ; for if it were unlike, it would be many and not one.)[2]

(7) So then it is eternal and infinite and one and all alike. And it cannot perish nor become greater, nor does it suffer pain or grief. For, if any of these things happened to it, it would no longer be one. For if it is altered, then the real must needs not be all alike, but what was before must pass away, and what was not must come into being. Now, if it changed by so much as a single hair in ten thousand years, it would all perish in the whole of time.

Further, it is not possible either that its order should be changed ; for the order which it had before does not perish, nor does that which was not come into being. But, since nothing is either added to it or passes away or is altered, how can any real

---

[1] This fragment is quoted by Simpl. *De caelo*, p. 557, 16 (R. P. 144). The insertion of the word " infinite " is justified by the paraphrase (R. P. 144 a) and by *M.X.G.* 974 a 11, πᾶν δὲ ἄπειρον ὂν ⟨ἓν⟩ εἶναι· εἰ γὰρ δύο ἢ πλείω εἴη, πέρατ' ἂν εἶναι ταῦτα πρὸς ἄλληλα.

[2] I have ventured to insert this, though the actual words are nowhere quoted, and it is not in Diels. It is represented in the paraphrase (R. P. 145 a) and in *M.X.G.* 974 a 13 (R. P. 144 a).

thing have had its order changed ? For if anything became different, that would amount to a change in its order.

Nor does it suffer pain ; for a thing in pain could not all be. For a thing in pain could not be ever, nor has it the same power as what is whole. Nor would it be alike, if it were in pain ; for it is only from the addition or subtraction of something that it could feel pain, and then it would no longer be alike. Nor could what is whole feel pain ; for then what was whole and what was real would pass away, and what was not would come into being. And the same argument applies to grief as to pain.

Nor is anything empty. For what is empty is nothing. What is nothing cannot be.

Nor does it move ; for it has nowhere to betake itself to, but is full. For if there were aught empty, it would betake itself to the empty. But, since there is naught empty, it has nowhere to betake itself to.

And it cannot be dense and rare ; for it is not possible for what is rare to be as full as what is dense, but what is rare is at once emptier than what is dense.

This is the way in which we must distinguish between what is full and what is not full. If a thing has room for anything else, and takes it in, it is not full ; but if it has no room for anything and does not take it in, it is full.

Now, it must needs be full if there is naught empty, and if it is full, it does not move. R. P. 145.

(8) This argument, then, is the greatest proof that it is one alone ; but the following are proofs of it also. If there were a many, these would have to be of the same kind as I say that the one is. For if there is earth and water, and air and iron, and gold and fire, and if one thing is living and another dead, and if things are black and white and all that men say they really are,—if that is so, and if we see and hear aright, each one of these must be such as we first decided, and they cannot be changed or altered, but each must be just as it is. But, as it is, we say that we see and hear and understand aright, and yet we believe that what is warm becomes cold, and what is cold warm ; that what is hard turns soft, and what is soft hard ; that what is living dies, and that things are born from what lives not ; and that all those things are changed, and that what they were and what they are now are in no way alike. We think that iron, which is hard, is

rubbed away by contact with the finger ; [1] and so with gold and stone and everything which we fancy to be strong, and that earth and stone are made out of water ; so that it turns out that we neither see nor know realities. Now these things do not agree with one another. We said that there were many things that were eternal and had forms and strength of their own, and yet we fancy that they all suffer alteration, and that they change from what we see each time. It is clear, then, that we did not see aright after all, nor are we right in believing that all these things are many. They would not change if they were real, but each thing would be just what we believed it to be ; for nothing is stronger than true reality. But if it has changed, what was has passed away, and what was not is come into being. So then, if there were many things, they would have to be just of the same nature as the one. R. P. 147.

(9) Now, if it were to exist, it must needs be one ; but if it is one, it cannot have body ; for, if it had body it would have parts, and would no longer be one. R. P. 146.[2]

(10) If what is real is divided, it moves ; but if it moves, it cannot be. R. P. 144 a.[3]

Theory of reality.

166. It has been pointed out that Melissos was not perhaps originally a member of the Eleatic school ; but he certainly adopted all the views of Parmenides as to the true nature of reality with one remarkable exception. He appears to have opened his treatise with a reassertion of the Parmenidean " Nothing is not " (fr. 1a), and the arguments by which he supported this view are those with which we are already familiar (fr. 1). Reality, as with Parmenides, is eternal, a point which Melissos expressed in a way of his own. He argued that since everything that has come into being has a beginning and an end, everything that has not come into being has no beginning or end. Aristotle is very hard on him for this simple conversion of a universal affirmative

[1] Reading ὁμουρέων with Bergk. Diels keeps the MS. ὁμοῦ ῥέων; Zeller (p. 613, n. 1) conjectures ὑπ' ἰοῦ ῥέων.

[2] I read εἰ μὲν οὖν εἴη with E F for the εἰ μὲν ὃν εἴη of D. The ἐὸν which still stands in R. P. is a piece of local colour due to the editors. Diels also now reads οὖν.

[3] Diels now reads ἀλλὰ with E for the ἅμα of F, and attaches the word to the next sentence.

proposition ; [1] but, of course, his belief was not founded on that. His whole conception of reality made it necessary for him to regard it as eternal.[2] It would be more serious if Aristotle were right in believing, as he seems to have done, that Melissos inferred that what is must be infinite in space, because it had neither beginning nor end in time.[3] As, however, we have the fragment which Aristotle interprets in this way (fr. 2), we are quite entitled to understand it for ourselves, and I cannot see anything to justify Aristotle's assumption that the expression " without limit " means without limit in space.[4]

167. Melissos did indeed differ from Parmenides in holding that reality was spatially as well as temporally infinite ; but he gave an excellent reason for this belief, and had no need to support it by such an extraordinary argument. What he said was that, if it were limited, it would be limited by empty space. This we know from Aristotle himself,[5] and it marks a real advance upon Parmenides. He had thought it possible to regard reality as a finite sphere, but it would have been difficult for him to work out this view in detail. He would have had to say there was nothing outside the sphere ; but no one knew better than he that there is no

Reality spatially infinite.

---

[1] Arist. *Phys.* A, 3. 186 a 7 (R. P. 143 a). The false conversion is also mentioned in *Soph. El.* 168 b 35 (R. P. *ib.*). So Eudemos *ap.* Simpl. *Phys.* p. 105, 24, οὐ γάρ, εἰ τὸ γενόμενον ἀρχὴν ἔχει, τὸ μὴ γενόμενον ἀρχὴν οὐκ ἔχει, μᾶλλον δὲ τὸ μὴ ἔχον ἀρχὴν οὐκ ἐγένετο.

[2] The real reason is given in the paraphrase in Simpl. *Phys.* p. 103, 21 (R. P. 142 a), συγχωρεῖται γὰρ καὶ τοῦτο ὑπὸ τῶν φυσικῶν, though Melissos himself would not have put it in that way. He regarded himself as a φυσικός like the rest ; but, from the time of Aristotle, it was a commonplace that the Eleatics were not φυσικοί, since they denied motion.

[3] Cf. especially *Soph. El.* 168 b 39, ὡς ἄμφω ταὐτὰ ὄντα τῷ ἀρχὴν ἔχειν, τότε γεγονὸς καὶ τὸ πεπερασμένον. The same point is made in 167 b 13 and 181 a 27.

[4] The words ἀλλ' ἄπειρόν ἐστι mean simply " but it is without limit," and this is simply a repetition of the statement that it has no beginning or end. The nature of the limit can only be determined by the context, and accordingly, when Melissos does introduce the subject of spatial infinity, he is careful to say τὸ μέγεθος ἄπειρον (fr. 3).

[5] Arist. *Gen. Corr.* A, 8. 325 a 14, ἓν καὶ ἀκίνητον τὸ πᾶν εἶναί φασι καὶ ἄπειρον ἔνιοι· τὸ γὰρ πέρας περαίνειν ἂν πρὸς τὸ κενόν. That this refers to Melissos has been shown by Zeller (p. 612, *n.* 2).

such thing as nothing. Melissos saw that you cannot imagine a finite sphere without regarding it as surrounded by an infinite empty space ; [1] and as, in common with the rest of the school, he denied the void (fr. 7), he was forced to say reality was spatially infinite (fr. 3). It is possible that he was influenced in this by his association with the Ionic school.

From the infinity of reality, it follows that it must be one ; for, if it were not one, it would be bounded by something else (fr. 5). And, being one, it must be homogeneous throughout (fr. 6a), for that is what we mean by one. Reality, then, is a single, homogeneous, corporeal *plenum*, stretching out to infinity in space, and going backwards and forwards to infinity in time.

Opposition to Ionians.   168. Eleaticism was always critical, and we are not without indications of the attitude taken up by Melissos towards contemporary systems. The flaw which he found in the Ionian theories was that they all assumed some want of homogeneity in the One, which was a real inconsistency. Further, they all allowed the possibility of change ; but, if all things are one, change must be a form of coming into being and passing away. If you admit that a thing can change, you cannot maintain that it is eternal. Nor can the arrangement of the parts of reality alter, as Anaximander, for instance, had held ; any such change necessarily involves a coming into being and passing away.

The next point made by Melissos is somewhat peculiar. Reality, he says, cannot feel sorrow or pain ; for that is always due to the addition or subtraction of something, which is impossible. It is not easy to be sure what this refers to. Perhaps it is to the theory by which Anaxagoras explained perception.[2]

---

[1] Note the disagreement with Zeno (§ 162).
[2] See p. 273. It is clear that Anaxagoras made considerable use of pain (πόνος), and it is possible that his doctrine, summed up in the words ἀεὶ πονεῖ τὸ ζῷον (Arist. *Eth. Nic.* H, 15. 1154 b 7) had a wider application than appears from his remains. Aristotle (*De caelo*, B, 1. 284 a 15) makes a point of the οὐρανός being ἄπονος.

Motion in general [1] and rarefaction and condensation in particular are impossible ; for both imply the existence of empty space. Divisibility is excluded for the same reason. These are the same arguments as Parmenides employed.

169. In nearly all accounts of the system of Melissos, we find it stated that he denied the corporeality of what is real, —an opinion which is supported by a reference to fr. 9, which is certainly quoted by Simplicius to prove this very point.[2] If, however, our general view as to the character of early Greek philosophy is correct, the statement must seem incredible. And it will seem even more surprising when we find that in the *Metaphysics* Aristotle says that, while the unity of Parmenides seemed to be ideal, that of Melissos was material.[3] Now the fragment, as it stands in the MSS. of Simplicius,[4] puts a purely hypothetical case, and would most naturally be understood as a disproof of the existence of something on the ground that, if it existed, it would have to be both corporeal and one. This cannot refer to the Eleatic One, in which Melissos himself believed ; and, as the argument is almost verbally the same as one of Zeno's,[5] it is natural to suppose that it also was directed against the Pythagorean assumption of ultimate units. The only possible objection is that Simplicius, who twice quotes the

(margin: Opposition to Pythagoreans.)

---

[1] The view of Bäumker that Melissos admitted ἀντιπερίστασις or motion *in pleno* (*Jahrb. f. kl. Phil.*, 1886, p. 541 ; *Das Problem der Materie*, p. 59) depends upon some words of Simplicius (*Phys.* p. 104, 13), οὐχ ὅτι μὴ δυνατὸν διὰ πλήρους κινεῖσθαι, ὡς ἐπὶ τῶν σωμάτων λέγομεν κτλ. These words were formerly turned into Ionic and passed off as a fragment of Melissos. They are, however, part of Simplicius's own argument against Alexander, and have nothing to do with Melissos at all.

[2] See, however, Bäumker, *Das Problem der Materie*, pp. 57 *sqq.*, who remarks that ἐόν (or ὄν) in fr. 9 must be the predicate, as it has no article. In his fifth edition (p. 611, *n.* 2) Zeller adopted the view here taken. He rightly observes that the hypothetical form εἰ μὲν ὂν εἴη speaks for it, and that the subject to εἴη must be ἕκαστον τῶν πολλῶν, as with Zeno.

[3] *Met.* A, 5. 986 b 18 (R. P. 101).

[4] Brandis changed the εἴη to ἔστι, but there is no warrant for this.

[5] Cf. Zeno, fr. 1, especially the words εἰ δὲ ἔστιν, ἀνάγκη ἕκαστον μέγεθός τι ἔχειν καὶ πάχος.

fragment, certainly took it in the sense usually given to it.[1] But it was very natural for him to make this mistake. " The One " was an expression that had two senses in the middle of the fifth century B.C. ; it meant either the whole of reality or the point as a spatial unit.   To maintain it in the first sense, the Eleatics were obliged to disprove it in the second ; and so it sometimes seemed that they were speaking of their own " One " when they really meant the other.   We have seen that the very same difficulty was felt about Zeno's denial of the " one." [2]

Opposition to Anaxagoras.   170. The most remarkable fragment of Melissos is, perhaps, the last (fr. 8). It seems to be directed against Anaxagoras ; at least the language seems more applicable to him than any one else. Anaxagoras had admitted (§ 137, *fin.*) that, so far as our perceptions go, they do not agree with his theory, though he held this was due solely to their weakness. Melissos, taking advantage of this admission, urges that, if we give up the senses as the test of reality, we are not entitled to reject the Eleatic theory. With wonderful penetration he points out that if we are to say, with Anaxagoras, that things are a many, we are bound also to say that each one of them is such as the Eleatics declared the One to be.   In other words, the only consistent pluralism is the atomic theory.

Melissos has been unduly depreciated owing to the criticisms of Aristotle ; but these, we have seen, are based mainly on a somewhat pedantic objection to the false conversion in the early part of the argument. Melissos knew nothing about the rules of conversion ; and he could easily have made his reasoning formally correct without modifying his system.   His greatness consisted in this, that not only was he the real systematiser of Eleaticism, but he was also able to see, before the pluralists saw it themselves, the only way in which the theory that things are a many could be

---

[1] Simpl. *Phys.* pp. 87, 6, and 110, 1.
[2] See above, § 159, p. 315, *n.* 3.

consistently worked out.[1] It is significant that Polybos, the nephew of Hippokrates, reproaches those " sophists " who taught there was only one primary substance with " putting the doctrine of Melissos on its feet." [2]

[1] Bäumker, *op. cit.* p. 58, *n.* 3 : " That Melissos was a weakling is a *fable convenue* that people repeat after Aristotle, who was unable to appreciate the Eleatics in general, and in particular misunderstood Melissos not inconsiderably."

[2] Περὶ φύσιος ἀνθρώπου, c. 1, ἀλλ' ἔμοιγε δοκέουσιν οἱ τοιοῦτοι ἄνθρωποι αὐτοὶ ἑωυτοὺς καταβάλλειν ἐν τοῖσιν ὀνόμασι τῶν λόγων αὐτῶν ὑπὸ ἀσυνεσίης, τὸν δὲ Μελίσσου λόγον ὀρθοῦν. The metaphors are taken from wrestling, and were current at this date (cf. the καταβάλλοντες of Protagoras). Plato implies a more generous appreciation of Melissos than Aristotle's. In *Theaet.* 180 e 2, he refers to the Eleatics as Μέλισσοί τε καὶ Παρμενίδαι, and in 183 e 4 he almost apologises for giving the pre-eminence to Parmenides.

CHAPTER IX

LEUKIPPOS OF MILETOS

Leukippos and Demokritos. 171. WE have seen (§§ 31, 122) that the school of Miletos did not come to an end with Anaximenes, and it is a striking fact that the man who gave the most complete answer to the question first asked by Thales was a Milesian.[1] It is true that the very existence of Leukippos has been called in question. Epicurus is reported to have said there never was such a philosopher, and the same thing has been maintained in quite recent times.[2] On the other hand, Aristotle and Theophrastos certainly made him the originator of the atomic theory, and they can hardly have been mistaken on such a point. Aristotle was specially interested in Demokritos, and his native Stageiros is not very far from Abdera, the seat of the Atomist school.

---

[1] Theophrastos said he was an Eleate or a Milesian (R. P. 185), while Diogenes (ix. 30) says he was an Eleate or, according to some, an Abderite. These statements are just like the discrepancies about the native cities of Pythagoreans already noted (Chap. VII. p. 283, *n.* 1). Diogenes adds that, according to others, Leukippos was a Melian, which is a common confusion. Aetios (i. 7. 1) calls Diagoras of Melos a Milesian (cf. *Dox.* p. 14). Demokritos was called by some a Milesian (Diog. ix. 34; R. P. 186) for the same reason that Leukippos is called an Eleate. We may also compare the doubt as to whether Herodotos called himself a Halikarnassian or a Thourian.

[2] Diog. x. 13 (R. P. 185 b), ἀλλ' οὐδὲ Λεύκιππόν τινα γεγενῆσθαί φησι φιλόσοφον οὔτε αὐτὸς (sc. Ἐπίκουρος) οὔτε Ἕρμαρχος. This led E. Rohde to maintain that Leukippos never existed (*Kl. Schr.* i. 205), but this is to make too much of a characteristic Epicurean sally. I suggest that Epicurus said something like Λεύκιππον οὐδ' εἰ γέγονεν οἶδα, which would be idiomatic Greek for "I (purposely) ignore him," "I decline to discuss him." (Cf. *e.g.* Dem. *De cor.* § 70 Σέρριον δὲ καὶ Δορίσκον καὶ τὴν Πεπαρήθου πόρθησιν . . . οὐδ' εἰ γέγονεν οἶδα.) That would be just like Epicurus.

The question is intimately bound up with that of the date of Demokritos, who said that he himself was a young man in the old age of Anaxagoras, a statement which makes it unlikely that he founded his school at Abdera much before 420 B.C., the date given by Apollodoros for his *floruit*.[1] Now Theophrastos stated that Diogenes of Apollonia borrowed some of his views from Anaxagoras and some from Leukippos,[2] which must mean that there were traces of the atomic theory in his work. Further, Diogenes is parodied in the *Clouds* of Aristophanes, which was produced in 423 B.C., from which it follows that the work of Leukippos must have become known before that date. What that work was, Theophrastos also tells us. It was the *Great Diakosmos* usually attributed to Demokritos.[3] This means further that what were known later as the works of Demokritos were really the writings of the school of Abdera, and included, as was natural, the works of its founder. They formed, in fact, a *corpus* like that which has come down to us under the name of Hippokrates, and it was no more possible to distinguish the authors of the different treatises in the one case than it is in the other.

Theophrastos found Leukippos described as an Eleate in some authorities, and, if we may trust analogy, that means he had settled at Elea.[4] It is possible that his emigration

[1] Diog. ix. 41 (R. P. 187). As Diels says, the statement suggests that Anaxagoras was dead when Demokritos wrote. It is probable, too, that this is what made Apollodoros fix his *floruit* just forty years after that of Anaxagoras (Jacoby, p. 290). We cannot make much of the statement of Demokritos that he wrote the Μικρὸς διάκοσμος 750 years after the fall of Troy ; for we cannot tell what era he used (Jacoby, p. 292).

[2] Theophr. *ap.* Simpl. *Phys.* p. 25, 1 (R. P. 206 a).

[3] This was stated by Thrasylos in his list of the tetralogies in which he arranged the works of Demokritos, as he did those of Plato. He gives Tetr. iii. thus : (1) Μέγας διάκοσμος (ὃν οἱ περὶ Θεόφραστον Λευκίππου φασὶν εἶναι) ; (2) Μικρὸς διάκοσμος ; (3) Κοσμογραφίη ; (4) Περὶ τῶν πλανήτων. The two διάκοσμοι would only be distinguished as μέγας and μικρός when they came to be included in the same *corpus*. A quotation from the Περὶ νοῦ of Leukippos is preserved in Stob. i. 160. The phrase ἐν τοῖς Λευκίππου καλουμένοις λόγοις in M.X.G. 980 a 8 seems to refer to Arist. *De gen. corr.* A, 8. 325 a 24, Λεύκιππος δ' ἔχειν ᾠήθη λόγους κτλ. Cf. Chap. II. p. 126, *n.* 1.

[4] See above, p. 330, *n.* 1.

was connected with the revolution at Miletos in 450–49 B.C.[1] In any case, Theophrastos says distinctly that he had been a member of the school of Parmenides, and his words suggest that the founder of that school was then still at its head.[2] He may quite well have been so, if we accept Plato's chronology.[3] Theophrastos also appears to have said that Leukippos " heard " Zeno, which is very credible. We shall see, at any rate, that the influence of Zeno on his thinking is unmistakable.[4]

The relations of Leukippos to Empedokles and Anaxagoras are more difficult to determine. It has become part of the case for the historical reality of Leukippos to say that there are traces of atomism in the systems of these men ; but the case is strong enough without that assumption. The chief argument for the view that Leukippos influenced Empedokles is that drawn from the doctrine of " pores " ; but we have seen that this originated with Alkmaion, and it is therefore more probable that Leukippos derived it from Empedokles.[5] Nor is it at all probable that Anaxagoras knew anything of the theory of Leukippos. It is true that he denied the existence of the void ; but it does not follow that any one had already maintained that doctrine in the atomist sense. The early Pythagoreans had spoken of a void too, though they had confused it with atmospheric air ; and the experiments of Anaxagoras with the *klepsydra* and the inflated skins would only have had any point if they were directed against the Pythagorean theory.[6] If he had really

---

[1] Cf. [Xen.] Ἀθ. πολ. 3, 11.   The date is fixed by *C.I.A.* i. 22 a.

[2] Theophr. *ap.* Simpl. *Phys.* p. 28, 4 (R. P. 185). Note the difference of case in κοινωνήσας Παρμενίδῃ τῆς φιλοσοφίας and κοινωνήσας τῆς Ἀναξιμένους φιλοσοφίας, which is the phrase used by Theophrastos of Anaxagoras (p. 253, *n.* 2). The dative seems to imply a personal relationship. It is quite inadmissible to render " was familiar with the doctrine of Parmenides," as is done in Gomperz, *Greek Thinkers*, vol. i. p. 345.

[3] See § 84.

[4] Cf. Diog. ix. 30, οὗτος ἤκουσε Ζήνωνος (R. P. 185 b) ; and Hipp. *Ref.* i. 12, 1, Λεύκιππος . . . Ζήνωνος ἑταῖρος.

[5] See above, Chap. V. p. 194, *n.* 3.

[6] See above, Chap. VI. § 131 ; and Chap. VII. § 145.

wished to refute Leukippos, he would have had to use arguments of a very different kind.

172. Theophrastos wrote of Leukippos as follows in the First Book of his *Opinions* :

Leukippos of Elea or Miletos (for both accounts are given of him) had associated with Parmenides in philosophy. He did not, however, follow the same path in his explanation of things as Parmenides and Xenophanes did, but, to all appearance, the very opposite (R. P. 185). They made the All one, immovable, uncreated, and finite, and did not even permit us to search for *what is not* ; he assumed innumerable and ever-moving elements, namely, the atoms. And he made their forms infinite in number, since there was no reason why they should be of one kind rather than another, and because he saw that there was unceasing becoming and change in things. He held, further, that *what is* is no more real than *what is not*, and that both are alike causes of the things that come into being : for he laid down that the substance of the atoms was compact and full, and he called them *what is*, while they moved in the void which he called *what is not*, but affirmed to be just as real as *what is*. R. P. 194.

173. It will be observed that Theophrastos, while noting the affiliation of Leukippos to the Eleatic school, points out that his theory is, *prima facie*,[1] just the opposite of that maintained by Parmenides. Some have been led by this to deny the Eleaticism of Leukippos altogether ; but this denial is really based on the view that the system of Parmenides was " metaphysical," coupled with a great reluctance to admit that so scientific a hypothesis as the atomic theory can have had a " metaphysical " origin. This is merely a prejudice, and we must not suppose Theophrastos himself believed the two theories to be so far apart as they

[1] The words ὡς δοκεῖ do not imply assent to the view introduced by them ; indeed they are constantly used in reference to beliefs which the writer does not accept. The translation " methinks " in Gomperz, *Greek Thinkers*, vol. i. p. 345, is therefore most misleading, and there is no justification for Brieger's statement (*Hermes*, xxxvi. p. 165) that Theophrastos dissents from Aristotle's view as given in the passage about to be quoted.

seem.[1] As this is really the most important point in the history of early Greek philosophy, and as, rightly understood, it furnishes the key to the whole development, it is worth while to transcribe a passage of Aristotle [2] which explains the historical connexion in a way that leaves nothing to be desired.

Leukippos and Demokritos have decided about all things practically by the same method and on the same theory, taking as their starting-point what naturally comes first. Some of the ancients had held that the real must necessarily be one and immovable ; for, said they, empty space is not real, and motion would be impossible without empty space separated from matter ; nor, further, could reality be a many, if there were nothing to separate things. And it makes no difference if any one holds that the All is not continuous, but discrete, with its parts in contact (*the Pythagorean view*), instead of holding that reality is many, not one, and that there is empty space. For, if it is divisible at every point there is no one, and therefore no many, and the Whole is empty (*Zeno*) ; while, if we say it is divisible in one place and not in another, this looks like an arbitrary fiction ; for up to what point and for what reason will part of the Whole be in this state and be full, while the rest is discrete ? And, on the same grounds, they further say that there can be no motion. In consequence of these reasonings, then, going beyond perception and overlooking it in the belief that we ought to follow the argument, they say that the All is one and immovable (*Parmenides*), and some of them that it is infinite (*Melissos*), for any limit would be bounded by empty space. This, then, is the opinion they expressed about the truth, and these are the reasons which led them to do so. Now, so far as arguments go, this conclusion does seem to follow ; but, if we appeal to facts, to hold such a view looks like madness. No one who is mad is so far out of his senses that fire and ice appear to him to be one ; it is only things that are right, and things that

---

[1] This prejudice is apparent all through Gomperz's *Greek Thinkers*, and seriously impairs the value of that fascinating, though somewhat imaginative work. It is amusing to notice that Brieger, from the same point of view, regards the custom of making Anaxagoras the last of the Presocratics as due to theological prepossessions (*Hermes*, xxxvi. p. 185).

[2] Arist. *De gen. corr.* A, 8. 324 b 35 (R. P. 193).

appear right from habit, in which madness makes some people
see no difference.

Leukippos, however, thought he had a theory which was in
harmony with sense, and did not do away with coming into being
and passing away, nor motion, nor the multiplicity of things. He
conceded this to experience, while he conceded, on the other
hand, to those who invented the One that motion was impossible
without the void, that the void was not real, and that nothing of
what was real was not real. " For," said he, " that which is
strictly speaking real is an absolute *plenum* ; but the *plenum* is
not one. On the contrary, there are an infinite number of them,
and they are invisible owing to the smallness of their bulk. They
move in the void (for there is a void) ; and by their coming
together they effect coming into being ; by their separation,
passing away."

In this passage Zeno and Melissos are not named, but
the reference to them is unmistakable. The argument of
Zeno against the Pythagoreans is clearly given ; and Melissos
was the only Eleatic who made reality infinite, a point which
is distinctly mentioned. We are therefore justified by
Aristotle's words in explaining the genesis of Atomism and
its relation to Eleaticism as follows. Zeno had shown that
all pluralist systems yet known, and especially Pythagoreanism, were unable to stand before the arguments from
infinite divisibility which he adduced. Melissos had used
the same argument against Anaxagoras, and had added, as
a *reductio ad absurdum*, that, if there were many things, each
one of them must be such as the Eleatics held the One to be.
To this Leukippos answers, " Why not ? " He admitted the
force of Zeno's arguments by setting a limit to divisibility,
and to each of the " atoms " which he thus arrived at he
ascribed all the predicates of the Eleatic One ; for Parmenides had shown that if *it is*, it must have these predicates
somehow. The same view is implied in a passage of Aristotle's *Physics*.[1] " Some," we are there told, " surrendered
to both arguments, to the first, the argument that all things

[1] Arist. *Phys.* A, 3. 187 a 1 (R. P. 134 b).

are one, if the word *is* is used in one sense only (*Parmenides*), by affirming the reality of what is not ; to the second, that based on dichotomy (*Zeno*), by introducing indivisible magnitudes." Finally, it is only by regarding the matter in this way that we can attach any meaning to another statement of Aristotle's that Leukippos and Demokritos, as well as the Pythagoreans, virtually make all things out of numbers.[1] Leukippos, in fact, gave the Pythagorean monads the character of the Parmenidean One.

Atoms.

174. We must observe that the atom is not mathematically indivisible, for it has magnitude ; it is, however, physically indivisible, because, like the One of Parmenides, it contains no empty space.[2] Each atom has extension, and all atoms are exactly alike in substance.[3] Therefore all differences in things must be accounted for either by the shape of the atoms or by their arrangement. It seems probable that the three ways in which differences arise, namely, shape, position, and arrangement, were already distinguished by Leukippos ; for Aristotle mentions his name in connexion with them.[4] This explains, too, why the atoms are called " forms " or " figures," a way of speaking which is clearly of Pythagorean origin.[5] That they are also called

[1] Arist. *De caelo*, Γ, 4. 303 a 8, τρόπον γάρ τινα καὶ οὗτοι (Λεύκιππος καὶ Δημόκριτος) πάντα τὰ ὄντα ποιοῦσιν ἀριθμοὺς καὶ ἐξ ἀριθμῶν. This also serves to explain the statement of Herakleides attributing the theory of corporeal ὄγκοι to the Pythagorean Ekphantos of Syracuse (above, p. 291, *n.* 3).

[2] The Epicureans misunderstood this point, or misrepresented it in order to magnify their own originality (see Zeller, p. 857, *n.* 3).

[3] Arist. *De caelo*, A, 7. 275 b 32, τὴν δὲ φύσιν εἶναί φασιν αὐτῶν μίαν. Here φύσις can only have one meaning. Cf. *Phys.* Γ, 4. 203 a 34, αὐτῷ (Δημοκρίτῳ) τὸ κοινὸν σῶμα πάντων ἐστὶν ἀρχή.

[4] Arist. *Met.* A, 4. 985 b 13 (R. P. 192); cf. *De gen. corr.* A, 2. 315 b 6. As Diels suggests, the illustration from letters is probably due to Demokritos. It shows, in any case, how the word στοιχεῖον came to be used for " element." We must read, with Wilamowitz, τὸ δὲ Z τοῦ H θέσει for τὸ δὲ Z τοῦ N θέσει, the older form of the letter Z being just an H laid upon its side (Diels, *Elementum*, p. 13, *n.* 1).

[5] Demokritos wrote a work, Περὶ ἰδεῶν (Sext. *Math.* vii. 137 ; R. P. 204), which Diels identifies with the Περὶ τῶν διαφερόντων ῥυσμῶν of Thrasylos, *Tetr.* v. 3. Theophrastos refers to Demokritos, ἐν τοῖς περὶ τῶν εἰδῶν (*De sensibus*, § 51). Plut. *Adv. Col.* 1111 a, εἶναι δὲ πάντα τὰς

φύσις [1] is quite intelligible if we remember what was said of that word in the Introduction (§ VII.). The differences in shape, order, and position just referred to account for the "opposites," the "elements" being regarded rather as aggregates of these (πανσπερμίαι), as by Anaxagoras.[2]

175. Leukippos affirmed the existence both of the Full The void. and the Empty, terms which he may have borrowed from Melissos.[3] He had to assume empty space, which the Eleatics had denied, in order to make his explanation of the nature of body possible. Here again he is developing a Pythagorean view. The Pythagoreans had spoken of the void, which kept the units apart; but they had not distinguished it from atmospheric air (§ 53), which Empedokles had shown to be a corporeal substance (§ 107). Parmenides, indeed, had formed a clearer conception of space, but only to deny its reality Leukippos started from this. He admitted, indeed, that space was not real, that is to say, corporeal; but he maintained that it existed all the same. He hardly, it is true, had words to express his discovery in; for the verb "to be" had hitherto been used by philosophers only of body. But he did his best to make his meaning clear by saying that "what is not" (in the old corporealist sense) "is" (in another sense) just as much as "what is." The void is as real as body.

176. It might seem a hopeless task to disentangle the Cosmo-cosmology of Leukippos from that of Demokritos, with logy. which it is generally identified; but that very fact affords a valuable clue. No one later than Theophrastos was able to distinguish their doctrines, and it follows that all definite

ἀτόμους, ἰδέας ὑπ' αὐτοῦ καλουμένας (so the MSS.: ἰδίως, Wyttenbach; ⟨ἢ⟩ ἰδέας, Diels). Herodian has ἰδέα . . . τὸ ἐλάχιστον σῶμα (Diels, Vors. 55 B 141). So Arist. Phys. Γ, 4. 203 a 21, (Δημόκριτος) ἐκ τῆς πανσπερμίας τῶν σχημάτων (ἄπειρα ποιεῖ τὰ στοιχεῖα). Cf. De gen. corr. A, 2. 315 b 7 (R. P. 196).

1 Arist. Phys. Θ, 9. 265 b 25; Simpl. Phys. p. 1318, 33, ταῦτα γὰρ (τὰ ἄτομα σώματα) ἐκεῖνοι φύσιν ἐκάλουν.
2 Simpl. Phys. p. 36, 1 (Diels, Vors. 54 A 14), and R. P. 196 a.
3 Arist. Met. A, 4. 985 b 4 (R. P. 192). Cf. Melissos, fr. 7 sub fin.
22

statements about Leukippos in later writers must, in the long run, go back to him.   If we follow this up, we shall be able to give a fairly clear account of the system, and we shall even come across some views which are peculiar to Leukippos and were not adopted by Demokritos.[1]

The fuller of the doxographies in Diogenes, which comes from an epitome of Theophrastos,[2] is as follows :

He says that the All is infinite, and that it is part full, and part empty.   These (the full and the empty), he says, are the elements.   From them arise innumerable worlds and are resolved into them.   The worlds come into being thus.   There were borne along by " abscission from the infinite " many bodies of all sorts of figures " into a mighty void," and they being gathered together produce a single vortex.   In it, as they came into collision with one another and were whirled round in all manner of ways, those which were alike were separated apart and came to their likes.   But, as they were no longer able to revolve in equilibrium owing to their multitude, those of them that were fine went out to the external void, as if passed through a sieve ; the rest stayed together, and becoming entangled with one another, ran down together, and made a first spherical structure. This was in substance like a membrane or skin containing in itself all kinds of bodies.   And, as these bodies were borne round in a vortex, in virtue of the resistance of the middle, the surrounding membrane became thin, as the contiguous bodies kept flowing together from contact with the vortex.   And in this way the earth came into being, those things which had been borne towards the middle abiding there.   Moreover, the containing membrane was increased by the further separating out of bodies from outside ; and, being itself carried round in a vortex, it further got possession of all with which it had come in contact. Some of these becoming entangled, produced a structure, which was at first moist and muddy ; but, when they had been dried and were revolving along with the vortex of the whole, they were then ignited and produced the substance of the heavenly bodies.

[1] Cf. Zeller, " Zu Leukippos " (*Arch.* xv. p. 138).

[2] Diog. ix. 31 *sqq.* (R. P. 197, 197 c).   This passage deals expressly with Leukippos, not with Demokritos or even " Leukippos and Demokritos." For the distinction between the " summary " and " detailed " doxographies in Diogenes, see Note on Sources, § 15.

The circle of the sun is the outermost, that of the moon is nearest
to the earth, and those of the others are between these. And all
the heavenly bodies are ignited because of the swiftness of their
motion ; while the sun is also ignited by the stars. But the
moon only receives a small portion of fire. The sun and the
moon are eclipsed . . . (And the obliquity of the zodiac is produced) by the earth being inclined towards the south ; and the
northern parts of it have constant snow and are cold and frozen.
And the sun is eclipsed rarely, and the moon continually, because
their circles are unequal. And just as there are comings into
being of the world, so there are growths and decays and passings
away in virtue of a certain necessity, of the nature of which he
gives no clear account.

As it comes substantially from Theophrastos, this passage
is good evidence for the cosmology of Leukippos, and it is
confirmed by certain Epicurean extracts from the *Great Diakosmos*.[1] These, however, give a specially Epicurean turn to
some of the doctrines, and must therefore be used with caution.

177. The general impression we get from the cosmology
of Leukippos is that he either ignored or had never heard of
the great advance in the general view of the world which was
due to the later Pythagoreans. He is as reactionary in his
detailed cosmology as he was daring in his general physical
theory. We seem to be reading once more of the speculations of Anaximenes or Anaximander, though there are traces
of Empedokles and Anaxagoras too. The explanation is not
hard to see. Leukippos would not learn a cosmology from
his Eleatic teachers ; and, even when he found it possible to
construct one without giving up the Parmenidean view of
reality, he was thrown back upon the older systems of Ionia.
The result was unfortunate. The astronomy of Demokritos
was still of this childish character. He believed the earth
was flat and rested on the air.

*Relation
to Ionic
cosmo-
logy.*

This is what gives plausibility to Gomperz's statement
that Atomism was "the ripe fruit on the tree of the old Ionic

---

[1] See Aet. i. 4 (*Dox.* p. 289 ; *Vors.* 54 A 24 ; Usener, *Epicurea,* fr. 308).
Epicurus himself in the second epistle (Diog. x. 88 ; Usener, p. 37, 7) quotes
the phrase ἀποτομὴν ἔχουσα ἀπὸ τοῦ ἀπείρου.

340   EARLY GREEK PHILOSOPHY

doctrine of matter which had been tended by the Ionian physiologists." [1]   The detailed cosmology was certainly such a fruit, and it was possibly over-ripe ; but the atomic theory proper, in which the real greatness of Leukippos comes out, was wholly Eleatic in its origin.   Nevertheless, it will repay us to examine the cosmology too ; for such an examination will serve to bring out the true nature of the historical development of which it was the outcome.

The eternal motion. 178. Leukippos represented the atoms as having been always in motion.   Aristotle puts this in his own way.   The atomists, he says, "indolently" left it unexplained what was the source of motion, and did not say what sort of motion it was.   In other words, they did not decide whether it was a "natural motion" or impressed on them "contrary to their nature." [2]   He even said that they made it "spontaneous," a remark which has given rise to the erroneous view that they held it was due to chance. [3]   Aristotle does not say that, however ; but only that the atomists did not explain the motion of the atoms in any of the ways in which he himself explained the motion of the elements.   They neither ascribed to them a natural motion like the circular motion of the heavens and the rectilinear motion of the four elements in the sublunary region, nor did they give them a forced motion contrary to their own nature, like the upward motion that may be given to the heavy elements and the downward that may be given to the light.   The only fragment of Leukippos which has survived is an express denial of chance.   "Naught happens for nothing," he said, "but everything from a ground and of necessity." [4]

---

[1] Gomperz, *Greek Thinkers*, vol. i. p. 323.
[2] Arist. *Phys.* Θ, 1. 252 a 32 (R. P. 195 a) ; *De caelo*, Γ, 2. 300 b 8 (R. P. 195) ; *Met.* A, 4. 985 b 19 (R. P. *ib.*).
[3] Arist. *Phys.* B, 4. 196 a 24 (R. P. 195 d).   Cicero, *De nat. d.* i. 66 (R. P. *ib.*).   The latter passage is the source of the phrase "fortuitous concourse" (*concurrere*=συντρέχειν).
[4] Aet. i. 25, 4 (*Dox.* p. 321), Λεύκιππος πάντα κατ' ἀνάγκην, τὴν δ' αὐτὴν ὑπάρχειν εἱμαρμένην. λέγει γὰρ ἐν τῷ Περὶ νοῦ· Οὐδὲν χρῆμα μάτην γίγνεται, ἀλλὰ πάντα ἐκ λόγου τε καὶ ὑπ' ἀνάγκης.

Speaking historically, all this means that Leukippos did not, like Empedokles and Anaxagoras, find it necessary to assume a force to originate motion. He had no need of Love and Strife or Mind, and the reason is clear. Though Empedokles and Anaxagoras had tried to explain multiplicity and motion, they had not broken so radically as Leukippos with the Parmenidean One. Both started with a condition of matter in which the " roots " or " seeds " were mixed so as to be " all together," and they therefore required something to break up this unity. Leukippos, who started with an infinite number of Parmenidean " Ones," so to speak, required no external agency to separate them. What he had to do was just the opposite. He had to account for their coming together, and there was nothing so far to prevent his return to the old idea that motion does not require any explanation at all.[1]

This, then, is what seems to follow from the criticisms of Aristotle and from the nature of the case ; but it is not consistent with Zeller's opinion that the original motion of the atoms is a fall through infinite space, as in the system of Epicurus. This view depends, of course, on the further belief that the atoms have weight, and that weight is the tendency of bodies to fall, so we must now consider whether and in what sense weight is a property of the atoms.

179. As is well known, Epicurus held that the atoms were naturally heavy, and therefore fell continually in the infinite void. The school tradition is, however, that the " natural weight " of the atoms was an addition made by Epicurus himself to the original atomic system. Demokritos, we are told, assigned two properties to atoms, magnitude and form, to which Epicurus added a third, weight.[2] On the

The weight of the atoms.

---

[1] Introd. § VIII.
[2] Aet. i. 3, 18 (of Epicurus). συμβεβηκέναι δὲ τοῖς σώμασι τρία ταῦτα, σχῆμα, μέγεθος, βάρος. Δημόκριτος μὲν γὰρ ἔλεγε δύο, μέγεθός τε καὶ σχῆμα, ὁ δὲ Ἐπίκουρος τούτοις καὶ τρίτον βάρος προσέθηκεν· ἀνάγκη γάρ, φησί, κινεῖσθαι τὰ σώματα τῇ τοῦ βάρους πληγῇ· ἐπεὶ (" or else ") οὐ κινηθήσεται;

other hand, Aristotle distinctly says that Demokritos held the atoms were heavier " in proportion to their excess," and this seems to be explained by the statement of Theophrastos that, according to him, weight depended on magnitude.[1] Even so, however, it is not represented as a primary property of the atoms in the same sense as magnitude.

It is impossible to solve this apparent contradiction without referring briefly to the history of Greek ideas about weight. It is clear that lightness and weight would be among the very first properties of body to be distinctly recognised as such. The necessity of lifting burdens must very soon have led men to distinguish them, though no doubt in a crude form. Both weight and lightness would be thought of as *things* that were *in* bodies. Now it is a remarkable feature of early Greek philosophy that from the first it was able to shake itself free from this idea. Weight is never called a " thing " as, for instance, warmth and cold are ; and, so far as we can see, not one of the thinkers we have studied hitherto thought it necessary to give any explanation of it at all, or even to say anything about it.[2] The motions and resistances which popular theory ascribes to weight are

---

ib. 12, 6, Δημόκριτος τὰ πρῶτά φησι σώματα, ταῦτα δ' ἦν τὰ ναστά, βάρος μὲν οὐκ ἔχειν, κινεῖσθαι δὲ κατ' ἀλληλοτυπίαν ἐν τῷ ἀπείρῳ. Cic. De fato, 20, " vim motus habebant (atomi) a Democrito impulsionis quam plagam ille appellat, a te, Epicure, gravitatis et ponderis." These passages represent the Epicurean school tradition, which would hardly misrepresent Demokritos on so important a point. His works were still accessible. It is confirmed by the Academic tradition in *De fin.* i. 17 that Demokritos taught the atoms moved " in infinito inani, in quo nihil nec summum nec infimum nec medium nec extremum sit." This doctrine, we are quite rightly told, was " depraved " by Epicurus.

[1] Arist. *De gen. corr.* A, 8. 326 a 9, καίτοι βαρύτερόν γε κατὰ τὴν ὑπεροχήν φησιν εἶναι Δημόκριτος ἕκαστον τῶν ἀδιαιρέτων. I cannot believe this means anything else than what Theophrastos says in his fragment on sensation, § 61 (R. P. 199), βαρὺ μὲν οὖν καὶ κοῦφον τῷ μεγέθει διαιρεῖ Δημόκριτος.

[2] In Aet. i. 12, where the *placita* regarding the heavy and light are given, no philosopher earlier than Plato is referred to. Parmenides (fr. 8, 59) speaks of the dark element as ἐμβριθές. Empedokles (fr. 17) uses the word ἀτάλαντον. I do not think that there is any other place where weight is even mentioned in the fragments of the early philosophers.

all explained in some other way. Aristotle distinctly declares that none of his predecessors had said anything of absolute weight and lightness. They had only treated of the relatively light and heavy.[1]

This way of regarding the notions of weight and lightness is clearly formulated for the first time in Plato's *Timaeus*.[2] There is no such thing in the world, we are told there, as " up " or " down." The middle of the world is not " down " but " just in the middle," and there is no reason why any point in the circum-ference should be said to be " above " or " below " another. It is really the tendency of bodies towards their kin that makes us call a falling body heavy and the place to which it falls " below." Here Plato is really giving the view taken more or less consciously by his pre-decessors, and it is not till the time of Aristotle that it is questioned.[3] For reasons which do not concern us here, Aristotle identified the circumference of the heavens with " up " and the middle of the world with " down," and equipped the elements with natural weight and lightness that they might perform their rectilinear motions between them. As, however, Aristotle believed there was only one world, and did not ascribe weight to the heavens proper, the effect of this reactionary theory on his cosmical system was not great ; it was only when Epicurus tried to combine it with the infinite void that its true character emerged. It seems to me that the nightmare of Epicurean atomism can only be explained on the assumption that an Aristotelian doctrine was violently adapted to a theory which really

[1] Arist. *De caelo*, Δ, 1. 308 a 9, περὶ μὲν οὖν τῶν ἁπλῶς λεγομένων (βαρέων καὶ κούφων) οὐδὲν εἴρηται παρὰ τῶν πρότερον.

[2] Plato, *Tim.* 61 c 3 sqq.

[3] Zeller says (p. 876) that in antiquity no one ever understood by weight anything else than the property of bodies in virtue of which they move downwards ; except that in such systems as represent all forms of matter as contained in a sphere, " above " is identified with the circumference and " below " with the centre. As to that, I can only say that no such theory of weight is to be found in the fragments of the early philosophers or is anywhere ascribed to them, while Plato expressly denies it.

excluded it.[1] It is totally unlike anything we meet with in earlier days.

This suggests at once that it is only in the vortex that the atoms acquire weight and lightness,[2] which are, after all, only popular names for facts which can be further analysed. We are told that Leukippos held one effect of the vortex to be that like atoms were brought together with their likes.[3] Here we seem to see the influence of Empedokles, though the " likeness " is of another kind. It is the finer atoms that are forced to the circumference, while the larger tend to the centre. We may express that by saying that the larger are heavy and the smaller light, and this will amply account for everything Aristotle and Theophrastos say ; for there is no passage where the atoms outside the vortex are distinctly said to be heavy or light.[4]

There is a striking confirmation of this view in the atomist cosmology quoted above.[5] We are told there that the separation of the larger and smaller atoms was due to the fact that they were " no longer able to revolve in equilibrium owing to their number," which implies that they had previously been in a state of " equilibrium " or " equipoise." Now the word ἰσορροπία has no necessary implication of

---

[1] The Aristotelian criticisms which may have affected Epicurus are such as we find in *De caelo*, A, 7. 275 b 29 *sqq.*   Aristotle there argues that, as Leukippos and Demokritos made the φύσις of the atoms one, they were bound to give them a single motion.   That is just what Epicurus did, but Aristotle's argument implies that Leukippos and Demokritos did not. Though he gave the atoms weight, even Epicurus could not accept Aristotle's view that some bodies are naturally light.   The appearance of lightness is due to ἔκθλιψις, the squeezing out of the smaller atoms by the larger.

[2] In dealing with Empedokles, Aristotle expressly makes this distinction. Cf. *De caelo*, B, 13, especially 295 a 32 *sqq.*, where he points out that Empedokles does not account for the weight of bodies on the earth (οὐ γὰρ ἤ γε δίνη· πλησιάζει πρὸς ἡμᾶς), nor for the weight of bodies before the vortex arose (πρὶν γενέσθαι τὴν δίνην).

[3] Diog. *loc. cit.* (p. 338).

[4] This seems to be in the main the view of Dyroff, *Demokritstudien* (1899), pp. 31 *sqq.*, though I should not say that lightness and weight only arose in connexion with the atoms of the *earth* (p. 35).   If we substitute " world " for " earth," we shall be nearer the truth.

[5] See above, p. 338.

weight in Greek. A ῥοπή is a mere leaning or inclination in a certain direction, which is the cause rather than the effect of weight. The state of ἰσορροπία is therefore that in which the tendency in one direction is exactly equal to the tendency in any other, and such a state is more naturally described as the absence of weight than as the presence of opposite weights neutralising one another.

Now, if we no longer regard the "eternal motion" of the premundane and extramundane atoms as due to their weight, there is no reason for describing it as a fall. None of our authorities do as a matter of fact so describe it, nor do they tell us in any way what it was. It is safest to say that it is simply a confused motion this way and that.[1] It is possible that the comparison of the motion of the atoms of the soul to that of the motes in a sunbeam coming through a window, which Aristotle attributes to Demokritos,[2] is really intended as an illustration of the original motion of the atoms still surviving in the soul. The fact that it is also a Pythagorean comparison[3] so far confirms this; for we have seen that there is a real connexion between the Pythagorean monads and the atoms. It is also significant that the point of the comparison appears to have been the fact that the motes in the sunbeam move even when there is no wind, so that it would be a very apt illustration indeed of the motion inherent

---

[1] This view was independently advocated by Brieger (*Die Urbewegung der Atome und die Weltentstehung bei Leucipp und Demokrit*, 1884) and Liepmann (*Die Mechanik der Leucipp-Demokritschen Atome*, 1885), both of whom unnecessarily weakened their position by admitting that weight is an original property of the atoms. On the other hand, Brieger denies that the weight of the atoms is the cause of their original motion, while Liepmann says that before and outside the vortex there is only a latent weight, a *Pseudoschwere*, which only comes into operation in the world. It is surely simpler to say that this weight, since it produces no effect, does not yet exist. Zeller rightly argues against Brieger and Liepmann that, if the atoms have weight, they must fall; but, so far as I can see, nothing he says tells against their theory as I have restated it. Gomperz adopts the Brieger-Liepmann explanation. See also Lortzing, *Bursians Jahresber.*, 1903, pp. 136 *sqq.*

[2] Arist. *De an.* A, 2. 403 b 28 *sqq.* (R. P. 200).

[3] *Ibid.* A, 2, 404 a 17 (R. P. 86 a).

in the atoms apart from the secondary motions produced by impact and collision.

The vortex.

180. But what are we to say of the vortex itself which produces these effects ? Gomperz observes that they seem to be " the precise contrary of what they should have been by the laws of physics " ; for, " as every centrifugal machine would show, it is the heaviest substances which are hurled to the greatest distance." [1] Are we to suppose that Leukippos was ignorant of this fact, which was known to Empedokles and Anaxagoras ? [2] We know from Aristotle that all those who accounted for the earth being in the centre of the world by means of a vortex appealed to the analogy of eddies in wind or water,[3] and Gomperz supposes that the whole theory was an erroneous generalisation of this observation. If we look at the matter more closely, we can see, I think, that there is no error at all.

We must remember that all the parts of the vortex are in contact, and that it is just this contact (ἐπίψαυσις) by which the motion of the outermost parts is communicated to those within them. The larger bodies are more able to resist this communicated motion than the smaller, and in this way they make their way to the centre where the motion is least, and force the smaller bodies out. This resistance is surely just the ἀντέρεισις τοῦ μέσου which is mentioned in the doxography of Leukippos,[4] and it is quite in accordance with this that, on the atomist theory, the nearer a heavenly body is to the centre, the slower is its revolution.[5] That is just the point which, as we have seen,[6] Anaximander would seem not to have observed. There is

---

[1] Gomperz, *Greek Thinkers*, i. p. 339.

[2] For Empedokles, see Chap. V. p. 237 ; Anaxagoras, see Chap. VI. p. 269.

[3] Arist. *De caelo*, B, 13. 295 a 10, ταύτην γὰρ τὴν αἰτίαν (sc. τὴν δίνησιν) πάντες λέγουσιν ἐκ τῶν ἐν τοῖς ὑγροῖς καὶ περὶ τὸν ἀέρα συμβαινόντων· ἐν τούτοις γὰρ ἀεὶ φέρεται τὰ μείζω καὶ τὰ βαρύτερα πρὸς τὸ μέσον τῆς δίνης.

[4] Diog. ix. 32. Cf. especially the phrases ὧν κατὰ τὴν τοῦ μέσου ἀντέρεισιν περιδινουμένων, συμμενόντων ἀεὶ τῶν συνεχῶν κατ' ἐπίψαυσιν τῆς δίνης, and συμμενόντων τῶν ἐνεχθέντων ἐπὶ τὸ μέσον.

[5] Cf. Lucr. v. 621 *sqq.*

[6] See p. 69.

no question of " centrifugal force " at all, and the analogy of eddies in air and water is in reality quite satisfactory.

181. When we come to details, the reactionary character of the atomist cosmology is very manifest. The earth was shaped like a tambourine, and floated on the air.[1] It was inclined towards the south because the heat of that region made the air thinner, while the ice and cold of the north made it denser and more able to support the earth.[2] This accounts for the obliquity of the zodiac. Like Anaximander (§ 19), Leukippos held that the sun was farther away than the stars, though he also held that these were farther away than the moon.[3] By this time the occultation of the planets by the moon must have been observed. There seems to be no very clear distinction between the planets and the fixed stars. Leukippos appears to have known the theory of eclipses as given by Anaxagoras.[4] Such other pieces of information as have come down to us are mainly of interest as showing that, in some important respects, the doctrine of Leukippos was not the same as that taught afterwards by Demokritos.[5]

The earth and the heavenly bodies.

182. Aetios expressly attributes to Leukippos the doctrine that the objects of sense-perception exist " by law " and not by nature.[6] This must come from Theo-

Perception.

---

[1] Aet. iii. 3, 10, quoted above, p. 79, *n.* 1.

[2] Aet. iii. 12, 1, Λεύκιππος παρεκπεσεῖν τὴν γῆν εἰς τὰ μεσημβρινὰ μέρη διὰ τὴν ἐν τοῖς μεσημβρινοῖς ἀραιότητα, ἅτε δὴ πεπηγότων τῶν βορείων διὰ τὸ κατεψῦχθαι τοῖς κρυμοῖς, τῶν δὲ ἀντιθέτων πεπυρωμένων.

[3] Diog. ix. 33, εἶναι δὲ τὸν τοῦ ἡλίου κύκλον ἐξώτατον, τὸν δὲ τῆς σελήνης προσγειότατον, ⟨τοὺς δὲ⟩ τῶν ἄλλων μεταξὺ τούτων.

[4] From Diog. *loc. cit.* (*supra*, p. 339), it appears that he dealt with the question of the greater frequency of lunar as compared with solar eclipses.

[5] Diels pointed out that Leukippos's explanation of thunder (πυρὸς ἐναποληφθέντος νέφεσι παχυτάτοις ἔκπτωσιν ἰσχυρὰν βροντὴν ἀποτελεῖν ἀποφαίνεται, Aet. iii. 3, 10) is quite different from that of Demokritos (βροντὴν . . . ἐκ συγκρίματος ἀνωμάλου τὸ περιειληφὸς αὐτὸ νέφος πρὸς τὴν κάτω φορὰν ἐκβιαζομένου, *ib.* 11). The explanation given by Leukippos is derived from that of Anaximander, while Demokritos is influenced by Anaxagoras. See Diels, 35 *Philol.-Vers.* 97, 7.

[6] Aet. iv. 9, 8, οἱ μὲν ἄλλοι φύσει τὰ αἰσθητά, Λεύκιππος δὲ Δημόκριτος καὶ Διογένης νόμῳ. See Zeller, *Arch.* v. p. 444.

phrastos ; for, as we have seen, all later writers quote
Demokritos only.　A further proof of the correctness of the
statement is that we also find it attributed to Diogenes of
Apollonia, who, as Theophrastos tells us, derived some of
his views from Leukippos.　There is nothing surprising in
this.　Parmenides had already declared the senses to be
deceitful, and said that colour and the like were only
" names," [1] and Empedokles had also spoken of coming into
being and passing away as only a name.[2]　It is not likely
that Leukippos went much further than this.　It would
probably be wrong to credit him with Demokritos's clear
distinction between " true-born " and " bastard " knowledge, or that between the primary and secondary qualities
of matter.[3]　These distinctions imply a definite theory of
knowledge, and all we are entitled to say is that the germs
of it were already to be found in the writings of Leukippos
and his predecessors.　Of course, these do not make Leukippos a sceptic any more than Empedokles or Anaxagoras,
whose remark on this subject (fr. 21a) Demokritos is said to
have quoted with approval.[4]

　　There appear to be sufficient grounds for ascribing the
theory of perception by means of *simulacra* or εἴδωλα, which
played such a part in the systems of Demokritos and
Epicurus, to Leukippos.[5]　It is a natural development of
the Empedoklean theory of " effluences " (§ 118).　It hardly
seems likely, however, that he went into detail on the subject,
and it is safer to credit Demokritos with the elaboration of
the theory.

　　[1] Chap. IV. p. 176.　The remarkable parallel quoted by Gomperz
(p. 321) from Galileo, to the effect that tastes, smells, and colours *non sieno
altro che puri nomi* should, therefore, have been cited to illustrate Parmenides rather than Demokritos.
　　[2] See p. 206, fr. 9.　　[3] For these see Sext. *Math.* vii. 135 (R. P. 204).
　　[4] Sext. vii. 140, " ὄψις γὰρ ἀδήλων τὰ φαινόμενα," ὥς φησιν Ἀναξαγόρας,
ὃν ἐπὶ τούτῳ Δημόκριτος ἐπαινεῖ.
　　[5] See Zeller, " Zu Leukippos " (*Arch.* xv. p. 138).　The doctrine is
attributed to him in Aet. iv. 13, 1 (*Dox.* p. 403) ; and Alexander, *De sensu*,
pp. 24, 14 and 56, 10, also mentions his name in connexion with it.　This
must come from Theophrastos.

183. We have seen incidentally that there is a wide
divergence of opinion among recent writers as to the place of Atomism in Greek thought. The question at issue is really whether Leukippos reached his theory on what are called " metaphysical grounds," that is, from a considera-tion of the Eleatic theory of reality, or whether, on the contrary, it was a pure development of Ionian science. The foregoing exposition will suggest the true answer. So far as his general theory of the physical constitution of the world is concerned, it has been shown, I think, that it was derived entirely from Eleatic and Pythagorean sources, while the detailed cosmology was in the main a more or less successful attempt to make the older Ionian beliefs fit into this new physical theory. In any case, his greatness consisted in his having been the first to see how body must be regarded if we take it to be ultimate reality. The old Milesian theory had found its most adequate expression in the system of Anaximenes (§ 31), but of course rarefaction and condensa-tion cannot be clearly represented except on the hypothesis of molecules or atoms coming closer together or going farther apart in space. Parmenides had seen that very clearly (fr. 2), and it was the Eleatic criticism which forced Leu-kippos to formulate his system as he did. Even Anaxagoras took account of Zeno's arguments about divisibility (§ 128), but his system of qualitatively different " seeds," though in some respects it goes deeper, lacks that simplicity which has always been the chief attraction of atomism.

CHAPTER X

ECLECTICISM AND REACTION

The "bank-ruptcy of science." **184.** WITH Leukippos our story should come to an end; for he had answered the question first asked by Thales. We have seen, however, that, though his theory of matter was of a most original and daring kind, he was not equally successful in his attempt to construct a cosmology, and this seems to have prevented the recognition of the atomic theory for what it really was. We have noted the growing influence of medicine, and the consequent substitution of an interest in detailed investigation for the larger cosmological views of an earlier time, and there are several treatises in the Hippokratean *corpus* which give us a clear idea of the interest which now prevailed.[1] Leukippos had shown that " the doctrine of Melissos," [2] which seemed to make all science impossible, was not the only conclusion that could be drawn from the Eleatic premisses, and he had gone on to give a cosmology which was substantially of the old Ionic type. The result at first was simply that all the old schools revived and had a short period of renewed activity, while at the same time some new schools arose which sought to accommodate the older views to those of Leukippos, or to make them more available for scientific purposes by combining them in an eclectic fashion. None of these attempts had any lasting importance or influence, and what we have to consider in

[1] Cf. what is said in Chap. IV. p. 150, *n.* 2, of the Περὶ διαίτης. The Περὶ ἀνθρώπου φύσιος and the Περὶ ἀρχαίης ἰατρικῆς are invaluable documents for the attitude of scientific men to cosmological theories at this date.   [2] Cf. Chap. VIII. p. 329, *n.* 2.

this chapter is really one of the periodical " bankruptcies of science " which mark the close of one chapter in its history and announce the beginning of a new one.

I. Hippon of Samos

185. Hippon of Samos or Kroton or Rhegion belonged to the Italian school of medicine.[1] We know very little indeed of him except that he was a contemporary of Perikles. From a scholiast on Aristophanes [2] we learn that Kratinos satirised him in his *Panoptai* ; and Aristotle mentions him in the enumeration of early philosophers given in the First Book of the *Metaphysics*,[3] though only to say that the inferiority of his intellect deprives him of all claim to be reckoned among them.

With regard to his views, the most precise statement is Moisture. that of Alexander, who doubtless follows Theophrastos. It is to the effect that he held the primary substance to be Moisture, without deciding whether it was Water or Air.[4] We have the authority of Aristotle [5] and Theophrastos, represented by Hippolytos,[6] for saying that this theory was supported by physiological arguments of the kind common at the time, and the arguments tentatively ascribed to Thales by Aristotle are of this kind (§ 10). His other views belong to the history of Medicine.

Till quite recently no fragment of Hippon was known to exist, but a single one has now been recovered from the

---

[1] Aristoxenos said he was a Samian (R. P. 219 a). In Menon's *Iatrika* he is called a Krotoniate, while others assign him to Rhegion (Hipp. *Ref.* i. 16) or Metapontion (Censorinus, *De die nat.* 5, 2). This variation implies that he belonged originally to the Pythagorean school. The evidence of Aristoxenos is, in that case, all the more valuable. Hippon is mentioned along with Melissos as a Samian in Iamblichos's Catalogue of Pythagoreans (*V. Pyth.* 267).

[2] Schol. on *Clouds*, 94 *sqq.*

[3] Arist. *Met.* A, 3. 984 a 3 (R. P. 219 a).

[4] Alexander in *Met.* p. 26, 21 (R. P. 219).

[5] Arist. *De an.* A, 2. 405 b 2 (R. P. 220).

[6] Hipp. *Ref.* i. 16 (R. P. 221).

Geneva Scholia on Homer.[1]　It is directed against the old assumption that the " waters under the earth " are an independent source of moisture, and runs thus :

The waters we drink are all from the sea ; for if wells were deeper than the sea, then it would not, doubtless, be from the sea that we drink, for then the water would not be from the sea, but from some other source.　But as it is, the sea is deeper than the waters, so all the waters that are above the sea come from it.　R. P. 219 b.

We observe here the universal assumption that water tends to rise from the earth, not to sink into it.

Along with Hippon, Idaios of Himera may just be mentioned.　We know nothing of him except from Sextus,[2] who says he held air to be the primary substance.　The fact that he was a Sicilian is, however, suggestive.

II. Diogenes of Apollonia [3]

Date.　186. After discussing the three great representatives of the Milesian school, Theophrastos went on to say :

And Diogenes of Apollonia, too, who was almost the latest of those who gave themselves up to these studies, wrote most of his work in an eclectic fashion, agreeing in some points with Anaxagoras and in others with Leukippos.　He, too, says that the primary substance of the universe is Air infinite and eternal, from which by condensation, rarefaction, and change of state, the form of everything else arises.　R. P. 206 a.[4]

---

[1] *Schol. Genav.* p. 197, 19.　Cf. Diels in *Arch.* iv. p. 653.　The extract comes from the 'Ομηρικά of Krates of Mallos.

[2] Sext. *Adv. Math.* ix. 360.

[3] Stephanos of Byzantion *s.v.* 'Απολλωνία says this was Apollonia in Crete, but that seems improbable.　Zeller doubted it on the ground that Diogenes wrote in Ionic, but Ionic was the regular dialect for scientific works, and we cannot found on that.　On the other hand, it seems much more likely in itself that he came from Apollonia on the Pontos, a Milesian colony which regarded Anaximander as its founder (p. 52, *n.* 1).　Aelian (*V. H.* ii. 31) calls him Διογένης ὁ Φρύξ, which shows that he took this view.

[4] On this passage see Diels, " Leukippos und Diogenes von Apollonia " (*Rhein. Mus.* xlii. pp. 1 *sqq.*).　Natorp's view that the words are merely those of Simplicius (*ib.* pp. 349 *sqq.*) can hardly be maintained.

This passage shows that the Apolloniate was somewhat later in date than the statement in Laertios Diogenes [1] that he was contemporary with Anaxagoras would lead us to suppose, and the fact that his views are satirised in the *Clouds* of Aristophanes points in the same direction.[2]

187. Simplicius affirms that Diogenes wrote several works, though he allows that only one survived till his own day, namely, the Περὶ φύσεως.[3] This statement is based upon references in the surviving work itself, and is not to be lightly rejected.   In particular, it is very credible that he wrote a tract *Against the Sophists*, that is to say, the pluralist cosmologists of the day.[4]   That he wrote a *Meteorology* and a book called *The Nature of Man* is also quite probable.   This would be a physiological or medical treatise, and perhaps the famous fragment about the veins comes from it.[5]

Writings.

188. The work of Diogenes seems to have been preserved in the Academy ; practically all the fairly extensive fragments which we still have are derived from Simplicius.   I give them as they are arranged by Diels :

The Fragments.

(1) In the beginning any discourse, it seems to me that one should make one's starting-point something indisputable, and one's expression simple and dignified.   R. P. 207.

(2) My view is, to sum it all up, that all things are differentiations of the same thing, and are the same thing.   And this is obvious ; for, if the things which are now in this world—earth, and water, and air and fire, and the other things which we see

---

[1] Diog. ix. 57 (R. P. 206).   The statement of Antisthenes, the writer of *Successions*, that he had " heard " Anaximenes is due to the usual confusion.   He was doubtless, like Anaxagoras, " an associate of the philosophy of Anaximenes."   Cf. Chap. VI. § 122.

[2] Aristoph. *Clouds*, 227 *sqq.*, where Sokrates speaks of " mixing his subtle thought with the kindred air," and especially the words ἡ γῆ βίᾳ | ἕλκει πρὸς αὑτὴν τὴν ἰκμάδα τῆς φροντίδος.   For the ἰκμάς, see Beare, p. 259.

[3] Simpl. *Phys.* p. 151, 24 (R. P. 207 a).

[4] Simplicius says Πρὸς φυσιολόγους, but he adds that Diogenes called them σοφισταί, which is the older word.   This is, so far, in favour of the genuineness of the work.

[5] Diels gives this as fr. 6 (*Vors.* 51 B 6).   I have omitted it, as it really belongs to the history of Medicine.

23

existing in this world—if any one of these things, I say, were different from any other, different, that is, by having a substance peculiar to itself ; and if it were not the same thing that is often changed and differentiated, then things could not in any way mix with one another, nor could they do one another good or harm. Neither could a plant grow out of the earth, nor any animal nor anything else come into being unless things were composed in such a way as to be the same. But all these things arise from the same thing ; they are differentiated and take different forms at different times, and return again to the same thing. R. P. 208.

(3) For it would not be possible for it without intelligence to be so divided, as to keep the measures of all things, of winter and summer, of day and night, of rains and winds and fair weather. And any one who cares to reflect will find that everything else is disposed in the best possible manner. R. P. 210.

(4) And, further, there are still the following great proofs. Men and all other animals live upon air by breathing it, and this is their soul and their intelligence, as will be clearly shown in this work ; while, when this is taken away, they die, and their intelligence fails. R. P. 210.

(5) And my view is, that that which has intelligence is what men call air, and that all things have their course steered by it, and that it has power over all things. For this very thing I hold to be a god,[1] and to reach everywhere, and to dispose everything, and to be in everything ; and there is not anything which does not partake in it. Yet no single thing partakes in it just in the same way as another ; but there are many modes both of air and of intelligence. For it undergoes many transformations, warmer and colder, drier and moister, more stable and in swifter motion, and it has many other differentiations in it, and an infinite number of colours and savours. And the soul of all living things is the same, namely, air warmer than that outside us and in which we are, but much colder than that near the sun. And this warmth is not alike in any two kinds of living creatures,

---

[1] The MSS. of Simplicius have ἔθος, not θεός ; but I adopt Usener's certain correction. It is confirmed by the statement of Theophrastos that Diogenes called the air within us " a small portion of the god " (de Sens. 42) ; and by Philodemos (Dox. p. 536), where we read that Diogenes praises Homer, τὸν ἀέρα γὰρ αὐτὸν Δία νομίζειν φησίν, ἐπειδὴ πᾶν εἰδέναι τὸν Δία λέγει (cf. Cic. Nat. D. i. 12, 29).

nor, for the matter of that, in any two men ; but it does not differ much, only so far as is compatible with their being alike. At the same time, it is not possible for any of the things which are differentiated to be exactly like one another till they all once more become the same.

(6) Since, then, differentiation is multiform, living creatures are multiform and many, and they are like one another neither in appearance nor in intelligence, because of the multitude of differentiations. At the same time, they all live, and see, and hear by the same thing, and they all have their intelligence from the same source. R. P. 211.

(7) And this itself is an eternal and undying body, but of those things [1] some come into being and some pass away.

(8) But this, too, appears to me to be obvious, that it is both great, and mighty, and eternal, and undying, and of great knowledge. R. P. 209.

That the chief interest of Diogenes was a physiological one, is clear from his elaborate account of the veins, preserved by Aristotle.[2] It is noticeable, too, that one of his arguments for the underlying unity of all substances is that without this it would be impossible to understand how one thing could do good or harm to another (fr. 2). In fact, the writing of Diogenes is essentially of the same character as a good deal of the pseudo-Hippokratean literature, and there is much to be said for the view that the writers of these curious tracts made use of him very much as they did of Anaxagoras and Herakleitos.[3]

189. Like Anaximenes, Diogenes regarded Air as the primary substance ; but we see from his arguments that he lived at a time when other views had become prevalent.

Cosmology.

---

[1] The MSS. of Simplicius have τῷ δέ, but surely the Aldine τῶν δέ is right.   [2] Arist. *Hist. An.* Γ, 2. 511 b 30.

[3] See Weygoldt, " Zu Diogenes von Apollonia " (*Arch.* i. pp. 161 *sqq.*). Hippokrates himself represented just the opposite tendency to that of those writers. His great achievement was the separation of medicine from philosophy, a separation most beneficial to both (Celsus, i. pr.). This is why the Hippokratean corpus contains some works in which the " sophists " are denounced and others in which their writings are pillaged. To the latter class belong the Περὶ διαίτης and the Περὶ φυσῶν ; to the former, especially the Περὶ ἀρχαίης ἰατρικῆς.

He speaks clearly of the four Empedoklean elements (fr. 2), and he is careful to attribute to Air the attributes of Nous as taught by Anaxagoras (fr. 4). The doxographical tradition as to his cosmological views is fairly preserved :

Diogenes of Apollonia makes air the element, and holds that all things are in motion, and that there are innumerable worlds. And he describes the origin of the world thus. When the All moves and becomes rare in one place and dense in another, where the dense met together it formed a mass, and then the other things arose in the same way, the lightest parts occupying the highest position and producing the sun.   [Plut.] *Strom.* fr. 12 (R. P. 215).

Nothing arises from what is not nor passes away into what is not.   The earth is round, poised in the middle, having received its shape through the revolution proceeding from the warm and its solidification from the cold.   Diog. ix. 57 (R. P. 215).

The heavenly bodies were like pumice-stone.   He thinks they are the breathing-holes of the world, and that they are red-hot.   Aet. ii. 13, 5 = Stob. i. 508 (R. P. 215).

The sun was like pumice-stone, and into it the rays from the aether fix themselves.   Aet. ii. 20, 10.   The moon was a pumice-like conflagration.   *Ib.* ii. 25, 10.

Along with the visible heavenly bodies revolve invisible stones, which for that very reason are nameless ; but they often fall and are extinguished on the earth like the stone star which fell down flaming at Aigospotamos.[1]   *Ib.* ii. 13, 9.

We have here nothing more than the old Ionian doctrine with a few additions from more recent sources.   Rarefaction and condensation still hold their place in the explanation of the opposites, warm and cold, dry and moist, stable and mobile (fr. 5).   The differentiations into opposites which Air may undergo are, as Anaxagoras had taught, infinite in number ; but all may be reduced to the primary opposition of rare and dense.   We may gather, too, from Censorinus [2] that Diogenes did not, like Anaximenes, speak of earth and water as arising from Air by condensation, but rather of blood,

---

[1] See Chap. VI. p. 252, *n.* 6.
[2] Censorinus, *de die natali*, 6, 1 (*Dox.* p. 190).

flesh, and bones. In this he followed Anaxagoras (§ 130), as it was natural that he should. That portion of Air, on the other hand, which was rarefied became fiery, and produced the sun and heavenly bodies. The circular motion of the world is due to the intelligence of the Air, as is also the division of all things into different forms of body and the observance of the " measures " by these forms.[1]

Like Anaximander (§ 20), Diogenes regarded the sea as the remainder of the original moist state, which had been partially evaporated by the sun, so as to separate out the remaining earth.[2] The earth itself is round, that is to say, it is a disc : for the language of the doxographers does not point to the spherical form.[3] Its solidification by the cold is due to the fact that cold is a form of condensation.

Diogenes did not hold with the earlier cosmologists that the heavenly bodies were made of air or fire, nor yet with Anaxagoras, that they were stones. They were, he said, pumice-like, a view in which we may trace the influence of Leukippos. They were earthy, indeed, but not solid, and the celestial fire permeated their pores. And this explains why we do not see the dark bodies which, in common with Anaxagoras, he held to revolve along with the stars. They really are solid stones, and therefore cannot be penetrated by the fire. It was one of these that fell into the Aigospotamos. Like Anaxagoras, Diogenes affirmed that the inclination of the earth happened subsequently to the rise of animals.[4]

We are prepared to find that Diogenes held the doctrine of innumerable worlds ; for it was the old Milesian belief, and had just been revived by Anaxagoras and Leukippos. He is mentioned with the rest in the *Placita*; and if Simplicius classes him and Anaximenes with Herakleitos as holding the Stoic doctrine of successive formations and destructions of

---

[1] On the " measures " see Chap. III. § 72.

[2] Theophr. *ap*. Alex. in *Meteor.* p. 67, 1 (*Dox.* p. 494).

[3] Diog. ix. 57 (R. P. 215).   [4] Aet. ii. 8, 1 (R. P. 215).

a single world, he has probably been misled by the " accommodators." [1]

Animals and plants. 190. Living creatures arose from the earth, doubtless under the influence of heat. Their souls, of course, were air, and their differences were due to the various degrees in which it was rarefied or condensed (fr. 5). No special seat, such as the heart or the brain, was assigned to the soul ; it was simply the warm air circulating with the blood in the veins.

The views of Diogenes as to generation, respiration, and the blood, belong to the history of Medicine ; [2] his theory of sensation too, as it is described by Theophrastos,[3] need only be mentioned in passing. Briefly stated, it amounts to this, that all sensation is due to the action of air upon the brain and other organs, while pleasure is aeration of the blood. But the details of the theory can only be studied properly in connexion with the Hippokratean writings ; for Diogenes does not really represent the old cosmological tradition, but a fresh development of reactionary philosophical views combined with an entirely new enthusiasm for detailed investigation and accumulation of facts.

III. ARCHELAOS OF ATHENS

Anaxagoreans. 191. The last of the early cosmologists was Archelaos of Athens, who was a disciple of Anaxagoras.[4] He is also said, by Aristoxenos and Theophrastos, to have been the teacher of Sokrates, and there is not the slightest reason for doubting it.[5] There is no reason either to doubt the tradition

---

[1] Simpl. *Phys.* p. 1121, 12. See Chap. I. p. 59.
[2] See Censorinus, quoted in *Dox.* p. 191 *sq.*
[3] Theophr. *de Sens.* 39 *sqq.* (R. P. 213, 214). For a full account, see Beare, pp. 41 *sqq.*, 105, 140, 169, 209, 258. As Prof. Beare remarked, Diogenes " is one of the most interesting of the pre-Platonic psychologists " (p. 258). [4] Diog. ii. 16 (R. P. 216).
[5] See Chiappelli in *Arch.* iv. pp. 369 *sqq.* Ion of Chios said that Sokrates accompanied Archelaos to Samos (fr. 73 Köpke). If this refers to the siege of Samos, it is interesting to think of the youthful Sokrates serving against a force commanded by Melissos.

that Archelaos succeeded Anaxagoras in the school at Lampsakos.[1] We certainly hear of Anaxagoreans,[2] though their fame was soon obscured by the rise of the Sophists, as we call them.

192. On the cosmology of Archelaos, Hippolytos[3] Cosmology. writes as follows :

Archelaos was by birth an Athenian, and the son of Apollodoros. He spoke of the mixture of matter in a similar way to Anaxagoras, and of the first principles likewise. He held, however, that there was a certain mixture immanent even in Nous. And he held that there were two efficient causes which were separated off from one another, namely, the warm and the cold. The former was in motion, the latter at rest. When the water was liquefied it flowed to the centre, and there being burnt up it turned to earth and air, the latter of which was borne upwards, while the former took up its position below. These, then, are the reasons why the earth is at rest, and why it came into being. It lies in the centre, being practically no appreciable part of the universe. (But the air rules over all things),[4] being produced by the burning of the fire, and from its original combustion comes the substance of the heavenly bodies. Of these the sun is the largest, and the moon second ; the rest are of various sizes. He says that the heavens were inclined, and that then the sun made light upon the earth, made the air transparent, and the earth dry ; for it was originally a pond, being high at the circumference and hollow in the centre. He adduces as a proof of this hollowness that the sun does not rise and set at the same time for all peoples, as it ought to do if the earth were level. As to animals, he says that when the earth was first being warmed in the lower part where the warm and the cold were mingled together, many living creatures appeared, and especially men, all having the same manner of life, and deriving their sustenance

---

[1] Euseb. *P. E.* p. 504, c 3, ὁ δὲ Ἀρχέλαος ἐν Λαμψάκῳ διεδέξατο τὴν σχολὴν τοῦ Ἀναξαγόρου.

[2] Ἀναξαγόρειοι are mentioned by Plato (*Crat.* 409 b 6), and in the Δισσοὶ λόγοι (cf. p. 29, *n.* 3). It is also to be noted that Plato (*Parm.* 126 a, b) represents certain φιλόσοφοι from Klazomenai as coming to Athens after the death of Sokrates for the purpose of getting an accurate account of the famous conversation between Parmenides and the young Sokrates (§ 84).

[3] Hipp. *Ref.* i. 9 (R. P. 218).

[4] Inserting τὸν δ' ἀέρα κρατεῖν τοῦ παντός, as suggested by Roeper.

from the slime ; they did not live long, and later on generation from one another began. And men were distinguished from the rest, and set up leaders, and laws, and arts, and cities, and so forth. And he says that Nous is implanted in all animals alike ; for each of the animals, as well as man, makes use of Nous, but some quicker and some slower.

It is clear from this that, just as Diogenes had tried to introduce certain Anaxagorean ideas into the philosophy of Anaximenes, so Archelaos sought to bring Anaxagoreanism nearer to the old Ionic views by supplementing it with the opposition of warm and cold, rare and dense, and by stripping Nous of that simplicity which had marked it off from the other " things " in his master's system. It was probably for this reason, too, that Nous was no longer regarded as the maker of the world.[1] Leukippos had made such a force unnecessary. It may be added that this twofold relation of Archelaos to his predecessors makes it very credible that, as Aetios tells us,[2] he believed in innumerable worlds ; both Anaxagoras and the older Ionians upheld that doctrine.

Con-
clusion.
193. The cosmology of Archelaos, like that of Diogenes, has all the characteristics of the age to which it belonged— an age of reaction, eclecticism, and investigation of detail.[3] Hippon of Samos and Idaios of Himera represent nothing more than the feeling that philosophy had run into a blind alley, from which it could only escape by trying to get back. The Herakleiteans at Ephesos, impenetrably wrapped up as they were in their own system, did little but exaggerate its paradoxes and develop its more fanciful side.[4] It was not enough for Kratylos to say with Herakleitos (fr. 84) that you cannot step twice into the same river ; you could not do

---

[1] Aet. i. 7, 14=Stob. i. 56 (R. P. 217 a).   [2] Aet. ii. 1, 3.
[3] Windelband, § 25. The period is well described by Fredrich, *Hippo-kratische Untersuchungen*, pp. 130 *sqq*. It can only be treated fully in connexion with the Sophists.
[4] For an amusing picture of the Herakleiteans see Plato, *Theaet.* 179 e. The new interest in language, which the study of rhetoric had called into life, took with them the form of fantastic and arbitrary etymologising, such as is satirised in Plato's *Cratylus*.

so even once.[1]   The fact is that philosophy, so long as it clung to its old presuppositions, had nothing more to say ; for the answer of Leukippos to the question of Thales was really final.

It will be observed that all these warring systems found their way to Athens, and it was there, and there alone that the divergent theories of Ionia and the West came into contact.   Such questions as whether the earth was round or flat, and whether "what we think with" was Air or Blood, must have been hotly debated at Athens about the middle of the fifth century B.C., when Sokrates was young.   On any view of him, it is surely incredible that he was not interested in these controversies at the time, however remote they may have seemed to him in later life.   Now, in the *Phaedo*, Plato has put into his mouth an autobiographical statement in which he tells us that this was actually the case,[2] and the list of problems there given is one that can only have occupied men's minds at Athens and at that date.[3]   All the scientific schools end at Athens, and it was the Athenian Sokrates who saw that the questions they had raised could only be met by making a fresh start from another point of view.

[1] Arist. *Met.* Γ, 5. 1010 a 12.   He refused even to speak, we are told, and only moved his finger.

[2] Plato, *Phaedo*, 96 a *sqq.*

[3] I have tried to show this in detail in my notes on the passage in my edition of the *Phaedo* (Oxford, 1911).   It is a remarkable proof of Plato's historical sense that he should have been able to give an account of the state of scientific opinion at Athens some twenty-five years before his own birth, without, so far as I can see, a single anachronism.

APPENDIX

ON THE MEANING OF Φύσις

THE account which I have given (pp. 10 *sqq.*) of the meaning of the term φύσις in early Greek philosophy has been criticised by Professor W. A. Heidel in a paper entitled Περὶ φύσεως, *A Study of the Conception of Nature among the Pre-Socratics.*[1] It is an exceedingly valuable paper, and I cannot find that it contains anything inconsistent with my view, though the writer apparently thinks it does. The only point at issue, so far as I can see, is that Professor Heidel assumes that the original meaning of φύσις is "growth," which seems to me extremely doubtful. No doubt the verb φύομαι (*i.e.* φυίομαι) with a long vowel means "I grow," but the simple root φυ is the equivalent of the Latin *fu* and the English *be*, and need not necessarily have this derivative meaning. There is an interesting article in support of my view by Professor Lovejoy in the *Philosophical Review,* vol. xviii. pp. 369 *sqq.*, and Mr. Beardslee has recently examined the use of the word φύσις in Greek writers of the fifth century B.C. in a Ph.D. dissertation (University of Chicago Press, 1918). Here again, while acknowledging the value of the work, I can only say that I do not find its results inconsistent with the account I have given. I have never questioned the obvious fact that the word φύσις had a history, and developed meanings quite different from that which it may have had for an Ionian.

I should almost be willing to rest the case for this on the fragment of Euripides quoted on p. 10, where the significant epithet ἀθάνατος καὶ ἀγήρως is given to φύσις, but it may be well to collect here some of the passages on which I also rely.

1. Plato, *Laws* 891 C 1, κινδυνεύει γὰρ ὁ λέγων ταῦτα πῦρ καὶ ὕδωρ καὶ γῆν καὶ ἀέρα πρῶτα ἡγεῖσθαι τῶν πάντων εἶναι, καὶ τὴν φύσιν ὀνομάζειν ταῦτα αὐτά. 892 C 2, φύσιν βούλονται λέγειν γένεσιν τὴν περὶ τὰ πρῶτα· εἰ δὲ φανήσεται ψυχὴ πρῶτον, οὐ πῦρ οὐδὲ ἀήρ, ψυχὴ δ' ἐν πρώτοις γεγενημένη, σχεδὸν ὀρθότατα λέγοιτ' ἂν εἶναι διαφερόντως φύσει.

[1] *Proceedings of the American Academy of Arts and Sciences,* vol. xlv. No. 4.

In 891 c 7 the use of φύσις here criticised is expressly said to be that of ὁπόσοι πώποτε τῶν περὶ φύσεως ἐφήψαντο ζητημάτων.

2. Ar. *Phys.* B, 1. 193 a 9, δοκεῖ δ᾽ ἡ φύσις καὶ ἡ οὐσία τῶν φύσει ὄντων ἐνίοις εἶναι τὸ πρῶτον ἐνυπάρχον ἑκάστῳ ἀρρύθμιστον καθ᾽ ἑαυτό, οἷον κλίνης φύσις τὸ ξύλον, ἀνδριάντος δ᾽ ὁ χαλκός. σημεῖον δέ φησιν Ἀντιφῶν ὅτι, εἴ τις κατορύξειε κλίνην καὶ λάβοι δύναμιν ἡ σηπεδὼν ὥστε ἀνεῖναι βλαστόν, οὐκ ἂν γενέσθαι κλίνην ἀλλὰ ξύλον.

Antiphon the Sophist was a contemporary of Sokrates.

3. Ar. *Phys.* A, 6. 189 b 2, οἱ μίαν τινὰ φύσιν εἶναι λέγοντες τὸ πᾶν, οἷον ὕδωρ ἢ πῦρ ἢ τὸ μεταξὺ τούτων. B, 1. 193 a 21, οἱ μὲν πῦρ, οἱ δὲ γῆν, οἱ δ᾽ ἀέρα φασίν, οἱ δὲ ὕδωρ, οἱ δ᾽ ἔνια τούτων, οἱ δὲ πάντα ταῦτα τὴν φύσιν εἶναι τὴν τῶν ὄντων. Γ, 4. 203 a 16, οἱ δὲ περὶ φύσεως ἀεὶ πάντες ὑποτιθέασιν ἑτέραν τινὰ φύσιν τῷ ἀπείρῳ τῶν λεγομένων στοιχείων, οἷον ὕδωρ ἢ ἀέρα ἢ τὸ μεταξὺ τούτων.

4. Ar. *Met.* Δ, 4. 1014 b 16, φύσις λέγεται ἕνα μὲν τρόπον ἡ τῶν φυομένων γένεσις, οἷον εἴ τις ἐπεκτείνας λέγοι τὸ υ.

There is no doubt that this means that, to Aristotle, φύσις did not immediately suggest the verb φύομαι. That has a long υ and φύσις has a short υ. We need not discuss the question whether Aristotle's difficulty is a real one or not. All that concerns us is that he felt it.

5. Aristotle, Προτρεπτικός, fr. 52 Rose (*ap.* Iambl. *Protr.* p. 38. 22 Pistelli), ὁμοίως δὲ καὶ τῶν περὶ φύσεως (ἐστί τις ἐπιμέλεια καὶ τέχνη)· πολὺ γὰρ πρότερον ἀναγκαῖον τῶν αἰτιῶν καὶ τῶν στοιχείων εἶναι φρόνησιν ἢ τῶν ὕστερον. οὐ γὰρ ταῦτα τῶν ἄκρων οὐδ᾽ ἐκ τούτων τὰ πρῶτα πέφυκεν, ἀλλ᾽ ἐξ ἐκείνων καὶ δι᾽ ἐκείνων τἆλλα γίγνεται καὶ συνίσταται φανερῶς. εἴτε γὰρ πῦρ εἴτ᾽ ἀὴρ εἴτ᾽ ἀριθμὸς εἴτε ἄλλαι τινὲς φύσεις αἴτιαι καὶ πρῶται τῶν ἄλλων, ἀδύνατον τῶν ἄλλων τι γιγνώσκειν ἐκείνας ἀγνοοῦντας· πῶς γὰρ ἄν τις ἢ λόγον γνωρίζοι συλλαβὰς ἀγνοῶν, ἢ ταύτας ἐπίσταιτο μηδὲν τῶν στοιχείων εἰδώς ;

The importance of this passage for our purpose is that it is from a popular work, in which the phraseology is Academic (*e.g.* the use of φρόνησις for what Aristotle himself called σοφία).

The usage of Theophrastos is the same, but of course he simply reproduces Aristotle.

INDEXES

I. ENGLISH

Aahmes, 18 sq., 46
Abaris, 81, 90 n. 2
Abdera, school of, 61, 330 sq.
Abstinence, Orphic and Pythagorean, 93, 95 ; Empedoklean, 250
Academy, 29 ; library of, 33, 116, 171 n. 3, 353
Accommodation (συνοικείωσις), 32, 142, 358
Achaians, 2 n. 1, 4, 81 ; of Peloponnesos, 92 ; dialect, 282 n. 4
Achilles and the tortoise, 318
Achilles, Εἰσαγωγή, Sources § 9 (p. 34), 191 n. 3, 292 n. 2, 298 n. 1
Adrastos, 24 n. 2
Aegean civilisation, survivals of, 2, 3, 15, 21 n. 2, 39, 80
Aether. See αἰθήρ
Aetios, Sources § 10 (p. 35)
Ages of the world, 5
Aigospotamos, meteoric stone of, 252, 269, 357
Ainesidemos, 152
Air, identified with mist or vapour, 62, 64, 68, 74 sq., 109, 110, 153, 187 n. 1, 216 n. 2, 219 n. 3, 228 n. 2, 246 n. 2 ; identified with the void, 109, 186, 194, 229 ; atmospheric, 109, 229, 266 sq., 269, 289, 293, 337
Akousmata, 96, 98, 283
Akousmatics, 94, 96, 98
Akragas, 3, 197 sqq.
Alexander, writer of Successions, Sources § 17 (p. 37)
Alexander Aetolus, 255
Alexander Aphrodisiensis, Sources § 7 (p. 33) ; on Anaximander, 64 ; on Xenophanes, 116 n. 1, 126 ; on the Pythagoreans, 107 n. 1, 288, 306 nn. 1 and 2 ; on Parmenides, 183 ; on Zeno, 320 n. 1 ; on Hippon, 351
Alkidamas, 86, 199 n. 5, 201 n. 2, 202, 257 n. 1, 278 n. 1, 312

Alkmaion of Kroton, 86, 110 n. 2, 153, 193-196, 202, 248, 282 n. 5, 296, 332
Allegorists, Homeric, 49 n. 1, 116 n. 2
Amasis, 40, 88
Amber, 48 n. 1, 50
Ameinias, 170
Anakreon and Kritias, 203 n. 3
Anaxagoras, 251-275 ; and Euripides, 10, 255 ; and Sokrates, 256, 267 ; and Perikles, 254 sqq. ; and Zeno, 349 ; and Anaximenes, 253, 266, 269, 270, 271 ; and Herakleitos, 264, 268 ; and Empedokles, 261, 264, 265, 267, 268, 273 sq. ; and Leukippos, 331 ; relation to the Eleatics, 182, 261, 310 ; on the rise of the Nile, 45 ; on the moon's light, 177 n. 1 ; on eclipses, 306 ; on πόνος, 326 n. 2 ; primitive cosmology of, 111, 297
Anaxagoreans, 29 n. 3, 359 n. 2
Anaximander, 50-71 ; as an observer in marine biology, 26 ; and Xenophanes, 114
Anaximenes, 72-79, 179 ; school of, 79, 253, 305, 330, 353 n. 1
Androkydes, 283
Andron of Ephesos, 87
Anecdotes, of Thales, 46 n. 4 ; of Xenophanes, 113 n. 2, 115 n. 3 ; of Herakleitos, 115 n. 3, 131 n. 4 ; of Empedokles, 200 n. 5
Animals, Anaximander, 26, 70 sqq. ; Empedokles, 242 sqq. ; Anaxagoras, 272 sq. ; Diogenes of Apollonia, 358
Antichthon, 297, 305 sq.
Antisthenes, writer of Successions, Sources § 17 (p. 37)
Antonius Diogenes, 87 n. 2
Apollo, an Achaian god, 4
Apollo Hyperboreios, 4, 81, 87 n. 3, 90, 200
Apollodoros, Sources § 21 (p. 38) ; on Thales, 44 n. 2 ; on Anaximander,

II. GREEK

THE END